fic Coast Line

Southern Pacific's Coast Line

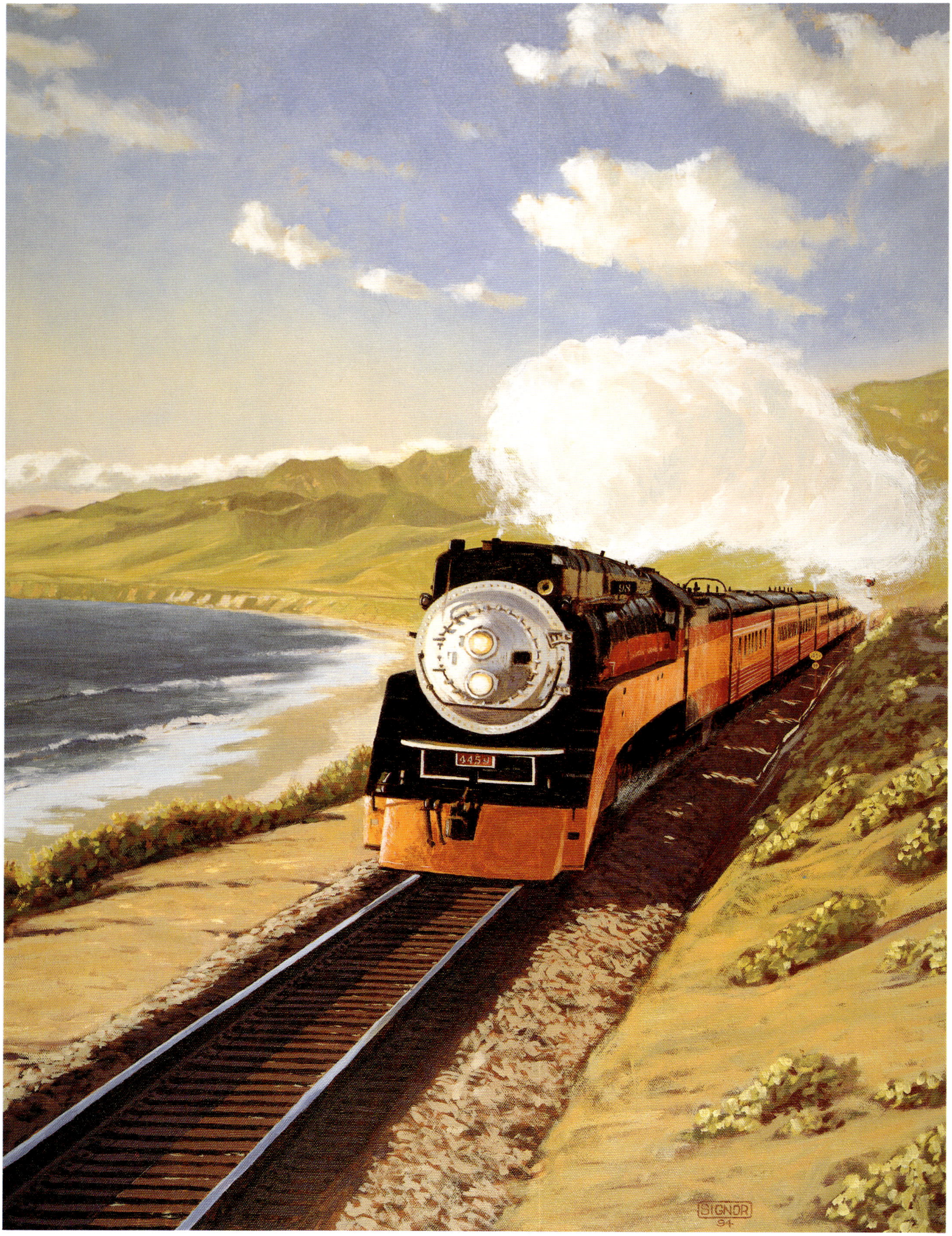
4459
SIGNOR
94

Southern Pacific's
Coast Line

JOHN R. SIGNOR

SIGNATURE PRESS
Wilton, California

Southern Pacific's Coast Line

Copyright © 1994 by John R. Signor
All rights reserved. No part of this publication may be reproduced or distributed
in any form or by any means, including photocopy, or stored in a database or
retrieval system, without the prior written permission of the publisher.

Published by Signature Press
Wilton, California 95693

Library of Congress Cataloging-in-Publication Data

Signor, John R.
    Southern Pacific's Coast Line

    p. cm.
    Includes bibliography and index.
    ISBN 0-9633791-3-5
      1. Southern Pacific Railroad Company. 2. Railroads-California
Southern.   I. Title

Frontispiece
In an original oil painting created by John Signor, Train No. 98, the *Coast Daylight*, races down
the Coast Line near Tajiguas in 1948. It was Jane Hollister Wheelwright, a descendent of the
historic Hollister ranching family, who wrote in 1979 that, unlike many of the incursions of man,
the *Daylight* "seemed to belong there, and did not jar the feeling of the Coast in the slightest."

Library of Congress Catalog Card No. 95-67525
ISBN No. 0-9633791-3-5

Signature Press
11508 Green Road
Wilton, California 95693

Second Printing, 2002
Printed in Hong Kong

Dedicated in memory of

George A. McCarron
Hired out April 28, 1941, promoted May 7, 1951

Coast Division engineer and life-long railfan, without whose interest
and dedication to the preservation of Coast Line legend and lore,
this project would not have been possible.

Acknowledgements

*A*S WITH ANY LARGE UNDERTAKING of this type, it would have been impossible to compile the story of Southern Pacific's Coast Line without the help and encouragement of many people. The majority are present and former SP employees, but much additional support was provided by railway enthusiasts, librarians, collectors, curators of public and private archives and other interested parties.

First and foremost, the author is indebted to George McCarron, a friend and longtime Coast Line engineer whose dedication to the preservation of Coast Line legend and lore started in the days when there were real "old timers," and to his daughter Margaret and son-in-law Joseph Hellen of Livermore, California, who generously made available George's life work for this project.

Out on the road, SP employees Robert McNeel, Vince "the Godfather" Cipolla, Dan Wolf, Benny Romano, Tom Dill, Vince McGinnis, Mike Jarel, Jim Escalante, Vaughn Savage, Art Laidlaw, Jess Trainer, Ray Ridgeway, Neal Vodden, Harold Soper, Ken Bruce, Jay Bell, John Edwards and Jim Hutton related stories from a "hoghead's" point of view, while Albert Snyder, M.A. "Bo" Golson, Jess Trainer, Danny Nagel, Arlon "Mickey" Shannon, Mike Robinson, Lee Barnet, Clyde Davis, Tony Grassel, Teddy Kadlubowski, Jack Graham, Don Titus and J.P. "Pat" Bray filled in details from the train service side.

Other rails involved included Phil Gosney from Amtrak; Malcolm "Mac" Gaddis, formerly an SP traveling electrician; Glen Icanberry from the Santa Fe; Scott Twist, towerman; Jamie Schmid and "Junior" Bedwell. Considerable assistance was received from Lynn Farrar, Jeff Root, Bruce Feld, Bob Hoppe, Ron Rang, Ray Tyler, Bart Nadeau, Mike Furtney and George Farosich at the Southern Pacific general office in San Francisco.

Outside the railroad industry, I found many individuals ready to assist me in my research. They were Steve Peery Jr., Jeffery Moreau, Jim Harrison, Lauren Ayers of Santa Paula, Bill Sanford, Steve Donaldson, Rick Reyes, Anthony Thompson and Robert J. Church.

There were stewards of public and private archives and collections that were so helpful, and I wish to acknowledge Kay Bost of the DeGolyer Library, Southern Methodist University, Dallas, Texas; Marilyn Stanley and Janice Pond of Holly Sugar Corporation; Mr. Donald Duke; Mrs. Alzora Snyder, archivist for the Pajaro Valley Historical Association; Virginia M. Crook, San Luis Obispo City and County Library; Joseph P. Samora, California State Archives; Mary Jean S. Gamble, John Steinbeck Library, Salinas; Charles Johnson, Ventura County Museum of Art & History; Mark P. Hall-Patton, San Luis Obispo Historical Society; William A. Meyers, Southern California Edison Company; Michael Redmon, Santa Barbara Historical Society; Alan Jutzi, Huntington Library, San Marino; and Gordon T. Bennett, Bennett-Loomis Archives, Arroyo Grande.

Unlike some of the districts the author has undertaken to document, there survives today a rich legacy of photography on the Coast Line from the early days forward. Although a blessing, this has made the task of image selection for this book very difficult. In the era prior to the Depression, many unsung commercial photographers documented the Coast Line for the railroad and other commercial concerns and their work is provided here courtesy Southern Pacific Lines. Those known are Piedmont photographer C.M. Kurtz who documented many SP engineering projects prior to 1920, and San Luis Obispo commercial photographers Virgil Hodges, McCurry and Aston, all who provided excellent views on the central coast. Gifted amateurs R.P. Middlebrook and R.H. McFarland each provided valuable action views along the Coast Line in the early days, and these are made available here through the generosity of Arnold S. Menke. E.E. Gale's work comes to us from Vernon Sappers and Stanley Palmer's early work on the Monterey Branch from Mallory Hope Ferrell.

As always, I am grateful for the work of skilled rail photographers Ted Benson, Dick Dorn, Don Hansen, Robert Morris, Tim Zukas, Donald Duke, John Roskoski, Bonnie Adams, David Lustig, Steve Patterson, Richard Steinheimer, John C. Illman, Jack Whitmeyer, Ed Workman, John Shaw, Grant Flanders, Stan Kistler and Bruce Veary.

Lastly I would like to thank my Julie for her continued support and Lynn Farrar, Mike Furtney, Bart Nadeau and Tony Thompson for proofreading.

John R. Signor
Dunsmuir, California
October, 1994

Southern Pacific Lines

Table of Contents

	Acknowledgements	vi
	Foreword by Anthony Thompson	ix
1	The Early Days: *Formation of the Coast Line*	1
2	By Rail on the Padre Trail: *Coast Line Operations prior to the Depression*	39
3	The Challenging Years: *Coast Line Operations through Depression and War*	83
4	Growth and Prosperity: *The Post-War Era on the Coast*	149
5	Decline & Rebirth: *Recent Coast Line Operations*	243
	Epilogue	276
	Station List, Southern Pacific Coast Line	279
	Bibliography	307
	Index	309

Foreword

THE COAST LINE of the Southern Pacific needs no qualification: it is indelibly the railroad of the California coast between Los Angeles and San Francisco. And though its images are legion, there is one which predominates: the streamlined *Daylight* train, in vivid red and orange paint. The steam enthusiast pictures a streamlined 4-8-4 locomotive on the head end, the diesel fan envisions an EMD E unit or an Alco PA, but the classic train is a constant, its appearance little changed from its introduction in 1937 until 1958.

Yet the Coast Line is much more. It is history, it is geography, it is freight as well as passenger trains, and it is people: the people who did the railroad's work, the people who lived along the line, and those who rode the trains, most of them Californians. For all of them, the richness of association they feel for the Coast Line is indeed much more than a single train, central though the *Daylight* may be.

The history, reaching back before the time of the American Revolution to the Spanish navigators, soldiers and padres who met the native Indians and explored and settled California, is long and rich. Yet as late as the Gold Rush in 1849, the non-Indian population of coastal California could be numbered only in the thousands. The development of towns, of agriculture and industry, and the emergence of the state's social fabric, were all dependent on the coming of the railroad, and for the California coast that railroad was the Southern Pacific.

Long reviled in the popular imagination as "The Octopus," from the title of Frank Norris's novel, the SP certainly has borne its share of opprobrium. Yet that 19th-century image is in many ways inaccurate and certainly too simple. In recent years, serious historians have re-examined the historical record, both favorable and unfavorable to the Southern Pacific, and are moving beyond the negative images conjured up in another time, to a more balanced view.

But whatever view is taken of the railroad, its effects on the land and towns along its routes, including the Coast Line, were profound. It brought both rapid and convenient personal transportation, and also effective movement of agricultural and manufactured products, both into and out of the coastal region and its towns and cities. This of course accelerated development and growth, and hastened the appearance of modern California.

Accordingly, any history of the Coast Line is also in part a history of California. The railroad and its territory were and are inextricably joined.

Among the most difficult topics for an historian to address for any railroad is operations. Many day-to-day practices were not written down and in some cases, were never officially blessed. Even official procedures can be dry and lifeless without interpretation. Interviews with present and former employees are thus essential in bringing to life the operating practices of the working railroad.

John Signor has included all these aspects of the Coast Line in this book. Drawing on many historical resources, but most dramatically on the extensive files of the Southern Pacific itself, he has produced a broad history of the SP in coastal California, illustrated with many photographs, published and unpublished. In the years before World War II, official photography provided much of the best coverage, but since that time, increasingly thorough amateur photography of the railroad and its activities provides far richer and more varied coverage. This book draws deeply on both kinds of sources. Signor's fine maps, as always, enliven and enrich the text, as do the railroad graphics and ephemera included here. This outstanding treatment is a welcome and very fitting addition to the history and lore of this part of the Southern Pacific, and indeed of the entire railroad. It will also enlarge understanding of the history of California and the West.

Anthony Thompson
Berkeley, California
November, 1994

One mile out of San Francisco, San Jose local passenger No. 28 roars out of tunnel No. 2 on the new Bayshore Cutoff in 1911. Completion of the Bayshore Cutoff in December, 1907, together with installation of signalling over the entire 470-mile route between San Francisco and Los Angeles in the period prior to 1908, gave Southern Pacific's Coast Line most of the track alignment, and the geographic and other features, which are associated with the route today.
Robert H. McFarland photo, Arnold S. Menke collection

1

The Early Days

Formation of the Coast Line

THE COMPLETION of Southern Pacific's famed Coast Line, linking San Francisco and Los Angeles by way of San Jose, Salinas, San Luis Obispo and Santa Barbara, came late in California's great railroad building era, yet a segment of this route was the first railroad projected in the state.

The Coast Line generally followed the route pioneered by the Spanish explorer Don Gaspar de Portolá during 1769. On July 14th of that year, Portolá and a band of 63 adventurers set out from San Diego in search of the Bay of Monterey, which Vizcaíno had described as an "unusually fine harbor." The trail they blazed north through virgin territory took them past the sites of Los Angeles and Saugus, then down the Santa Clara River to its mouth, near Ventura. From that point, Portolá and his men followed the coast for many miles, passing Carpinteria, Gaviota, Point Concepcion, Guadalupe, San Luis Obispo and Morro Bay before turning inland above San Simeon. Along the way, Portolá and his diarist, Father Juan Crespi, bestowed names on many of the locations, landmarks and topographical features they encountered, names which are still with us today.

Extremely rough terrain was encountered north of San Simeon and after much hardship the party crossed over the divide into the Salinas River Valley near present-day King City. From this point the Salinas River was traced to its mouth on Monterey Bay, the very object of their search. Portolá failed to recognize Monterey Bay, however, and pushed further north along the coast, eventually reaching the site of San Francisco in late October, before returning to San Diego.

While it was the heroic Portolá who actually blazed the coast trail, it was the indomitable Father Junípero Serra who stayed on for 15 long years to establish the chain of settlements along the route. By 1781, the missions that Serra had founded dotted the coast road "like the beads of a rosary, and each he had dedicated to the Glory of God;" while the chain that joined them he named "El Camino Real," popularly translated as "the King's highway" (though in Spanish times it merely meant "the public road").

Three-quarters of a century later, the missions were in ruins and the pastoral California of the padres was fast fading into the legend of the Old West. The land, once the domain of "the heathen," had passed through the hands of the Spaniards and Mexicans and was now Yankee territory. America was stretching her boundaries ever westward and along with this spirit of expansion came a new breed of explorer, the railway surveyor.

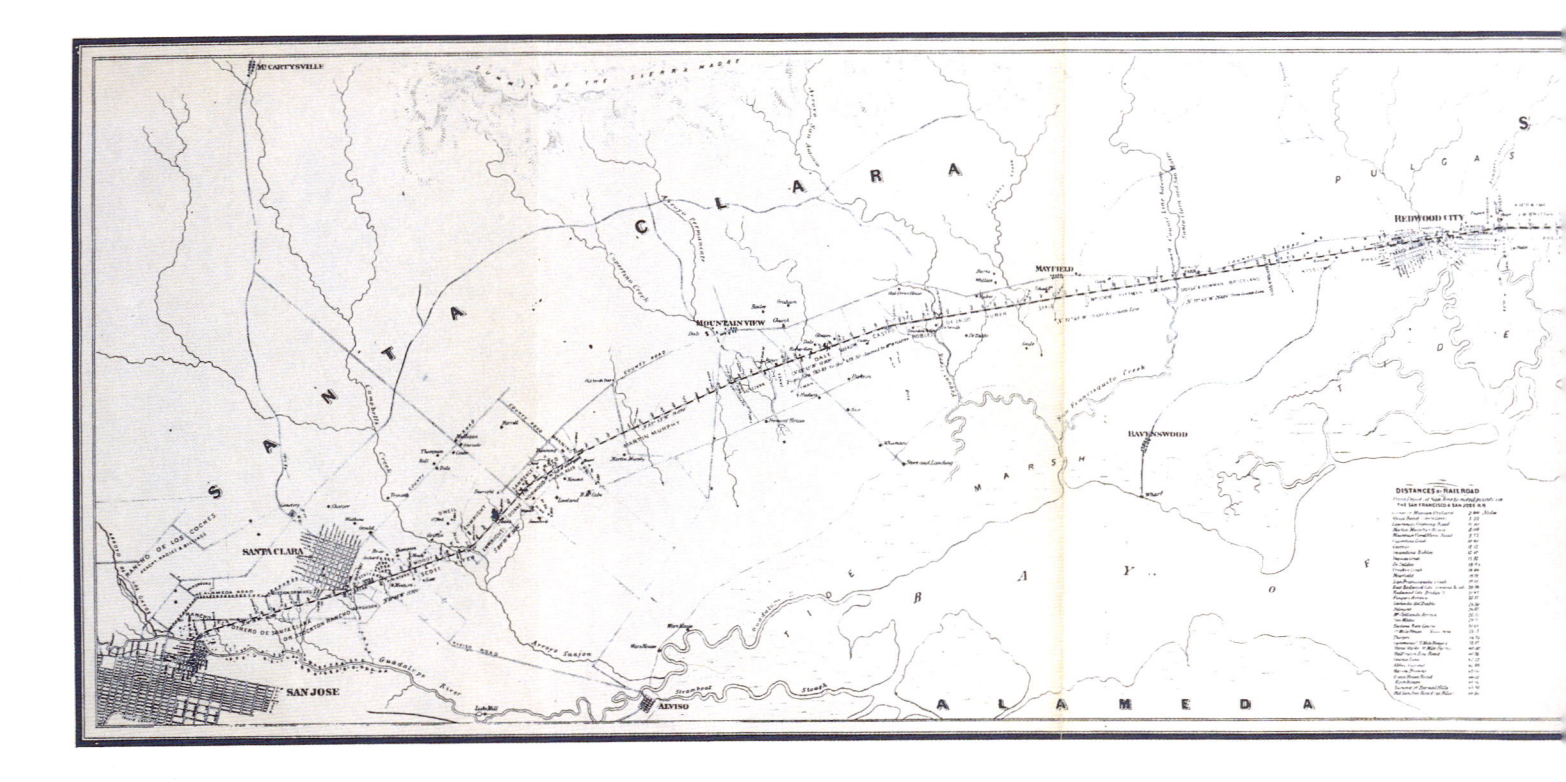

Realizing the value that railways could provide in binding the growing nation together, Congress, on March 3, 1853, passed the first of several Pacific Railroad Acts. These were designed to promote "explorations and surveys to ascertain the most practicable and economical route for a railroad from the Mississippi River to the Pacific Ocean." While transcontinental routes were the main focus of this endeavor, a number of other surveys were made.

And so it was that on November 20, 1854, Lt. John G. Parke and a party of scientists and engineers, acting under the authority of Congress, set out from Benicia, California, intent on determining the practicability of locating a line of railroad from the Bay of San Francisco to Los Angeles, lying wholly west of the Coast Range. The actual survey work began at the Pueblo of San Jose, from which point they advanced south past Gilroy to the Pajaro River and thence down to its opening on Monterey Bay.

Parke and his men then moved to the Salinas River and ascended it to a point nineteen miles above the mission of Soledad where the party was divided. One took the wagon road over the hills via Mission San Antonio and the other continued up the valley, the two parties reuniting at the mission of San Miguel. The old road was then followed to Rancho Santa Margarita, where a camp was established. From there, various explorations were extended and surveys made.

Thirty days later, the survey was pushed over "San Luis Pass" and down to the mouth of the Arroyo Grande. Turning south, Parke and his men passed through the Nipomo Rancho, across the Guadalupe Largo to the mission of Santa Inez. From here three lines were run connecting the valley of Santa Inez with the Guadalupe Largo. Camp was then moved to Gaviota Pass. A survey of the pass was made, and also one following the shoreline by way of Points Arguello and Concepcion (later usually spelled "Conception"). The surveyors then traced a route through Santa Barbara, the Rincon, Mission San Buenaventura, and up the Santa Clara River to San Fernando and Los Angeles.

In the end, Lt. Parke's explorations and surveys resulted in a location which essentially followed what was then called "the old coast road," the El Camino Real. Two routes were suggested between Tres

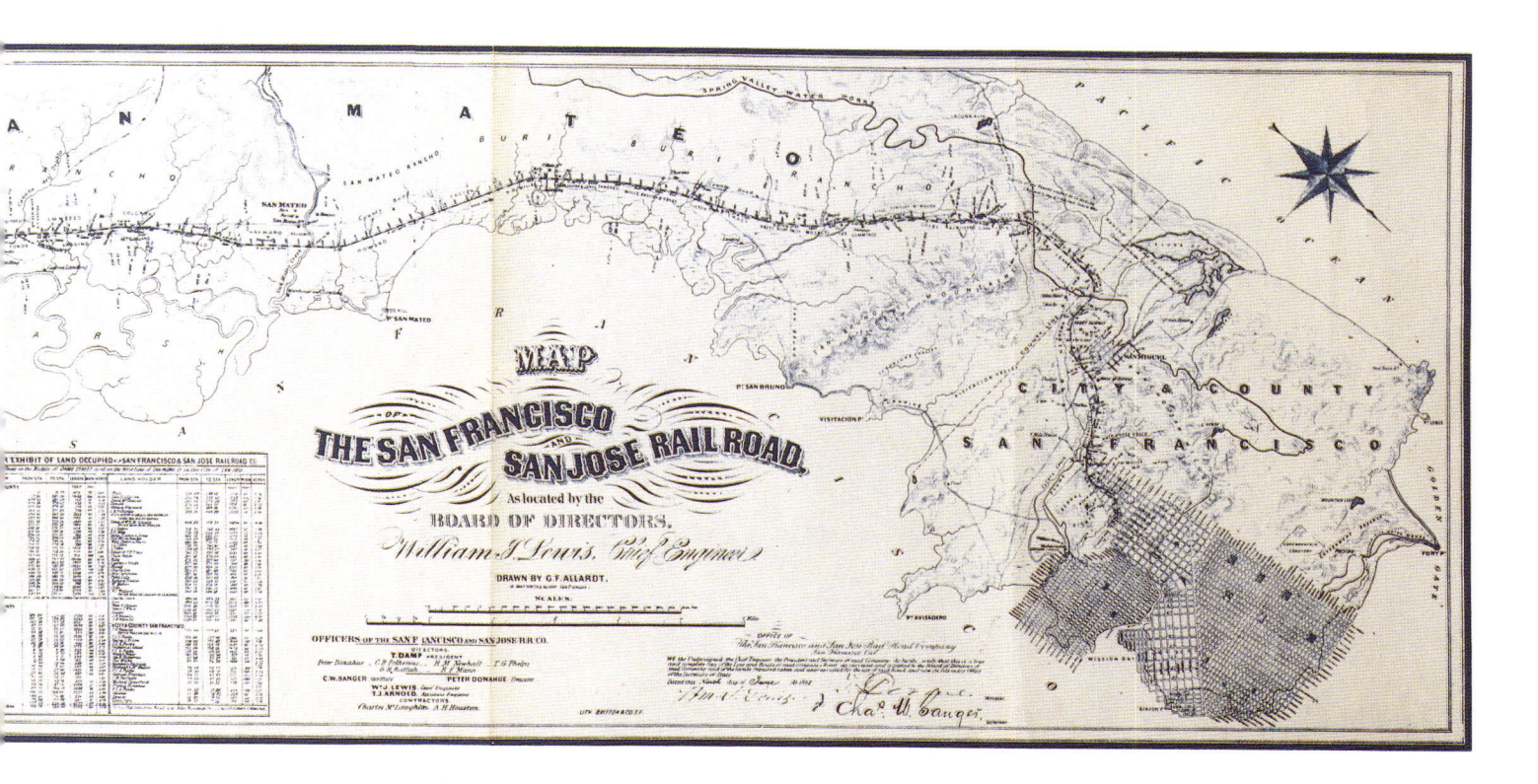

Filing map of the San Francisco and San Jose Railroad Company, dated June 6, 1862.
Courtesy Southern Pacific Lines

Alamos and the mouth of Gaviota Creek, one by way of Gaviota Pass, and the other along the coastal terrace through Point Conception. The latter was thirteen and three-quarters miles longer but the difficulties to be encountered in constructing a road through Gaviota Pass seemed to balance the cost.

The results of these surveys, and others throughout the west, were published in a series of reports during 1857, and became the blueprint for many of the railway construction projects that were beginning to take shape on the west coast.

Meanwhile, during 1849, while the Gold Rush was in full swing, a group of San Franciscans had launched the scheme of building a railroad down the peninsula to San Jose and, it was hoped, later extending it to the Mississippi River. By the fall of 1851, the Pacific and Atlantic Railroad was formally organized with this in mind, yet little was accomplished. It was difficult to attract investors, as the gold fields offered greater opportunities for profit. Reorganizations in 1853, and again in 1859—when the name was changed to The San Francisco and San Jose Rail Road Company—turned out to be no more successful.

It was the fourth reorganization of this company, on August 18, 1860, that finally met with some success. Contracts were let that October and, following a vote of the counties of Santa Clara, San Mateo and San Francisco in April, 1861, a total of $600,000 was subscribed to the project. Surveys of the route were conducted in 1861 by Col. William J. Lewis, Chief Engineer, and T. J. Arnold, Chief Assistant Engineer.

Construction of the road began in both directions at San Francisquito Creek in what is now Menlo Park during May, 1861, under the direction of W.J.L. Moulton, Superintendent of Construction. Operation of trains began October 19, 1863, running from 25th and Valencia Streets, San Francisco, to Big Trees Station (now Menlo Park.) At this point, while the road was still under construction to San Jose, the Company held its first formal opening near two large redwood trees on the banks of the same creek between Menlo Park and Palo Alto. Governor Leland Stanford and other speakers addressed a crowd of several thousand people assembled for the occasion.

Although the road was not yet completed into downtown San Francisco, the opening of the road through from the Race Track to San Jose on January 16, 1864, was celebrated with fitting ceremonies at the new brick station on San Pedro Street in San Jose. Practically the entire town's population was on hand to greet the two excursion trains that arrived from San Francisco. Timothy Dame, president of the railroad, reviewed the history of his company and told of the difficulties encountered in completing the project. He went on to prophesy that "the time was not far distant when the 'iron horse' would be shouting his cry of joy on the hills and through the valleys of the great plain that separates us from the homes of our childhood."

On February 13, 1864, operation of the northern end of the line was extended from 25th Street via private right-of-way to 22nd and Harrison, thence along Harrison Street to 16th where a small engine terminal with a six-stall roundhouse, turntable and machine shop was built to service all rolling stock. From this point tracks were further extended to Fourth and Brannan Streets, San Francisco, where Company terminal facilities were established occupying about a quarter of a block. Trains were operated to this point under a special permit from the City of San Francisco for several years, as the Fourth and Townsend Streets property, which was owned by the Company, was under water. Later, the Southern Pacific leased the Market Street Railway's tracks from Valencia and 16th to its junction with Market Street. Here several lots were purchased and in 1866, the road's freight and passenger depots were established. For a short time, SP operated steam trains down Market Street to the Ferry Building but gave up the practice after the city fathers raised an uproar. The depot remained at Brannan until 1869 when the land at Townsend Street was filled in and made the permanent San Francisco terminal. The Company's large station and office building on Townsend between 3rd and 4th Streets was opened in 1875.

The San Francisco and San Jose Rail Road was not the only rail operation beginning to take root in California. The Sacramento Valley Rail Road Company, California's first, had been opened from Sacramento to Folsom in 1856. The Central Pacific Rail Road Company of California began construction east out of Sacramento in January, 1863. The Western Pacific Railroad, incorporated in December, 1862, by Timothy Dame and others interested in the San Francisco and San Jose Rail Road, was to build from San Jose to a connection with the Central Pacific near Sacramento. This Western Pacific had no connection with the WP completed in 1909.

Yet another enterprise, the Southern Pacific Railroad Company, was incorporated December 2, 1865, under the laws of California to build from San Francisco Bay south through the counties of Santa Clara, Monterey, San Luis Obispo, Tulare, Los Angeles and San Diego, thence east through San Diego County to a junction with a contemplated road from the Mississippi River. Little headway was made in the plans of this new company until it was recognized as a part of a second transcontinental railroad by the act of Congress in July, 1866. The following January, the company filed a map designating the general route it proposed to take from San Francisco through San Jose, Gilroy and Tres Pinos in the Santa Clara and San Benito valleys, thence across the Coast Range into the San Joaquin Valley near the site of present-day Coalinga. This road was projected to cross the Tehachapi and be built as far as the Colorado River.

The first step of the Southern Pacific Railroad was to acquire the line already in operation between San Francisco and San Jose. Stock that San Francisco County held in the San Francisco and San Jose Rail Road Company was purchased following authorization of the state legislature on March 30, 1868. Three weeks later, on April 21, ground was broken at 4th Street in San Jose for extension of the line to Gilroy. This work was carried out under the authority of the Santa Clara and Pajaro Valley Rail Road Company and was completed about April 13, 1869. Beyond Gilroy, construction proceeded in the name of the Southern Pacific Railroad, and trains were operated to Hollister on July 13, 1871, and to Tres Pinos on August 12, 1873.

Meanwhile, Governor Stanford and his associates in the Central Pacific had acquired a controlling interest in the budding young railroad company. The first indication of the close relationship between the two lines came on September 25, 1868, when Collis P. Huntington, vice president of the Central Pacific,

Reflecting the continued growth in suburban traffic, the Southern Pacific had by 1890 erected this much larger station one block to the east at Third and Townsend Streets, San Francisco.
Southern Pacific Lines

The property at Fourth and Townsend Streets in San Francisco had been purchased for terminal grounds by the San Francisco and San Jose Rail Road Company in the early 1860s. Because the location was under water at the time (pending filling of the bay), it was not until 1870 that a simple frame station (**left**) was erected on the site. By this time, the Southern Pacific Railroad was taking shape and the company took the opportunity to build their general office building nearby (**below**).
Left, Arnold S. Menke collection; below, Vernon J. Sappers collection

Reflecting the change in ownership of the San Francisco and San Jose Rail Road, a 15-car special, drawn by an unidentified Southern Pacific American-type locomotive, and operated for the benefit of General U.S. Grant and party, pauses at Belmont (**above**) in 1882. More typical of the era, a south-bound passenger train, drawn by Southern Pacific 4-4-0 No. 73 (**below**) rolls through open country near Oak Grove (now Burlingame) in 1884. The Peninsula line had been open now for twenty years, yet much of the route was still rural. The San Francisco and San Jose Rail Road roster was absorbed by the SP and No. 11, *Menlo Park* (**left**) built by Wm. Mason in 1870, wound up as SP No. 1167 before being scrapped in 1898.

Above, Vernon J. Sappers collection;
left and below, courtesy DeGolyer Library;

transmitted to the Secretary of the Interior the annual report of the Southern Pacific Railroad Company. This became a matter of official record on October 12, 1870, when The San Francisco and San Jose Rail Road Company, the Santa Clara and Pajaro Valley Rail Road Company and the California Southern Railroad Company (incorporated January 22, 1870, to build from Gilroy to Salinas), were consolidated to form a new Southern Pacific Railroad Company.

During this period in which the Southern Pacific Railroad Company came into existence, the Central Pacific was pushing forward extensions from its main line in California north into the Sacramento Valley and south into the San Joaquin Valley. This latter line, upon which work commenced at Lathrop on December 31, 1869, became the main thrust of the combined companies' push to the Colorado River. The proposed line from Tres Pinos south over the Coast Range was never built, and most of the land grants were given up.

Work did continue, however, on what was eventually to become the Coast Line. Four days after the line was completed to Hollister, forces were transferred to a point two miles south of Gilroy and on July 17, 1871, ground was broken on the "Watsonville Branch." Work was carried out by the Contract and Finance Company, the construction arm of the "Big Four" (Huntington, Stanford, Charles Crocker and Mark Hopkins), and the pace was to be brisk: 25 miles through the difficult Chittenden Pass country in 90 days.

The Los Angeles *Star* reported on August 18th that "a heavy force of workmen is employed on the railroad between Gilroy and Salinas City and the work will be completed by the first of November. The road...passes within five miles of San Juan, south of the Pajaro River. A bridge across the river is now being built and [the road] runs down the Pajaro River Valley one mile from Watsonville, thence to Salinas City." The *Star* went on to editorialize that the route "will probably be down Salinas Plains to San Luis Obispo, to Santa Barbara and Los Angeles."

The road was opened for traffic to Pajaro (now Watsonville Junction) on November 27, 1871, and to Salinas on November 1 of the following year. From Salinas, construction continued south another 25 miles to Soledad under the name of the Southern Pacific Branch Railroad Company. This company had been organized to build south through the Salinas Valley and over Polonio Pass into the Tulare Valley and a connection with the Valley Line at Poso near Bakersfield. A similar company, by the name of The Southern Pacific Branch Railway Company, was to build south from a point at or near San Miguel to a connection in Los Angeles County with the projected line over Tehachapi Pass. All of this road was built in later years except the portion from San Miguel into the Tulare Valley.

By August 12, 1873, the road was in operation to Soledad where construction was halted for a number of years. During this period, the Southern Pacific Railroad was aggressively pushed through to Los Angeles from Goshen via Mojave and on east across Arizona and New Mexico, eventually completing a through route to New Orleans in 1883. Additional effort was expended in pushing a through line north from Redding toward Oregon. It was not until the spring of 1886, as Pacific Improvement Company forces labored in the Siskiyou Mountains toward an eventual completion of the Shasta Route, that Southern Pacific was again ready to resume work on the Coast Line.

The Southern Pacific started construction south from San Jose through the Santa Clara Valley, reaching Tres Pinos on August 12, 1873. From this point, the line was originally projected over the Coast Range to the San Joaquin Valley. But the Big Four elected to build south in the San Joaquin from Lathrop, and the line beyond Tres Pinos was never built.

Southern Pacific Lines

The Southern Pacific was opened for traffic to Salinas City (**above**) on November 1, 1872. This view of Salinas looking north from Main St. dates from 1905.

California State Library

The Pacific Improvement Company, a construction company controlled by SP interests, developed the celebrated Del Monte Hotel (**below**) on 7,000 acres of land adjacent to the Monterey Branch. With its own station (**left**), the Del Monte was for over half a century the destination for the wealthy and socially prominent seeking relaxation on the Pacific Coast.

Both, California State Library

SOUTHERN PACIFIC RAILROAD,
(NORTHERN DIVISION.)

Commencing Monday, April 21st, 1879, Passenger Trains
WILL LEAVE AS FOLLOWS:

FROM SAN FRANCISCO.

DAILY P.M.	DAILY, Sundays Excepted P.M.	P.M.	P.M.	SUNDAYS ONLY P.M.	DAILY A.M.	SUNDAYS ONLY A.M.	DAILY A.M.	Distance from SAN FRAN.	STATIONS	Distance from SOLEDAD	DAILY A.M.	DAILY, Sundays Excepted A.M.	A.M.	A.M.	SUNDAYS ONLY A.M.	DAILY A.M.	DAILY P.M.	SUNDAYS ONLY P.M.
Lv.	Lv.	Lv.	Lv.	Lv.	Lv.	Lv.	Lv.				Ar.	Ar.	Ar.	Ar.	Ar.	Ar.	Ar.	Ar.
6.30	5.00	4.25	3.30	3.30	10.40	9.30	8.20	0	**San Fran.** Townsend St.	142-9	6.40	8.30	9.10	10.00	10.00	3.40	6.40	8.15
6.45	5.14	4.39	3.45	3.45	10.55	9.46	8.36	3-4	Valencia St.	139-5	6.25	8.16	8.56	9.46	9.46	3.25	6.25	8.00
6.50	5.18	*....	*....	†3.49	10.59	9.49	8.40	4-6	BERNAL	138-3	6.20	8.13	*....	*....	†9.42	3.20	6.21	7.55
6.56	5.23	*....	*....	†3.54	11.04	9.55	8.48	6-9	SAN MIGUEL	136-0	6.13	8.08	*....	*....	†9.37	3.15	6.15	7.50
7.03	5.28	*....	*....	†3.59	11.09	10.01	8.55	9-2	COLMA	133-7	6.05	8.02	*....	*....	†9.32	3.10	6.08	7.44
7.10	5.34	4.57	*....	†4.05	11.16	10.08	9.03	12-2	BADEN	130-7	5.56	7.55	*....	*....	†9.26	3.02	6.00	7.36
7.17	5.39	*....	*....	†4.10	11.21	10.14	9.10	14-3	SAN BRUNO	128-6	5.48	7.50	*....	*....	†9.22	2.57	5.53	7.31
7.25	5.45	5.07	4.15	4.15	11.28	10.21	9.17	17-0	MILLBRAE	125-9	5.40	7.44	8.29	9.17	9.17	2.50	5.45	7.25
7.30	5.51	*....	*....	†4.20	11.33	10.26	9.21	19-2	OAK GROVE	123-7	5.31	7.39	*....	*....	†9.12	2.45	5.36	7.19
7.39	5.55	5.15	4.24	4.24	11.38	10.31	9.25	21-1	SAN MATEO	121-8	5.25	7.34	8.21	9.09	9.09	2.40	5.30	7.13
7.48	6.03	*....	†4.31	†4.31	11.48	10.41	9.34	25-1	BELMONT	117-8	5.10	7.25	*....	†9.02	†9.02	2.30	5.21	7.03
7.55	6.11	5.27	4.38	4.38	11.56	10.50	9.41	28-6	REDWOOD	114-3	5.02	7.18	8.08	8.55	8.55	2.21	5.12	6.54
					P.M.													
8.00	6.16	*....	*....	†4.43	12 01	10.56	9.46	30-9	FAIR OAKS	112-0	4.54	7.13	*....	*....	†8.50	2.15	5.05	6.48
8.05	6.20	*....	4.47	4.47	12 05	10.59	9.49	32-1	MENLO PARK	110-8	4.50	7.10	8.01	8.47	8.47	2.12	5.01	6.44
....	....	5.41	4.53	4.53	12 12	11.06	9.56	34-9	MAYFIELD	108-0	....	....	7.55	8.41	8.41	2.05	4.53	6.37
....	....	5.48	5.01	5.01	12 22	11.15	10.05	39-1	MTN. VIEW	103-8	....	....	7.48	8.34	8.34	1.56	4.44	6.27
....	....	*....	†5.07	5.07	12 29	11.23	10.11	41 9	MURPHYS	101-0	....	....	†7.42	*....	†8.29	1.49	4.38	6.20
....	....	†5.57	*....	†5.11	12 34	11.28	10.16	43-9	LAWRENCES	99-0	....	....	†7.37	*....	†8.25	1.44	4.33	6.15
....	....	6.04	5.17	5.17	12 43	11.36	10.24	47-4	SANTA CLARA	95-5	....	....	7.30	8.19	8.19	1.36	4.26	6.06
....	....	6.10	5.23	5.23	12 55	11.43	10.30	50-0	SAN JOSE	92-9	....	....	7.25	8.13	8.13	1.30	4.20	6.00
....	....	....	†5.49	....	1 15	....	....	57-3	EDEN VALE	85-6	....	....	....	†7.47	....	1.04	....	....
....	....	....	†5.58	....	1 27	....	....	62-8	COYOTE	80-1	....	....	....	†7.37	....	12.53	....	....
....	....	....	†6.04	....	1 34	....	....	65-8	PERRYS	77-1	....	....	....	†7.31	....	12.46	....	....
....	....	....	6.10	....	1 40	....	....	68-8	MADRONE	74-1	....	....	....	†7.25	....	12.40	....	....
....	....	....	†6.15	....	1 46	....	....	71-5	TENNANTS	71-4	....	....	....	†7.20	....	12.34	....	....
....	....	....	6.42	....	2 20	....	....	80-3	GILROY	62-6	....	....	....	7.04	....	12.15	....	....
																P.M.		
....	....	....	....	....	2.26	....	....	82-5	CARNADERO	60-4	....	....	....	*....	....	11.55	....	....
....	....	....	†6.55	....	2.35	....	....	86 5	SARGENTS	56-4	....	....	....	†6.38	....	11.45	....	....
....	....	....	†7.18	....	2.59	....	....	96-5	VEGA	46-4	....	....	....	†6.15	....	11.23	....	....
....	....	....	7.25	....	3.05	....	....	99-4	PAJARO	43-5	....	....	....	6.10	....	11.16	....	....
....	....	....	....	....	3.30	....	....	109-7	CASTROVILLE	33-2	....	....	....	....	....	10.52	....	....
....	....	....	....	....	4.00	....	....	117-6	SALINAS	25-3	....	....	....	....	....	10.35	....	....
....	....	....	....	....	4.35	....	....	128-5	CHUALAR	14-4	....	....	....	....	....	9.47	....	....
....	....	....	....	....	4.55	....	....	134-5	GONZALES	8-4	....	....	....	....	....	9.28	....	....
....	....	....	....	....	5.20	....	....	142-9	Ar SOLEDAD Lv	0	....	....	....	....	....	9.00	....	....
																A.M.		

☞ *Trains do not stop. †Trains stop only on signal or to leave passengers. ☜

The 10.40 A.M. Train Connects at { PAJARO (Daily) with the Santa Cruz R. R. for Aptos Soquel and Santa Cruz.
{ SALINAS (Daily) with the M. & S. V. R. R. for Monterey.
On Saturdays Only—The 3.30 P.M. Train Connects at { PAJARO with the Santa Cruz R. R. for Aptos, Soquel and Santa Cruz.
{ SALINAS with the M. & S. V. R. R. for Monterey.

TRAINS BETWEEN GILROY AND TRES PINOS.

Dist.	SOUTHWARD. Trains Leave	DAILY.	DAILY, Sundays Excepted	Dist.	NORTHWARD. Trains Leave	DAILY, Sundays Excepted	SUNDAYS ONLY.
0	Gilroy	2.25 P.M.	6.50 P.M.	0	Tres Pinos	5.55 A.M.	10.45 A.M.
14-	Hollister	2.55 "	7.50 "	6-2	Hollister	6.10 "	11.00 "
20-2	Tres Pinos....arrive	3.10 "	8.15 "	20-2	Gilroy....arrive	6.45 "	11.50 "

STANDARD OF TIME............,............Trains are run by Anderson & Randolph's (San Francisco) Time.

Courtesy Southern Pacific Lines

This is not to imply that railroad construction stopped completely on the coast in the interim. Following the arrival of Southern Pacific in the Salinas Valley in the early 1870s, several lines were developed to tap surrounding communities of importance. Responding to perceived inequities in freight rates, a group of local citizens organized, on March 5, 1874, The Monterey and Salinas Valley Rail Road Company. Construction began on April 20, 1874, and the 18.5-mile narrow-gauge road was completed between Salinas (City) and the port of Monterey on October 23, 1874. Drought, flood and intense competition from the Southern Pacific took their toll, however, and in August of 1879, the Pacific Improvement Company purchased the narrow-gauge line, on behalf of the SP, at a foreclosure sale. Shortly after, Charles Crocker sold the entire Monterey and Salinas Valley's physical plant, including locomotives, rolling stock, turntables, water tanks and nineteen miles of track hardware to the Nevada Central Railway. The Pacific Improvement Company was at this time engaged in building a road from Castroville (later Del Monte Junction) to Monterey. In this work, a twelve-mile stretch of the narrow gauge right-of-way, from the Salinas River crossing at Bardin into Monterey, was rehabilitated as standard

Work on the line south in the Salinas Valley was done in stages. In the spring of 1886, work commenced at Soledad on the extension south. The railroad was in operation to San Miguel (**left**) on October 18th and to Paso Robles (**above**) on October 31, 1886. Once Templeton was reached in November, work was shifted to the southern end of the Coast Line at Saugus.

Two photos, San Luis Obispo County Historical Society

gauge, and the completed line was opened in January of 1880.

Even as the branch was nearing completion, the "Big Four" were at work capitalizing on their investment. Through their construction company, the Pacific Improvement Company, some 7,000 acres of land were acquired in the vicinity of Monterey and in September 1880, the Hotel Del Monte opened for business. Catering to San Francisco's elite the sprawling resort, surrounded by formal British gardens, was rendered in an amalgam of the "Swiss" Stick Style and Queen Anne, with towers and turrets, lacy stickwork verandas and half-timbering. Well publicized by the railroad, the Del Monte quickly earned a place in the lore of the Old West. The Monterey Branch was later extended to Pacific Grove and Lake Majella. For this purpose, The Monterey Extension Railroad Company was organized, and after consolidating with the SP, extended the line as far as the mouth of the Carmel River. The final 4.4 miles of the 16-mile extension were built by the SP, and Lake Majella was reached on August 1, 1889.

The Santa Cruz Branch was formerly the narrow-gauge road of the Santa Cruz Railroad Company, which had been organized during the summer of 1873 under circumstances similar to the Monterey operation. The 21-mile road from the Southern Pacific at Watsonville Junction (formerly Pajaro) was opened to Santa Cruz on May 18, 1876. The inevitable bankruptcy followed soon after and the road, after passing to the Pacific Improvement Company, was in Southern Pacific hands by November, 1882. Broad-gauging was accomplished in 1883.

Resumption of construction on the extension of the road south of Soledad was announced on April 11, 1886, and by July 20th, the line was in operation to King's City; to San Miguel on October 18th; to Paso Robles on October 31st; and to Templeton on November 16, 1886. Once Templeton was reached, the graders were moved to Newhall (near Saugus) where work had already begun on the extension westward through the "Santa Paula Valley" to Ventura and Santa Barbara. Travelers wishing to continue to Santa Barbara south from Templeton were required to continue their journey via stage, although after 1887 the narrow-gauge Pacific Coast Railway offered another transportation option between San Luis Obispo and Los Olivos.

Work on the southern end of what was to become the "Coast Line" had first been attempted in April, 1886, but it was not until the middle of September that work was begun in earnest. The survey followed the bottom country along the Santa Clara River from Saugus to the coast. The Los Angeles *Times* kept close tabs on the progress. The rails reached Piru on December 18, 1886; Sespe on December 25th; and Santa Paula on January 18, 1887. Strong rains in February and a shortage of rail impacted progress but by March 3, 1887, the rails were within one quarter of a mile of Saticoy. The trains finally arrived at Ventura on May 18th. Meanwhile, advance crews of Chinese graders were deployed along the more difficult stretches of work at Rincon Point and Ortega Hill, chipping away a ledge in the rocky cliffs.

Scheduled passenger trains began operating to Carpinteria on July 1, 1887. At this point, the absence of rail from the east delayed further progress and it was not until early August that the construction trains were within earshot of Santa Barbara. By August 13th, the track layers had reached the depot site. But the grand jubilee commemorating the 100th anniversary of the founding of Santa Barbara and the arrival of the railroad was reserved for Saturday, August 20, 1887.

While Santa Barbara celebrated, railroad building continued. By early October, "the Front" was at Hope Ranch and on December 21, 1887, the "Ventura Division" of the Southern Pacific was opened to Ellwood, eleven miles west of Santa Barbara. But it was here, for a number of reasons, that work was suspended for what eventually became nearly 14 years. There was little business between Santa Barbara and San Luis Obispo to justify the

In the fall of 1886, grading began at Saugus on the southern end of the Coast Line, along the Santa Clara River. Fillmore (**above**) was reached in December, 1886.
Ventura County Museum of Art & History

A crew of SP surveyors poses for the camera at Ventura (**above**) in the spring of 1887. Trains finally reached the coast near Ventura that May, while advance crews of Chinese graders were preparing a route along the cliffs at Rincon Point and Ortega Hill.
Southern Pacific Lines

SP locomotive 84 poses with a Los Angeles-bound local passenger train at the old Victoria St. station in Santa Barbara about 1890. The railroad reached town in August of 1887, but construction of the "Ventura Division" of the Southern Pacific continued only as far as Ellwood, where work was again suspended for nearly 14 years.
Robert McNeel Collection

considerable expense of construction. The Oregon extension was sapping much of the available cash, and to make things worse, considerable anti-railroad legislation was cropping up in California, and the United States government, in hopes of proving some sort of wrongdoing, had initiated the Pacific Railroad Hearings.

Beyond Ellwood, construction would be more costly, as the terraced land bordering on the ocean was cut by a series of deep lateral ravines which would require much bridging. Then too, there was the choice of routes suggested by the Pacific Railroad Reports; that of the coast route by way of points Conception, Arguello and Purisima, and the inland route via Gaviota Pass. Surveys were conducted through the pass during the summer of 1886, by Joseph Hood, brother of SP's chief engineer William Hood, and again in September, 1887, by W.B. Story (who later left Southern Pacific for the Atchison, Topeka & Santa Fe), but no action was taken. By May 1890, the local press was reporting that Gaviota Pass had been "practically abandoned as a route" because the line along the coast would have more favorable grades.

While residents of San Luis Obispo waited anxiously for the trains to arrive, workers pose at the west end of the 3,610-foot tunnel No. 1 at the summit of the Cuesta Grade during the summer of 1893, a period when construction in the Santa Lucia Range was at its peak.
San Luis Obispo Public Library

The crossing of the Santa Lucia Range was the other major obstacle to completion of the Coast Line. Mr. Story favored Lieutenant Parke's survey via the head of Corral de Piedra Creek which avoided the mountains entirely, and was quoted in the local press, saying "If we were permitted to leave this town [San Luis Obispo] out, the problem would be solved; but we are directed to find a route through the city of San Luis Obispo."

Company officials were hazy about plans to complete the gap between Templeton and Ellwood. The *Alta California* quoted Collis Huntington in April, 1888 regarding the matter. "Yes," he said, "we propose to go on with the construction of the coast line between Templeton...and Santa Barbara, but the exact route has not been decided. It will take some time to complete the road as there is a great deal of heavy work to be done this side of Santa Barbara. We desire, however, to complete that road as soon as possible." That June C.F. Crocker, son of Charles Crocker, was more specific, projecting that work might commence "sometime this fall or winter."

Indeed, during October 1888, the railroad gathered about 175 men at Templeton to begin work on the extension south. By December, the force numbered over 1,000 and the road was open for operation through broken country to Santa Margarita on January 13, 1889. From this point, heavy construction was encountered in the rugged Santa Lucia Range and it would be another five years before San Luis Obispo, 17 miles distant, would be reached. On April 9, 1889, Collis Huntington and a party of officials came to San Luis Obispo. They had come by train as far as Santa Margarita, then by stage through the Cuesta to the Ramona Hotel. That evening, he addressed a large gathering at the recently opened agricultural pavilion. Speaking frankly he said "Now, we are sixteen miles from here, and if you were to give us the right-of-way, and it was all straight and the title was perfect and the ground that we would want for the shops and depot purposes was provided, I expect we might commence work at the building of the road...As far as I am personally concerned, I would just as soon you would be ten years about it as not; in fact, rather." Both Huntington and associate C.F. "Fred" Crocker intimated that the expense and difficulty of building tunnels through the Cuesta was discouraging, without local support.

Cuesta Grade

A "committee of 21" was quickly organized to come up with a plan to comply with the railroad's demands but it was not until eighteen months later, on October 23, 1890, that a satisfactory agreement was worked out between the railroad and the counties of San Luis Obispo and Santa Barbara. For the central coast communities, having waited so long for rail connections to the outside world, had banded together in their negotiations with the railroad. Finally, early in 1891, the news came that the Pacific Improvement Company would begin work in the first five miles of the Coast Division gap south of Santa Margarita about January 15th. The company was calling for bids on the construction of two tunnels, one 3,600 feet long, and the other 1,400 feet.

The work was slow and intermittent, however, and a year later a force of barely forty men was at work on the line between Santa Margarita and the mouth of the first tunnel. Much of the preliminary work that had been done in this area during 1889 was now repeated as the earlier road had disappeared in thickets and high grass. It was not until October, 1892, that contracts were settled for the construction into San Luis Obispo, setting the stage for the big

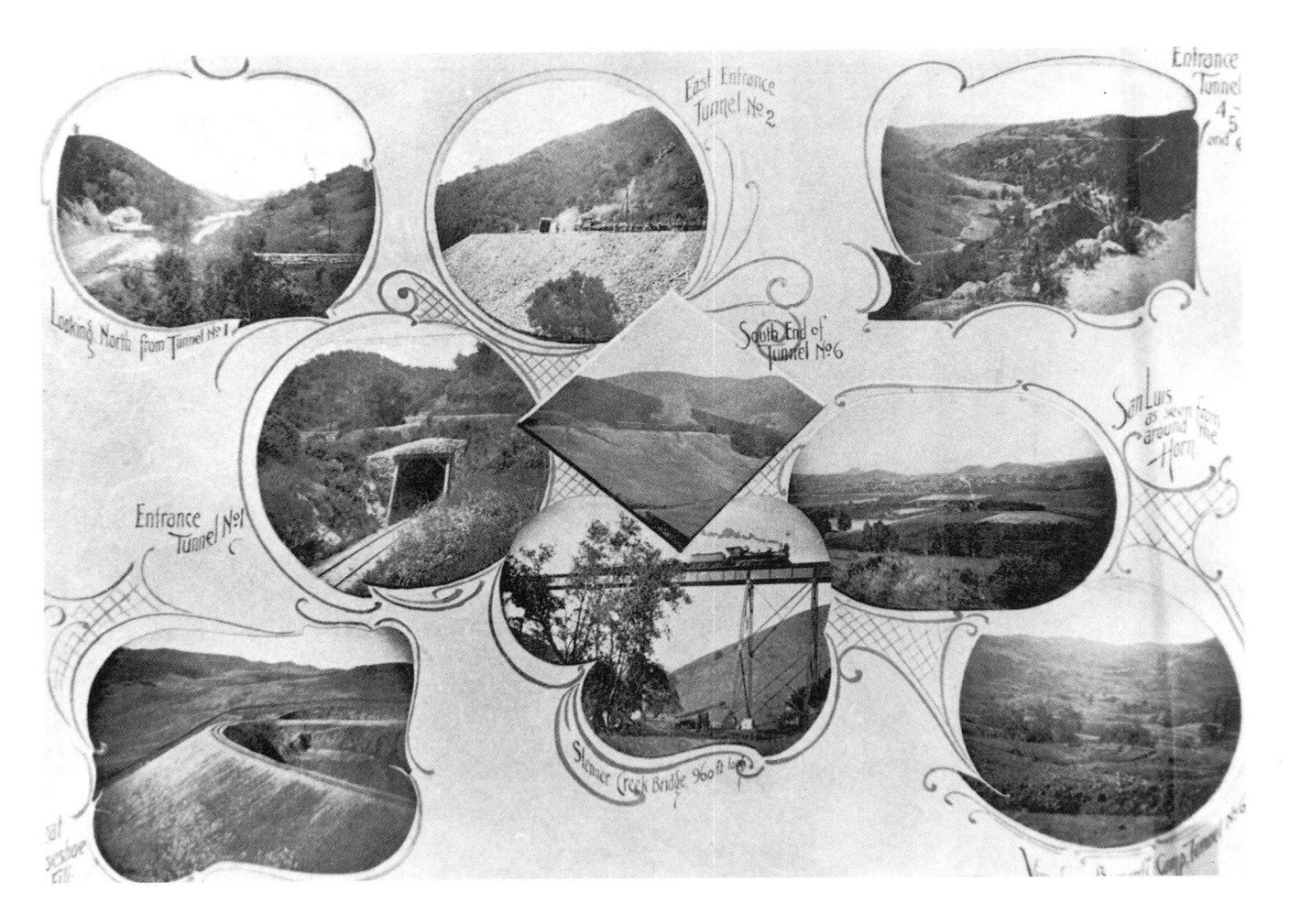

The most costly work to be undertaken on the entire Coast Line occurred on the 17-mile Cuesta Grade between Santa Margarita and San Luis Obispo. Here the builders penetrated the ridge of the rugged Santa Lucia Mountains with a great tunnel before descending over eleven hundred feet to San Luis Obispo.

San Luis Obispo Public Library

push the following spring. The Oakland *Tribune* reported that the contract price was said to be $3 million, or nearly $300,000 per mile.

By May, 1893, it was reported that 1,200 men were at work on the Cuesta grade. The final alignment, as located by Chief Engineer William Hood, was spectacular. After piercing the saddle at the summit with a long tunnel, six more tunnels were required as the line dropped down grade following along a side hill which was generally steep and frequently precipitous. Many deep cuts and deeper fills were required as the road wound its way down the mountain side. Perhaps the most astounding feature of the Cuesta Grade occurred where the westernmost point of the alignment was reached near Chorro Creek. From this point, the line reversed itself to describe a giant loop which stretched out for several miles, returning at last almost to the starting point, a few hundred feet lower in elevation. Below this point, the line led straight to a precipice and sailed off "into the atmosphere" eighty feet above the earth (Stenner Creek) before landing on an adjacent hillside. "The great Tehachapi Loop," the San Luis Obispo *Tribune* crowed, "will pale before the present costly piece of engineering."

A tight securities market, followed by the panic in the economy during mid-summer 1893, resulted in layoffs among the work force but the momentum was regained in the fall and at last, on January 19, 1894, the summit tunnel was "holed through." One by one the lesser tunnels were opened up until all that was left to extend the road into San Luis Obispo was the completion of the massive Stenner Creek viaduct. In late March, word came down the

As the road wound its way down the south side of the slope, many deep cuts, additional tunnels and fills were required (**above**). Near Chorro Creek the line reached its greatest feature, describing a great loop (**right**) before leading to a high steel viaduct over Stenner Creek, some 80 feet below. Railroad usage for a number of years was "Steiner Creek," but the geographic name, "Stenner," eventually prevailed. Local landmark Cerro Romualdo looms in the distance (**below**) as a westbound train works upgrade over the viaduct several year after construction.

Top, Robert H. McFarland, author's collection;
right, San Luis Obispo Public Library;
below, San Luis Obispo County Historical Society

Southern Pacific reached San Luis Obispo on May 5, 1894, and immediately began construction of yards and engine facilities. The railroad reservation was above and to the east of the main part of town as shown by these two views taken that summer. SP's new Coast Line cuts across the foreground (**above**) as Cerro San Luis Obispo rises to the west of the growing community of the same name. From the outset the new Southern Pacific depot (**left**) was the scene of much activity.
Both, San Luis Obispo Public Library

grade that the structural parts for the bridge had arrived from Pittsburgh. They occupied fifty or more freight cars that were scattered along the tracks from the mouth of the summit tunnel all the way back to Templeton.

Track was laid to Stenner Creek by April 6, 1894, and long trains pulled by two or three engines dumped 100 carloads of ballast a day along the track bed. It was discovered at the time construction of the bridge was begun that some parts had not arrived yet and work was delayed while a search was conducted for the side-tracked cars. Some were found as far away as New Orleans. The time was fast approaching when the trains would reach San Luis Obispo. On May 3rd, 10,000 feet of track were laid from Stenner Creek trestle to within a stone's throw of the community. At last, at 3:25 PM, May 5, 1894, the first train steamed triumphantly into San Luis Obispo.

Railroad construction continued in and around the vicinity of town for some time after the trains began running from San Francisco into San Luis Obispo. The yards, depot grounds and turntable site were located on a side hill which required moving and leveling tons of earth. By early fall, the brick roundhouse was taking shape and the contractors began cutting and scraping roadbed south of town. By November rails and ties were on hand and a force of sixty men was brought in to start laying track. By Christmas, 1894, some advanced graders had moved

Despite the fact that a 56-mile gap remained in the Coast Line, ranchers, merchants and communities along the line of advancing rails still reaped great benefit from greatly improved transportation. By the mid-'nineties, traffic to and from the coast counties had increased enormously. Witness the first solid trainload of lima beans (**above**) ever shipped out of Ventura County, which departed Ventura in October, 1890. In another view of prosperity, engine No. 1631 and a long freight pause at San Ardo (**right**) in the upper Salinas Valley about 1898.
Top, Ventura County Museum of Art & History; right, Henry Clark photo, courtesy George McCarron

across the Santa Maria River onto the Guadalupe plains.

By January 14, 1895, track was completed to the edge of Pismo; to Oceano by January 27th; and on July 1, 1895, regular trains began running over the Santa Maria River on a temporary trestle into Guadalupe. Meanwhile, contracts had been let early in 1895 for the construction of a permanent bridge across the Santa Maria River. Progress was slow. At one point over 300 men were at work on the 1,283-foot steel structure before the bridge was completed in late June, 1896.

Keeping up the momentum, Southern Pacific began selling tickets to a new place eleven miles south of Guadalupe, called Someo, or Casmalia, on January 30, 1896. The seven miles from Casmalia through Antonio and Narlon was opened to Los Alamos Creek on April 6, 1896. On June 1st, regular operations were extended to Tangair and by the tenth of June the rail head was on the north bank of the Santa Ynez River.

The community of Bridgeport, peopled mainly by railroad and bridge workers, sprang up on the south bank of the river. Using a temporary bridge across the Santa Ynez River, the rails reached the new station of Surf, 304 miles from San Francisco, on August 18, 1896. A few months later, all the buildings from Bridgeport had been moved the few hundred feet south to the new station.

The gap on the Coast Line had now been narrowed to the 56 miles between Surf and Ellwood but progress on this final section was not immediately forthcoming. This would be a costly piece of railroad to construct, involving heavy fills, two tunnels and nine steel trestles. Poor financial conditions and maturing debt obligations within the Company itself diverted capital from the Coast Line project. During the remainder of 1896, and the years 1897 and 1898, little progress was made except for some seven miles of grading between Surf and Cañada Honda.

Even so, there was an increase in through passenger business. Due to the heat in the Central

During the summer of 1896, Bridgeport, the railroad construction camp on the Santa Ynez River, bustles with activity (**above**). That August, the camp was moved south, when the road was opened to Surf. "The Gap" was now 56 miles.

Lompoc Valley Historical Society

Below Surf, construction proceeded across coastal terraces on the Robert Sudden Ranch (**above**) but slow progress was made beyond the Cañada Honda. To close The Gap between Surf and Ellwood required tunnels, heavy fills, and large steel trestles, all taking considerable time and money (**left**).
Above, Southern Pacific Lines; two at left, Lompoc Valley Historical Society

Valley, many San Francisco-Los Angeles passengers began taking the train to Surf, thence by stage to Santa Barbara and then by train to Los Angeles. Others might get off at San Luis Obispo and take the Pacific Coast Railway to Los Olivos and then the stage to Santa Barbara. The resulting journey was considerably slower, but cooler.

At last, in November of 1898, with financial conditions improving and the Company's internal debt crisis resolved, work was resumed at Surf on the extension south. Track was laid to Honda by mid-December, 1898. The viaduct across the Cañada Honda was not ready until the end of July, 1899. Meanwhile, graders were at work further down the line, including the 811-foot tunnel near Sudden, so that once the viaduct at Honda was opened, track laying proceeded rapidly, reaching Jalama Creek at the end of October.

For many years, the Company had been content to pursue intermittently the construction of the Coast Line from the north, extending it southward as conditions would permit. But in the spring of 1899, in order to hasten the completion of the Coast Line, it was decided to work from both ends of the gap. Accordingly, on March 27, 1899, ground was broken at Ellwood on the extension north. Although the original 1887 alignment ended some ways beyond the station at Ellwood, the graders began their work on an entirely new alignment that straightened out many of the curves on either side of the station of Ellwood before setting out into new territory in the direction of Gaviota.

By October, 1899, there were over 1,000 men at work along the line engaged in filling some of the immense canyons draining into the sea and spanning others with large steel viaducts. The 451-foot bridge across the canyon at Jalama Creek was completed in January, 1900, and by April 10th, Southern Pacific was accepting commercial freight as far south as Concepcion. Track laying had commenced at Ellwood in late March and by June 30, 1900, all that remained was a gap just shy of 18 miles between Cuarta Canyon (Sacate) and Gato Canyon (between Naples and Capitan.)

As this final push to complete "The Gap" gathered momentum, work was also going forward on several important Coast Line branches. The Lompoc Branch, opened for service on July 28, 1899, extend-

An SP local works the Union Sugar Company mill at Betteravia about 1903 (**left**). Southern Pacific completed its branch from Guadalupe to Betteravia (**below**) on August 1, 1899. The SP later sold the five-mile line to the Santa Maria Valley Railroad, which still operates the line as of this writing.

Aston photos, courtesy Bennett-Loomis Archives

ed for nine miles from Surf to Lompoc, in the center of the rich Santa Ynez Valley. Founded in 1874 as a temperance colony, Lompoc had matured into a ranching and farming center of some significance. The exploitation of a large diatomaceous earth deposit in the adjacent White Hills, beginning in 1894, no doubt also influenced Southern Pacific officials to build into the valley. Limestone (needed for processing) in San Miguelito Canyon also attracted Union Sugar Company of nearby Betteravia, which received its own Southern Pacific rail service about the same time.

The Union Sugar Company, organized in September, 1887 by a group of five San Francisco businessmen, was named to indicate the union of the counties of San Luis Obispo and Santa Barbara as one beet-growing territory. Their new mill, to be built in the Santa Maria Valley, was the connecting link. Settled on the shores of Lake Guadalupe, five miles southeast of the town of Guadalupe, Union Sugar erected the town of Betteravia (from the

Ellwood, some 11 miles west of Santa Barbara, had remained end of track since December, 1887. Finally, on March 27, 1899, work resumed on the line north as construction crews rushed to close The Gap on the Coast Line. This view of Ellwood dates from 1895.

William A. Myers collection

The American Beet Sugar Company mill, built at Oxnard in 1898, prompted the construction of a four-mile branch line that left the main line at Montalvo near Ventura. It was this branch, built to exceedingly high standards, that was soon developed into the Montalvo Cutoff: the new Coast Route main line over Santa Susana Pass into Los Angeles.

Ventura County Museum of Art & History

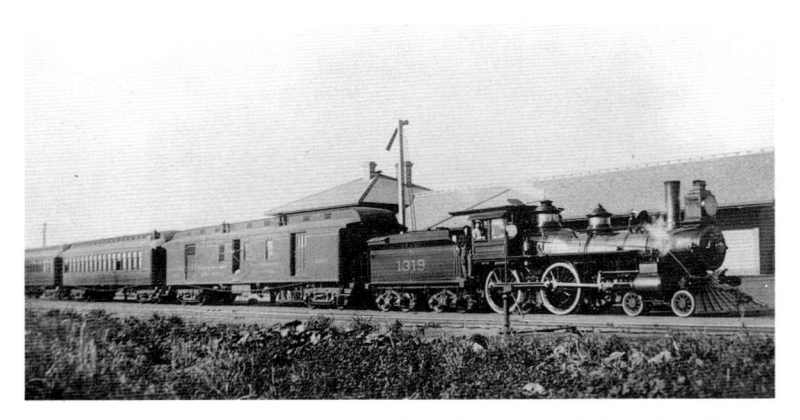

A Los Angeles-bound local pauses at Saticoy in 1898. This pastoral line through the Santa Clara River Valley would soon be relegated to branch-line status with the completion of the Montalvo Cutoff.

Robert McNeel collection

French *betterave*, meaning "beet root"). The mill and refinery itself were ready for operation in 1897, and Southern Pacific completed its branch from Guadalupe through Iremel to Betteravia on August 1, 1899.

Beet sugar refineries also figured in the construction of two other Coast Line branches just prior to the turn of the century. Spreckels Sugar Company began the construction of an immense sugar beet refinery on 122 acres southwest of Salinas in January 1897. As the project was nearing completion in the spring of 1899, Southern Pacific built a 3.3-mile spur from the main line at Spreckels Junction, just south of Salinas, out to the mill site.

Similarly, the development activities of the Oxnard brothers and the erection of their $2 million American Beet Sugar Company refinery on 100 acres at Oxnard in 1898 prompted the construction of a four-mile branch from the main line at Montalvo that was completed to the mill site on April 15, 1898. The costly bridging of the Santa Clara River, required in order to reach Oxnard, suggested that there might be more in store for this line than just a factory spur.

Other branches off the Coast Line completed prior to 1900 included the 22-mile Burbank Branch. This extended through the San Fernando Valley developments of Lankershim, Encino, Reseda and

Owensmouth to Chatsworth Park and was opened on September 30, 1893. Another connected the isolated community of Nordhoff (now called Ojai) with a 15-mile branch off the Coast Line just north of Ventura. Originally constructed by Capt. John Cross as the Ventura and Ojai Valley Rail Road using second-hand Southern Pacific ties, rails and rolling stock (in exchange for bonds), this branch was opened for operation on May 1, 1898. The previous month, Southern Pacific had acquired all of the stock in the operation and on June 27, 1899, this trackage became the Ojai Valley Branch.

It was during this period, in late March, 1900, that C.P. Huntington and William Hood chose to make an inspection trip to the end of the line aboard a special train from Los Angeles. Questioned by the press during the trip, Huntington was in an agreeable mood and touched on a variety of subjects. One story in connection with this inspection trip never made the papers, however. Years later, J.A. Small, then train master at Ellwood (who subsequently rose to the rank of President of the Southern Pacific of Mexico), related the following story through the pages of the old *Railroad Man's Magazine.*

"Our instructions on handling [Huntington's] train were frequent, detailed and exacting, or as the Mexican says, 'muy duro.' The track had been completed to about one mile north of Ellwood station, with an additional uncompleted mile, the rails being laid, but only the joint and center tie spiked, to permit our moving the rail and ties forward by man-powered push cars.

"My instructions were to be sure to stop the train at Ellwood, but someone on board had different ideas and the special found itself stopped on the last inch of unspiked track. Everyone of the party was happily oblivious of this fact, all except William Hood, Chief Engineer who, as soon as he hit the ground, realized the position with a bang. Returning to Ellwood on a hand car...his temper became shorter with each turn of the wheels and by the time he got to me, both the wheels and Hood were plenty hot. In no vague terms he told me what he thought of me as a railroader, and promised that unless I got that special train back over the unspiked track without the President and the directors discovering the facts, I could consider myself fired.

"I laid my delicate position before Dudley the conductor. He thought for a minute as he spat a fine fluid arch in the direction of the special train and said, 'Well, son, we might get the gang out and spike the track, but that would take several hours and the big shots would surely catch on to what had happened. The other way would be to run her back as we ran her out, with care and prayer.'

" 'All right Dud,' I answered, 'you furnish the care and I'll furnish the prayer.' And together Dudley and I got that train back to Ellwood without a derailment."

Work continued steadily. By September, the tracklayers were nearing Capitan. Grading was complete by mid-October, and all that remained were the completion of the steel trestles at Arroyo Hondo and Cementario Canyon. The Arroyo Hondo bridge was finished first, in late November, and at last, on December 30, 1900, the last rail was laid and the last spike driven—directly on the Cementario Canyon bridge, about one mile east of Gaviota. The line was not opened immediately for service, however, as the track had to be ballasted and surfaced, buildings and water facilities erected, and a multitude of other details worked out before operations could commence. Several specials did move over the entire route, including those of Henry Huntington (Collis' nephew) and of former President of the U.S. Rutherford B. Hayes. Finally, in the middle of March, E.O. McCormick, Passenger Traffic Manager of the Southern Pacific, announced that the Coast Line would be opened on Sunday, March 31, 1901. Collis P. Huntington had not lived to see completion of the line, dying suddenly on August 13, 1900.

Initially, through service over the line was limited to the *Sunset Express*, Nos. 19 and 20, which were moved over from the San Joaquin Valley main line and operated on a 17-hour schedule nightly between Los Angeles and San Francisco. A second set of trains, Nos. 1 and 2, the *Santa Barbara Passenger*, operated between San Francisco and Santa Barbara, with other local passenger trains filling in between Santa Barbara and Los Angeles, San Francisco and Monterey, Salinas, San Luis Obispo and Lompoc.

The goal of linking Los Angeles and San Francisco by rail via the Coast Line had finally been

GAP CLOSED

The operation of through trains between San Francisco and Los Angeles, via Surf and Santa Barbara, commenced ON SUNDAY, MARCH 31, 1901,

ON THE NEW COAST LINE

Two Through Trains Daily. The COAST LINE LIMITED leaving each terminal in the morning, equipped with elegant cafe and parlor cars, makes daylight trips through the most picturesque, varied and entertaining scenes on the continent. There is no grander trip. Inquire for particulars of agents of the

SOUTHERN PACIFIC

E. O. McCORMICK
Passenger Traffic Manager, S. F.

T. H. GOODMAN
General Passenger Agent, S. F.

This modest advertisement appeared in the April, 1901 number of *Sunset*, proclaiming the opening of the Coast Line. *Sunset Magazine* was founded by SP in 1898 and continued in railroad ownership until it was sold in 1914. The Lane family, whose company is the present publisher of *Sunset*, acquired it in 1928.

Richard Buike collection

achieved. It had been a long time coming–more than 36 years–since the first rails had crept south from San Francisco, and the coastal counties that the completed line served now looked forward to a prosperous new era. Southern Pacific, however, was far from through with its Coast Line construction work. Once the Coast Line was completed and through trains were running, it was quickly realized that the route had a number of physical limitations that prevented the exploitation of the line to the fullest extent.

From the outset, the response from the public was gratifying, yet it was difficult to accommodate the heavy trains and volume of traffic in a timely fashion. The Coast Line had been built over a lengthy period, with some segments dating back to 1863. Railway technology had changed in the intervening years and rail weight, bridge size, gradient and curvature that might have been entirely suited to the light traffic of the 1880s was fast becoming inadequate to support the faster and heavier trains of the new century. Thus within ten years of the opening of the Coast Line, the 50-mile line from San Francisco to San Jose over the San Bruno hills would be upgraded, double-tracked, and a portion of the route south out of the City entirely changed in location. Nearly 100 miles of railroad between Ellwood and Burbank on the southern end of the line would be upgraded through line changes and the building of 61 miles of entirely new railroad. In addition, many minor reductions in curvature and gradient were undertaken throughout the length of the route, most notably in the 91 miles between Salinas and Santa Margarita.

It was on the district between Santa Barbara and Los Angeles that the first project of significance began to take shape. The operating problems in this section certainly warranted attention. Out of Los Angeles, trains destined for the Coast Line had to make their way up the thickly congested valley line to San Fernando, then take on a helper for the run over the summit at Tunnel before diverging onto the Coast Line at Saugus. From here on to Santa Barbara, the line, subject to frequent washout, meandered down the Santa Clara Valley to the coast before turning north. Excessive curvature and street running in the city of Santa Barbara slowed trains down even more.

Montalvo Cutoff
1899-1904

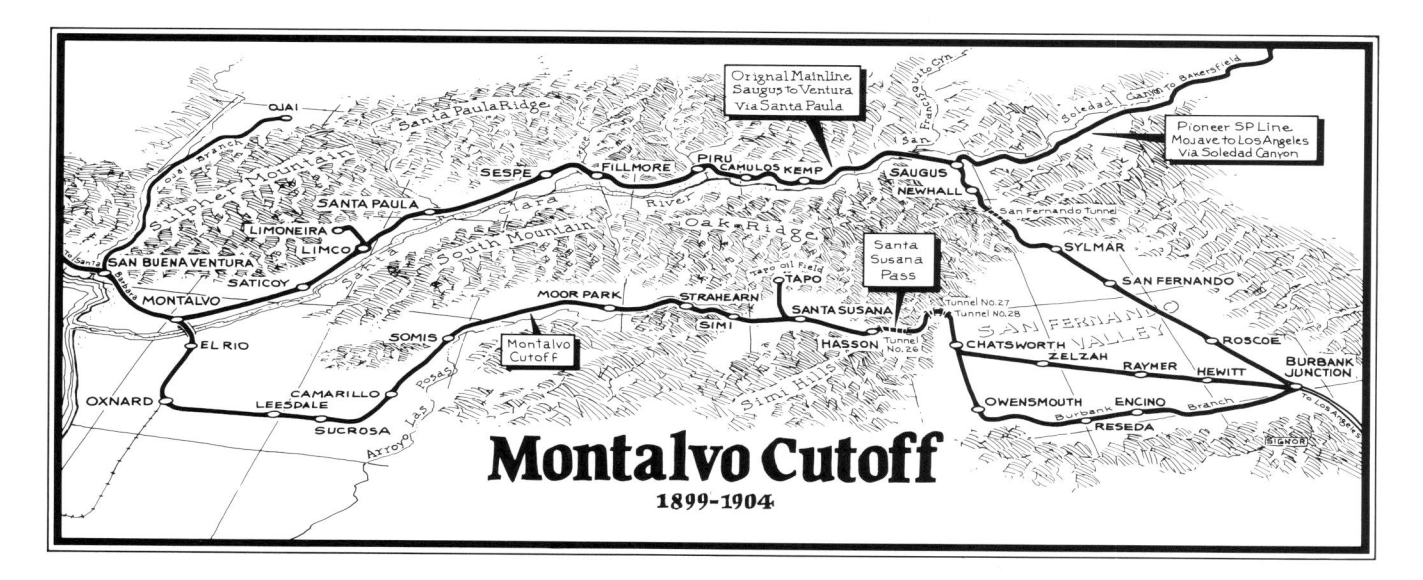

The road as originally constructed through Santa Paula was not the only practicable route between the Los Angeles basin and the Ventura County coast. Indeed, as early as 1854, Lt. Parke in the Pacific Railroad Reports had indicated a preference for a route which crossed the Santa Clara River below San Buenaventura (now Ventura), then followed the broad expanse of coastal plain east before threading wide canyons leading to "Semi Pass." Although a tunnel of 3,960 feet, 600 feet below the crest, would be required to pierce the sharp summit, beyond lay the vast expanse of the San Fernando plain which presented no obstacles the rest of the way to Los Angeles. Yet when the time came to build, the economy of opening a line down the Santa Clara Valley, entirely devoid of costly tunnels, won out.

It was on the San Fernando plain that Southern Pacific began building a branch from Burbank west towards this pass in the fall of 1887. The following June, as the work progressed, the Los Angeles *Times* reported that railroad officials had announced a survey of a short cut through "Santa Susana Pass" and Simi. After the branch was completed to Chatsworth Park in the summer of 1893, the Santa Monica *Outlook* editorialized that a wiser choice would be to locate the line from Ventura along the coast to Santa Monica and Los Angeles, saving twenty miles and passing immediately by the wharf at "Port Los Angeles." Huntington would not be swayed by such arguments, even though he had a big stake in the Santa Monica wharfage. He continued

During the fall of 1899, as The Gap on the Coast Line was closing rapidly, work began on an entirely new line between Montalvo and Burbank that would replace the original line via Santa Paula. The most difficult work on the new "Montalvo Cutoff" was encountered in Santa Susana Pass. Work is well underway during the summer of 1900 as these graders widen a cut at the east end of tunnel No. 28 (**right**) above Chatsworth. An even deeper cut (**above**) was required near the longest tunnel, No. 26.
Two photos, Southern Pacific Lines

23

Completed and placed in service on March 20, 1904, the "Montalvo Cutoff" saved just six miles over the old line via Santa Paula but reduced the maximum gradient from 2.1 percent to one percent and reduced the maximum curvature to six degrees. Soon after the Cutoff opened, a westbound passenger emerges (**left**) from tunnel No. 28 and sweeps around a familiar curve (**above**) on the way to tunnel No. 27. It was in this area, so close to Hollywood, yet remote in character, that many early motion pictures featuring trains and the Old West were filmed.

Top and left, Southern Pacific Lines

An inspection speeder poses at the entrance to tunnel No. 27 shortly before the Montalvo Cutoff was opened for service. Three tunnels were required in the Santa Susana, the longest being 7,369 feet, at that time the longest on the Pacific Coast.

Southern Pacific Lines

to favor the route through Santa Susana Pass, although the project would have to wait until better times.

At last, in the fall of 1899, as the Coast Line was nearing completion, Huntington authorized work to begin on the short cut. Since the branch from Montalvo had been opened to Oxnard in April, 1898, it only remained to extend it across the broad, level plain towards the mouth of the pass. The project moved forward rapidly for a time and the "Montalvo Cutoff," as it came to be known, was in operation to Somis in August, 1899, to Strathearn, some 29 miles, by June, 1900 and at the mouth of the great tunnel at Hasson in March, 1901. Work on the Santa Susana tunnel itself had begun on July 16, 1900—one month prior to Huntington's death—and this and subsequent projects undertaken in connection with the Coast Line were soon under the influence of the energetic Edward Henry Harriman, who assumed the presidency of the Southern Pacific on September 26, 1901.

The long bore at Hasson, tunnel No. 26, totalling some 7,369 feet, was blasted for the most part through solid rock and took over three years to complete. Drilled from the two ends, the headings met on August 18, 1903, but there was much still to be accomplished before through service could commence. Two additional tunnels of 994 and 599 feet had to be completed further south in difficult country, and Harriman, not content with the existing facilities between Burbank and Chatsworth Park via Owensmouth (now Canoga Park), ordered an entirely new line built direct-as-the-crow-flies across the valley from the mouth of the pass at Chatsworth to Burbank Junction.

Completed and open for service on March 20, 1904, the "Montalvo Cutoff" saved just six miles over the old line via Santa Paula but reduced the maximum grade from 2.1 percent to one percent, and the sharpest curvature from 10 degrees to six.

Seventeen additional line changes were made between Santa Barbara and Montalvo and between Santa Barbara and Ellwood. Santa Barbara itself was the subject of a line change commencing in

Oxnard, already a station of considerable importance due to the large American Beet Sugar factory complex, took on added significance and prosperity with the completion of the Montalvo Cutoff, because it was now on the main line between San Francisco and Los Angeles. Whaleback tenders were part of the distinctive style of SP steam power.

Ventura County Museum of Art & History

The crown jewel of the Santa Barbara relocation project was this handsome new station, designed by Santa Barbara architect Francis Wilson in the Mission style. The interior featured a bas-relief of Padre Junípero Serra over the fireplace in the women's waiting room (**left**) and was outfitted with simple but elegant wooden furniture rendered in the popular "Craftsman" style. In fact, *The Craftsman* magazine praised the new Santa Barbara station as well as the Burlingame station as "...charming examples of the evolution of railway architecture." The Santa Barbara line change was placed in service on January 1, 1906, although the yards and roundhouse would take several more years to complete. These photos by renowned Oakland commercial photographer C.M. Kurtz, and commissioned by Southern Pacific, were taken on January 28, 1906. They include exterior views of the south or track side (**bottom, left**) and the east side (**bottom, right**), while the train arriving (**top**) is local No. 21 from Los Angeles.

Four photos, C.M. Kurtz, Southern Pacific Lines

After completion of the Montalvo Cutoff, additional line changes were made between Montalvo and Ellwood, including major work in Santa Barbara. Since the time the line was built through open country in 1887 (**above**), Santa Barbara had grown considerably, and the original alignment had become congested due to its location in city streets. This route was largely abandoned in favor of a 1.63-mile line change to the west. The new alignment, cutting diagonally across city streets, featured double track, as shown (**right**) looking north near Bath Street.
Top, Santa Barbara Historical Society; right, Southern Pacific Lines

November, 1904, that saw the Coast Line removed from its convoluted and frequently congested location in the city streets. The new alignment, cutting diagonally across the west side of town, paralleled the coast from Rancheria and Gutierrez Streets to the bird refuge, a distance of 1.63 miles. Freight yards were laid out along the new tangent and plans unveiled for a new roundhouse (not completed until 1910.) A grand new station, designed by Santa Barbara architect Francis Wilson in the Mission style, complete with gardens, rounded out the construction on the relocation project, which was opened on January 1, 1906. Soon after, the main line was removed from Rancheria Street and the whole affair within the city limits of Santa Barbara was eventually double tracked.

Even as the Montalvo Cutoff was nearing completion, work was progressing on the 50-mile line between San Francisco and San Jose. The principal problem on the district was the southern entrance into San Francisco. Opened for service in October, 1863, this narrow, twisting right-of-way ran for a

Completion of double track down the Peninsula in 1905 and the implementation of faster and more frequent train service hastened development of suburbs along the line. Suburban train No. 86 pauses at San Mateo (**top**) about 1910, while patrons await another San Jose-bound local at Redwood City (**left**) in 1915. Another San Jose local pauses at the San Bruno station (**below**) about 1907. Further improvements to service were to come with the completion of the Bayshore Cutoff which started just above San Bruno, eliminating the old line into San Francisco via Harrison Street.

Top and below, R.H. McFarland photos, Arnold S. Menke collection; left, Southern Pacific Lines

Opened in 1863, the Harrison Street line had been the least expensive line to build into San Francisco. By the turn of the century, however, the presence of at least 18 passenger trains a day each way operating on city streets, as well as a considerable freight business, had rendered the twisting and steeply graded line obsolete. But SP's plan to double-track through the Mission District raised the cries of outraged residents along the route. The city had grown considerably along with the railroad's business, and the presence of triple-headed freight trains blasting through residential districts, much as this one is doing at 21st and Harrison in 1905 (**above**), was becoming intolerable. Cutting diagonally across city streets (**right**), an outbound train approaches Valencia Street station. Outbound double-headed train No. 28, the *Del Monte Express*, enters the curve leading to private right-of-way on Harrison Street near 21st in 1907 (**below**). Helpers were frequently required as the grade was nearly 2 percent.

Three photos, Robert H. McFarland, Arnold S. Menke collection

Train No. 42, a San Jose suburban train, rounds the bend at 11th and Bryant Streets in 1907 (**left**). Behind the fence at right is SP's San Francisco engine terminal. The tent at left is evidence that aftereffects of the devastating 1906 earthquake and fire were still being felt.

Robert H. McFarland photo, Arnold S. Menke collection

Southern Pacific's engine terminal in San Francisco at 16th and Harrison Streets bustles with activity. Having outgrown the north roundhouse, originally built by the San Francisco & San Jose (**left, below**), and with traffic into the City growing dramatically, SP was forced to build a second roundhouse (**right** and **lower right**) adjacent to and south of the original. In these views, taken between 1903 and 1907, suburban and light freight engines are turned.

Three photos, R.H. McFarland, Arnold S. Menke collection

30

Once out of the City, the old Harrison Street line passed through some pastoral countryside. Local No. 42 (**top**) works upgrade near the summit at Oceanview, while a heavier No. 24, the San Luis Obispo passenger (**left**), double-heads through Bernal Cut. Another local train (**below**) approaches Elkton station; note the Geneva Ave. street cars to the right. All of these views were taken during 1907, just prior to all through traffic being shifted to the Bayshore Cutoff.

Three photos, Robert H. McFarland, Arnold S. Menke collection

considerable distance through a thickly populated section of San Francisco. In many cases, the tracks were laid across city blocks and directly in streets heavy with traffic. The need for conforming to public right-of-way had resulted in heavy grades and sharp curves. Further, the line made a wide detour to the west and helpers were required out of San Francisco to the 291-foot summit at Oceanview. The ruling grade south was 158 feet to the mile, or 3 percent, although this represented only some 300 feet near the summit. (The bulk of the grade was a mere 1.72 percent.) If this wasn't enough, traffic had grown enormously since the 1860s. The advent of the railway had caused rapid suburban settlement of the district and by the summer of 1886, eighteen passenger trains a day hustled commuters into and out of the City. It is interesting to note that six of these trains terminated or originated at Menlo Park.

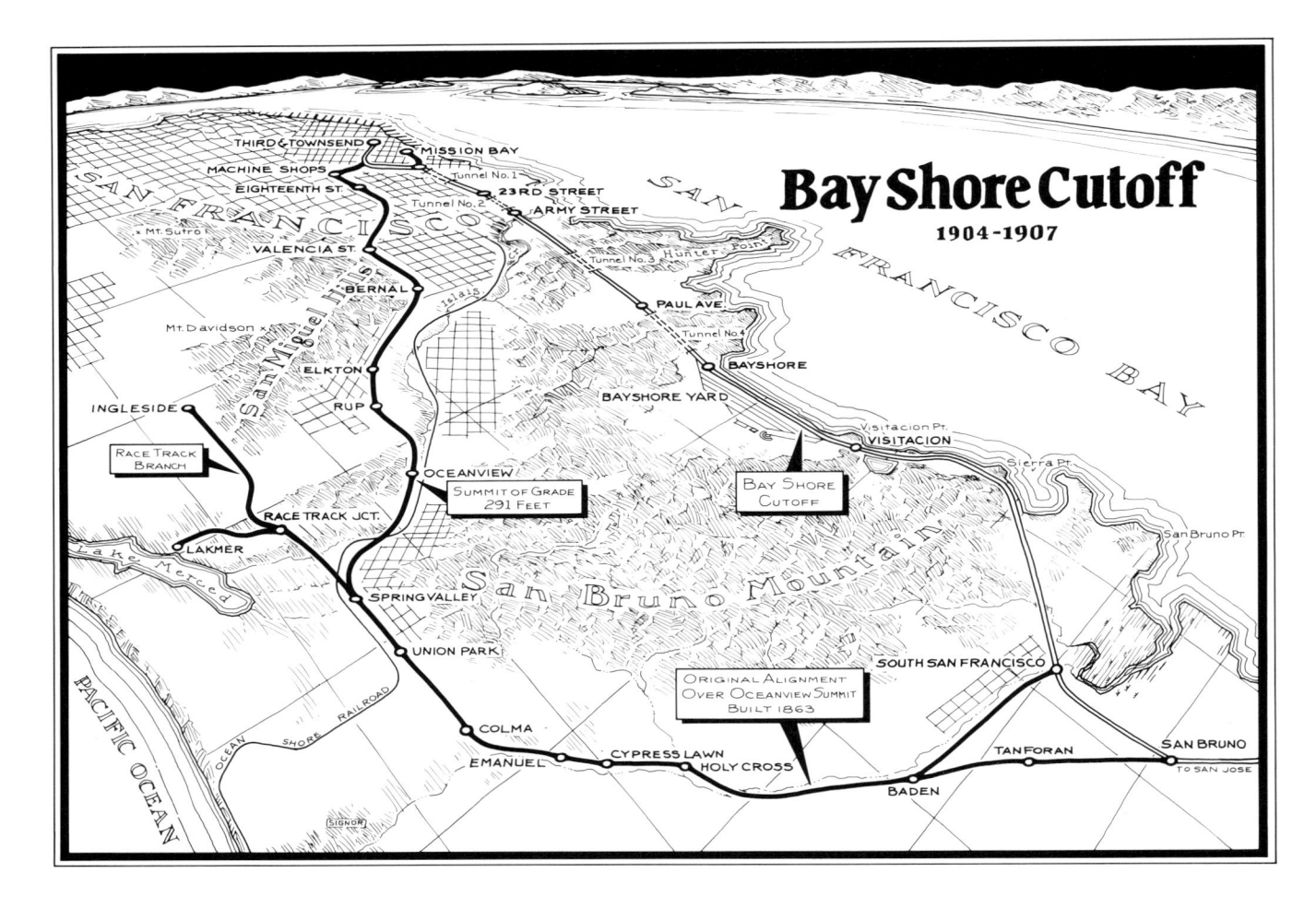

Apparently the railroad never had a franchise for operation along Harrison Street. And by 1898, the residents along this line were up in arms over the railway's stated intent of double-tracking the line through the Mission District. As things turned out, the double track never got below 19th and Harrison Streets. By December 1901, the frequency of first class trains over this segment had reached 29, half of which terminated at Palo Alto–and all this over a single-track line requiring helpers!

The lack of capacity on the flat and featureless line south of San Bruno was quickly addressed. *Railway Age* reported on October 30, 1903, that a second track had been completed between San Bruno and San Jose–some 39 miles–and that trains were running. Signalling was of course included in the project. But simply extending the second track into the City wouldn't do. Nothing short of a radical new location would solve the larger problems encountered on the line over San Bruno Mountain.

Feasibility studies for just such a relocation were conducted as early as 1873 and again in 1878. The route of preference was as nearly a direct line between San Francisco and San Bruno as it was

Work began on the Bayshore Cutoff in October, 1904, and by the following March, this temporary trestle (**above**) was in place to facilitate the filling of Visitacion Bay. Here a huge modern freight terminal was planned, later called Bayshore Yard. The material used to fill the bay at this location came from bay dredging, from the many tunnels being built, and from the massive Visitacion Point cut (**left**), upon which work is underway in September, 1905. St. Joseph's Orphanage stands prominently on the hill above tunnel No. 3 (**below**) as excavation is in progress during December, 1905. Five major tunnels were needed for the Cutoff.

Three photos by C.M. Kurtz, courtesy Southern Pacific Lines

practicable to make. Starting at Seventh and Townsend Streets in San Francisco, the projected route ran southwest along the base of the Potrero Hills and along San Francisco Bay, touching at Visitacion Point, Macdonald Point and Sierra Point before cutting inland to South San Francisco and San Bruno. Much cutting and filling would be required as well as five tunnels and at least one major trestle. The estimated cost in 1878 was said to be an exorbitant $1 million per mile, yet the advantages to be gained were many. The proposed route would save more than three miles, reduce maximum curvature from twelve to four degrees, and be virtually gradeless (three-tenths of one percent) compared to the existing alignment.

E.H. Harriman recognized the absolute necessity of the line change but other large works competed for available capital and it was not until October, 1904, that ground was broken on the "Bay Shore Cutoff," as it was originally termed; the name soon became "Bayshore." The task ahead was formidable. Fully twenty percent of the line was in tunnels. The

An important element in the overall plan of the Bayshore Cutoff, the yards at Visitacion Bay, are rapidly taking shape. In a view taken April 9, 1909, looking south from the end of tunnel No. 4 (**above**), much of the initial unit of the yard, including the hump, is in place. By January, 1910, work is underway on the new roundhouse (**left**) which will replace the old facilities at 16th Street. The following February, in a view looking north (**below**), the Bayshore roundhouse is finished, but much additional trackage and shop buildings remain to be built.

Three photos, C. M. Kurtz, Southern Pacific Lines

Despite setbacks such as the 1906 earthquake and fire, and with some finishing work still to be done, the Bayshore Cutoff was placed in service in December, 1907. The following March, photographer Kurtz composed this shot of the new line sweeping around Sierra Point. The large cut at Visitacion Point is clearly visible in the middle distance. The two-track line entering the main line is the freight lead from Bayshore Yard.

Three photos, C. M. Kurtz, Southern Pacific Lines

cut at Visitacion Point, 95 feet in depth, required the removal of some 750,000 cubic yards of material, all of which was used to fill in the cove known as Visitacion Bay, north of the cut. But Harriman, planning for the future growth of the San Francisco region, directed his engineers to take the project several steps further than originally envisioned by the planners of Huntington's day.

The entire line was built with two main tracks, yet it was designed throughout to accommodate up to four tracks—except for four of the five tunnels—as traffic might warrant. A modern freight terminal, designed to replace the old machine shops at 16th Street and the car repair and roundhouse facilities at Mariposa Street on the old line into San Francisco, was planned to occupy over 200 acres on the great fill at Visitacion Bay. The new yards, some 8,400 feet long, would include a roundhouse, machine and car shops, and a hump, the second to be built on the Pacific Coast (the first was at Roseville, California, on SP's Sacramento Division).

One final element of Harriman's plans for Southern Pacific's terminal facilities on San Francisco Bay addressed the problem of easy freight access to San Francisco from the Ogden and Shasta routes. As matters stood, those lines terminated at Oakland, from which freight cars had to be transferred to car ferries for the trip across the bay, or moved on land around the south end of the bay by a "wishbone" route nearly 100 miles long. Taking

Tunnel No. 2, March 25, 1908 (**above**). The Cutoff was designed as a four-track line, but was built with two main tracks, leaving room for others to be added as traffic warranted. There were 3,600 feet of bridge and trestles on the line, the most important of which was this structure (**below**) carrying the road over Islais Creek, near Army St., San Francisco.

35

Although not directly a part of the main Coast Line, the Dumbarton Cutoff, an 11-mile connection between SP's Peninsula and East Bay lines, was to have a great impact on traffic levels into the San Francisco terminal district. The Cutoff featured a causeway and bridge across a narrow point in San Francisco Bay, and opened between Redwood Junction and Dumbarton Point (Newark) on September 12, 1910. These photos were taken one month after opening.

Three photos, C.M. Kurtz, Southern Pacific Lines

Emerging from the north end of tunnel No. 2 on the Bayshore Cutoff is an inbound local (**right**). With the Cutoff in place, as well as the double-tracking of the remainder of the Peninsula line, the average commuter between San Jose and San Francisco gained 17 minutes on his daily run. Over the next several decades, the stretch of Coast Line from Redwood City to Bayshore would consistently be the busiest stretch of track on the entire SP system.

It was not only passenger traffic that benefited from the Cutoff; freight trains from the south, east or north could now run directly into San Francisco and with much lighter power. Witness this long freight train (**left**) passing by Bayshore Yard about 1909 with a single Mogul in charge.

Two photos, Robert H. McFarland, Arnold S. Menke collection

advantage of a narrow gap in southern San Francisco Bay, Harriman's engineers designed an eleven-mile cutoff between Redwood City, on the Peninsula, and Newark on the East Bay line. The bulk of the project entailed the construction of a long causeway and a swingspan bridge across the tidal flats between Dumbarton Point and Ravenswood. Preliminary work on this project, which included an additional five miles of trackage between Newark and Niles in the East Bay, was underway even as the Bayshore Cutoff neared completion.

After several major setbacks, including the intervention of the great 1906 San Francisco earthquake (see p. 58) which collapsed tunnel No. 2, the Bayshore Cutoff was opened for service on Sunday, December 8, 1907. Peninsula commuter schedules were quickly adjusted and nineteen towns from San Francisco to San Jose became seventeen minutes closer to the City. Work continued on the yards at Visitacion Bay (later Bayshore) and the Dumbarton Cutoff which was opened between Niles Junction and Newark in May, 1909, and between Newark and Redwood Junction on September 12, 1910. The old route into San Francisco via Oceanview was relegated to branch line status, and was eventually to be severed in the middle during October, 1942.

These great projects, together with the complete signalling of the 470-mile route between San Francisco and Los Angeles in the period prior to 1908, gave the Coast Line most of the alignment and features which we associate with the route today. But more importantly, it gave Southern Pacific a Coast Line that was first class in many respects, as safe as technology would allow and well equipped to handle the rise in traffic that could be expected in the rapidly expanding territory it served. ❏

Train No. 77, the *Shore Line Limited*, works its way north along the Santa Barbara County coast near Miramar. Here, as well as at other points along the Coast Line, oil rigs extending out onto the coastal shelf dominate the scene. California's burgeoning oil industry provided a vital source of freight revenue for Southern Pacific.
Southern Pacific Lines

2

By Rail on the Padre Trail

Coast Line Operations prior to the Depression

PRIOR TO THE COMPLETION of the Coast Line as a through route between San Francisco and Los Angeles in 1901, the northern and southern segments of the line were operated independently of each other. The branch from Saugus to Ellwood was referred to as the "Ventura Division" but in reality its operation was governed through the office of the San Joaquin Division superintendent at Bakersfield, whose jurisdiction extended all the way to Los Angeles. A crew could cover the distance between Los Angeles and Santa Barbara in a single tour of duty. The delights of the seashore, and the growing importance of Santa Barbara as "a gem city of the Pacific Coast for tourists and invalids" had, by 1887, provided enough patronage to support two passenger trains a day each way. Some agriculture began to take root following the completion of the railway, but freight traffic was light and pastoral in its implications along the southern portion of the coast.

The railroad south from San Francisco attracted a much greater volume of business from the outset. Once organized as part of the Southern Pacific Railroad, the line down the Peninsula was designated the Northern Division, with headquarters at San Francisco. As the line was extended southward into the Santa Clara and Salinas valleys, additional mileage was added until the Northern Division encompassed over 221 miles of main line between San Francisco and Templeton. Tributary branches to Almaden, Tres Pinos, Santa Cruz, Loma Prieta, Monterey and Spreckels added considerably to division mileage as well.

As previously discussed, the rapid suburbanization of San Mateo County greatly increased the volume of passenger traffic immediately south of San Francisco. By November 13, 1887, eighteen passenger trains a day were arriving and departing San Francisco for points south–primarily Menlo Park–but other schedules terminated or originated at San Mateo, San Jose, Hillsdale (Almaden Branch trains) and Castroville (Monterey Branch trains).

Such gains in passenger traffic were certainly welcomed by the railroad but it was freight that offered the greater opportunity for profit. The Northern Division main line passed through the Santa Clara

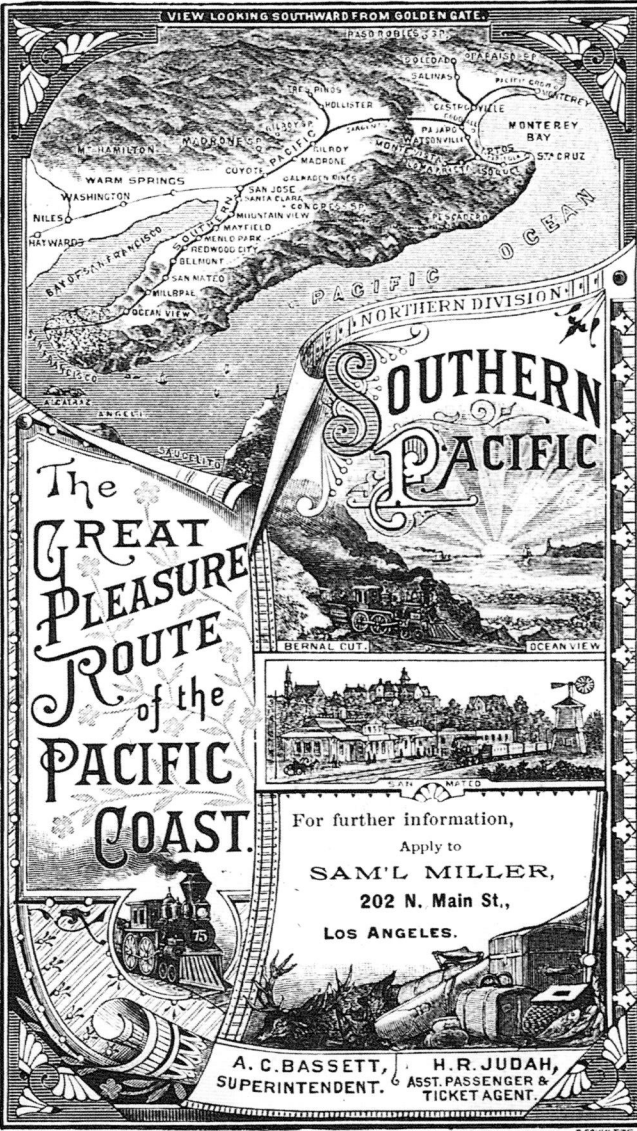

Valley, dotted with orchards, and penetrated the vast Salinas River Valley which, with the coming of the railroad, had made a rapid conversion from grazing land into "one great field of grain from the coast almost to Soledad." Staked out in 1868, Salinas City was, by 1872, the county seat, a grain town, and terminal of the Southern Pacific Railroad.

Nearly every growing town along the division had its "team track" where local farmers brought the produce of their fields to the railhead for shipment to consumers. And the same track provided a convenient point for receiving incoming freight of all kinds including farm implements and building materials, especially lumber. The Santa Cruz and Loma Prieta branches tapped thick stands of redwood which were felled, cut up into dimensioned lumber, and shipped north to feed the insatiable demand for construction materials in San Francisco and its growing suburbs. Mine timbers were needed too in the mercury mines at Almaden, ten miles southwest of San Jose on the slopes of Bache Mountain. These mines, discovered in 1845, had, with the completion of the branch railroad in 1886, become the most productive of their type in the country.

During the summer of 1893, SP surveyed an eight-mile spur from the main line at Spring Valley, eight miles southeast of San Francisco, west towards the beach thence north to Golden Gate Park, where elaborate plans were being made for a "Midwinter Exhibition." By September crews were busy laying track as far as the Park & Ocean Railway's line, over whose standard-gauge tracks SP trains would move 2.8 miles to gain entrance into the park. The spur was placed in operation on October 14, 1893 and a gaily decorated train loaded with celebrities arrived at the park from the depot at Fourth and Townsend Streets at 3:00 PM. Virtually all of the exhibits, some of which came from as far away as Chicago, were moved by rail through Lathrop and Niles to San Jose, then up the Coast Division to Spring Valley for delivery by rail to the Exposition site. Much of this branch was dismantled in 1896.

By 1894, with the terminus of the Coast Line at San Luis Obispo, the Northern Division had become the Coast Division of the Southern Pacific Railroad. Freight crews were now operating between San Luis Obispo and Salinas, a distance of 135 miles, and between Salinas and San Francisco, some 118 miles.

From about 1873 until 1891, the segment of the Coast Line between San Francisco and the end of track in the Salinas Valley was known as the Northern Division. This public folder dates from December, 1888.
Southern Pacific Lines

40

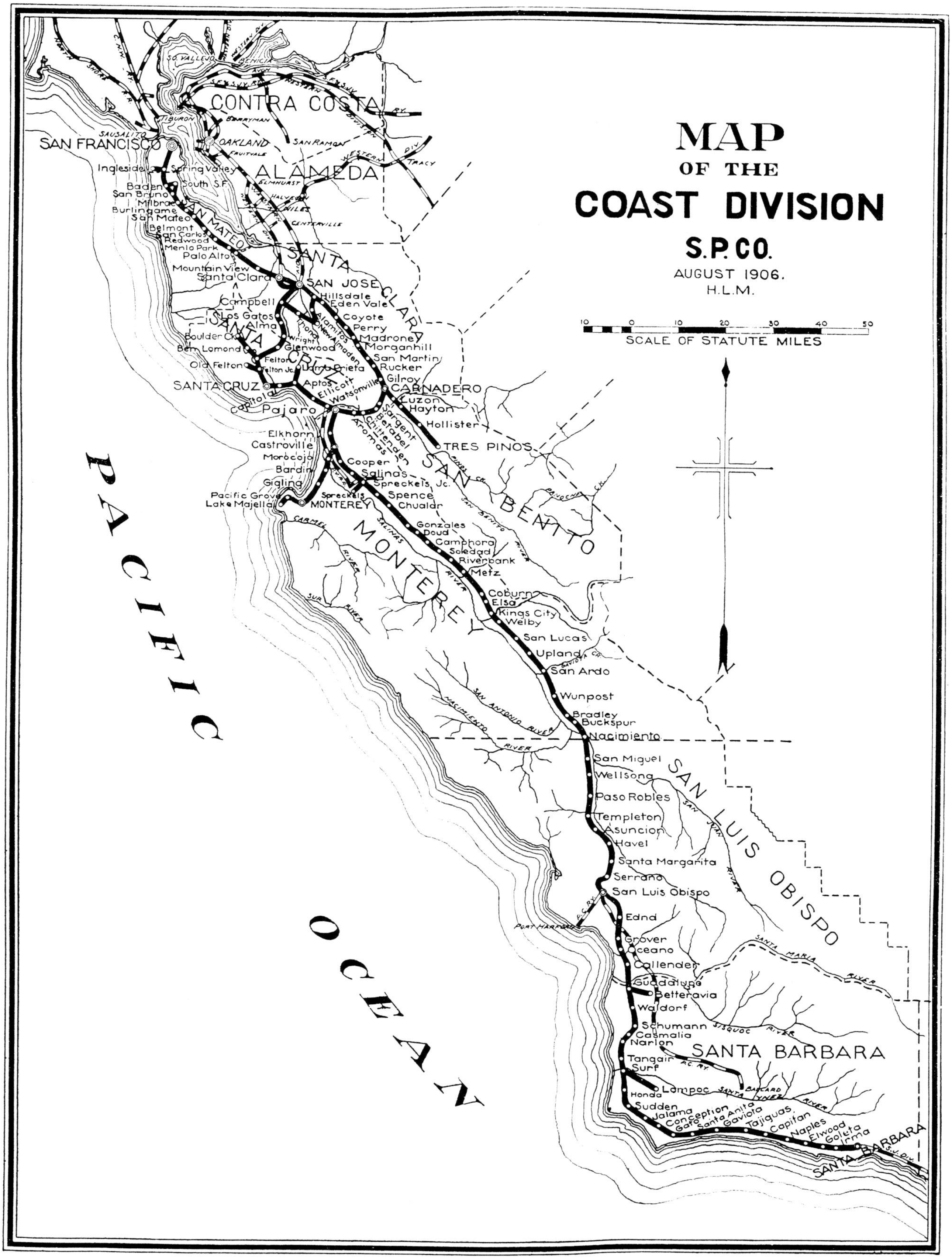
MAP
OF THE
COAST DIVISION
S.P.CO.
AUGUST 1906.
H.L.M.
SCALE OF STATUTE MILES
10 0 10 20 30 40 50
PACIFIC
OCEAN
CONTRA COSTA
ALAMEDA
SAN MATEO
SANTA CLARA
SANTA CRUZ
SAN BENITO
MONTEREY
SAN LUIS OBISPO
SANTA BARBARA
SAN FRANCISCO
SAUSALITO
TIBURON
OAKLAND
SAN RAMON
TRACY
FRUITVALE
ELMHURST
HALVERSON
NILES
CENTERVILLE
Ingleside
Spring Valley
South S.F.
Baden
San Bruno
Milbrae
Burlingame
San Mateo
Belmont
San Carlos
Redwood
Menlo Park
Palo Alto
Mountain View
Santa Clara
SAN JOSE
Hillsdale
Eden Vale
Coyote
Perry
Madrone
Morganhill
San Martin
Rucker
Gilroy
CARNADERO
Luzon
Hayton
Hollister
TRES PINOS
Campbell
Los Gatos
Alma
Wright
Glenwood
Boulder Ck.
Ben Lomond
Felton
Felton Jc.
Old Felton
SANTA CRUZ
Capitola
Aptos
Ellicott
Watsonville
Pajaro
Elkhorn
Castroville
Morocojo
Bardin
Gigling
Pacific Grove
Lake Majella
MONTEREY
Spreckels
Cooper
Salinas
Spreckels Jc.
Spence
Chualar
Gonzales
Doud
Camphora
Soledad
Riverbank
Metz
Coburn
Elsa
Kings City
Welby
San Lucas
Upland
San Ardo
Wunpost
Bradley
Buckspur
Nacimiento
San Miguel
Wellsona
Paso Robles
Templeton
Asuncion
Havel
Santa Margarita
Serrano
San Luis Obispo
PORT HARFORD
Edna
Grover
Oceano
Callender
Guadalupe
Betteravia
Waldorf
Schumann
Casmalia
Narlon
Tangair
Surf
Lompoc
Honda
Sudden
Jalama
Conception
Gato
Santa Anita
Gaviota
Tajiguas
Capitan
Naples
Elwood
Goleta
Irma
SANTA BARBARA
CARMEL RIVER
SUR RIVER
SALINAS RIVER
SAN BENITO RIVER
SAN ANTONIO RIVER
NACIMIENTO RIVER
SANTA MARIA RIVER
SISQUOC RIVER
SANTA YNEZ RIVER

Period rolling stock, including what is believed to be Southern Pacific's passenger equipment exhibit, crowds the rail yards at San Francisco's Midwinter Exhibition in 1893. To deliver exhibits, construction materials and people to the fair held at Golden Gate Park, Southern Pacific utilized an eight-mile line comprising 5.2 miles of new rail built from the main Coast Line at Spring Valley as far as Park & Ocean Junction, from which SP trains continued on over a street railway to the exhibition site. The Electric Tower rises in the middle distance. Electricity, at that time still very much a novelty, was a main feature at the fair.

Two photos, Southern Pacific Lines

As the railhead was extended slowly south during the 1890s, each additional segment was added to the Coast Division's jurisdiction until with the completion of the Coast Line in March 1901, Coast Division crews began operating over the 117-mile district between San Luis Obispo and Santa Barbara. Here, the Coast Division's jurisdiction ended. The actual division point was fixed at Arrellaga Street, on the northern fringe of the city, so that the Santa Barbara yards and the terminal remained the responsibility of the Superintendent of the San Joaquin Division. That continued until 1912, when Saugus became the termination point of the San Joaquin Division, and the main line from Santa Barbara to Los Angeles, together with the Santa Paula Branch, was added to the Los Angeles Division.

The new Coast Line was slow to develop a strong through freight business. The country it spanned was young and growing, compared with the long-established territory to the east which was served by SP's San Joaquin Valley Line. The two lines paralleled each other down the state and even served the same terminals. The Valley Line had the Tehachapi to contend with, but overall, the inland route was relatively flat and featureless compared to the more challenging profile of the Coast Line. Consequently, the bulk of the heavy freight business moving north and south in the state stayed east of the Coast Range and it was passenger trains that provided the bulk of the through traffic during the early years of the Coast Line. And yet in the fullness of time, the Coast Line was to handle a considerable freight business of its own.

A glimpse of the future, and the Coast Line's first major test of capacity, occurred during the summer of 1915. An unfortunate fire in tunnel No. 15 in the Tehachapi Mountains blockaded the San Joaquin Division from May 14th to June 9th. For the duration, the Coast Line handled, in addition to its own trains, which were already considerable due to the Panama-Pacific Exposition, all freight and passenger traffic usually routed via the San Joaquin Valley Line, including those of the Santa Fe! During the 27-day tie-up, the Coast Line moved an unprecedented 470 through passenger trains and 295 freight trains. A bottleneck occurred on the 17-mile Cuesta Grade where all trains required help. During the emergency, San Luis Obispo roundhouse turned a record 908 helpers, 886 passenger locomotives and 870 freight engines. A number of train and engine men and telegraph operators were borrowed from the San Joaquin Division, and temporary offices were set up in some cases to expedite the movement of trains.

The tunnel No. 15 disaster had dramatically increased the level of freight traffic on the Coast Line overnight, but steady gains in routine freight business were already under way. The harvesting and refining of sugar beets was an early industry to develop along the coast, and the *Southern Pacific Bulletin* reported that a new record was set during the 1913 beet sugar season on the Coast Division. A total of 1,586 cars were moved from the loaders at Camphora, Elsa, Gonzales, Harlem, King City, Molus, Neponset, Nema, Plantel, Spence and Sargent. Nearly half the movement originated at Camphora and Sargent. Three immense beet sugar factories were now in place

Widely circulated postcards from the 'teens recount the delights of travel along the Coast Line, where the popular fancy with "the California missions combined pleasantly with the temperate climate of the coast to create a vacation paradise."

All, Roger Titus Collection

This spread of Post Cards distributed by the Pacific Novelty Company depict the mission at Santa Barbara (**upper left**), the hotel at Paso Robles Hot Springs (**left**) and the flower-lined roadbed (**above**) at Miramar.

Santa Barbara station (**right**) achieved some renown as the gateway to the winter playground that the Central Coast country was for socialites and the rich of the East. Many eventually settled here or at nearby Montecito.

Alas, by the mid-'twenties, the "Good Roads" movement had developed enough momentum that Southern Pacific's dominance as a passenger carrier on the coast was beginning to wane. Henceforth, vacationists would often choose the motor car. In this view (**left**), the former plank road at Rincon has been freshly surfaced with asphalt.

Renowned Bay Area artist Maurice Logan was commissioned by the Southern Pacific to paint a series of images which could be used in passenger advertising. They were reproduced in brochures, posters and magazine advertisements; these two are from a 1928 brochure. At this time, the Coast Line was considered part of the Sunset Route, as exemplified by the *Sunset Limited*'s run between San Francisco and New Orleans, and thus was one of SP's "Four Great Scenic Routes."
Southern Pacific Lines

The Santa Ynez Range looms in the hazy distance as a southbound passenger train rolls through rich agricultural lands near Ellwood. The sheltered coastal valleys of Santa Barbara and Ventura counties were well suited to walnut and lemon production. *Southern Pacific Lines*

on the Coast Line: the American Beet Sugar factory at Oxnard which, by 1913, was employing 600 people during the 100-day-long campaign and producing an output, largely granulated sugar in 100-pound sacks, which was valued at $3.7 million; the huge Union Sugar plant at Betteravia; and the factories of Claus Spreckels, first established as the Western Beet Sugar Company at Watsonville in 1888, and subsequently at the sprawling Spreckels Sugar factory, opened near Salinas in the summer of 1899. This last facility was served by a 3.3-mile Southern Pacific spur, completed on May 11, 1898, which left the main line at Spreckels Junction, two miles south of Salinas.

There were other encouraging developments along the main line as well. By 1919, San Jose canneries were shipping some 1,450 carloads of prunes annually, 375 carloads of dried fruits and 2,250 carloads of canned fruits. The surrounding Santa Clara Valley had over 100,000 acres devoted to fruit orchards. The Logan rock quarry, already a supplier of ballast and crushed rock for railroad work, was now the principal source for state highway projects developing in the south bay region. Thousands of carloads of apples were shipped annually from the Watsonville district. A whaling station was in operation near Del Monte Junction, where as many as nineteen whales were caught in one week. The oil derived from them was shipped east in tank cars for various purposes and carloads of fertilizer were another by-product.

Infusorial or diatomaceous earth, a product of the White Hills near Lompoc, contributed 1,550 carloads to the Coast Line in 1919. By this time, the original 1907 spur to the first Celite Company mill site had become inadequate, and plans were afoot to construct a four-mile branch, south from Lompoc up San Miguelito Canyon to the present mill. The Celite Company organized the Pacific Southwestern Railroad in 1922 to build and operate the line and construction commenced in May, 1923. Southern

Pacific arranged to share the burden of construction, finish the line to higher standards, and eventually, in 1928, acquired full title to the railroad which became known as the White Hills Branch. The mills of the Celite Company (later Johns-Manville) became Santa Barbara County's largest industry, with agriculture running a close second.

Sheltered coastal valleys in Santa Barbara and Ventura counties were well suited to orchard production. Walnuts matured in great quantities in the district between Naples and Santa Barbara. But further south, the citrus industry predominated, largely in the growing of lemons. By 1913, 10,000 acres in the Ojai Valley were devoted to lemon production. Other lemon-producing districts included Camarillo, Simi, Moorpark, Terre Haute, Sespe, Fillmore and Santa Paula. Just west of Santa Paula, The Limoneira Ranch, reputed to possess the largest lemon plantings on a single holding in the world, built a 2.5-mile spur from Limco to the ranch compound in 1910. Another spur extended from the mainline near Santa Susana two miles north to the Patterson Ranch near the mouth of Tapo Canyon. With such development, it was no wonder that Ventura County's citrus crop was valued at $1.4 million in 1913.

Oil production was another important traffic producer. Indeed, California's petroleum industry had its beginnings on the coast. Producing oil fields sprouted along the Coast Line at Ellwood, Dulah and Seacliff. Small refineries were in operation at Newhall, Ventura and Santa Paula by the mid-1870s. Oil was first tried as a locomotive fuel in 1894 when a Southern California Railway locomotive was converted in the Union Oil shops at Santa Paula. Southern Pacific began the conversion to oil fuel in 1900. The first solid train of asphalt departed Santa Paula for New York in 1897. The Santa Paula Branch passed through a rich oil district and loading docks clustered at Santa Paula, Sespe, Fillmore and Piru. The "Tapo Spur," built to serve citrus packing sheds, also served the Tapo Canyon oil field. Southern Pacific also handled a good deal of traffic to and from the Santa Maria and Cat Canyon fields, although they were off line, located on the Pacific Coast Railway.

A seven-car SP passenger train bound for Los Angeles approaches the Pacific Coast Railway crossing at Hadley Tower in 1914 (**above**). The industrial activity at Hadley, served by both standard and narrow gauge rail, consisted of the the California Liquid Asphalt Company on the left (formerly located at Avila Beach) and the Baker Ensign Refinery on the right. Petroleum and its many derivatives contributed markedly to Coast Line freight revenues.
Aston photo, courtesy Bennett-Loomis Archives

Mission Bay roundhouse (**above**), built about 1906, was located close to downtown San Francisco to service commuter and other passenger power. Mission Bay yard (**right**) was the focal point for rail service to over 300 industries in the City's industrial switching district. Both facilities were reached from the mainline at Potrero Tower (at far right in upper view).
Two photos, Vernon J. Sappers collection

The movement of troops and materials during World War I brought increased traffic loads to the Coast Line. This was especially true during the period of federal control from December 28, 1917, through March 1, 1920. Under a doctrine of "joint use" to promote the highest efficiency in the movement of freight, the USRA (United States Railway Administration) instructed on July 17, 1918 that the Dumbarton Bridge line and Peninsula line be opened to freight traffic of the Western Pacific Railroad, traffic formerly moved across the bay on barges.

By 1925, the Coast Division was handling 7.3 million gross tons of freight annually between San Luis Obispo and Santa Barbara, 8 million between Watsonville and San Luis Obispo, 9.5 million between Watsonville and San Jose, 10.2 million between Santa Barbara and Burbank, and a whopping 22 million gross tons between Redwood Junction and Bayshore Yard!

Located close to the heart of the great city, Bayshore Yard was, by the fall of 1921, handling nearly 42,000 cars monthly, requiring an average of 14 switch engines a day to work the yard's 25 outbound tracks, 39 inbound tracks and 21 repair tracks. In all, more than 30 engines and crews were needed to switch the great industrial district stretching from South San Francisco to Mile Post 0.

Drumm Street Station, located at the intersection of Broadway, Drumm Street and the Embarcadero, handled all export and import freight. Pier 5 was used exclusively for Southern Pacific's Sacramento River steamers, and over 300 industries were served by private spurs in the San Francisco switching district—74 in the vicinity of Drumm Street alone—from flour mills to steel shipbuilding. Southern Pacific completed a six-story concrete grocers terminal, each floor 600 by 1000 feet, on Channel St. between Third and Fourth in 1921. On November 27, 1927, the steamer

By the fall of 1921, when these photos were taken, the car repair and heavy locomotive erecting shops were in place and fully operational at Bayshore Yard near San Francisco. And with the 21-mile segment of the Coast Line between Redwood Junction and Bayshore shouldering an incredible 22 million gross tons per year–the SP system's busiest stretch of track–Bayshore was now handling almost 42,000 cars a month, requiring a fleet of switch engines to work the yard's 64 outbound and inbound tracks and 21 repair tracks.

Two photos, Vernon J. Sappers collection

S.S. *Limon* became the first ship of United Fruit Company's "Great White Fleet" to dock at the new Southern Pacific banana terminal. Its cargo of 30,000 bunches of bananas was loaded into refrigerator cars spotted on eight spur tracks, capacity 47 cars, built at the facility. Prior to the opening of this terminal, all banana shipments had been unloaded at New Orleans. Plans were for a banana steamer to dock every Monday at San Francisco.

All this activity required an increasing number of freight trains to be operated on the Coast Line, many of them running extra, but it was the passenger trains that were the most visible to the general public. When the December 6, 1901 timecard was placed in effect, three through trains were indicated: Nos. 1 and 2, the all-coach *Coast Line Limited*; Nos. 9 and 10, the night *Sunset Express*; and the tri-weekly *Sunset Limited*, Nos. 125 and 126. The latter two trains were trans-continental in scope, linking San Francisco with New Orleans via the Sunset Route. In addition, trains No. 3 and 4 provided daily local service between San Francisco and San Luis Obispo. The *Coast Line Limited* and the *Sunset Limited* both were allowed fourteen hours and 45 minutes over the entire 483-mile line between San Francisco and Los Angeles, while the *Sunset Express* required nineteen hours to cover the same distance.

On November 15, 1902, the seasonal *Sunset Limited* became a daily train, Nos. 9 and 10, but the *Sunset Express* was dropped from the timetable. The

A King City Local rolls homeward past the mission at San Miguel in the upper Salinas Valley. The popular interest in the romance of the missions and California's rich Spanish heritage was a strong drawing card for tourists to travel Southern Pacific's Coast Line.
Southern Pacific Lines

The 36-inch refractor telescope at Lick Obervatory on Mt. Hamilton near San Jose, was a popular side trip for Coast Line travelers laying over at San Jose. The observatory was reached by stage and automobile and tourists, having endured the four-hour trip from the railroad station, normally spent the night.
Southern Pacific Lines

Coast Line Limited was renumbered to be Nos. 21 and 22. On February 28, 1906, this train became the *Coaster*, and the next day the *Shore Line Limited*, train Nos. 19 and 20, was added to the schedule. On May 8, 1910, the celebrated *Lark*, Nos. 75 and 76, was established, providing night sleeping car service on the thirteen hour, 45-minute run between Los Angeles and San Francisco. Service changes occurred frequently, but always the trend was towards more trains and by June 30, 1916, ten long distance trains were regularly operating over the Coast Line: Nos. 17 and 18, the *Seashore Express*; Nos. 21 and 22, the *Coaster*; Nos. 23 and 24, the San Luis Obispo local; Nos. 75 and 76, the *Lark*; and Nos. 77 and 78, the *Shore Line Limited*.

These trains were consistently well patronized and frequently operated in sections. The delights of the California coast were a particularly attractive drawing card and on weekends during the season, it was common to find three to five special trains tied up at Santa Barbara with special tour groups from the east. The private cars of the monied and socially elite crowded the spurs built in downtown Santa Barbara adjacent to such prestigious hotels as the Potter, and for the Ambassador, the Neal, and the Arlington. In northern California, Del Monte was yet another favorite destination.

By 1910, a sophisticated and well funded promotional campaign spearheaded by Southern Pacific's publication of the widely-distributed *Sunset Magazine*, and augmented by colorful brochures and advertising, had placed the attractions of the Coast Line firmly in the minds of the nation's traveling public. A brief and pleasant side trip by auto stage from San Jose would provide the tourist with a close-up view of the thirty-six-inch refractor telescope at the Lick Observatory on Mt. Hamilton. A daily stage transported the invalid some thirteen miles from the main line to sample the "remarkably curative properties" of Gilroy Hot Springs. The seaside resort of Santa Cruz, and the Hotel Del Monte, "the finest seaside resort in the world," were well known and widely patronized. But the railroad was also quick to popularize such lesser known attractions as Paraiso Springs, a "Carlsbad of America," just an hour's ride from Soledad, where arsenic, soda and sulfur springs could "cure almost anything." And the new (1908) Pinnacles National Monument was easily accessed by auto stage from Soledad or Hollister, while the world-renowned health and pleasure resort Hotel El Paso De Robles was yet another frequent destination. People suffering from any of a long list of nervous, circulatory and skin disorders had only to take of the waters, mud-baths and sand baths and be cured here so readily "that crutches and similar badges of discouragement are like drugs on the market in Paso Robles—unnecessary."

Southern Pacific also helped popularize the missions which dotted the Coast Line at frequent intervals, publishing many articles of both fact and fiction on the subject. The road distributed thousands of pamphlets that promoted the railroad as an excellent way to visit these relics of a more romantic and picturesque era in California history. Following in the main the route of the El Camino Real, the Coast Line provided convenient access to the missions at San Buenaventura, Santa Barbara, San Luis Obispo, San Miguel, San Antonio, Carmel, Santa Clara and San Francisco and all were frequented by tourists who clearly had a fascination for the old ruins.

This popular fancy with the missions and the Spanish heritage of California led Southern Pacific to adopt the "Mission Revival" style of architecture when designing new stations and facilities along the route, each complete with palmettos and lush gar-

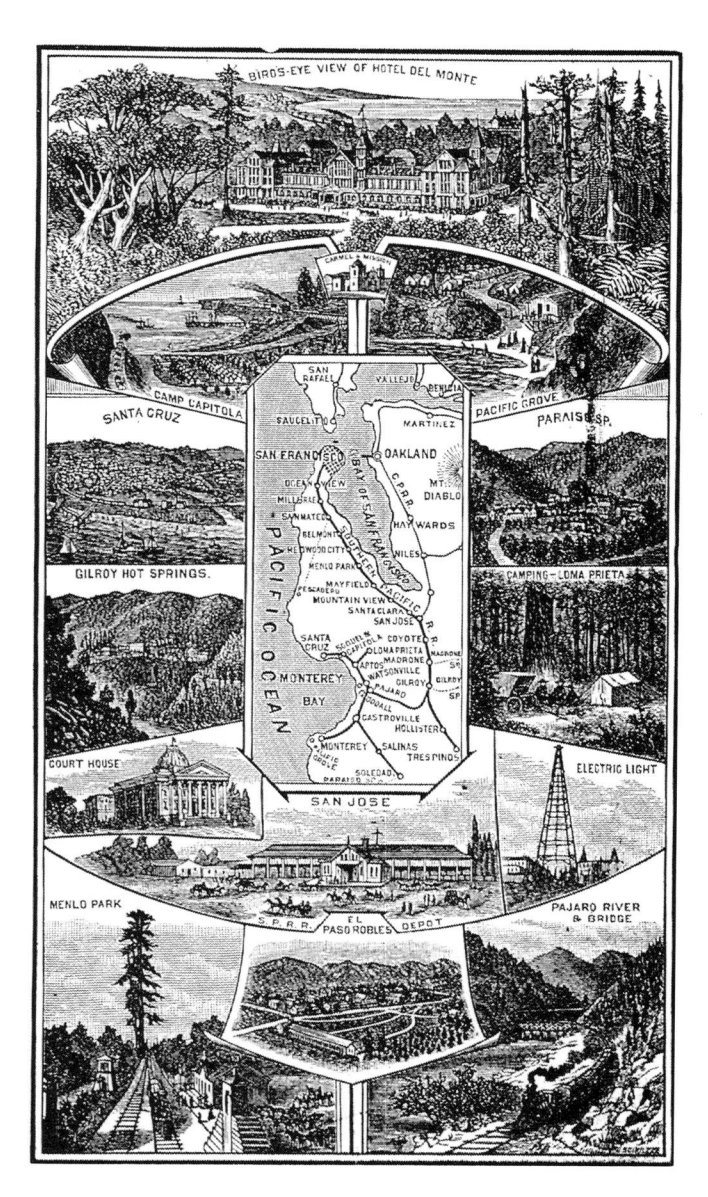

An 1883 tourist pamphlet promotes scenic attractions accessable from SP's Northern Division, including the Hotel Del Monte, Gilroy Hot Springs, Paraiso Springs, El Paso Robles and camping in the Santa Cruz Mountains. These and other recreational opportunites were "just three short hours from San Francisco."
Southern Pacific Lines

The popular fascination with California's Spanish heritage led Southern Pacific to adopt the Mission Revival style of architecture for its new stations along the Coast Line. The Burlingame station (**above**) is now accepted to be the first building erected in this style in California. This view of the historic structure was taken on August 12, 1939. In time, other stations were built in the Mission Revival style along the coast. The Atascadero station (**below**) was opened on May 6, 1922, while the shelter at Del Monte (**left**) was opened in 1926. That year, the Del Monte Hotel, having been leveled in September, 1924 by a disastrous fire, was itself rebuilt in the Mission Revival style.

Top and left, Benny Romano collection;
below, Southern Pacific Lines

Southern Pacific took the occasion of the Panama-Pacific International Exposition, held in San Francisco during 1915, to upgrade and rebuild its old passenger station at 3rd and Townsend Streets. Designed by SP's own architects, the new facility, opened early in 1915, was perhaps the most important station on the Coast Line to be built in the Mission Revival style. At the same time, the Company improved the track layout. Built with six rows of umbrella sheds (**right**), the terminal itself was revised to include fifteen tracks. Car repair tracks were located at 7th Street (**below**), where the main line turned toward the south and the Bayshore Cutoff. These photos date from 1920.

Three photos, Vernon J. Sappers collection

The grounds of the Panama-Pacific International Exposition glisten in the California sun near the Presidio in San Francisco. The SP estimated that over a million and a half visitors toured their building during the ten-month event, held during most of the year 1915. With the Exposition heavily promoted in the east, the influx of tourists created an unprecedented density of train movements on the SP system.
Author's collection

dens. The handsome station at Burlingame, formally opened on October 10, 1894, by the Southern Pacific and the Burlingame Country Club, is today officially recognized as the first permanent structure to be built in this style in the state of California. Stations reflecting the Mission Revival style or with "Spanish" or "Moorish" influence were eventually built at Santa Barbara, Gilroy, Atascadero, San Luis Obispo, Glendale, Burbank, Los Angeles and San Francisco.

The latter station was an imposing building, constructed of reinforced brick and covered in a rich stucco. Designed by Southern Pacific's architectural bureau, the San Francisco station was patterned after the general features of missions, employing a pastiche of bell towers, gables and arches, topped with a heavy tile roof. The station faced Third Street between King and Townsend and had six rows of umbrella sheds and paved platforms which extended from the station to Fourth Street. The passenger terminal itself had fifteen tracks–extending from Third Street Station to Fifth Street–and each was long enough to hold an entire train. A system of double ladder tracks and diamond crossings permitted practically any train movement without the possibility of a tie-up. A Union Switch & Signal electro-pneumatic interlocking protected the entire plant and was controlled from a new interlocking tower erected at Fourth Street, also in the Mission Revival style.

When completed early in 1915, twenty-five regular passenger trains were scheduled to enter San Francisco terminal daily and the same number were scheduled to depart. The facility was designed to handle a great deal more business than this, however, and the opportunity was not long in coming.

The Panama-Pacific International Exposition was held in San Francisco from February 20 until December 14, 1915. This 635-acre, $25 million extravaganza celebrated the completion of the year-old Panama Canal, "the eighth wonder of the world." A Panama-California Exposition was staged simultaneously in San Diego and together the two pageants generated a passenger traffic boom of unprecedented proportions on the Coast Line, as ever-curious easterners flocked west by the thousands. Southern Pacific took full advantage of the occasion to promote its own activities.

In addition to underwriting a significant share of the exposition, the railroad erected its own million-dollar auditorium, an imposing two-story structure seventy feet in height, which was dedicated March 10, 1915. Built in the "Renaissance" style, the facade was set off by a series of Corinthian columns, while the interior featured the "Sunset Theater" with a seating capacity of four hundred, equipment displays (including the historic locomotive *C.P. Huntington* and the latest articulated Mallet design), and a series of miniature dioramas depicting highlights along "The Road of a Thousand Wonders."

Of course, as its name implies, the principal attraction of the Coast Line has always been the marvelous vistas and cool marine air of the Pacific Ocean. For nearly 107 miles, from Surf to Ventura, the railroad hugs the rugged bluffs and sandy beaches immediately adjacent to the coast. The trains to take in the 'twenties were Nos. 77 and 78, the *Shore Line Limited*, the only ones to make the trip in daylight. Train No. 77 is seen approaching Miramar (**right**) and later (**above**) passing Point Arguello and its historic lighthouse. In an earlier view (**below**) train No. 77 pauses at Surf about 1908, as the station's namesake pounds the coast to the west.

Three photos, Southern Pacific Lines

The second section of the westbound *Lark* lies in the ditch (**above**) at "Stony Point," near Metz (north of King City), on July 13, 1910, a victim of excessive speed. It was incidents like this that led in 1923 to the construction of tunnel No. 5-1/2, and elimination of a restrictive curve.
George McCarron collection

Wreckage litters the sand dunes at Honda on May 11, 1907 in the aftermath of the worst tragedy ever to occur on the Coast Line. The wreck of the "Shriner's Special," operating as the third section of train No. 21, the *Coaster*, claimed the lives of 36, most of whom were just sitting down to lunch in the diner.
Two photos, George McCarron collection

The Southern Pacific estimated that over a million and a half visitors toured their building during the ten-month exposition. The movement of business to and from the event caused a density of train movements hitherto unknown on the system. The peak came in mid-July when a record 29 passenger trains were handled between Watsonville Junction and San Jose on a single day. During the same period, the double-track Peninsula line between San Francisco and San Jose handled 76 trains on several successive days, while the record over Santa Susana Pass and the Cuesta stood at 27 and 30, respectively. During July, the *Lark* was run in three or four sections every day northbound and in two sections southbound, while the *Shore Line Limited* was run in two sections northbound, and extra equipment was run on all other trains. For a time it was necessary to deadhead empty trains between San Francisco and Los Angeles. It was a credit to Coast Line employees that the entire business, plus a considerable movement of freight traffic, was handled without a single serious mishap.

This was not to say that the Coast Line did not have its share of tragedies. The route was plagued by a series of unfortunate accidents in the early years of through operation. At 11:10 AM on March 4, 1902, locomotive 1701, operating as an eastbound caboose hop, suffered a boiler explosion a mile and a half south of Waldorf, killing two men and severely injuring another. Excessive speed was blamed for the derailment of the first section of the *Lark* a mile and a half east of Santa Margarita on October 2, 1911, which killed the fireman on the helper and injured eight others. Speed also was the culprit when the engine and five cars of a druggists' special operating as the second section of the westbound *Lark* left the rails while rounding "Stony Point" curve near Metz on July 13, 1910. Engineer Dixon and fireman Ernst were crushed to death beneath the wreckage but passenger injuries were moderate, despite sensational press reports to the contrary, due to the soft silt of the adjacent Salinas River cushioning much of the impact. It was the fireman once again who suffered the worst in the unfortunate derailment of the *Seashore Express* at Gonzales on April 10, 1915; the cause, a broken switch.

But unquestionably the worst tragedy to occur on the Coast Line took place at the lonely siding of Honda, six miles south of Surf, on May 11, 1907. On that fateful day, a "Shriner's Special," operating as the third section of train No. 21, the *Coaster*, with engine 2412, was approaching Honda at the authorized speed of 55 miles per hour when suddenly engineer Charles "Fred" Champlain heard something snap and the locomotive left the track. The derailment sent the engine headlong into a ditch, burying its pilot in the sand and telescoping the trailing cars into its boiler, resulting in an explosion and fire. The dining car, where most of the dead were found, slid 150 yards on its side, lifting a stretch of rail off the ground like a knife shaving wood. Only one car remained on the track. The catastrophe took place at 12:10 PM and the train's conductor, William John, shortly telegraphed the first news of the wreck into San Luis Obispo by shinnying up a telegraph pole and employing a special "Telegraphone" to tap a signal up the line.

Rescue trains were dispatched from Santa Barbara and San Luis Obispo and the first men on the scene saw nothing but chaos and carnage. A millionaire from Buffalo was wandering incoherently along the tracks, asking people if his tie was straight. (He left the scene in a strait jacket.) The flagman's wife was tending to the victims using her wedding linen to bandage their wounds, and everywhere the pitiful cries of the critically injured mixed with the hiss of escaping steam. Third-degree burns were the primary cause of death. The remains of those found dead at the scene were removed to Santa Barbara. Twenty-three wounded were transported back to San Luis Obispo but nine of the passengers died en route. In the end, the wreck of the Shriner's Special claimed 36 lives. Coroner's juries in both San Luis Obispo and Santa Barbara disagreed as to the cause of the wreck–defective equipment leased from the Pennsylvania Railroad, a boulder in the track, or reasons unknown–and litigation over the incident was prolonged and bitter. It was largely because of this "unexplained" tragedy that railroad men began to regard this segment of the Coast Line as a "treacherous piece of track." Indeed, the wreck of the Shriner's Special would haunt the district around Honda for years.

Derailments were not the only problems the Coast Line experienced in the early years. Sometimes the forces of nature, over which even the Southern Pacific had little control, combined to wreak havoc on its operations. Shortly after five in the morning on

The great San Francisco earthquake of April 18, 1906, did great damage to the Coast Line. Large rocks fell from the hillside and rails were twisted (**top**) in Chittenden Pass, and train No. 334, en route to Salinas, was derailed by the quake midway between the quarry at Logan and Aromas (**bottom**).

Two photos, John G. Snyder, courtesy Alzora Snyder

April 18, 1906, an earthquake of extraordinary violence shook San Francisco to its very foundations. The tremors lasted for 65 horrifying seconds, and were felt hundreds of miles away, but clearly San Francisco took the full force of the quake's energy. Fires broke out and, with the water mains broken in the streets, soon merged into a great conflagration which raged unchecked for three days and nights. The entire business part of the city, some five square miles, was reduced to heaps of smoldering ruins.

For a time, Southern Pacific's entire Coast Division operations were demoralized. System headquarters at Fourth and Townsend streets–which also housed the officers and dispatchers of Coast Division–was thrown into chaos, then succumbed to the fire. Where the main line directly crossed the fault line, the force of the quake was pronounced. On Valencia Street hill, just south of the financial district, the rails were badly contorted and shifted laterally by the quake. Between Sargent and Watsonville, the tracks crossed the fault through Chittenden Pass. Local freight No. 334, en route to Salinas, was midway between Logan's rock quarry and Aromas at the exact instant the quake struck. Without warning, the tank of No. 334's locomotive jumped the track along with the first eighteen cars of the train. The bridge across the Pajaro River in Chittenden Pass had shifted on its footings, as had several bridges on the Peninsula line. The earthquake also collapsed the SP sand shed located west of Aromas (which was subsequently torn down), as well as tunnels No. 2 and 5, on the then-abuilding Bayshore Cutoff.

Although the railroad was hard hit, operations were reorganized to meet the emergency. Temporary offices were established at Oakland and Alameda Piers and the Ferry Building. Tracks were inspected and repairs made where necessary. Within twelve hours of the quake, Southern Pacific and the Harriman Lines had been given over wholly to the work of relief. Trains of emergency supplies and refugees were given free transportation and the right-of-way over all other trains. On Thursday, April 19th, Southern Pacific moved 1,073 carloads of refugees out of the stricken city, and nearly as many on the 20th. Between April 18th and May 3rd, 1,409 cars of supplies were brought in for the benefit of sufferers. And all of these movements funneled along the Peninsula line between San Jose and San Francisco.

The clean-up job was tremendous. SP consigned 30 heavy wagons with their teamsters, then engaged on the Bayshore Cutoff, to the military authorities to be used in hauling supplies. Tracks were laid directly on the city streets and work trains were organized to haul away the rubble. It was some time before operations on the north end of the Coast Line were back to normal.

There were other acts of God which periodically struck the Coast Line. Severe storms in March, 1889 closed the Ventura Division for several weeks, and again in March, 1893. The spring of 1905 found a series of storms disrupting operations over a wide area, from Elkhorn Slough on the north to Santa Paula. The west side of Ventura was under water and slides blocked the Coast Line at Punta Gorda and Seacliff. These, together with a washout at Rincon Creek, stranded a freight train in Ventura for a week.

But these storms were modest in comparison with the great flood of 1914, the worst gale to hit the Coast Line in 38 years. The month of January, 1914, started out wet and by mid-month, Southern Pacific was experiencing trouble keeping its schedules. Saturday night, January 14th, the northbound *Sunset Express* was detained at Santa Barbara due to washouts and flooding and as the days wore on, delays continued to mount. The record-breaking rains continued and eventually culminated in a deluge which began in the wee hours of Saturday, January 24th. A full 8.48 inches of rain was dumped on the coast in 72 hours, half of which fell in two devastating hours on Sunday afternoon. Before the weekend was over, large segments of the Southern Pacific in Oregon and California were affected. The Pajaro, Salinas, Santa Ynez, Ventura and Santa Clara Rivers, together with hundreds of minor tributaries, were all swollen to overflowing. Damage to bridges and roadbed halted two trains in Santa Barbara, another in Carpinteria and several hundred passengers were marooned in San Luis Obispo.

With the Coast Line crippled, Southern Pacific took unusual steps to rescue stranded passengers. The coastwise steamer *Santa Clara* took port at San Luis Obispo and gathered passengers destined for Los Angeles, while the steamer *Bear*, already on its regular run from San Pedro to San Francisco, was chartered by the Company and took on stranded passengers at Santa Barbara and San Luis Obispo, allowing them to complete their journey north. After much effort and expense, through train service was eventually restored on February 3rd. While this work was under way, repairs on some branch lines were delayed until the main line could be opened.

The Ojai Valley Branch was particularly hard hit. During the height of the storm, before the lines went down, the section foreman in charge of the branch wired Superintendent W. H. Whalen at Los Angeles that "the river is where the railroad was." The loss of the entire eight miles of railroad between Ventura Junction and Nordhoff was a heavy blow to the ranchers of the Ojai Valley, who were deeply concerned with how to bring their 1914 citrus crop to market. It was estimated that it would take three months to restore the railroad to the old grade, and by that time, the crop would be lost. At a mass meeting in Ventura on February 1st, the growers pressed for quicker action. It was pointed out that a temporary track could be laid down in about two weeks and thus save the crop. Assistant General Manager H.V. Platt was in attendance, and lost no time in arranging for the work to be carried out. Within days, 283 men were on the job and after just eight days of determined effort, the temporary line was opened on February 10th. The Nordhoff Branch was eventually rebuilt in its entirety, much on new alignment, but for the moment the lemon crop was saved.

The Santa Clara Valley, one ridge to the south, was to suffer a similar, though man-made, disaster a little over a decade later. Just before midnight, March 12, 1928, the Los Angeles Department of Water and Power's St. Francis Dam suffered a massive and near-instantaneous failure. Located in San Francisquito Canyon, a remote gorge tributary to the Santa Clara River northeast of Castaic, the failure of the dam unleashed a 185-foot wall of water which then wreaked death and destruction as it made its way to the sea. Power outages in metropolitan Los Angeles, and most of Ventura and Santa Barbara counties, were the first indication that something was amiss.

Southern Pacific's Santa Paula Branch lay squarely in the path of the advancing water. Seventeen railroaders were drowned without warning as the flood swept over the section quarters at Castaic; the bodies were found thirty miles downstream at Santa Paula. Around 2:00 AM, railroad officials were appraised of the situation and the threat it posed not only to the branch but to the main Coast Line at Montalvo. Orders were issued to hold all trains at either Montalvo or Ventura on the north and Oxnard on the south. By 4:00 AM, the advancing wall of water, now fanned out and just 35 feet high, hit Saticoy. And soon the debris-choked water poured in a great arc over the Montalvo Bridge, washing out its southern approach, but the bridge held. As the first rays of dawn illuminated the Santa Clara Valley, the full horror of the disaster was felt. Great tracts of land between Camulos and Fillmore were "swept as bare as a pool table." The death toll hovered just above 400, and about twenty miles of the Santa Paula Branch were badly washed out; about eight miles of line and four bridges were completely obliterated.

Two Southern Pacific officials, Assistant General Manager T. H. Williams and Los Angeles Division Superintendent G.E. Gaylord, hurried to the scene from Los Angeles. Within a few hours, large crews of men and materials were under way. SP handled relief supplies, stricken people and bodies without charge. A little over twelve hours after the disaster the main Coast Line was up and running. About the same time, train service was restored to Fillmore and later to Piru, but the shadow of that catastrophe was to

The station grounds at Santa Barbara are littered with flood debris following the epic storms of January, 1914. Over four inches of rain fell in two devastating hours on January 25th alone, closing the Coast Line for ten days.
Robert McNeel collection

Just after midnight on February 24, 1910, the east end of tunnel No. 10 (**top**) between Thyle and Nova on the Cuesta grade collapsed without warning. The incident, which occurred just moments after the eastbound *Sunset Express* had passed through, effectively closed the Coast Line for what came to be twenty days. The night trains were annulled or diverted to the San Joaquin Valley Line, but some semblance of service was maintained by running the day trains up to the collapsed bore from either side and having the passengers transfer between trains by means of an old construction road (**above**) built around the tunnel in the 'nineties.

Two photos by Aston, Bob McCarron collection

hang over this beautiful valley for many years to come. And it would be months before the Santa Paula Branch would be reopened through to Saugus.

Yet another significant disruption to the Coast Line in the early years occurred on the Cuesta Grade above San Luis Obispo during the winter of 1910. For some time, work had been in progress on relining the Cuesta tunnels with concrete when suddenly, at 12:45 AM on February 24th, forty-six feet of the east end of tunnel No. 10, located between Thyle and Nova, caved in. The cave-in came without the slightest warning, but no one was caught in the tunnel. Train No. 10, the *Sunset Express*, had passed through the tunnel southbound only moments before and would be the last through train on the Coast Line for over two weeks. Train No. 18 tied up at Santa Margarita and No. 9 in San Luis Obispo.

The work of removing the mass of dirt, rock and broken timbers was begun almost immediately and soon three hundred men were at work on the tunnel. The following day, train No. 22, the *Coaster*, and train No. 24, the San Luis Obispo local from San Francisco, were consolidated at Santa Margarita and run to the west end of tunnel No. 10. The passengers and mail were then transferred around the tunnel to a waiting train on the other side. Tunnel No. 10 was comparatively short, and it required but little time for the passengers to walk around it over a well-graded trail (originally a construction haul road) from one end to the other. The Company would not run the risk of such transfers at night, so annulled train Nos. 9, 10, 17, 18, 19 and 20.

At first, work proceeded with the intent of holding the slide and reconstructing the tunnel, but by the afternoon of the 26th, it had been decided to abandon the bore entirely and make a huge cut instead. Accordingly, the torch was applied to what remained of tunnel No. 10 at 12:01 AM, February 27th, and within an hour, the timbers had burned enough to allow the rest of the tunnel to cave in.

Once the full impact of the slide was known, the Company took steps to restore some sort of service to the Coast Line. On February 26, it was announced that until further notice, train Nos. 21, 22, 23, and 24 would run via the Coast Line, transferring at tunnel No. 10. Train Nos. 9 and 10 were annulled and Nos. 17 and 18 were detoured via the Western Division and San Joaquin Valley Line. Through freight service was to be operated on the schedules of manifest trains Nos. 243 and 244 between San Francisco and Santa Margarita, and between San Luis Obispo and Santa Barbara.

Ten days later, much progress had been made but the line was still out of service. The provisional stations of Owlville and Curran had been established on the north and south sides of the tunnel, respectively. Curran had the advantage of a spur track, a station building and a telegraph office. A daily paper was issued, by means of pen and ink, setting forth in bright, crisp items, the events of the preceding twenty-four hours.

The inconvenience of the foot path around the stricken tunnel cut across all classes. The San Luis Obispo *Morning Tribune* of March 8, 1910, reported that "Andrew Carnegie passed through San Luis Obispo yesterday afternoon on train No. 21. When the train arrived at the site of tunnel No. 10, he was forced to walk around the cave-in in the same manner as the poorest passenger." The *Tribune* went on to mention that he was en route to Monterey where his private car awaited him.

At last, on the morning of March 14, 1910, the first train–a Palmer Oil Company special en route to Santa Maria and the Cat Canyon oil fields–passed by the former site of tunnel No. 10. Normal operations were quickly resumed and another crisis on the Coast Line had been overcome. Yet there were more difficulties, of an on-going nature, to contend with.

The Coast Line, by its very name, implies a close interaction with the Pacific Ocean. Between Pismo Beach and Oxnard, and at many other points along the way, the sea itself or its traces are directly visible from the train. Indeed, for nearly 107 miles between Surf and Ventura the railroad hugs the rugged bluffs and sandy beaches immediately adjacent to the coast. Erosion caused by the relentless pounding of the waves has made it necessary to construct at Honda, Lento, Concepcion and several other points, over 8,200 lineal feet of concrete seawalls similar to a design used by the Company at Galveston, Texas. Wind-blown sand has created other problems for the railroad, particularly in the 50-mile stretch between Pismo Beach and Honda. Sand dunes blown inland, at points to an altitude of 1,000 feet, seriously encroached on farmlands and railroad property. Steam shovels and work trains were used to clear drifting sand from the tracks. But to stop the drifting, the Southern Pacific employed a technique that was used to reclaim waste ground at Golden Gate Park in San Francisco. In the particularly troubled areas between Honda and Surf, and between Narlon and Callender, adobe (or oil) was spread over the sand and bent grass and acacia trees were planted over a wide area.

The same sand that proved so troublesome to operations, could also provide a source of revenue for the railroad, and sand pits were worked to advantage at numerous places along the line. The dunes themselves attracted recreationists and motion picture producers seeking desert locales.

Cecil B. De Mille's 1923 costume spectacle *The Ten Commandments* was filmed for Paramount just west of Guadalupe. Even though SP trains were not in the film, the Coast Line nevertheless played a major role in the production. Over twenty-five thousand people and three thousand animals, together with food and equipment, and twenty-one four-ton sphinxes were transported the 200 miles from the Hollywood studios to Guadalupe. Over 550,000 feet

For the epic film *The Ten Commandments*, made by Cecil B. De Mille in 1923, SP's Coast Line was used to transport the men, materials and equipment necessary to build a huge set depicting locations in ancient Egypt on the great sand dunes west of Guadalupe.

Southern Pacific Lines

While a scenic asset, the Coast Line's close proximity to the Pacific Ocean caused a multitude of problems for the railroad. Erosion caused by storm runoff as well as the relentless pounding of the waves undermined right-of-way and caused slides. Wind-blown sand encroached on railroad property. In slide-prone territory, such as two miles west of Tajiguas (**above**), SP oiled the hillside and installed slide-detection fencing. A more permanent solution to the problem was found in the construction of concrete seawalls. Over a period of ten years, from the mid-'twenties through 1935, SP constructed over 8,200 feet of concrete seawalls at such vulnerable points as Honda, tunnel No. 12 near Sudden (**left**), Concepcion, Sacate (**below**) and Lento.

Three photos, Southern Pacific Lines

"The Devil's Jaw" claims another victim, this time the steamer *Santa Rosa*, crashed on the rocks at Honda in July, 1911. Since the days of the Spanish navigators, the Point Conception area has been known as the Graveyard of the Pacific.
Virgil Hodges photo, Southern Pacific Lines collection

of lumber was hauled in, and De Mille's production company built an enormous set representing ancient Egypt on the dunes west of town. When it was all through, De Mille simply buried the set. It is interesting to note that, as this is written, efforts are under way to locate these long-abandoned sphinxes with sophisticated ground-penetrating radar in hopes of restoring and displaying them.

The Southern Pacific's Coast Line interacted with the sea in yet another, more heroic way. In the twenty-two-mile stretch between Tangair and Concepcion the railroad was, with the exception of a handful of isolated ranches and a lighthouse or two, the only incursion of man, and more importantly, the only means of rapid transportation and communication. This same range of coastline between Points Purisima and Concepcion was particularly treacherous to navigation. Mariners, almost since the days of Cabrillo, had tacked far to seaward to avoid the strong winds, pounding waves and jagged reefs characteristic of the area. But there were many who fell victim to its hazards and the place eventually became known as the "Graveyard of the Pacific." Even with advancements in navigational aids and steam propulsion, the toll continued to mount. And so it was inevitable that once the Coast Line was completed through the area in the late 'nineties, that the closest open Southern Pacific office would be the first point of contact in case of a disaster at sea.

The opportunity was not long in coming. The barkentine *Robert Sudden* went adrift in heavy seas at the mouth of the Santa Ynez River in 1905, within sight of the station at Surf where the alarm was first raised. The ship's cargo of 80,000 feet of lumber was sold to merchants in nearby Lompoc, and for many years, the ribs of the unfortunate vessel stuck up through the sand, bearing mute testimony to the tragedy. Another lumber ship, the *Sibyl Marston*, went aground on the beach a mile and a half south of Surf, on January 12, 1909, and it was a lonely SP track walker who was first on the scene.

But it was opposite Point Pedernales (Spanish for "flints"), near the siding at Honda, that the worst disasters occurred. Ships traveling south along the coast turned landward at this point in order to enter the Santa Barbara Channel. An error in navigation here

Without question, the worst nautical tragedy to occur along the Coast Line took place on September 8, 1923. On that foggy night the destroyer *Delphy*, on the mistaken belief they were turning into the Santa Barbara Channel, ordered a 55-degree course change and led seven of a flotilla of 14 Navy destroyers straight into the submerged volcanic rocks off Pt. Pedernales. The first men ashore assumed they were aground on San Miguel Island, and it was with some rejoicing that the wail of a steam whistle was heard in the night. SP track walkers were the first to respond to the tragedy and, as the fog lifted the next morning rescuers were greeted with this grisly scene. The Cañada Honda trestle is in the background.

Two photos, Vernon J. Sappers collection

might lead to the dreaded "La Guijada del Diablo"–the Devil's Jaw–a treacherous projection of partially submerged volcanic rocks that jutted out into the sea some 500 yards. It was in the Devil's Jaw that the passenger vessel *Santa Rosa* came to rest in 1911 with great loss of life and complete loss of the ship. Southern Pacific section men played a part in this tragedy and the morning after the incident, a special SP train picked up the survivors. The steamer *Harvard* met a similar fate in 1931, but unquestionably, the worst nautical tragedy to occur here, and one which would put the remote siding at Honda before the nation for many months, befell a flotilla of Navy destroyers speeding south to San Diego on the night of September 8, 1923.

There were 14 four-stackers in all, under the command of Captain Edward H. Watson. As the fog closed in around them, they raced at a steady 20 knots after the flagship *Delphy*. At 2100 hours, Watson ordered a 55-degree course change to enter the Santa Barbara Channel. Instead the *Delphy*–some forty miles off course–soon hit the rocks at Honda. On the mistaken belief that they were aground on San Miguel Island, the *Delphy* radioed the following destroyers to alter their course to the east, thereby sealing their doom! Within minutes, the *S.P. Lee*, the *Young*, the *Woodbury*, and the *Nicholas* followed the *Delphy* into the rocks. The crew of the destroyer *Farragut*, realizing that something was amiss, reversed engines only to be struck amidships by the following *Fuller*. The *Fuller*, after striking the *Farragut*, came to rest in the outermost rocks where the waves began to break it apart. The *Percival* and *Somers* hit submerged reefs but escaped serious damage, while the *Chauncey* was not as fortunate. Caught by the waves, its hull was cut by *Young*'s propellers,

64

and then it became impaled on a reef. All in all, seven of the fourteen destroyers, together with some 800 men, fell into the clutches of the Devil's Jaw on that terrible night.

The first men ashore were from the badly broken *S.P. Lee*. The last to leave the ship was Captain Morris. At this instant, the lonesome call of a deep-toned whistle came through the fog-shrouded night. "It's a train!" they shouted. "Thank God for that," said Captain Morris fervently, "thank God we're not on San Miguel Island. Has anyone got the time?" "Yes, Commodore," replied Commander Toaz, "just twenty-five minutes past ten." "Then I'm afraid we've just missed the *Lark* northbound to San Francisco..." They learned later that it was train No. 17, the *Seashore Express*.

The destroyers were wrecked at a point about a quarter of a mile from the tracks, and opposite the Honda section house. At 8:46 PM, section foreman John Giorvas heard a crash and two minutes later heard another. He ran to the second story of his home and looking out the window saw a light toward shore. All too familiar with the nautical hazards of the area, Giorvas gathered his sixteen men and made for the beach. There he could make out the form of a destroyer impaled on the rocks. The shouts of the crew could be heard, but no one could be seen. Returning to his section house, Giorvas flashed the alarm by telephone to the operator at Surf who, in turn, notified Trainmaster T. J. Foley in San Luis Obispo. Foley immediately made arrangements for the sending of doctors, surgical supplies, food, blankets and clothing to the scene of the wreck. Soon relief teams were speeding towards Honda aboard the southbound *Lark*.

The first doctors on the scene came from Lompoc aboard a section motor car, and Giorvas and his men, together with the local fence and steam shovel gangs, did their best to bring the stricken men ashore. A rope was thrown to the *Delphy* and some of the men started for shore, where the half-naked survivors gathered at the Honda section houses around great bonfires. The *Lark* arrived at 3:00 AM and traded its cargo of relief supplies and medical help for thirteen of the more seriously wounded, who were taken to hospitals in Santa Barbara. Throughout the night, the only woman on the scene was Mrs. Charles A. Atkins, or "Ma" Atkins, as the sailors called her, wife of the third-trick operator at Surf. A true angel of mercy, she distinguished herself with her hot coffee, her help in dressing wounds and her general willingness to do anything that would make the "boys" comfortable.

The following afternoon, a special from San Francisco arrived to take the remaining survivors, some 38 officers and 517 enlisted men, on to the naval base at San Diego. All told, twenty-three sailors lost their lives in "The Tragedy at Honda," the greatest pile-up in Navy annals and one of the most heroic chapters in Coast Line history.

The misadventures of the Navy at Honda occurred in 1923, a time when passenger traffic on the Coast Line was approaching its very zenith. On April 15th of that year, another night train was inaugurated between the San Francisco bay district (Oakland) and Los Angeles. The new trains, Nos. 73 and 74, called the *Padre*, were planned as a companion to the *Lark*, matching that famous train in speed and equipment. To generate publicity, before the

Train No. 21, the *Coaster*, rolls through Oceano in 1916. Established on February 28, 1906, the *Coaster* was one of ten long-distance passenger trains regularly operating over the Coast Line during the summer of 1916. Although discontinued that fall, the *Coaster* continued to operate intermittently as a night train on the Coast Line for many years.

Bennett-Loomis Archives

*The Sunset Limited races north along the Peninsula near Millbrae in 1926 (**above** and **opposite**). From the opening of the completed Coast Line until World War II, the Sunset Limited operated over the Coast between New Orleans and San Francisco. Two photos, Southern Pacific Lines*

northbound *Padre* departed on its inaugural run, it was taken to the historic old Mission San Gabriel Archangel a few miles east of Los Angeles and officially christened, with the Mission Players taking a prominent role in the colorful ceremonies.

As was the case everywhere on the Southern Pacific, all trains heading toward San Francisco were designated as railroad "westward," whether headed geographically south, west, or north; similarly trains moving away from San Francisco were "eastward."

The inauguration of the *Padre*, together with the resumption of the Friday- and Saturday-only *Daylight Limited*, Nos. 71 and 72, brought the number of regularly scheduled first-class trains plying the Coast Line to twelve, six each way. The *Daylight Limited* had begun operation the previous spring (April 22, 1922) on a 13-hour schedule Fridays and Saturdays only, but had been discontinued through the winter; the train operated daily after July 12th. The other trains making up the timecard for the summer of 1923 included Nos. 77 and 78, the *Shoreline Limited*; Nos. 75 and 76, the *Lark*; Nos. 101 and 102, the *Sunset Limited*; No. 110, the *Sunset Express*, and No. 17, the *Seashore Express*. As incredible as it may seem, even with this offering of frequent and convenient service, the Company was compelled to operate numerous special movements.

Regularly scheduled trains routinely operated in sections during peak holiday travel periods but many more were operated for specific business, fraternal and political organizations. The Democratic convention in San Francisco in 1920 and the Rotary Convention in Los Angeles the same year drew thousands of conventioneers to the Pacific Coast. But when it came to operating special trains, it was difficult to top the Shriners. The Mystic Shrine Convention that was conducted in San Francisco during June 1922 was typical. Sixty-two special trains crowded into the City over a 24-hour period on June 11 and 12th. With hotel occupancy at the breaking point, ten trains, totaling 107 cars, were parked at Fourth and Brannan Streets for the convenience of the Shriners. When it was all over, 42 extra trains departed the City on June 15th and 16th. The bulk of these specials operated between San Francisco and Oakland Pier by way of the Dumbarton Cutoff. But the entire Coast Line handled a heavy business as well. Thirty-one specials operated between San Francisco and Los Angeles as sections of the *Sunset Limited*, the *Lark*, and other regular trains. Similarly, the Los Angeles Shrine Convention of 1925 saw 27 specials operate via the Coast Line the night of June 4-5. Twenty-two more operated out of San Francisco over the Dumbarton Cutoff.

By the mid-'twenties, the annual rivalry between the University of California and Stanford University, known as the "Big Game," played in alternate years at Stanford Stadium in Palo Alto, was generating a heavy traffic in "Football Specials." The peak came in 1929, when Stanford's schedule included home games against both the University of Southern California, on October 26th, and the University of California on the 23rd of the following month. In addition to a number of specials operated over the Coast Line for the boosters from Southern California, 18 Football Specials departed San Francisco for Palo Alto on October 26th. Again on November 23rd, 27 specials were operated over the 31-mile stretch between San Francisco and Stadium station. After the crowds detrained, the specials continued on to Mayfield, where they backed around the wye. During the game, the specials were parked on the Los Altos Branch where they were backed up for seven miles! Over the course of twelve hours beginning at 8:00 AM, November 23rd, an incredible 607 movements were recorded through the Fourth Street interlocking plant in San Francisco.

This flood of traffic was in addition to the regular through and commute movements on the Peninsula.

Football Specials line up at Third and Townsend Street station in San Francisco during the 1926 season. Each year the number of Specials intensified with the peak year being 1929. On November 23rd that year, in addition to a number of specials from the East Bay, 27 Specials were operated from San Francisco to Stadium Station in Palo Alto to accommodate fans taking in the "Big Game" between Stanford and the University of California.

Southern Pacific Lines

As of September 6, 1925, the number of commuter trains operating daily each way between San Francisco and San Jose had risen to 34. During peak hours, these trains departed their respective terminals on ten-minute headways. This could only be accomplished by shortening the signal blocks and also increasing the number of blocks. In addition, four fast trains were introduced that spring. Two were non-stop, operating on a one hour and five minute schedule between the two cities. No wonder then, that on June 28, 1921, Southern Pacific President William Sproule directed his Chief Engineer, Geo. W. Boschke, to consider what measures, including electrification and multiple main lines, could be carried out to ease congestion on the Peninsula and accommodate what appeared to be a business with unlimited growth potential.

After consulting with Alan Babcock, the Company's electrical engineer and others, Boschke reported on July 6th that electrification of the suburban line, from Third and Townsend Streets to Market Street station, San Jose, using existing double track and coaches, but including the acquisition of new electric locomotives, would cost $1.5 million.

Electrification alone would not solve congestion on the Peninsula entirely, so several proposals were advanced for additional tracks. In the construction of the Bayshore Cutoff, Harriman had wisely planned for the eventuality of a four-track main line. It was suggested that for an additional $7.3 million, two additional tracks could be built from San Francisco to San Bruno, and one additional track could be built between San Bruno and Redwood City for the heavy freight business funneling over the Dumbarton Cutoff into the City.

To these proposals, Boschke further councilied a week later that "might it not be...advisable to get a franchise from 8th and Townsend Streets to 8th and Market Streets in San Francisco for a subway in 8th Street. This subway would be double track, looping at Market Street, so trains could be rapidly handled ... and enable us to run the electric suburban business to Civic Center."

In any case, it was felt that the necessary right-of-way should be acquired now with an eye towards an ultimate four-track railroad between San Francisco and San Jose. It was pointed out that the United Railways paralleled the SP from San Bruno to San

Mateo with a double-track electric line and that the operation was not in sound financial condition. A purchase of this right-of-way might be a good investment for these improvements.

By October of 1921, President Sproule had come to the opinion that he had "no faith in the suggestion that we could operate the Peninsula lines more cheaply by electric traction." Nor was there enough business to justify the large capital expenditures for a subway in 8th Street. Nevertheless, planning for additional tracks continued and was now expanded to consider, in addition to a four-track line at least as far as Palo Alto, built along the existing alignment, that a new double-track freight line also be built on the marshes, skirting the towns to the east of Burlingame and San Mateo. Furthermore, if this new line were extended below the Dumbarton Cutoff, through mostly hay fields and pasture land, to Santa Clara, the right-of-way could be obtained rather cheaply and later developed to advantage. Congestion on the existing Peninsula line could be further reduced by diverting all through passenger business to the east.

The scheme was not without its problems. Where the line passed through the marshes, heavy filling, estimated to the depth of 27 feet, would be required to keep the road stable in the soft ground. Moreover, an expensive drawbridge would be neces-

Southern terminus of the Coast Line was, after June 12, 1915, the new Central Station in Los Angeles. Designed by Parkinson & Bergstrom of that city, the new terminal (**top**) was shared with the Los Angeles and Salt Lake Railroad (after 1921, a wholly-owned part of the Union Pacific System). It replaced the outdated and inadequate River Station. Although Central Station had its station yard on private ground, trains to and from the Coast Line reached the terminal by long stretches of street running. Train No. 110, the *Sunset Express*, just in from San Francisco, rolls down Alameda Street on October 3, 1917 (**above, right**), en route to Central Station.

Top, Southern Pacific Lines collection;
right, R.P. Middlebrook photo, Arnold S. Menke collection

Located at milepost 303, near the mouth of the Santa Ynez River, the station of Surf (**top**) figured importantly in Coast Line operations. Not only was it the key water station between Santa Barbara and Guadalupe, but it was also the junction of the Lompoc Branch. In fact, for a brief time in the late 'teens, Surf was known as Lompoc Junction.

Lompoc Valley Historical Society

Train No. 173, one of three daily scheduled mixed trains, prepares to depart Lompoc (**above**) in 1912, and later clips through Baroda (**below**), nearing the end of its 9.7-mile run to Surf. Primarily an agricultural branch when placed in service on July 1, 1899, the Lompoc Branch was, after 1907, a major source of shipments of diatomaceous earth, generating over 1,500 carloads annually.

Two photos, Lompoc Valley Historical Society

sary where the road crossed Redwood Creek, as that stream was considered navigable for ordinary schooners. As the debate continued, Southern Pacific, in the spring of 1922, quietly purchased from the Peninsular Railway Company a number of properties situated between Redwood City and San Mateo, properties which might fit in with their plans for additional trackage.

By the summer of 1926, the plan had been adjusted to provide for a four-track railroad from the vicinity of Seventh and Townsend Streets to Visitacion; six tracks from Visitacion to Broadway (with the double-track freight line line crossing the passenger tracks at Visitacion Tower at grade in order to gain entrance into Bayshore Yard); and from Broadway to Santa Clara, a divergent line of four tracks located to the east along the shore line as far as Santa Clara.

Here the paper trail stops, and for whatever reasons (probably lack of sufficient capital) no additional tracks were ever built on the Peninsula. There were other grand ideas dreamed up for the Coast Line in the 'twenties as well. Considerable study was given to a great tunnel that would pierce the summit of the Santa Lucia Range on a tangent south-west axis between the west switch at Cuesta, and the existing grade at a point on the upper or "little" horseshoe curve near Serrano. The savings in distance, grade and curvature could be enormous.

Similarly, a Sargent-to-Salinas cutoff was investigated at one point. The proposed alignment, some 22 miles in length, included an 8,000-foot tunnel through the Gabilan Range (in dangerous proximity to the line of the San Andreas Fault). The cost for the project, which, though never built, would have followed approximately the present route of Highway 101, was estimated at $3.3 million in 1929.

The object of most of these proposals was to create as short and fast a railroad as possible between the Bay Area and Los Angeles for the expedited movement of passenger trains, the Coast Line's principal traffic. It was a time of unbounded optimism, but capital was becoming tight and dark clouds were soon to form over the Coast Line and the railroad industry as a whole. There would be little of comfort or progress in the coming decade. ❏

It was in Ventura County that Coast Line trains from the south first encountered the Pacific Ocean. After departing Oxnard, the road crossed the Santa Clara River (**below**) on a pile trestle near the mouth of the river. Just beyond was the seaside resort town of Ventura itself (**above**), and the junction of SP's Ojai Valley Branch. Mission San Buenaventura, established in 1782, was visible from the coaches. West of Ventura, the railroad cut through some difficult country between Pitas Point and Rincon Point (**right**), occupying a narrow shelf directly above the plank road and beach. In the early days, the old stage road was directly on the beach and travelers were often caught by the surf.

Top, Roger Titus collection;
right and below, Ventura County Museum of Art & History

71

The yard and engine crew of an afternoon goat pose for the camera (**top**) at San Luis Obispo in an age when the engine foreman routinely wore a suit coat and vest. There clearly are no "students" among the crew, as the mild climate of the central coast and the nature of the work led the high seniority men to bid on available jobs. All was not work, however, as the circle of captain's chairs and a stray deck of cards under the palm on the right would attest.

Aston photo, Bennett-Loomis Archives

The original Southern Pacific frame depot at San Luis Obispo, built in 1894, as it appeared in the mid-1930s (**above**). Similar structures were erected at Colton, California, and Salem, Oregon.

Robert H. McFarland

San Luis Obispo, located midway between Los Angeles and San Francisco at the foot of Cuesta Grade, was a major Coast Line division point. The local yards and roundhouse were first laid out during the summer of 1894, and with the opening of the Coast Line in 1901, facilities were greatly expanded. Train and engine crews changed here and helpers were added to trains heading over the Santa Lucia range. By 1906, when these two views (**above** and **right**) were taken, the yards were teeming with life and SP's 15-stall roundhouse serviced hundreds of locomotives a month.

Above, McCurry photo, Bennett-Loomis Archives; right, E.G. Gale photo, Vernon Sappers collection

Power and crews pose for the camera in the San Luis Obispo yards in 1906 (**left**).
E.G. Gale photo, Vernon Sappers collection

A double-headed westward freight train labors upgrade past the buildings and farms of the California Polytechnic School near Hathaway in 1907. Hathaway was the first station outside San Luis Obispo on the 17-mile Cuesta Grade.
Roger Titus collection

Train No. 21, the *Coaster*, rumbles across the Stenner Creek Viaduct (**above**) about 1914. The train is double-headed for the Cuesta Grade. Train No. 19, the *Shore Line Limited*, departs San Luis Obispo (**left**) shortly after the train was added to the Coast Line timecard on February 28, 1906.
Above, Aston photo, Harold Soaper collection;
left, E.G. Gale photo, Vernon Sappers collection

The Horseshoe Curve above San Luis Obispo has attracted photographers for years. In this view (**above**), released as a popular postcard by Aston Studio of San Luis Obispo in 1909, four Harriman Consolidations pound upgrade and around the curve with a heavy freight. On another day, train No. 72, the *Daylight* (**right**) drops downgrade around the loop followed by a heavy freight (**below**), both exposed in 1932.

Above, Aston photo, author's collection; right and below, Robert H. McFarland

Train No. 78, the *Shore Line Limited*, emerges from tunnel No. 10 above Chorro about 1928 (**left**).
George McCarron collection

An westward train works its way uphill midway on the Cuesta Grade (**below**) in the "Little Horseshoe" curve below Serrano.
Robert H. McFarland

Serrano, ten miles out of San Luis Obispo on the Cuesta Grade, was an important water stop on the east side of the hill. The siding had double crossovers to facilitate cutting out eastward helpers, if needed to return uphill for another help out of Santa Margarita. With retainers in constant use, Serrano also served as a required wheel-cooling and train inspection point. Serrano was a train order office as well, from 1901 until the end of World War I. This photo (**left**) dates from 1917.
Benny Romano collection

This view (**right**) of Cuesta looking west toward Santa Margarita dates from about 1906. Located just north of the summit of the Santa Lucia Range, Cuesta was primarily a maintenance of way point providing water, communications and facilities for receiving incoming freight. The station, with the telegraph call of CX, dated from the 'nineties when Cuesta was end of track. Once the line was opened to San Luis Obispo, Cuesta ceased to be a train order office.

E. G. Gale photo, Vernon Sappers collection

Although quiet in this view–and little changed today–Santa Margarita (**above**), located 16.6 miles above San Luis Obispo, was an extremely important station at the west end of the Cuesta Grade. Helpers out of San Luis Obispo were turned here and the train order office was busy 24 hours a day. Train No. 19, the *Shore Line Limited*, pauses at Santa Margarita in 1915 (**right**) while a helper is removed after the long climb over the summit of Cuesta Grade.

Two photos, Benny Romano collection

77

When the branch to Monterey was opened in 1880, SP established a station at the junction and named it Castroville. In 1893, SP renamed the station Del Monte Junction, as the resort was gaining wide acceptance and was easily the most popular station on the branch. The station remained Del Monte Junction until 1933 when, with the resort in decline, the station was once again named Castroville. This view was taken on Oct. 24, 1938 (**left**).

Benny Romano collection

A Southern Pacific local train picks its way along the rocky shoreline near Monterey about 1915. As late as 1921, six passenger trains a day operated each way over the 18-mile Monterey Branch between Del Monte Junction and the seaside resort of Pacific Grove, including Nos. 27 and 28, the *Del Monte Express*. First mentioned in April, 1889, the *Del Monte Limited* was the longest-running name train to operate anywhere on the Southern Pacific.

Southern Pacific Lines

Historic Monterey (**right**), first visited by the Spaniards in 1602, was the original capital of California. SP reached the site in 1880 and built this functional station. Although Monterey was a resort in its own right, SP derived most of its revenue at Monterey from the many canneries.

Benny Romano collection

Stanley Palmer captured these glimpses of pastoral Monterey Branch operations in and around Pacific Grove about 1905. The train (**above**) is presumably No. 281, the *Pacific Grove Mixed*, while one of the six daily westward locals prepares to depart Pacific Grove (**right**) for the main line. Note the trolley of the Monterey and Pacific Grove Railway.

Two photos, Stanley Palmer, courtesy Mallory Hope Ferrell

79

Train No. 30, the "Watsonville Junction Local," makes its way down 4th Street (**left**) in San Jose about 1914. Running for over 15 blocks directly in the streets of San Jose, the increasingly busy main line of the Coast Division was having problems coexisting with an increasing number of automobiles operating on the city streets.

F.M. Beckett photo, Ross Regier collection

Fourth St. Tower (**above**) was the point where the main Coast Line, entering San Jose from the south on 4th Street, joined the line coming in from Oakland via Milpitas. Just beyond was San Jose Market Street Station. Signs liberally decorate the building at left. An eastward (southbound) Coast Line freight (**left**) has departed College Park yard and is preparing to enter 4th Street. Both views date from 1906.

Two photos, Robert H. McFarland, Arnold S. Menke collection

In the early days, Southern Pacific's San Jose terminal facilities were limited to a small area near the center of town and Guadalupe Creek. The Market Street Station (**above**) was located along Julian St. at Market, east of the creek, while College Park Yard (**right**) was west of the creek. The San Jose engine terminal (**below**), which served both the main Coast Line and the Coast Division's narrow-gauge line to Santa Cruz, was located at Lenzen Avenue. This arrangement was, by the 1920s, hopelessly inadequate. To relieve the pressure on College Park, SP opened a new freight yard at Santa Clara with over nine miles of trackage during November, 1927, and plans were laid to remove the Coast Line from 4th Street and build a modern passenger terminal.

Above, Southern Pacific Lines;
right and below, R.H. McFarland, Arnold S. Menke collection

Running as 2nd No. 70, the new *Daylight* consist speeds south along the Santa Barbara County coast during a test run in early March, 1937. No other trains were so closely identified with the Coast Line as these colorful streamliners, whose introduction climaxed an otherwise cheerless decade in the history of the route.
Southern Pacific Lines photo, Vernon Sappers collection

3

The Challenging Years

Coast Line Operations through Depression and War

AS THE DECADE of the 1920s was drawing to a close, the territory served by Southern Pacific's Coast Line was rapidly developing into the nation's "salad bowl." The climate and soils of the Salinas, Pajaro, Santa Ynez and Santa Clara river valleys were particularly conducive to vegetable and lettuce production but prior to 1915, lettuce produced in California was of a nondescript, leafy type with little marketing potential. That year's crop yielded but five carloads, shipped from the Imperial Valley. It was not until seed companies had perfected the "Iceberg" variety (from seed imported from France in 1901) that production began to increase.

The first 37 carloads of lettuce from the Salinas-Watsonville district moved east in 1921. The Santa Maria-Guadalupe district joined the producing areas in 1922 with 203 carloads, but by the early 1930s most of this production was being hauled by truck to Los Angeles markets. Rail, however, continued to be the preferred way to ship perishables long distances. By 1930, 42,059 cars of lettuce were shipped east by Southern Pacific, with fully 74 percent of that total originating in the fertile valley of the Salinas River.

Despite hard economic times, lettuce production soared during the 1930s. By 1935, over 500 square miles were devoted to lettuce plantings in the Salinas-Watsonville district alone. Six switch engines were required around the clock at Salinas to work the town's 41 packing sheds; fourteen jobs worked Watsonville. The lettuce "Deal" on the Coast began about March 10th, and lasted through December. During the course of the 1935 "Deal," the Salinas-Watsonville district shipped 23,749 carloads. The peak day, May 5th, saw 368 cars dispatched in 99-car blocks over a 24-hour period. The peak day in 1936 was a whopping 465 carloads!

The Coast Line lettuce traffic was augmented by increasing carloads of other vegetables such as cauliflower from the Santa Maria-Guadalupe and Monterey-Santa Cruz districts, and cabbage, broccoli, carrots and later artichokes. A 1923 traffic agreement with the Union Pacific ensured that perishables originating north of Santa Margarita were funneled through Watsonville destined for the Overland Route, while traffic originating below San Luis Obispo was routed east over the Sunset Route.

Train No. 96, the eastward *Noon Daylight*, creeps across the just-completed Pajaro River bridge near Logan in September, 1941. Unique to the system, this bridge also crossed the volatile San Andreas fault at this point and was set on rockers so that the slightest movement of the fault would throw protective signals red.
Benny Romano collection

It was during this period that much attention was given to improving the capacity of the Coast Line in the vicinity of San Jose south. The situation in this territory was becoming critical. A number of inbound passenger trains passed over this section within a comparatively short time each morning on single track. For some time it had been possible to keep eastward traffic moving against these passenger trains, which frequently ran in many sections, by use of passing tracks but with the large increases in perishable business, especially during peak seasons, delays mounted. It was estimated that movements out of the Salinas Valley had increased almost 400 percent between 1923 and 1928 alone.

Moreover, something had to be done in San Jose. The original route, constructed in the 1860s, was laid in 4th Street, now one of the principal streets of the rapidly growing city. And the old College Park yard was entirely inadequate to serve the needs of San Jose's bustling cannery industry. To address these problems, plans were unveiled for a new classification yard between College Park and Santa Clara, the construction of second track between Watsonville Junction and San Jose, and numerous line changes to reduce curvature, together with a major rearrangement of tracks in San Jose.

The new San Jose freight terminal, later called Newhall Yard, contained a total of 9.13 miles of track, arranged in twelve tracks of 85 cars each. Together with a yard office and the new Santa Clara interlocking plant, it cost $400,000 and was opened November 15, 1927. (More capacity was added in 1928.) Fourteen local freights arrived and departed daily. The yard also switched nine through freight trains daily—18 during the busy season—and altogether a total of 105 to 114 trains was handled daily. Just prior to the completion of the new yard, during October 1927, San Jose Terminal handled 60,000 freight cars. On the average, 32 to 35 yard engines worked daily around San Jose in the late 1920s, and their movements were governed by five interlocking plants: Santa Clara Tower, College Park Tower, San Jose, West San Jose Tower and Valbrick, where the Western Pacific crossed the main line of the Coast Division.

In the fall of 1928, Southern Pacific unveiled plans for an ambitious $3.25 million re-design and expansion of the terminal facilities at San Jose, to be completed over the next two years. An entirely new double-track line was to be built on the west side of the city, together with the erection of a modern and artistic passenger station. For the moment, however, attention was directed to increasing capacity on the line between San Jose and Watsonville Junction. Expenditures totaling $5,875,263 were authorized in 1928, 1929 and 1930 for double-tracking.

Work on the seven-mile stretch of double track between Watsonville Junction and Logan was begun in May 1929, and was completed in October the same year. Early in 1930, 9.6 miles of new second track were completed between Lick and Coyote. Three 100-car center sidings were planned for Coyote, Gilroy and Chittenden. Double track was completed from Gilroy to Sargent on December 26,

Continuing difficulties with sinking right-of-way caused top Coast Division staff to assemble at Elkhorn Slough, between Watsonville Junction and Castroville, on August 4, 1931. From left, the railroaders were F.H. Depew, roadmaster; J.J. Jordan, superintendent; F.L. Guy, division engineer; H.R. Hughes, trainmaster; and W.D. Lamprecht, superintendent's secretary. Jordan, a Coast Division fixture for over 33 years, had just been advanced to superintendent that January. While Lamprecht went on to become vice president of operations, Jordan, who had a penchant for clams and marine air, stayed on as superintendent until his retirement in 1956.
Southern Pacific Lines

1930, but the rest of the project on to Logan through Chittenden Pass was never completed even though footings were placed for a second track at the new steel bridge across the Pajaro River (completed in September, 1941). The completion of this segment of the second track and the new line through San Jose were impacted by the Great Depression of the early 1930s. Litigation by the city of San Jose and the newly-formed community of Willow Glen further delayed progress on the San Jose by-pass line.

In the long view of history, it is difficult to appreciate the full impact that the Great Depression had on Southern Pacific, and the Coast Line in particular. Actions taken by the railroad during this difficult period are well documented, as are the marked decreases in traffic. But there was another, more human side to the story that is perhaps better expressed in John Steinbeck's classic novel of the Depression era, *East of Eden*. Written and set in the Salinas Valley during the 'thirties, Southern Pacific

Always one to keep his hand in things, Superintendent Jordan's business car *Coast* could be seen spotted up and down the line while the "old man" was about the business of supervising his district. Frequently seen on the varnish, the 119 was equally accustomed to the consist of the Coast Peddler. Although treated gently on such occasions, there was an embarrassing incident regarding an unscheduled "drop" of Jordan's car at King City. This view of the car at San Luis Obispo dates from 1952.
Art Laidlaw

The Rexall Company's unique blue and white convention train pauses at San Francisco (**left** and **below**) on May 26, 1936, in the midst of its 29,000-mile, 144-city tour of the United States. Later that summer, on June 8th, Union Pacific's revolutionary *City of Los Angeles* (**above**) was placed on display at Third and King Streets in San Francisco. These special trains, and Great Britain's *Royal Scot*, all operated over the Coast Line, providing much-needed diversion at a time when the country was in its sixth year of economic malaise.

Three photos, Southern Pacific Lines

trains form part of the fabric of life as this story is played out.

But for the record, gross ton-miles slid more than a third between 1928 and 1932–the bottom of the Depression. Branch line traffic decreased an incredible 74 percent! Trains were discontinued or downgraded. The *Sunset Limited* lost its all-Pullman status in 1930. Both the *Shore Line Limited* and the *Padre* were discontinued on September 15, 1931. Consists dwindled. On Cuesta Grade, freight helper miles decreased 25 percent, and passenger helper miles decreased 33 percent. These economies were gained primarily due to lighter trains and the new practice of permitting 2-10-2 engines to shove behind a steel-frame caboose, which allowed for a quicker "turn" of the helpers.

The economic situation had impacted the railway to be sure, but better times, no matter how distant they seemed at present, were inevitable. What concerned railway officials more was the rising tide of automobile and motor truck competition, made possible by the funding of the California State Highway system. Indeed, work on the first California State Highway contract had begun in SP's own back yard between South San Francisco and Burlingame in August, 1912. And by 1930, California's system of hard-surface roads had grown to such an extent that Southern Pacific was seriously challenged by the aggressive trucking industry.

Recognizing the trucker's ability to deliver "dock to dock," Southern Pacific took steps to meet this threat head-on and organized Pacific Motor Transport Company in 1928 to act as a feeder and distributing agency for the railroad in Southern California. This was followed in 1933 with the organization of Pacific Motor Trucking (PMT), which actually owned its own fleet of trucks. Coordinated train-truck service was expanded rapidly and by 1935 was available over a wide area between Marshfield, Oregon, and Tucson, Arizona.

Trucking subsidiaries were only part of the solution. Faster rail service was also necessary and the Coast Line between Los Angeles and San Francisco was the first district to benefit. On January 1, 1933, SP placed in operation certain "miscellaneous mixed trains" which began handling merchandise freight in baggage car equipment operating on passenger train schedules. An overall savings of 24 hours in transit

For many years, Southern Pacific maintained a nursery opposite the Goleta station adjacent to the Coast Line. All kinds of trees and shrubs were grown here. Plants, set out in flats, were loaded into baggage cars on a nearby spur for distribution throughout the system's many depot parks and grounds. During the Depression, the nursery staff was cut to one gardener who divided his time between the property at Goleta and the Santa Barbara depot grounds. By the late 'forties, it was all but forgotten.
Benny Romano collection

With a freshly-built concrete highway bridge in the foreground, a pre-streamlined *Daylight* rumbles across the Tajiguas Creek trestle along the coast west of Santa Barbara. California began work on its State Highway System in 1912 and by 1930, the "Coast Highway" was seriously challenging Southern Pacific's transportation dominance in the Los Angeles-San Francisco corridor.
Roger Titus collection

A PMT truck rolls through the industrial section of Los Angeles in November, 1938, gathering LCL freight for the new *Overnight* fast merchandise run on the Coast. At this time, the trucks were painted entirely in red. To meet the competition, Southern Pacific entered the trucking business during 1928 and by 1933, had organized Pacific Motor Trucking to own and operate a fleet of trucks in order to provide feeder service to its rail lines in Oregon, California and Arizona. In the background towers the Los Angeles City Hall, completed in 1928 and for many years the tallest building in the city.
Southern Pacific Lines

time was achieved on the Coast Line with train Nos. 69 and 70, the *Coaster*, providing through merchandise service with coordinated truck pickup and delivery at Los Angeles and San Francisco.

At first the expedited service was operated as a through train, but before long, time was found to set out a car at San Luis Obispo for coordinated truck service as well. Connecting truck service had been established from Watsonville Junction to Santa Cruz on December 12, 1932, and this service was expanded to include Salinas, Monterey and Pacific Grove on February 5, 1934. This operation was short-lived, however, because on August 5, 1934, the Company established another special merchandise train which served the same points. This new train, known as the "Monterey Merchandise," or "M&M Local," originated every night at Watsonville Junction, handling cars directly off the *Coaster* for local delivery.

By the fall of 1935, the concept of the fast merchandise train had been so well received on the Coast Line that it was time to provide a dedicated train for this service. Thus, on October 22, 1935, SP inaugurated its new *Overnight*, on the San Francisco-Los Angeles run. Dubbed "the fastest freight train in the West," the *Overnight* offered first morning delivery of LCL (less than car load) freight through Pacific Motor Trucking.

Operating as second 78, with engine 4357, enthusiasm ran high as the *Overnight* prepared to depart Third Street terminal on its initial run south. J.J. Jordan's business car *Coast* was attached to the rear. "Yes sir," boomed the Coast Division superintendent, "she's got a tight schedule, and I'm riding her out tonight, just to see how tough it is! I've been

Merchandise gathered from all over Southern California was brought to the Southern Pacific Company freight sheds near River Station (**top**) and transloaded into boxcars (**below, left**) for the dash up the Coast Line on the westward *Overnight*. Many of the boxcars (**right, below**) were 1920s veterans, with their original wood sheathing newly replaced with steel.

Three photos, Southern Pacific Lines

After receiving orders (**above**) and departing the freight sheds at Fourth and King Streets in San Francisco in 1938 (**right**), this *Overnight* is running as a section of the *Coaster*. It wasn't until after World War II that the *Overnights* received schedules of their own.

Two photos, Southern Pacific Lines

89

SP's *Overnight* (**above**), fresh in from the Coast and running as a second section of the *Sunset Limited*, rolls past Taylor Yard on the last lap of its dash to Los Angeles on a fine spring morning in 1938. Having experimented for several years with expedited service, SP inaugurated the *Overnight* fast merchandise service along the Coast Line on October 22, 1935.
Southern Pacific Lines

These black box cars with orange lettering and striping (**left**) were rebuilt for the early days of the *Overnight* service. Converted from existing wood-sheathed boxcars, more than 200 were rebuilt beginning in 1935, with steel sheathing welded to their "outside bracing" and high-speed steel wheels and axles applied at SP's Sacramento shops. Additional cars were also steel sheathed for passenger express service and painted Dark Olive green.
Paul Darrell photo, Anthony Thompson collection

90

waiting for this moment a long time," he continued. "We're going to put this train over the road and give those traffic department boys a service that certainly ought to sell." With that, Engineer Joseph De Nobble opened the throttle, and with Conductor Charles Pelletier in charge, the *Overnight* glided from the yard and accelerated into the night.

At the same time, the Oakland section of the *Overnight* was leaving West Oakland to consolidate with the San Francisco train at San Jose. Steel baggage cars were used initially, but 45 wood-sheathed box cars were quickly reconditioned in the Sacramento car shops for *Overnight* service, painted passenger green with gold lettering and fitted with high-speed rolled steel wheels and axles. These interim cars were first placed in operation during November, 1935.

Late in 1935, however, a program was begun of converting single-sheathed box cars from classes B-50-15 and B-50-16, for *Overnight* use. These were rebuilt with steel sheathing welded to their superstructure frames, received high-speed steel wheels, and were painted black with orange lettering and trim. As these were completed, the initial 45 cars were withdrawn from the service. Later, some steel-sheathed rebuilds were assigned to express service.

While SP moved aggressively to compete with the truckers for freight traffic, the road was content to abandon much of its money-losing branch passenger traffic to the "motor coach." Indeed, SP's own subsidiary, the Pacific Motor Transport Company, engaged in the "motorized transportation of passengers, mail, baggage and express." More often than not, the buses substituted for unprofitable local and branch passenger trains. One of the contract carriers was Pickwick Stage Lines. Early in 1929, Pacific Motor Transport, Pickwick and several other companies merged their bus operations to form what eventually became Pacific Greyhound Corporation. The SP owned a one-third interest in the new firm.

The Company, however, was not about to give up on intercity rail passenger service. And it was on the Coast Line during the Depression that SP's most famous train was developed. The *Daylight*, already the fastest train in the west, became the most distinctive when on April 18, 1930, the train dropped its conventional olive green livery and blossomed forth in new spring dress of pearl gray. The latest type club car was added coincident with the new color. Although short-lived, the gray scheme caused a sensation and by February, 1936, with the new numbers 98 and 99, the *Daylight's* running time had been cut to eleven hours. But this was just the beginning. During the darkest days of the Depression, plans were afoot to transform the *Daylight* into one of the fastest and most colorful trains in the West.

In July, 1936, after three years of research and development, SP unveiled plans for a new high-speed daily streamliner daytime service over the Coast Line. Orders were placed with Pullman Company for two entirely new trains, which together with new motive power, would cost $2 million. Lighter in weight than conventional equipment, the fully air-conditioned twelve-car trains were built of Cor-Ten steel, sheathed in corrugated stainless steel, and were to bear the famous name *Daylight*. Distinctively colored in red, orange and black, the entire train was 978 feet eight and one quarter inches long and weighed 29.7 percent less than conventional equipment. A low center of gravity, heat-treated axles with special lubrication, tight-lock couplers and rubber draft gear allowed for high-speed operation. The consist of a chair-baggage car, one full chair car, three two-car articulated chair car units, a coffee shop-tavern car,

During April 1930, the *Daylight* dropped its staid Dark Olive for new spring colors of pearl gray. Here the unconventional train prepares to negotiate Horseshoe Curve above Goldtree on the Cuesta Grade. By the end of 1930, the train reverted to green; gray showed dirt too badly.
Vernon J. Sappers collection

The new streamlined *Daylight* streaks through Aromas (**above** and **left**) on March 6, 1937, operating as second No. 70 on a trial run. The train's vivid oranges and reds became a lasting image of the Coast Line and of California itself.

Above, Southern Pacific Lines, Lee Barnett collection; left, Albert & Alzora Snyder

The inaugural run of No. 98 attracts a crowd at San Luis Obispo (**below**) on March 21, 1937.

George McCarron collection

Amidst appropriate fanfare, Olivia de Havilland christens the new *Daylight* at Los Angeles's Central Station on March 21, 1937. Standing with her is Father Joachim De Prada of Mission San Gabriel, while SP Vice President Felix S. McGinnis (immediately behind the film star) look on.

Two photos, Southern Pacific Lines

diner, parlor car and parlor observation could accommodate 465 passengers with a crew of 45.

Along with the new trains would come new power. Sleek new GS class 4-8-4's were ordered from Lima Locomotive Works with a top speed of 90 mph. Costing about $136,000 apiece, these new engines were designed with a "skyline casing" and a paint scheme that would carry the *Daylight*'s vivid colors in unbroken lines from pilot to observation car. Capable of operating through between San Francisco and Los Angeles, only two were needed to protect the "streamliner" service, but the others would operate in Coast Line service as helpers on Cuesta Grade and as back-up so that the *Daylight*'s exterior coloring and streamlining would be retained at all times.

At last, in the early spring of 1937, the equipment was delivered from the builders and several trial trips were arranged to determine, among other things, the accuracy of the new schedules. The train's brilliant orange and red paint contrasted beautifully with the adjacent green hills as the *Daylight* made its first test run from Los Angeles to San Francisco on March 4th, then returned on the 6th. There followed a number of trial trips on the 71-mile district between Los Angeles and Montalvo. Repeated tests were made of the new electro-pneumatic brakes, the air conditioning and heat control apparatus, and generators, trucks, wheels, and diaphragms.

During the testing phase, the colorful trains created quite a sensation among the press and public, and huge crowds attended inaugural ceremonies when service began on Sunday, March 21, 1937. Christening ceremonies were held both in San Francisco and Los Angeles. The National Broadcasting Company divided a 15-minute period between the two events. SP's President A.D. McDonald, Vice President J.H. Dyer and his daughter, Miss Lorene Dyer, were the principal participants in San Francisco. Asked by the NBC announcer what he thought of the train, President McDonald replied, "The important thing is what the public is going to think of it. Certainly we built it to meet their demand for speed, with safety and comfort and what you might call eye-appeal. Someone has called these trains 'rainbow trains.' That seems very apt, not only because the new *Daylight* suggests the vivid colors of our California coastline, but also because they are symbols of better times."

At Los Angeles, Vice President Felix S. McGinnis, Warner Brothers studio star Olivia de Havilland, and Franciscan Father Joachim De Prada, pastor of Mission San Gabriel, took the leading roles. Then at exactly 8:15 AM, the trains glided smoothly from their terminals. Posted running times for the new trains was nine hours 45 minutes between San Francisco and Los Angeles. In towns and cities along

Enormously popular from the outset, the *Daylight* frequently ran in sections. In fact it was necessary to operate at least a second section every day during July, 1939–and sometimes a third! The fog has lifted and GS-3 class No. 4425 bites into the curve at Seventh Street, San Francisco, that summer with the second section of No. 98.
Robert H. McFarland

As the sun dips in the west, No. 99 rounds the big curve near Moss Landing during the winter of 1939, and track gangs stand aside to watch the streamliner's passage.
Benny Romano collection

For the first few years, so that the sleek lines of the *Daylight* might remain unbroken, a GS-class engine was assigned at San Luis Obispo to assist the streamliner over Cuesta Grade (**left** and **above**). The big 4-8-4's assigned to the new *Daylights* were designed to handle a twelve-car train unassisted up a two percent grade. Thus, the modest ascent over Santa Susana Pass (**below**) proved no obstacle.

Left and above, Southern Pacific Lines;
below, Southern Pacific Lines, Dan Wolf collection

One of the most photogenic spots along the Coast Line is at Stenner Creek trestle. In this pair of 1939 photos which Southern Pacific used both for postcards sold on board the *Daylight*, and also for advertising, No. 98 is shown descending toward San Luis Obispo behind a 2-10-2 helper (**top**), while all fourteen cars of No. 99 are visible at Chorro siding above Stenner Creek, with a *Daylight* 4-8-4 helper (**center**).

Top and center, Southern Pacific Lines

The timetable allowed just three minutes at San Luis Obispo, believe it or not, for the *Daylight* to load and unload passengers and baggage, water and (if necessary) service the road engine, and add or remove a helper locomotive. Here engine No. 4450 on train No. 98 is almost ready to depart eastward on February 9, 1952 (**bottom**). Even the servicing carts were painted in *Daylight* colors.

Bottom, Jack Whitmeyer

96

Publicity photos of the *Daylight* naturally emphasized the attractions of scenic California. Nearly new engine No. 4449, just delivered for Southern Pacific passenger service, is shown near Santa Barbara in the summer of 1941 (**top**), "surrounded by California flowers," as the press release stated it. In a view which SP marketed as a postcard (**center**), the train rolls past the spring blossoms of a Santa Clara Valley orchard. In another photo from the 1939 series (**bottom**), the westward *Daylight* is shown as it leaves Montecito and passes alongside the Clark Bird Refuge in east Santa Barbara, only a minute or two from the depot, with the morning sun bright on the summits of the Santa Ynez Range to the north.

All, Southern Pacific Lines

Jane Hollister Wheelwright, a descendent of the same Hollister family who deeded much right-of-way to the Southern Pacific Coast Line, reminisced about the *Daylight* of her youth in her 1979 memoirs, *The Ranch Papers*. The *Daylight*, she wrote, "seemed to belong there, and did not jar the feeling of the coast in the slightest." The pictures on these two pages admirably bear that statement out. The *Daylight* was captured on film by the Company photographer in 1937 just west of Gaviota (**above**), on the Cañada de Alegria trestle approaching Sacate (**right, above**), and rolling along the coast at Sacate siding (**right, below**).
All, Southern Pacific Lines, Vernon J. Sappers collection

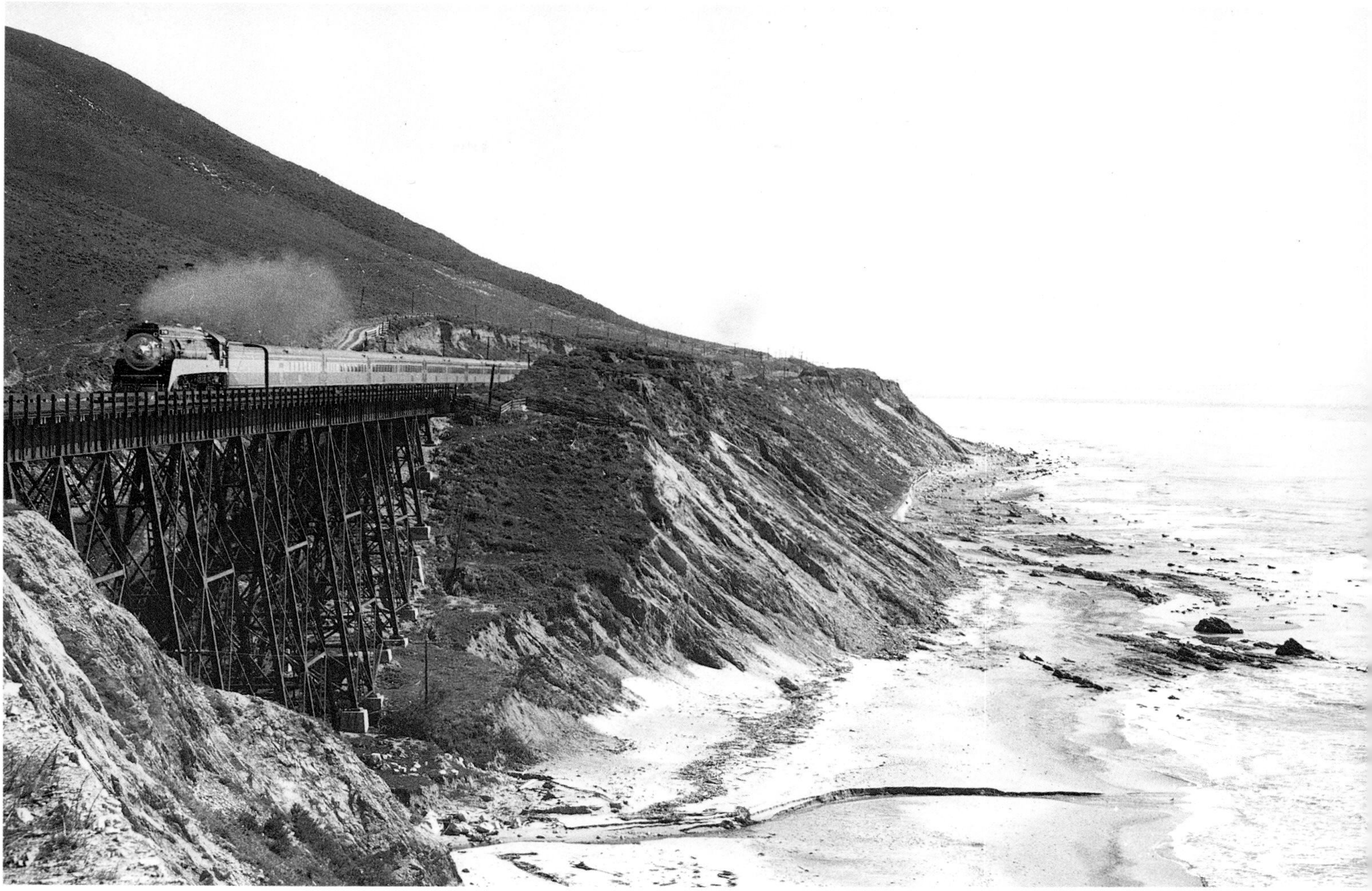

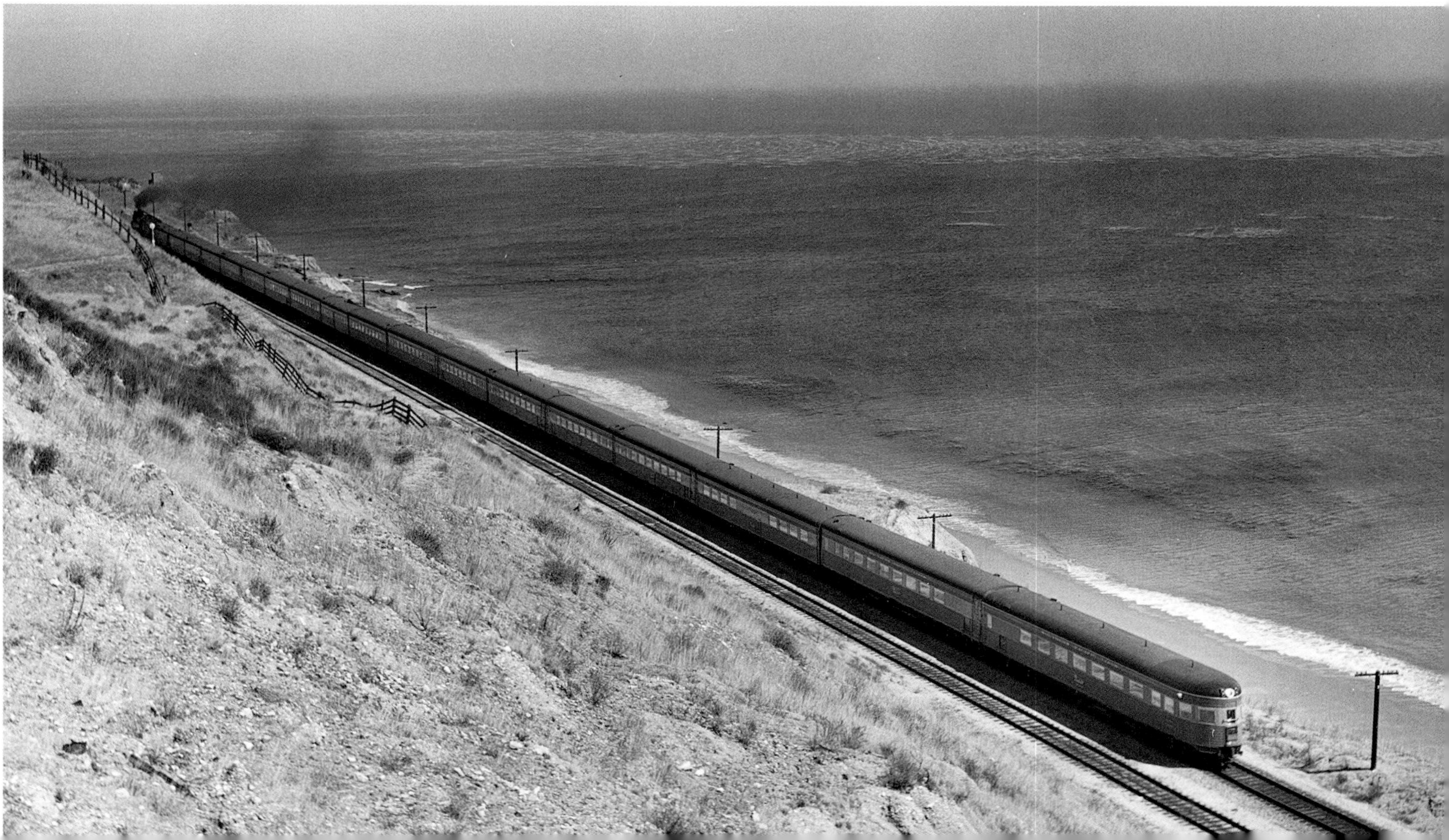

San Jose Improvements 1928-1935

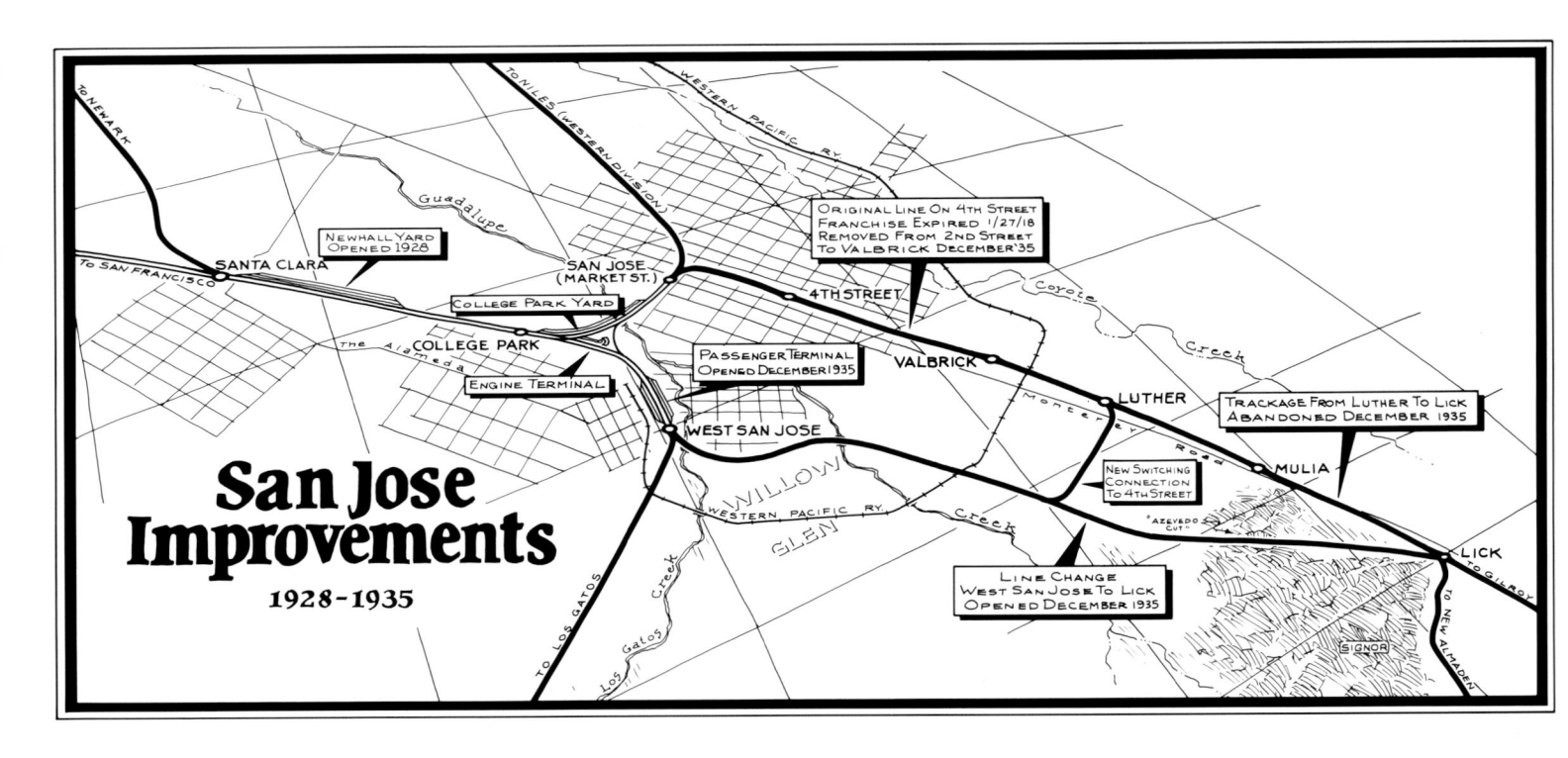

The great San Jose line change of the early 1930s utilized a small segment of the old South Pacific Coast right-of-way which led over the mountains to Santa Cruz. This modest station, dating back to the early days, became the site of the grand new Cahill Street Station.
Robert H. McFarland photo, Arnold S. Menke collection

the route, particularly at San Jose, Salinas, San Luis Obispo, Santa Barbara and Glendale–the points where the new *Daylights* stopped–people lined the tracks to wave friendly greetings and take part in the auspicious occasion.

The faster schedules of the new streamlined *Daylight* and those of other Coast Line trains such as the *Sunset Limited*, *Coaster*, and *Lark*–which was cut 30 minutes to make its run in 12 hours flat–were made possible by sweeping improvements to the Coast Line route. Nearly 80 miles of new 112- and 131-pound rail replaced sections of lighter rail. Numerous curves between Metz and Santa Margarita and between Montalvo and Chatsworth Junction were realigned. Crushed rock ballast was reinforced in places. Several key sidings were lengthened. Nearly 300 special yellow oval-shaped speed boards were installed that applied to the streamliners only.

A significant savings in running time was achieved with the the new $3.25 million San Jose Line Change. Although considerable work had been done at San Jose in the late 1920s (see p. 84), work on the Line Change was not begun until the darkest days of the Depression. Delays impeded progress on the project and it was not until December, 1935, that the new line was turned over to the operating department. The San Jose Line Change involved six miles of new line which left the old main at Polhemus Street on the north side of the city and proceeded along the route of the Santa Cruz branch, where an imposing new station was built on the site of the old South Pacific Coast depot. From the new station yard, the Line Change diverted to the southeast over six grade separations and through a saddle (Azevedo Cut) in the hills south of the city to a connection with the old main at Lick. In all, nine grade separations, seven subways and one overhead were required.

Peninsula commuter No. 137 prepares to depart San Jose's Market Street Station (**above**) on December 12, 1935. Sixteen days later, this station became obsolete with the opening of the $3.25 million San Jose Line Change. Keystone of the project was the imposing station erected on Cahill Street (**right**) in the Italian Renaissance style. The interior featured a mural painting (**below**) celebrating the history of San Jose and the Santa Clara Valley, from the Spanish period to the modern day, not neglecting the railroad. The new line, diverting to the south of San Jose's business district, required nine grade separations including this one (**lower right**) over Julian Street.

Four photos, C. M. Kurtz, Southern Pacific Lines

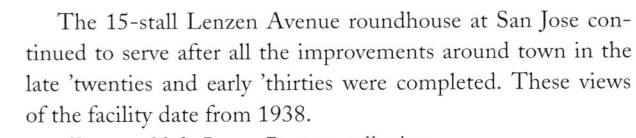

The 15-stall Lenzen Avenue roundhouse at San Jose continued to serve after all the improvements around town in the late 'twenties and early 'thirties were completed. These views of the facility date from 1938.
*Above and left, Benny Romano collection;
below, R. H. McFarland photo, Arnold S. Menke collection*

102

The morning commute fleet has long since departed as train No. 98, the *Daylight*, rolls into the Cahill Street station at San Jose on a crisp fall day in 1948. Goat No. 1221, an 0-6-0, was a fixture in town for many years.
Southern Pacific Lines

Portions of the old line through San Jose, south of the city, were retained for industrial switching purposes. Here a diesel-powered local works the old main line at Alma St. near Valbrick in 1950.
Benny Romano collection

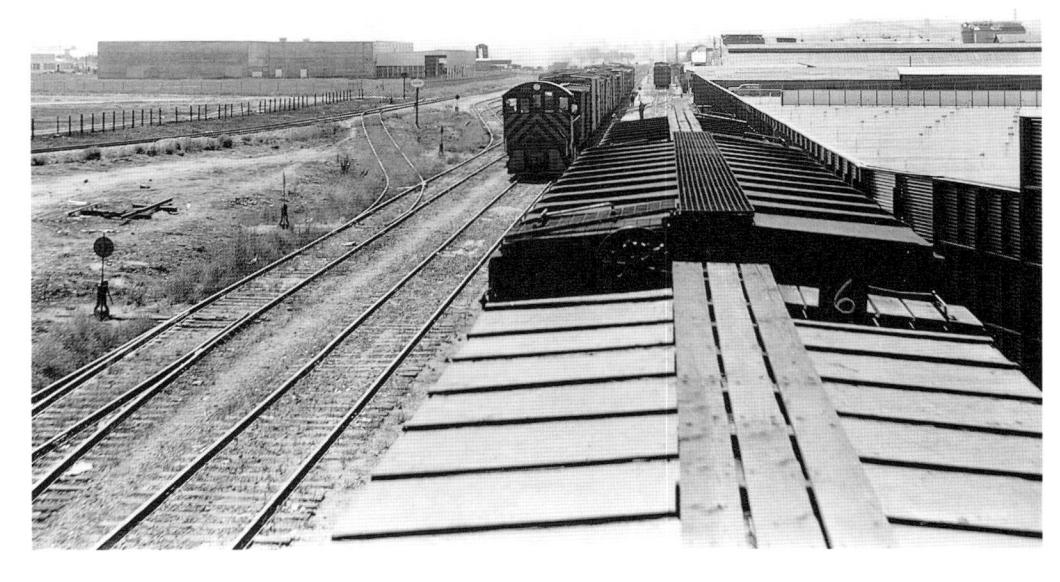

During an average business day at Burlingame in the late 1930s, 33 passenger trains passed through town each way including the *Lark*, *Sunset Limited*, *Del Monte*, *Daylight*, *Coaster* and other long-distance trains, as well as the Peninsula commute trains and locals to Santa Cruz. It is August 17, 1939, and morning commuters board train No. 125 (**above**) at 8:07 AM for the 16-mile ride to San Francisco. Thirty minutes later (**left**) the platform is quiet as train No. 98, the *Daylight*, approaches at speed. Burlingame residents wishing to board the train would have to go to nearby San Mateo.

Two photos, Benny Romano collection

Peninsula local No. 162 departs Palo Alto on October 1, 1937. An elaborate underpass project for University Avenue (the foreground street) made it necessary to relocate the main line for a distance, and in the process a modern stucco depot replaced this structure, familiar to generations of Stanford students. The new facilities were opened with much fanfare on March 8, 1941.
W. C. Whittaker

The architectural style of San Jose's new passenger station on Cahill Street was of the Italian Renaissance. Exterior walls were built in a tapestry of brick, enriched with terra cotta trim, varied in shades of red and sunset. The structure itself was an imposing 390 feet in length and varied between 40 and 78 feet in width. The interior featured marble wainscot with Caen stone plaster above and beamed ceilings. A mural painting depicting the historical background and development of San Jose and the Santa Clara Valley decorated the north wall over the ticket counter.

The station yard had four platform tracks, baggage, mail and express tracks, and a five-track storage and cleaning yard with a capacity of up to 71 suburban coaches. Three main tracks between College Park and the new station were controlled by College Park Tower. And a CTC installation between the new station and Lick was controlled by the operator at the new station.

Following gala opening festivities on the 30th, regular operations over the new San Jose line commenced at 12:01 AM, December 31, 1935. The first train south to use the new station was No. 38, arriving at 1:30 AM, while the *Sunset Limited* was the first northbound train, arriving at 6:52 AM.

Los Angeles, the southern terminus of the Coast Line, also received new passenger terminal facilities during the 1930s. The new "Union Passenger Terminal" opened on May 7, 1939, serving not only the Southern Pacific, but the Union Pacific, Santa Fe and Pacific Electric as well. The idea for the terminal grew out of a California State Railroad Commission study published in 1920 on the elimination of grade crossings in Los Angeles.

Over the years, Southern Pacific trains had used two important stations in Los Angeles; the original Arcade Depot and, after 1914, the Central Station. Both were located on Alameda Street in what was becoming an increasingly congested part of the city's commercial district. Of the several locations considered for the new terminal, the "Plaza Site" was deemed the most suitable. Located seven blocks north of Central Station, the new terminal would face Alameda Street just a stone's throw from the old Plaza of the City of Our Lady of the Angels. After much debate, ground was finally broken on the project in 1933.

In keeping with Los Angeles's heritage, the architecture was Mediterranean in character with massive stucco walls, paneled and beamed ceilings and tiled courtyards. Focal point of the new terminal

Opened May 7, 1939, the $11 million Los Angeles Union Passenger Terminal (**left**), with its graceful architecture in the Spanish-Mediterranean motif, its quiet patios and courtyards, and its decorative plantings, elegantly reflected the heritage of the city it was to serve. Operationally, the new terminal removed rail traffic from congested city streets and funneled the name trains of the Santa Fe, Union Pacific and the Southern Pacific—including Coast Line trains—through this six-track throat (**top**) into the terminals, 16 tracks for trains and 17 tracks for mail, express, private cars and switching. The seventh track in the throat is a switching stub. On opening day, Terminal Tower, standing at left in the panorama above, handled 700 moves in 24 hours.

Two photos, Southern Pacific Lines

106

was to be the 128-foot high clock tower set off with decorative palmetto plantings. The terminal itself, which was situated on 40 acres, was of the stub-end type with a six-track throat, eight platforms, sixteen tracks for passenger trains, and seventeen for mail, baggage, express and switching. The last Coast Line train to use the old Central Station did so the night of May 6, 1939, and after three days and nights of celebration and pageantry, the new $11 million terminal opened early the following morning.

These were good times for the SP's Coast Line. The *Daylight* continued to be America's most heavily patronized long-distance coach train. In fact, it was necessary to operate a second section of the train every day in July, 1939, and the train often was operated in three sections. Nearly 46,000 persons rode the *Daylight* or one of its sections during July, 1939, the peak of the World's Fair on Treasure Island in San Francisco Bay. Following the delivery of two new trains from Pullman in January, 1940, and the overhaul of the original *Daylight* trains, SP inaugurated two new *Noon Daylights* on March 30, 1940. The existing *Daylights* were designated *Morning Daylights* and 15 minutes was trimmed from existing schedules, allowing for a run north in nine hours and 30 minutes and south in nine hours and 40 minutes. And in July, 1941, the *Lark* was re-equipped with completely new streamlined cars, painted in a distinctive two-tone gray color scheme. The new train sets featured a triple-unit "Lark Club" dining-lounge-dormitory car.

But the late 1930s were also times of trouble with the forces of nature. Heavy storms once again struck the Coast Line early in 1938. Following days of incessant rain the Pajaro River broke its banks on February 11th, flooding thousands of acres and covering the tracks at Sargent, Betabel, and the entire Watsonville Junction yard. Communications and signal lines were downed by high winds, and the normally docile Salinas River cut savagely into railroad embankments near Metz. But things were only to get worse as the month progressed.

A six-day storm that began manifesting itself February 27th over the region from Santa Barbara to the Mexican border dumped 11.06 inches of rain in Los Angeles, 6.03 inches of which fell in a 24-hour period ending 4:30 AM, March 3rd. The lower end of the Coast Line was severed the evening of March 2nd. Water was running over tops of bridges east and

These two photos (**above**) show the situation at Watsonville Junction on February 12, 1938, after the Pajaro River had broken its banks flooding thousands of acres, including the railroad yards for a considerable distance.
Two photos, Benny Romano collection

The Los Angeles Division segment of the Coast Line was particularly hard hit by the 1938 storm. The afternoon of March 2nd, the raging Los Angeles River took out this key bridge at Dayton Avenue. For the next several years, the river was the focus of an extensive concrete channeling project.
Southern Pacific Lines

Trolley car bodies used for housing track workers cluster around the Concepcion depot (**above**) in this 1942 view. The Coast Line was operated under the time-honored method of timetable and train orders, transmitted from the dispatcher by telegraph. Train order offices strung out along the line formed the connecting link. Here telegraphers Eldon and Grace Sandy (**left**) copied orders to "flimsies" which were then "handed up" in front of the depot (**below**) to passing trains.

Top, Gordon Campbell; left and below, John Roskoski collection

west of Carpinteria, 75 feet of the bridge at Hewitt had washed out, wires were down, and slides blocked the tracks at Summerland and at tunnel No. 26. But the most serious threat was to the bridge across the Santa Clara River at Montalvo. The debris-littered waters of the raging Santa Clara had knocked one of the piers out of alignment and threatened to take the entire bridge out.

The *Sunset* and *Lark* were stormbound at Santa Susana as were the northbound *Daylight* and train No. 71 near Hewitt, 25 miles out of Los Angeles. The southbound *Daylight* and train No. 72 were held at Santa Barbara. All Southern California rail lines were hard hit–especially the San Joaquin Valley and Beaumont Hill lines–but the Coast was the first to return to service. On the evening of March 4, after two days and nights of persistent effort, the Montalvo bridge was saved and reopened. Then for more than a week after, the Coast Line, as the only through route into the embattled Los Angeles basin, experienced a heavy load of rerouted freight and passenger traffic from not only stricken SP lines but the Union Pacific and Santa Fe as well.

That all this rerouted traffic was handled without incident over the predominantly passenger-oriented Coast Line was testimony to the route's potential, as yet untapped, as a freight artery of high capacity. Prior to the 1941 war, through freight trains, of the

Originally called Pajaro, Watsonville Junction was made a terminal in 1912, when operations were transferred from Salinas, and by 1943, when this photo (**above**) was taken from the vantage point of a water tank, the yards had been developed to their greatest extent. Train No. 187 (**right**) the Santa Cruz local, connected with both train No. 99 and No. 72. The original Pajaro depot (**bottom**), located at the Santa Cruz Branch wye, was still serving admirably in 1939.
Above, Southern Pacific Lines;
right, John Snyder photo, collection Alzora Snyder;
bottom, Benny Romano collection

type and volume common to the San Joaquin Line, were few in number and, with few exceptions, were run as extras. With the exception of small sections of CTC near San Jose (and later on the Cuesta Grade) the Coast Line was operated in the classic tradition by timetable and train order. With this system, "running extra" was a simple way to move trains when their frequency and irregular operation did not warrant a more rigid schedule. Numbered freights on the coast were not entirely unknown, however. Through the first two decades of the twentieth century, train Nos. 243 and 244, the so-called "Sunset Manifest," operated as third- and second-class trains, respectively. The popular *Overnight* simply operated as second sections of first-class trains. But as late as 1937, there was only one through freight train schedule on the Coast: eastward train No. 766.

Operating districts on the Coast Line remained stable after 1912, with Coast Division passenger crews holding down runs between San Francisco and

Watsonville Junction
October 1947

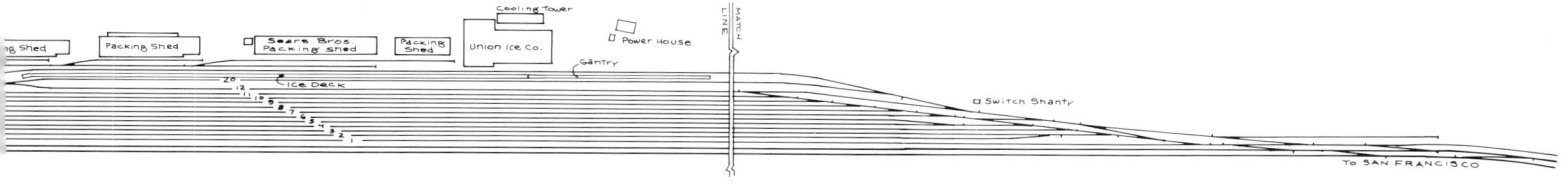

This is Watsonville Junction as it appeared during the latter half of the 1930s, a time when eleven local freights operated out of town during the season to such divergent points as Hollister, Santa Cruz, Davenport, Salinas, Monterey and King City. To stable the motive power necessary for all this activity, as well as the through freight power that required servicing, Southern Pacific built a concrete roundhouse (**right**) at the Junction in 1916. Up until World War II, Horrigan Road crossed right through the center of the yards near the yard office, and it was from this vantage point that the view looking railroad west (**top**) and railroad east (**opposite page**) were exposed in 1936. Even with all this activity, the roundhouse foreman (**bottom right**) still had time to smell the flowers.

Center photo at right, Guy Dunscomb; all othes, Benny Romano collection

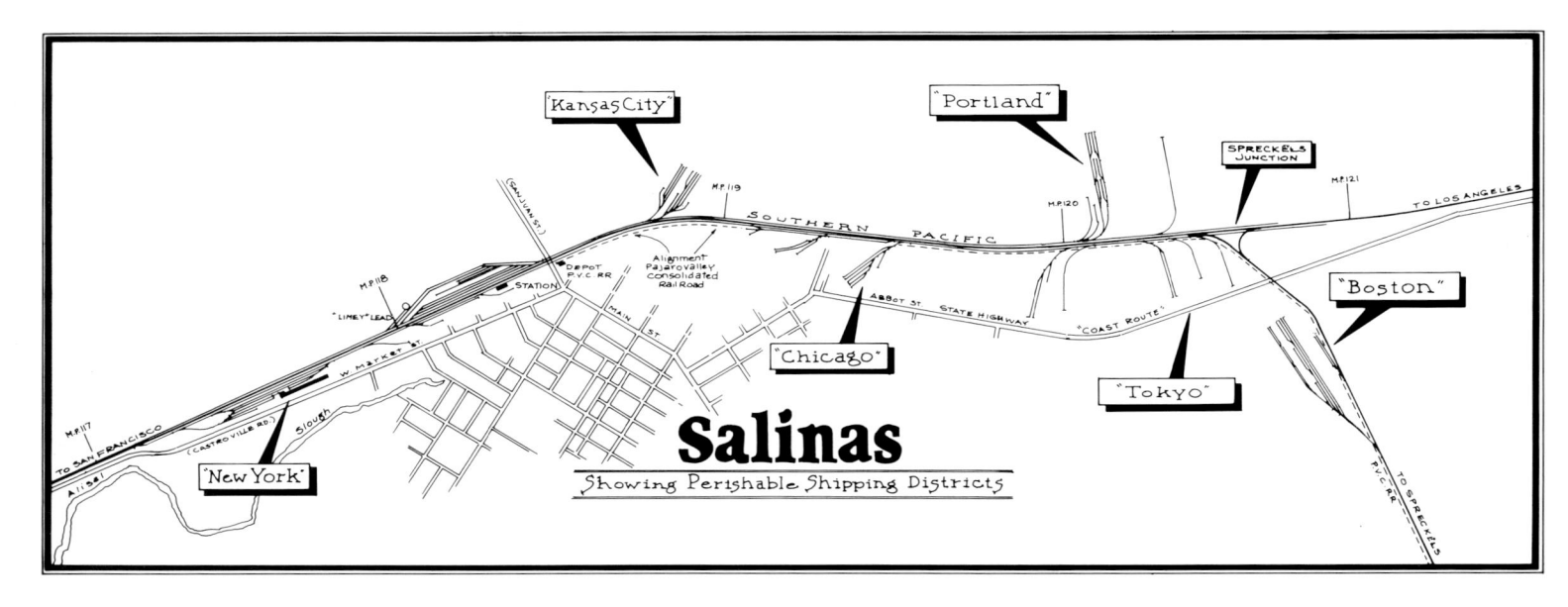

Salinas
Showing Perishable Shipping Districts

San Luis Obispo, and between San Luis Obispo and Santa Barbara, while Los Angeles Division passenger crews handled the 104-mile district between Santa Barbara and Los Angeles. On the Coast Division, engine crews (both through freight and passenger) and through freight train crews operated over the 100-mile San Francisco Subdivision between San Francisco/Bayshore and Watsonville Junction; the 152-mile Salinas Subdivision between Watsonville Junction and San Luis Obispo; and the 118-mile Guadalupe Subdivision between San Luis Obispo and Santa Barbara. On the Los Angeles Divison side, surprisingly, the engineer jobs belonged to the San Joaquin Division—a throwback to the days when the infant "Ventura Division" was administered by the superintendent at Bakersfield. Hence San Joaquin engine crews operated over the 104-mile Santa Barbara Subdivision between Santa Barbara and Los Angeles while Los Angeles Division train crews handled the same territory. Watsonville Junction, San Luis Obispo and Santa Barbara were all vital division points.

Watsonville Junction at its zenith was the hub of local activity in the Pajaro Valley-Monterey Bay region. The terminal boasted of a nine-stall concrete roundhouse and seventeen-track main yard. The parade of daily local freights and haulers called out of this busy terminal included three for the Santa Cruz Branch: the 7:00 AM Sand job, the 8:00 AM Davenport job, and the 4:30 PM Davenport job that did the perishable work. On the Monterey Branch, the Monterey Local was called for 8:00 AM, the Ord Local at 11:00 AM and the M&M Local after the departure of No. 76.

There were the 5:00 AM, 10:00 AM and 4:00 PM Salinas haulers which dragged the empty refrigerator cars over to the sheds, and returned with solid perishable trains destined for the east. In addition, there was the Hollister local (two during the perishable season) and the afternoon express perishable that might handle six to eight express cars of fresh strawberries. During the beet season, another local was called to work the beet loaders between Logan and Gilroy. Yard men worked all the sheds in Watsonville. Empty reefers were pre-iced, and loads re-iced, at the Pacific Fruit Express deck in Watsonville for the surrounding area, until most of the shippers in Salinas built their own docks and plants. Indeed, much of Watsonville's activity was tied to that of Salinas.

Operations around Salinas were seasonal in nature and dependent on the crops. By the late 'thirties, over 35,000 acres were planted to lettuce with the first crop being harvested in March, the second crop in August, and the third in late September. Celery, cauliflower and broccoli was harvested from April through December, as was the high value crop of strawberries.

The first sheds at Salinas congregated along the west side of the yard north of the depot on what was

112

Looking north from San Juan Street—now known as Main Street—during the winter of 1930 (**top**), the tracks are empty and the old yard at Salinas sleeps. Looking south, all is quiet as a lounger basks in the winter sun on the Pajaro Valley Consolidated Railroad depot platform (**bottom**). But by late February, the yards are choked with colorful reefers in anticipation of yet another lettuce "Deal." By mid-summer, with the season in full swing, six switch engines were required around the clock to work Salinas's 41 packing sheds. The nerve center for all this action was the depot (**right**), seen about 1936, in which both Southern Pacific and Pacific Fruit Express maintained extensive forces.

Top and bottom, Benny Romano collection; right, Southern Pacific Lines

Conductor "Chualar" Bill Nissen waves from his caboose (**right**), express trucks and all, on the "Honey Dipper" at Soledad in 1936.
Right, John Snyder photo, Alzora Snyder collection

The crew of the "Kansas City" switcher poses for the camera (**above**) at Salinas in October, 1942. From left, they were conductor George Ritchie, brakemen Olin Vansandt and Stanley Kerns, fireman Clarence Zimmerman and, in the gangway of the 2933, engineer Harold Soaper.
Above, Harold Soaper collection

No. 2920 works the yard at Salinas in November, 1939. The elderly 4-8-0 Twelve Wheelers found a home at Salinas because they were powerful, yet weighed less than most 2-8-0 Consolidations and consequently did less damage to light shed trackage.
Robert McNeel

Light-duty trucks bring lettuce in from the field (**left** and **below**) as the local's switch engine maneuvers an ice reefer in the packing shed district at Salinas. Once loaded, the reefers were assembled into trains (**top**) and rushed east. The first carloads of lettuce moved east from the Salinas Valley in 1921, and by 1935, with over 500 square miles devoted to lettuce production in the Salinas-Watsonville district alone, nearly 25,000 carloads were shipped east.

Three photos, Southern Pacific Lines

For over 125 miles the Coast Line follows the Salinas River, from the vast and enormously productive alluvial lands around Salinas (**top**), through San Ardo (**left**)–these views were taken on June 2, 1936–and on to Santa Margarita. San Miguel (**bottom left**) was the principal water stop for freight trains operating on this district. Water was usually taken directly off the main line as the siding at San Miguel was just 33 cars long. Most of the strategic meets and passes were accomplished in the two generous sidings at McKay, five miles to the west. This view of town facing north from 11th Street dates from November, 1945. Bradley (**bottom right**) was another valley station that took on added importance during World War II.

Bottom right, Robert H. McFarland;
top, left, and bottom left, Benny Romano collection

known as the "Limey Lead." But over time, Salinas grew in complexity and developed a number of important shipping districts, each with its own identity. The "Tokyo" district was opened by Japanese, then were built "New York," "Chicago," "Kansas City," "Portland" and later, "Boston"—and each had an engine assigned. Extra "haulers" worked Spreckels during the beet season from July through October and on occasion, the King City Local, when not called out of Watsonville Junction. Salinas had an old armstrong turntable. A carryover from the early days, the table was just large enough to accommodate the light Moguls and Consolidations that held down most assignments around Salinas. An exception to this were the 2900-series Twelve Wheelers assigned during the heavy summer and fall months. Less powerful than Consolidations, the 2900's were good switchers nevertheless, and their lighter weight and 54-inch drivers were easy on curves and admirably suited to the light trackage in the shed districts.

On the low grade run between Watsonville Junction and San Francisco, Moguls, Ten Wheelers and Consolidations held freight assignments and, as late as 1946, Pacifics and Consolidations were fre-

Train No. 97, the *Noon Daylight*, charges upgrade at the west switch at Chorro (**top**), while later in the day, No. 98, the *Daylight*, drops downgrade at tunnel No. 7 (**above**) on July 20, 1941.

Two photos, George McCarron collection

quently employed in through freight service. During the season, there were four 125-car perishables a night out of Salinas, with the first departing around 5:00 PM. These long and heavy trains had to be pushed out of the yard at Watsonville Junction by a switch engine and a helper was double-headed all the way to Morgan Hill, at which point it was cut off on the fly and run ahead to duck in the spur at Madrone. Out of San Jose, regular helpers were used up to Morgan Hill on loaded sugar beet trains only. But the trend towards ever-longer trains meant larger power would be needed.

On the 17-mile Cuesta Grade, helper power was traditionally the heaviest engines available. By the early 1920s this meant 2-8-0 Consolidations, but early in 1926, five old 4-6-6-2 Mallet Mogul engines, then numbered in the 4200 series, were assigned to helper service out of San Luis Obispo. A wye had to be built to accommodate them east of the round house. At first, local officials were enthusiastic over the idea, but when it came down to the press of regular business and the necessity of shortening passenger schedules, already the fastest of any division on the Southern Pacific, the Mallets began to manifest their shortcomings. At a maximum speed of 20 mph, the old compounds were just too slow for passenger trains which were allowed 30 mph on the hill. Within a year they were transferred to Beaumont Hill, where they continued to plague operating officers by slowing down fruit blocks.

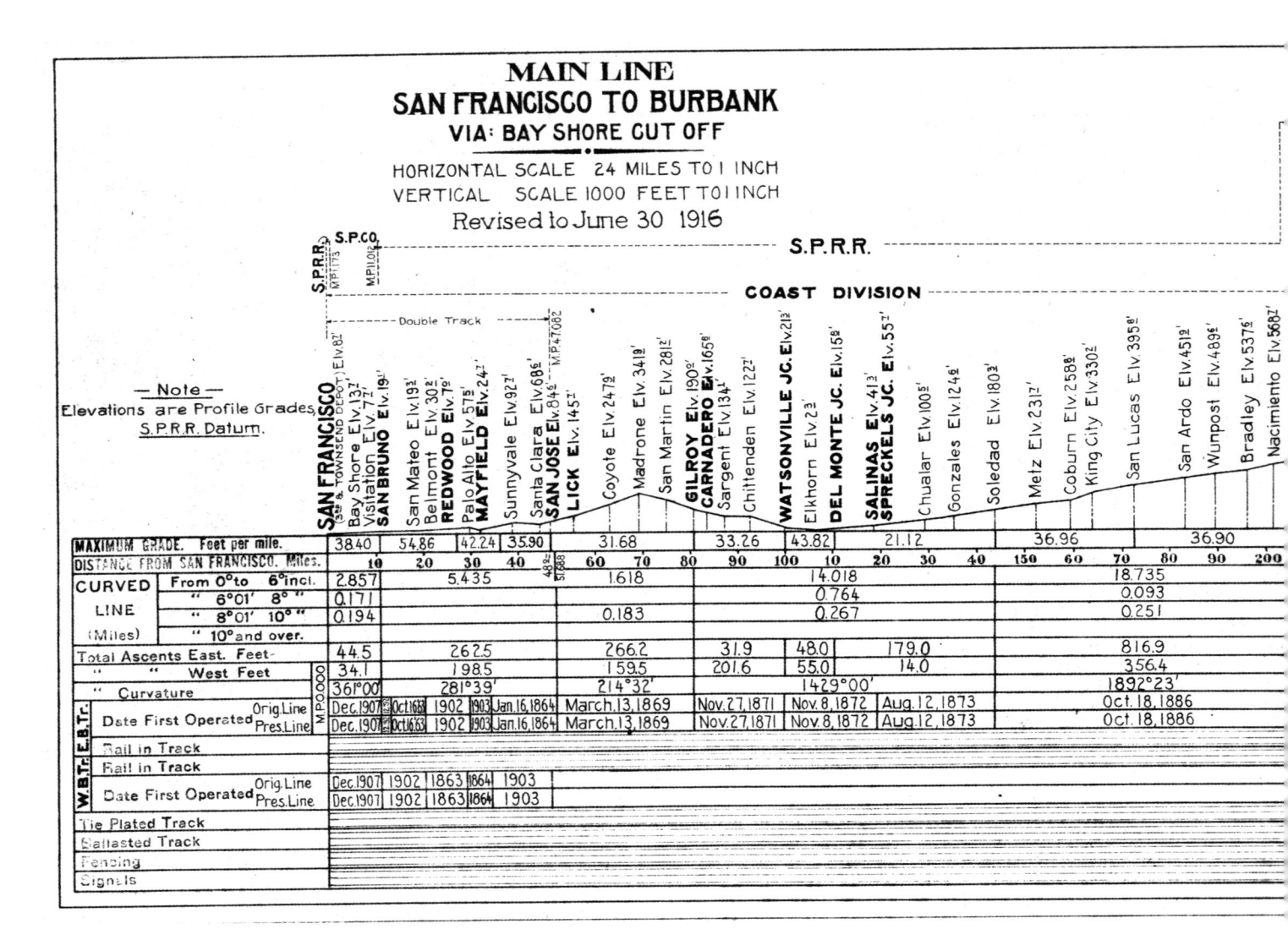

What was really needed on the hill were 2-10-2's or 2-8-2's, but they were too new and were earning their keep on the east end of the Salt Lake Division and elsewhere. Thus it was not until late 1927 that the first 2-10-2's were assigned to the Cuesta Grade. In a few years they would become standard power.

Departing San Luis Obispo westward with 99 cars and a 2-10-2 on the point, the first helper would be cut in 40 cars deep from the head end, the second helper (usually two 2-10-2's coupled together) would be cut in another 40 cars deeper, with the rear helper (or two) just ahead of the caboose. Swing men were used to work the retainers and dropped off at Santa Margarita to assist in cutting out helpers at the double crossover between Santa Margarita siding and Cushing. Once at Santa Margarita, they would "swing" (catch another crew) back to San Luis Obispo.

The Depression's traffic slump released additional 2-10-2's (always called "Decks" on the SP) from other divisions, and they found a home in through freight work on the coast, primarily on the 150-mile district between Watsonville Junction and San Luis Obispo where a single 2-10-2 could take a tonnage train on the long, steady ascent as far as Santa Margarita unassisted. Water stops were fewer. If stopped for operating reasons, eastward trains would sometimes take water at Soledad, but tanks were always replenished at San Miguel where there was a good supply of water. On arriving at Santa Margarita, the caboose was cut off "on the fly," then the train was pulled up to the east water plug (Union Oil crossover) to take water. Two more 2-10-2's were cut in for the short but steep climb to Cuesta. Retainers were set up as the brakemen worked the car tops leaving Santa Margarita. Then, depending on conditions, the helpers were either cut out at Thyle or Serrano–to return to Santa Margarita to assist another eastward

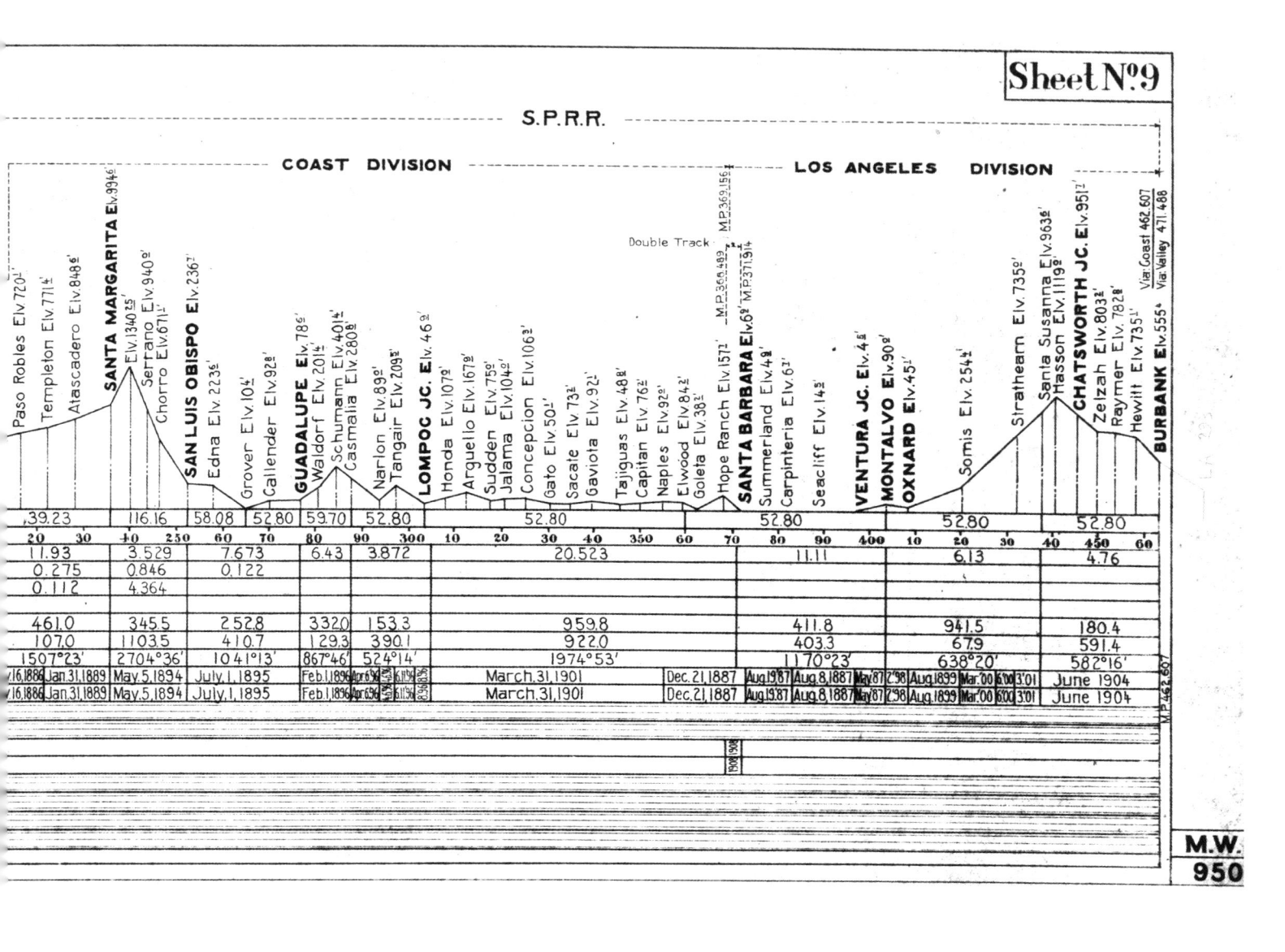

By the late 'thirties the popular *Daylights* were attracting more and more photographers to the Coast Line. The Horseshoe Curve above San Luis Obispo was a favorite location. No. 98 rolls off the curve and over Stenner Creek viaduct (**top**) at Goldtree, while No. 98 works upgrade around the loop (**bottom**) with a double-headed set of red and orange 4-8-4's.

The *Daylights* were colorful, but couldn't match the power and action of a five-engine freight working upgrade through the same territory, as this drag is doing (**center**) on June 29, 1941.

Top and bottom, Robert McFarland; center, Art Alter

Extra 3727 west works upgrade through Serrano, mid-way on the south slope of Cuesta Grade (**top**). The time is the summer of 1939, and the mounting pressure of war in Europe has lengthened the average freight train operating on the Coast Line. In response, SP has assigned a few of the massive AC-class articulateds to San Luis Obispo helper service (**left**).
Two photos, Robert H. McFarland

OVERLEAF: Five engines led by heavy 2-10-2 No. 3709 boost a 99-car freight, mostly PFE refrigerator cars, around Horseshoe Curve in the spring of 1940. By the mid-'thirties, 2-10-2's were standard power on Cuesta Grade.
Aston photo, Frank Wintering collection

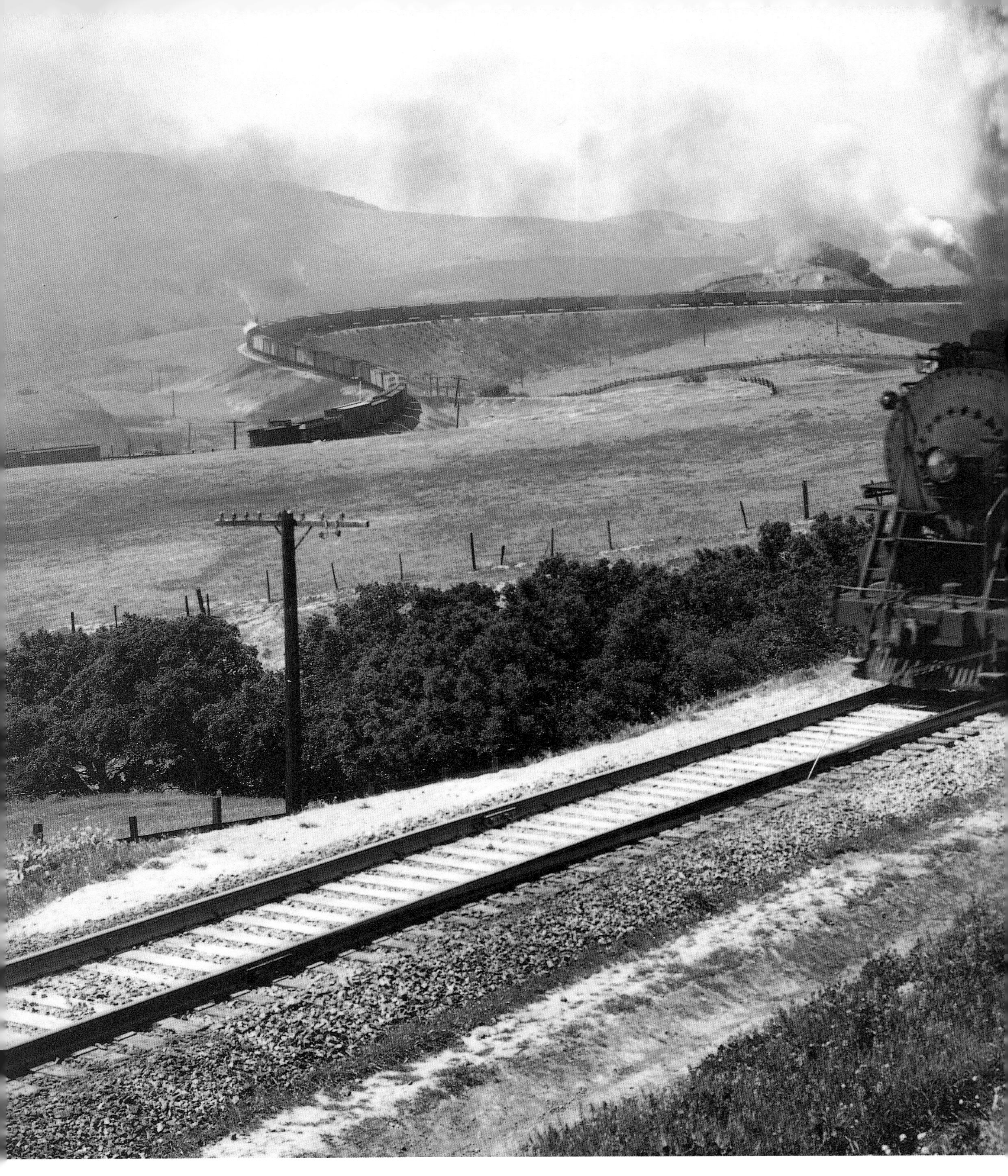

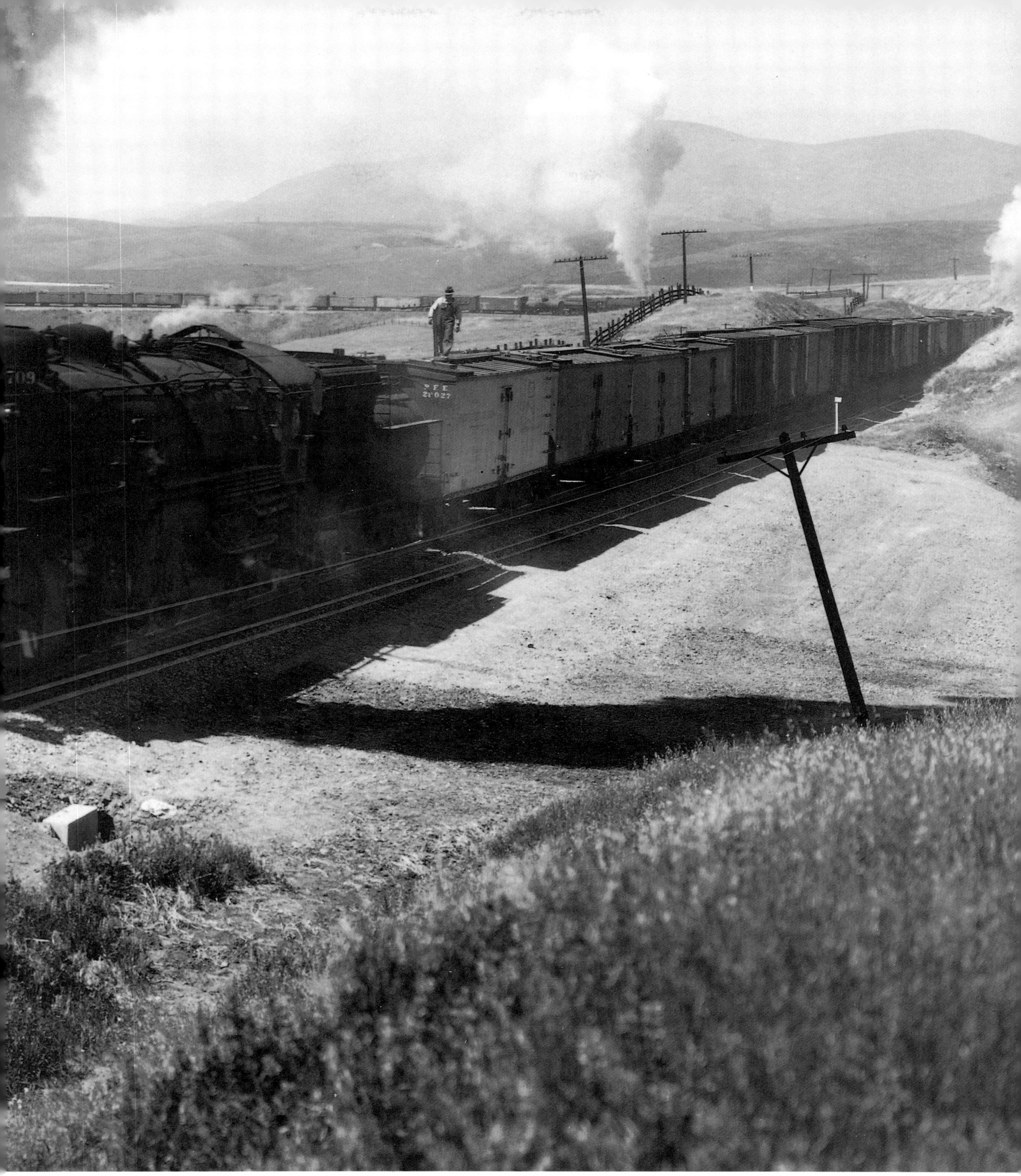
709
P F E
21027

The turntable, machine shop in roundhouse stalls 11 and 12, power house (twin stacks), engine servicing, and other details of the San Luis Obispo engine facilities lay quiet on a Sunday afternoon in October, 1940. It's difficult to tell from these views, but even then events in Europe and Asia were beginning to make a dramatic impact on the Coast Line.

All, Benny Romano collection

Atop Terrace Hill, one could get a general view (**top**) of the San Luis Obispo roundhouse facilities to the west, dominated by the oil fuel tank at the right. At its zenith, the roundhouse at San Luis Obispo employed 44 men including machinists, pipefitters, boiler makers, brickmen, laborers, hostlers, stationary engineers, cellar packers, engine crew dispatchers and foremen. There was plenty to do, with as many as 18 helper jobs on the Cuesta Grade as well as the locals, yard engines and the *Daylight* protection engines (**bottom**) to take care of. Yet another helper rolls in off the grade (**right**) by the depot in 1939.

*Top and right, George McCarron collection;
bottom, Benny Romano collection*

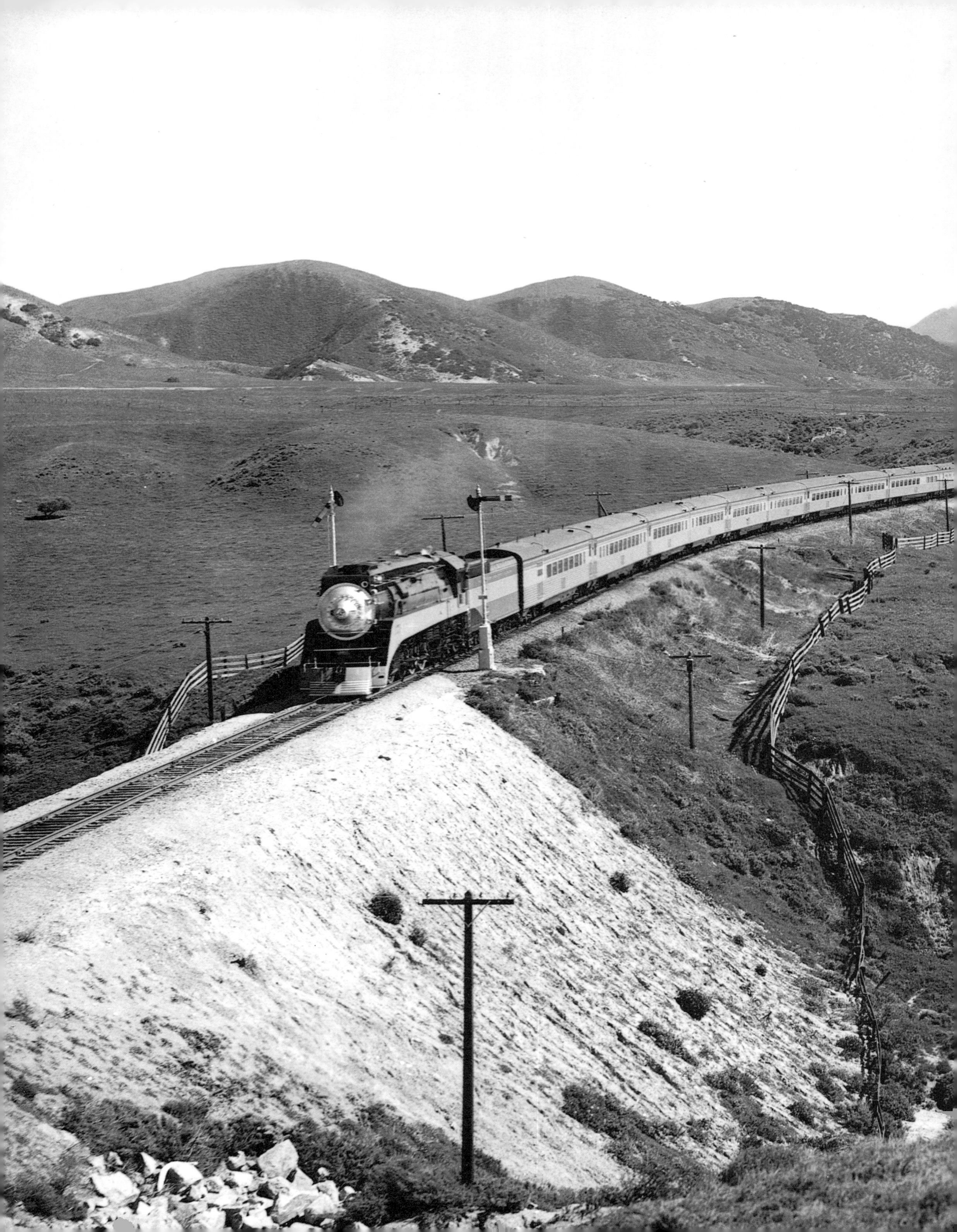

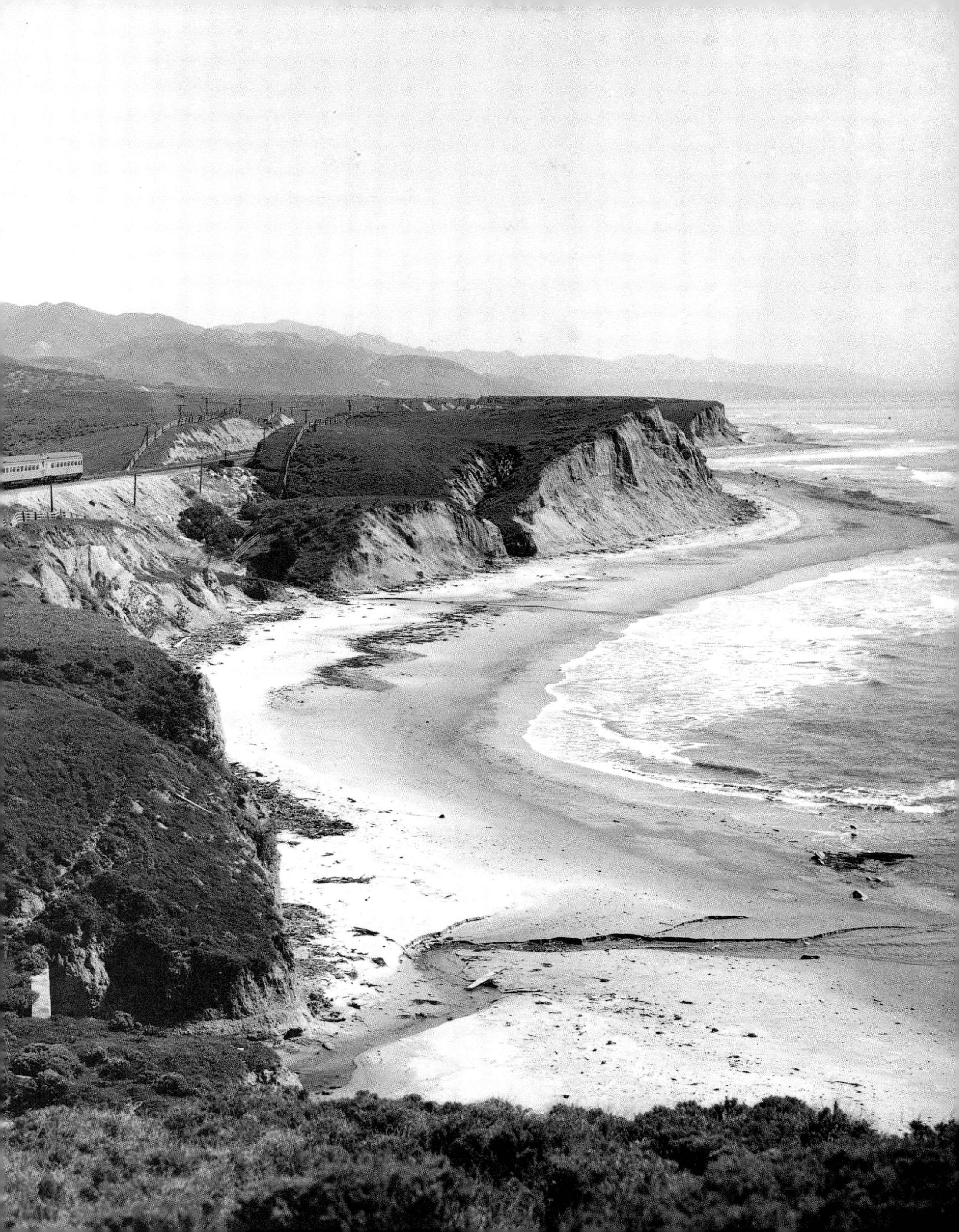

Surf, with its two sidings and an ample water supply, was a key operating point on the central coast. With the cab-forwards in use, the average freight train operating between San Luis Obispo and Santa Barbara could make it to Surf–the midway point–for water, unless the eastward train had to work Guadalupe. These views of Surf date from 1940. The white building to the right in the upper photo is the Surf store.
Top, Gordon Campbell;
above, Bancroft Library, University of California, Berkeley

PREVIOUS PAGES: Train No. 99, the *Daylight*, often heralded as the "Most Beautiful Train in the World," rolls through some of the most spectacular scenery west of Gaviota in 1937.
Southern Pacific Lines, Vernon Sappers collection

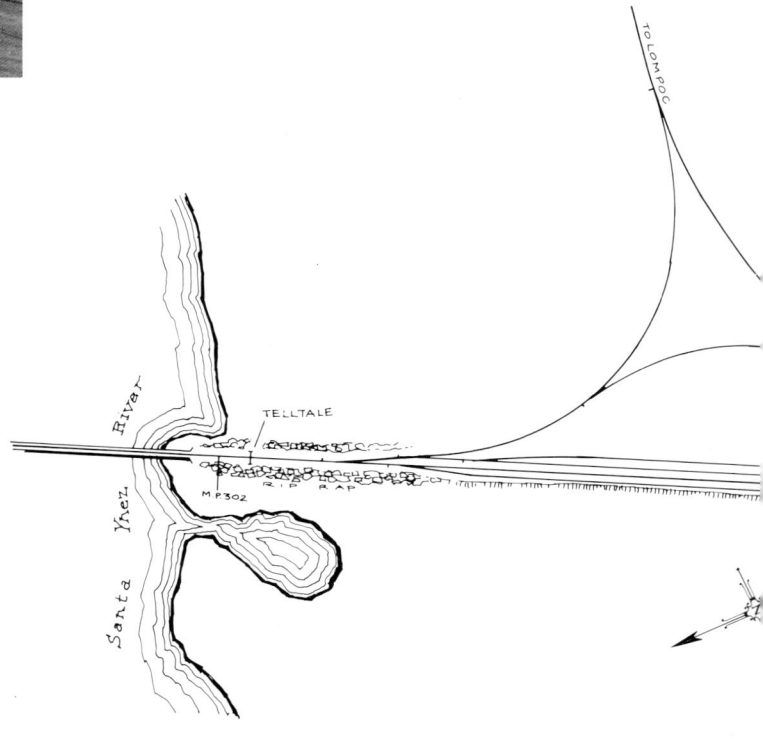

128

The second section of No. 763 (above), a block of empty "OK" reefers destined for Guadalupe, thunders through Honda. Up front is AC-6 No. 4137, a 4-8-8-2. By 1940, the distinctive articulateds were the preferred power on the "stormy end" of the Coast Line between San Luis Obispo and Santa Barbara.
Southern Pacific Lines

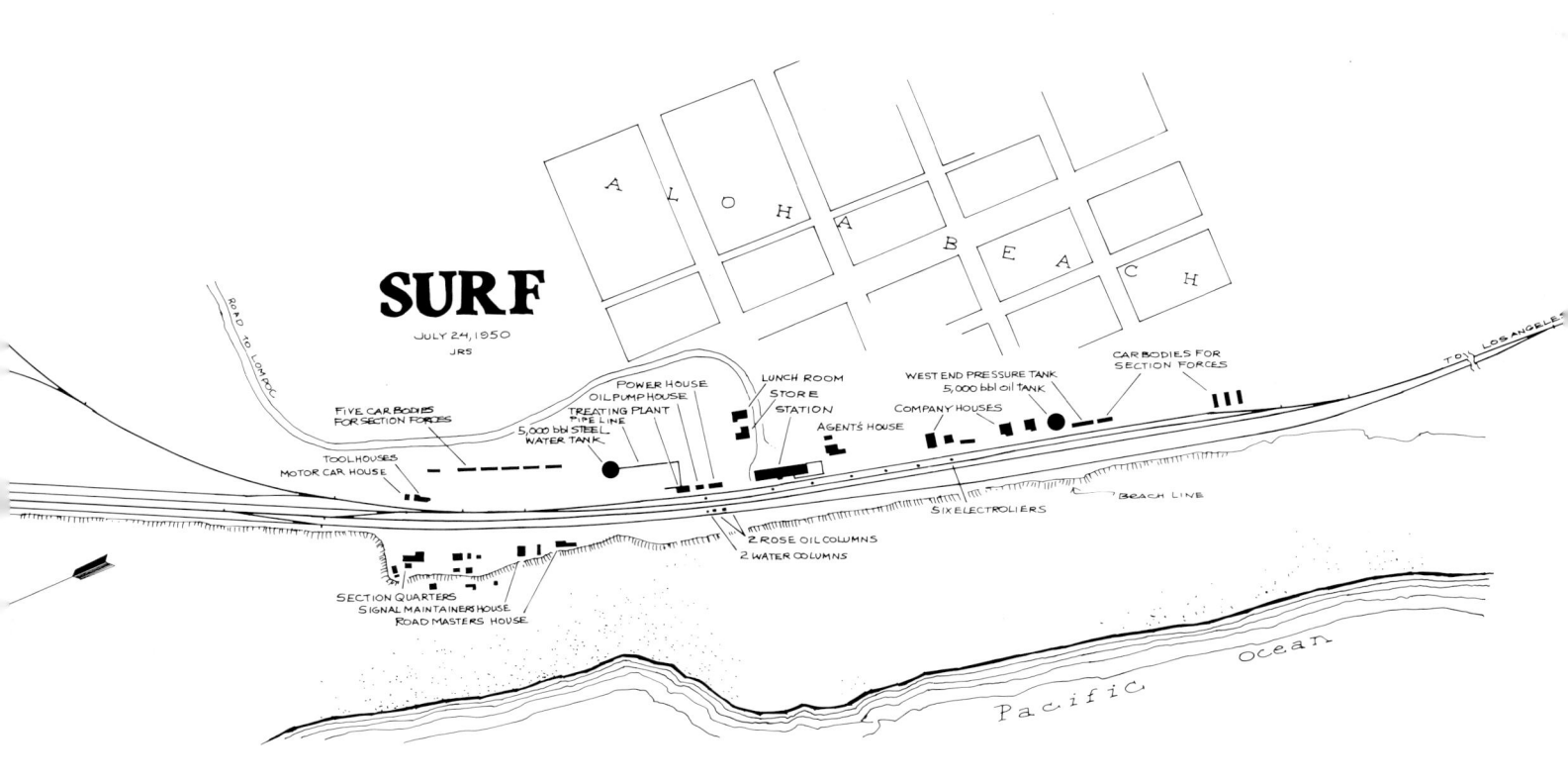

From the rubble of the June, 1925 earthquake rose much of what we know as the Spanish-style Santa Barbara of today, fashioned by local visionaries and dictated by strict building codes. SP's traditional brick roundhouse toppled in the quake (**top**), and in its place SP built a new structure whose design was inspired by the bull ring at Seville, Spain. SP engineer Robert McNeel took this general view of the Santa Barbara roundhouse (**center**) in 1940.
*Top, Southern Pacific Lines;
center, Robert McNeel*

As viewed from Cabrillo Street, the back of the Santa Barbara roundhouse was (as intended) very difficult to distinguish from a Spanish bullring, complete with decorative flags and plantings.
Robert McNeel

Although 4-6-2 Pacifics were usually used as helpers eastbound over Santa Susana Pass on the night Pullman trains, these two engines (**top**) are preparing to depart west out of Santa Barbara in 1945. At left is the old yard office where telegraphers for both the Coast and Los Angeles divisions were stationed.
Top, Robert McNeel

In 1940, the gardens around the Santa Barbara station were still well planted and maintained (**center**). Perhaps the most distinctive tree on the station grounds was the Moreton Bay Fig tree. This tree (**left**), which was planted in 1877, is native to Moreton Bay near Brisbane, Australia and is related to both the commercial fig and rubber trees but is unique in that it produces neither figs nor rubber. At the time of this 1936 photo, it had a branch spread of 124 feet. By the time SP donated the tree and the one-third acre parcel which contains it to the City of Santa Barbara in 1977, it had grown to 160 feet.
Two photos, Robert McNeel

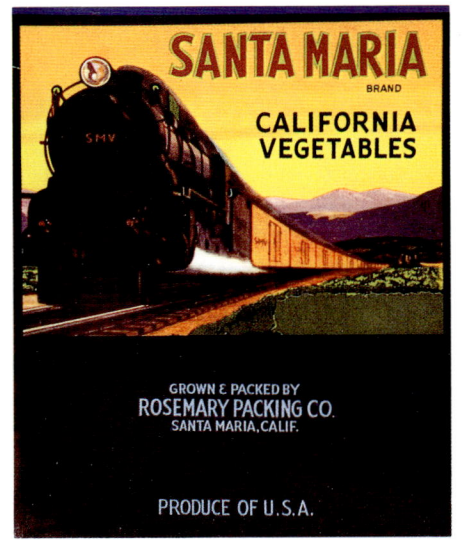

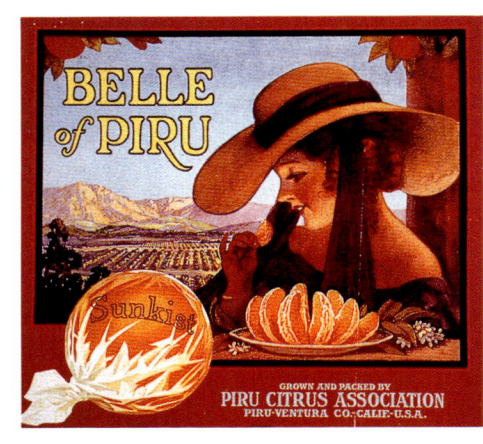

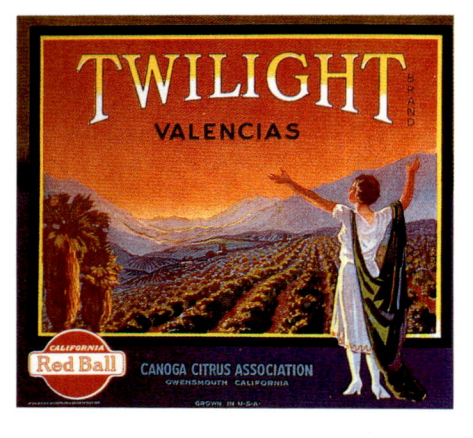

Every produce-growing region had its own characteristic labels for fruit and vegetable boxes, with size and proportions characteristic of the box ends. Shown here are lemon and orange labels, graded according to the Sunkist convention ("Sunkist" with the tissue-wrapped fruit was top grade, "Red Ball" was second or middle grade). The enlarged lettering of the vegetable labels from the Guadalupe-Santa Maria area reflect a post-1930 "commercial" label style.

All, courtesy Jim Seagrave, except Limoneira and Santa Maria labels, author's collection

FACING PAGE: The Pacific Ocean beaches were a constant attraction in the scenic route of the *Daylight*. Here, No. 98 rolls past the State Beach facilities at the mouth of Cañada del Refugio (**opposite, bottom**). It's a little after 3 PM, and in less than 30 minutes, passengers with Santa Barbara tickets will be stepping onto the platform.

Opposite, bottom, Southern Pacific Lines

132

FIRST WITH PICK-UP AND DELIVERY!

In 1929, long before any other western railroad, Southern Pacific pioneered the pick-up and delivery of less-carload freight. This service was rapidly expanded until today it is available at practically every station served by Southern Pacific and its connections in the eleven western states. At most stations, this service is performed by a reliable local drayman under contract to Southern Pacific. At other stations, the service is performed by Pacific Motor Trucking Company, a Southern Pacific subsidiary.

FIRST WITH OVERNIGHT MERCHANDISE TRAINS!

Southern Pacific was the first western railroad to establish overnight merchandise trains—trains moving on passenger train schedules—so fast that waybills have to be teletyped ahead! Today this fleet of 18 "hotshots" links important western shipping centers with a merchandise service faster, in many cases, than the U. S. Mail! In conjunction with pick-up and delivery and co-ordinated truck lines, the "Overnights" offer western shippers a merchandise service as fine as any in the nation.

FIRST WITH CO-ORDINATED TRUCKING SERVICE!

Southern Pacific was the first western railroad to offer a trucking service co-ordinated with its merchandise trains. Today Southern Pacific's subsidiary, the Pacific Motor Trucking Company, operates 418 big red trucking units over 4,136 miles of western highways, giving hundreds of smaller communities the same responsible, fast, cheap merchandise service enjoyed by the larger centers. These trucks have regular routes and schedules, just like the merchandise trains.

Shown here (**left** and **above**) are examples of graphics from Southern Pacific's promotion in the 1930s for the *Overnight* merchandise service. The "double wing" logo was extensively used in advertising, and was even considered for application to the boxcars assigned to the service, but in fact was never applied to any cars, even as a test.

Left and above, Southern Pacific Lines brochure

Santa Barbara

April 27, 1920

train—or were operated into San Luis Obispo itself.

The situation was somewhat different on the "stormy end" between San Luis Obispo and Santa Barbara. This 118-mile district passed through a more broken country with a number of minor (one percent) grades. These occurred in Price Canyon (eastward), at Callender, Shuman, Tangair, Surf, Arguello, Jalama, and westward out of Santa Barbara up to Hope Ranch. On tonnage freight, double-headed Consolidations were the rule until larger power became available. By 1940, the massive AC class Mallets (or a combination of power to equal the maximum tonnage of 3,450 tons) were the preferred power on the district. Water was a problem on the central coast. It was hard to find and usually highly mineralized. Emergency supplies were available at Oceano, Gaviota and Naples but an abundant and good quality supply was available at Surf, nearly midway on the district. Thus Surf was usually the only water stop for freight trains—in both directions—unless work had to be done at Guadalupe.

Operations on the southern end of the Coast Line were centered around Santa Barbara and Oxnard. At its zenith, during the second World War, over 250 people were employed in the SP yards at Santa Barbara. In addition to a large clerical staff, there was a "Coast" and a "Los Angeles" telegrapher each shift in the old freight house. Though the yard was small, just five tracks, it did a booming business. There was a switch engine on duty 'round the clock, with another called for midnight. Two locals, the Surf (Gaviota) local, and the Oxnard "Brady" local (so named for long-time Los Angeles Division conductor J.R. Brady), worked west and east out of town. Principal local industry was the huge shed complex of the Johnson Brothers Fruit Company located on the stem of the old main line. The ten-stall roundhouse was kept busy servicing local engines, passenger helpers and through freight power that might need attention. The largest engine able to turn on the table at Santa Barbara was a 4400-series 4-8-4. On the rare occasion when a Mallet had to be turned, it was done at Montalvo's wye, 32.5 miles away!

The local that worked the Ojai Branch was based at Oxnard as was the Santa Paula local. However, during the season, the Saticoy local was based at Fillmore and worked west to Montalvo, picking up all perishable across the branch, primarily lemons, and set them out at Montalvo for the "Brady Local" to take back to Santa Barbara for the "Smokey."

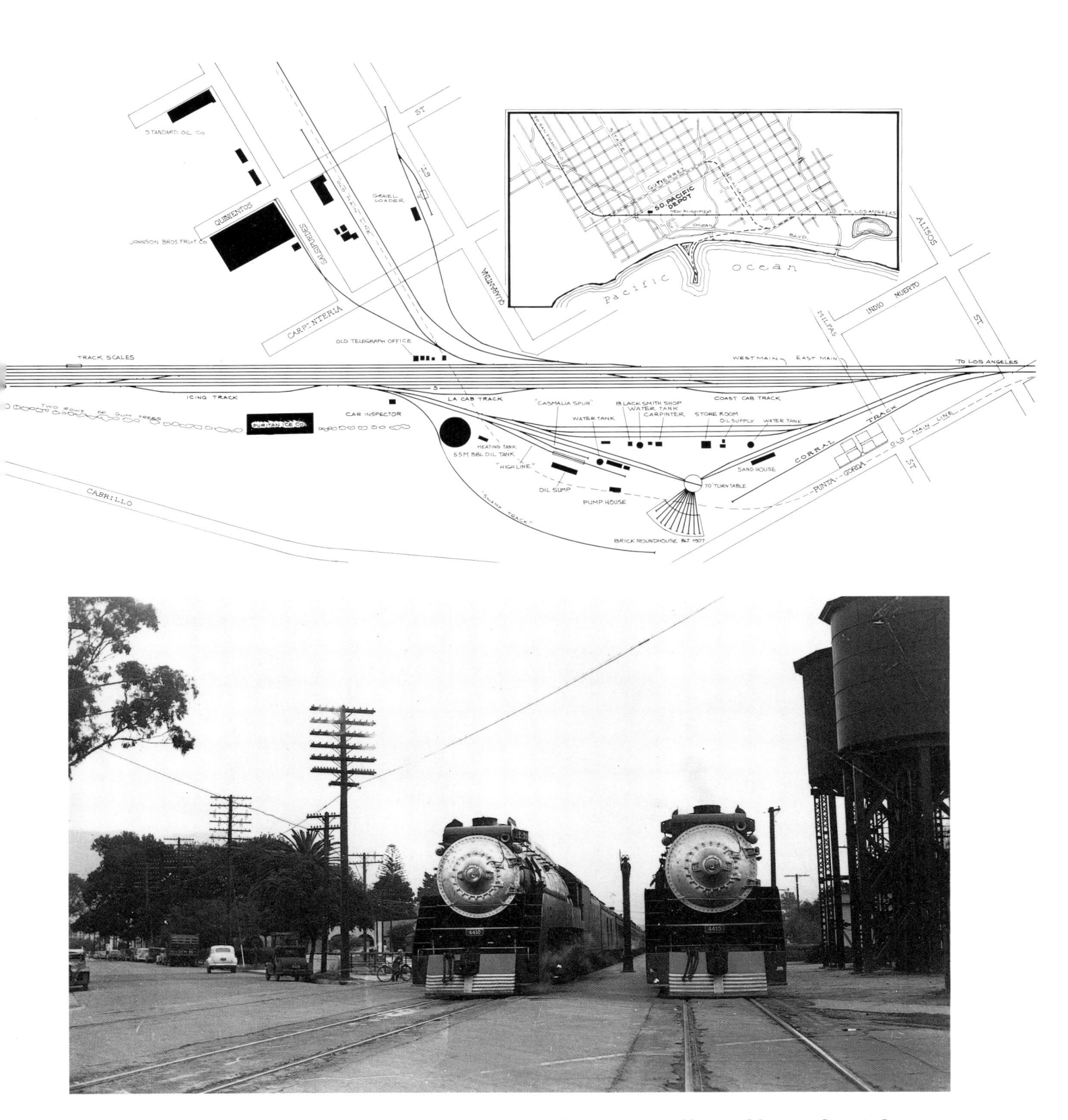

In a routine repeated daily in the early 'forties, the second section of No. 99 overtakes No. 71 at Montecito Street in Santa Barbara. No. 71 would arrive ahead of the *Daylight* and cross over to the eastbound main to work the mail.
Robert McNeel

A massive cab-forward moves out of Santa Barbara with westward tonnage in 1940 (**left**). Just up the line on another day (**top**), two cab-forwards meet at West Santa Barbara. The ACs allowed for longer trains and eliminated the practice of doubling the train or using helpers on the short but stiff grade up to Hope Ranch.

Two photos, Robert McNeel

136

With the Santa Ynez Mountains forming a delightful backdrop, No.98 steams past the Clark Bird Refuge at east Santa Barbara in 1939.
Southern Pacific photo, Dan Wolf collection

During the peak of the rush, the Santa Paula Branch was also worked by the Fillmore local out of Los Angeles, via Saugus, which at times was so heavy that helpers dropped down from Saugus to Fillmore in order to help the local, now essentially a fruit block, east to Saugus and over the summit at San Fernando Tunnel. On the main line, sheds in the Simi Valley and on the Tapo Spur near Santa Susana were worked by the daily Los Angeles-Oxnard local.

Perishable work from San Luis Obispo south was handled by the "Smokey." Called as a caboose hop out of San Luis Obispo with a pool crew—and in later years usually running as second 834—the "Smokey" picked up at Oceano, Guadalupe, Surf, Ellwood, La Patera, and Goleta, then pulled into the ice deck at Santa Barbara where the train was "filled" (cars added) and loads re-iced if needed. The "Smokey" did no work between Santa Barbara and Los Angeles.

Unlike the Cuesta Grade, freight and passenger trains normally did not require help over Santa Susana Pass, the other significant grade on the Coast Line. For manifest trains, the tonnage limit for one AC-class Mallet was established at 3,650 tons. There were exceptions, however. The Imperial Valley-Betteravia sugar beet trains usually double-headed from Los Angeles to Santa Barbara, and to get over the summit of Santa Susana Pass, frequently required a rear helper which was cut off at Hasson. Sugar beet trains originating in the San Joaquin Valley were able to avoid the pass by taking the Santa Paula Branch. The normal procedure was for through San Joaquin Division trains to set out the beets on the east passing track at Saugus. These were handled in turn by the Oxnard-Saugus beet hauler and taken around the wye at Montalvo to Holly Sugar in Oxnard.

It was necessary for about eight or ten years, beginning in the late 'thirties, to bulletin a regular helper at Santa Barbara to assist eastward passenger

An eastward freight, heavy with coastal oil, departs rural Santa Susana (**above**) for the pass in 1940. A little while later, a long westward freight, swollen with war materials, passes the same location. One AC-class cab-forward was rated for 3,650 tons on the grade over Santa Susana Pass, and frequently handled trains of this size and more without help.

Two photos, Southern Pacific Lines

138

A pre-streamlined *Daylight* powered by an Mt-class Mountain, leans into a familiar curve on the south slope of Santa Susana Pass near Chatsworth. The 4300 up front could handle the all-coach train over the pass with ease but often required a helper working the *Lark* and *Sunset Limited,* as these trains usually ran heavy with Pullmans in the same territory.
Southern Pacific Lines photo, Vernon Sappers collection

trains. Even with the large GS (4-8-4) and Mt or Mountain (4-8-2) class engines, the *Lark* and *Sunset Limited* couldn't make the time over Santa Susana Pass if handling twelve or more Pullmans. Two or three 4-6-2 Pacifics, usually Nos. 2445, 2448 and 2412, were used in this service only on the west slope. The normal procedure was to hold the helper in a spur just east of the Santa Barbara station, and add it to the point of the train while it was making its station stop. Once over the hill the helper was cut off at Chatsworth, turned on the wye, watered, and run light back to Santa Barbara.

This policy regarding tonnage ratings on Santa Susana Pass came under scrutiny when a Mallet, an inexperienced fireman, and other factors culminated in tragedy within 7,369-foot tunnel No. 26 on November 19, 1941. It was just after midnight when Extra 4193 West, with 51 loads and 45 empties totaling 3,550 tons, departed Chatsworth for the pass.

Leading train No. 71, ex-EP&SW Pacific No. 3126 pounds into Chatsworth on August 18, 1940.
Frank J. Peterson photo, Robert McNeel collection

139

Train No. 76, the celebrated *Lark*, flies through Chatsworth at 8:09 AM on August 18, 1940, on the last lap of its all-night dash from San Francisco to Los Angeles.
Frank J. Peterson photo, Robert McNeel collection

About 5,000 feet east of the east portal of tunnel No. 26, the engine slipped wildly and stalled. After taking slack twice, the train was able to proceed into tunnel No. 26, where it stalled once again about midway within the bore. When the slack ran out, a coupler knuckle broke at the 75th car, placing the train in emergency. Because the engine was working hard at the time it stalled, the tunnel quickly filled with voluminous smoke and gas which overcame the crew. Fuel oil dripping from the fire box ignited, enveloping the cab of No. 4193, and spread to trailing equipment, killing the engineer, the fireman, the second brakeman and twelve cars of livestock on the head end. It took three days to put the fire out. For the interim, through traffic was diverted via Santa Paula.

The horrible events that befell Extra 4193 West at Hasson in the fall of 1941 occurred as the nation was preparing for war. Soon memories of the tragedy would fade as the crush of troop trains and defense-related traffic made its impact on Coast Line operations.

Coast Line personnel received practical experience in the handling of troops and military equipment during July and August of 1939, as Southern Pacific moved 6,000 troops and officers of the California National Guard in eleven extra trains totaling 200 coaches to annual training at Camp San Luis Obispo at Goldtree siding, just below the Horseshoe Curve on Cuesta Grade. The following summer even larger maneuvers were conducted. In fact, what was to be the greatest peacetime movement of western troops in the nation's history began just

With the chaos that ensued following Pearl Harbor, the *Noon Daylight* and the *Sunset Limited* (between San Francisco and Los Angeles) were discontinued on January 5, 1942 to free up equipment and relieve congestion. The *Noon Daylight* had but one season under its belt, but the *Sunset Limited*, seen near Chatsworth in 1940 (**top**), had operated almost continuously on the Coast Line since 1902. In their place was an endless stream of troop trains funneling men to the many training camps that had sprung up along the Coast Line. Even before the passenger train discontinuances, a new schedule, Nos. 37 and 38, was added to the time card between San Luis Obispo and San Francisco, catering primarily to military personnel. No. 37 is seen climbing Cuesta Grade at Serrano (**right** and **below**) during 1941.

Top, Southern Pacific Lines; right, W.C. Whittaker; below, George McCarron collection

Due to congestion at San Miguel, the main gateway to Camp Roberts, troops on special maneuvers disembark at San Lucas during May, 1940, en route to Camp Roberts. In a four-day period of that pre-war month, 27 troop trains operated on the Coast Line. With the outbreak of war in the Pacific, such scenes as this would become commonplace on the Coast Line.
Three photos, Southern Pacific Lines

after midnight, Sunday, August 4, 1940. Against a backdrop of disturbing events in Europe and Asia, over 40,000 men of the National Guard and regular Army congregated at Ft. Lewis, Washington, from seven western states for maneuvers and war games. Forty special trains operated over the Coast Line in conjunction with the operation. That October, two 14-inch, railroad-mounted coastal defense guns fired out to sea at Naples, as had also been done in 1937.

By the fall of 1940, a huge defense program buildup was under way on the west coast. Within the span of several months, the Coast Line was bristling with defense-related projects, and lumber, concrete and other building materials poured into the region.

For a $5 million expansion at Camp Clayton, near Monterey, inbound shipments of 12 million board feet of lumber were needed just to erect buildings. The resulting facility, dubbed Fort Ord, was to be the new home for the Seventh Army, with an eventual personnel of 30,000 men. Camp San Luis Obispo, which had opened in the late 1920s as a summer camp, was the subject of a $2 million expansion plan designed to garrison 17,000 permanent personnel. Similar projects were under way at Camp Roberts near McKay, Camp McQuaide near Watsonville, and at the Naval station at Port Hueneme near Oxnard.

During March, 1941, the War Department took options on approximately 90,000 acres in the

Lompoc-Guadalupe-Santa Maria area. The remoteness of the varied terrain, and its proximity to the ocean, offered a perfect setting for artillery training and tank maneuvers. The Coast Line passed through the reservation, named Camp Cooke, which encompassed the spread of land from Point Sal south to Point Arguello, including the town of Surf. Tangair was established as the supply point for the camp, and the first troops began to arrive in October, 1941.

In the first seven weeks following Pearl Harbor, Southern Pacific handled 573 "main trains," as troop trains were known, and these, together with the already heavy traffic in defense materiel, placed a staggering load on the Coast Line—the "Burma Road of the West." In anticipation of this crush of traffic, the *Noon Daylight*, the *Sunset Limited* (between San Francisco and Los Angeles), and the *Overnight* were all discontinued for the duration on January 5, 1942.

Even Peninsula commuter trains were affected. Many of the suburban cars used in this operation were inducted into military service as well. In their place came lounges, observations, dining cars and anything else on wheels that would run and hold passengers. Nineteen cars were even leased from the Central Railroad of New Jersey. As one military veteran commented, "one morning we would be sitting in a beautiful lounge car and on the return trip we would find ourselves in an old tourist car with a stove at one end."

Southern Pacific quickly took steps to speed up operations and create more capacity. Oil-buffered spring switches were installed at sidings, at the ends of double track—especially in the bustling district between Lick and Watsonville—and at the east switches at Ortega, Oxnard, Camarillo and Hasson, and at the west switch of Chatsworth. Train order offices were opened at critical points like west Watsonville (Aromas, and later Vega) and Tangair (Camp Cooke). Numerous siding extensions were already underway. Work also began in September, 1941 on 16.6 miles of Centralized Traffic Control between San Luis Obispo and Santa Margarita. This project was completed in August of 1942, relieving a tremendous bottleneck. An assistant superintendent was placed at San Luis Obispo during the war with an office staff of seventy, including train dispatchers, crew dispatchers, callers, and yard clerks. With as many as 18 helper jobs bulletined out of San Luis

Camp Roberts, near McKay in the upper reaches of the Salinas Valley, was one of many military camps rushed to completion along the Coast Line during the early days of World War II (**top**). SP established a shelter station adjacent to the main line at the west garrison on December 15, 1941 (**above**). Although lacking in amenities, it was one of the busiest intermediate stations on the Coast Line as long as the war lasted.
*Top, George McCarron collection;
above, Benny Romano collection*

Obispo during the peak of hostilities, the roundhouse force also swelled to a peak of 44, mostly men but including a few women.

By 1943, traffic levels had more than doubled over the previous high levels of 1929 in the district between Santa Barbara and San Jose, and the segment of Coast Line between San Francisco and Redwood Junction was the busiest piece of railroad on the system, with 46.5 million gross ton-miles. To relieve congestion further, some dispatching districts were split (Watsonville Junction-San Luis Obispo at King City) and a system of freight train schedules was set up to make some order out of the mounting chaos. Coast Division timetable No. 151, issued

Solid trains of war materiel, mostly M3 half-tracks of the 7th Infantry Division, choke the yards at San Luis Obispo during the summer of 1943. Traffic levels that year on the Coast Line were double those of 1929, which had previously been the greatest in the history of the route.
Southern Pacific Lines

While equipment is handled directly from rail cars at San Luis Obispo (**top left**) or at the Camp (**top right**), troops disembark at Goldtree (**above**) for the short march to Camp San Luis Obispo. Started as a summer training camp for the National Guard in the 1920s, Camp San Luis Obispo was greatly expanded at the outbreak of war. Despite its close proximity to the main line, railway operations went on as usual. In a regular routine, *Daylights* with 2-10-2 helpers meet at Chorro (**left**) on the hillside above Camp San Luis Obispo in 1943. This siding, along with many others up and down the coast, had recently been extended.

All, Southern Pacific Lines

With so much of the Coast Line visible from the ocean, SP employees were urged to "keep it dark" during blackouts. Special hoods were fashioned from sheet metal and fitted to headlights, signals and markers throughout the Pacific territory. The hoods are in evidence on these locomotives at Santa Barbara in June, 1942. The engine on the left is a leased Pacific from the Chicago, Burlington and Quincy Railroad, pressed into service for the duration.
Two photos, Robert McNeel

Trick dispatcher J. M. Baggett works the CTC machine at the San Luis Obispo depot in August, 1944. In order to expedite traffic, spring switches were installed at many points along the Coast Line, and Centralized Traffic Control was installed on the 17 miles between San Luis Obispo and Santa Margarita. Completed in August 1942, the CTC greatly increased the capacity and performance of the railroad over Cuesta Grade.
Southern Pacific Lines

March 7, 1943, listed six scheduled freights (which were frequently run in many sections) each way. Second-class train No. 766 was joined by Nos. 768 and 770 eastward, and new third-class trains Nos. 763, 765 and 767 were carded westward.

As the war shifted in emphasis to the Pacific Theater, Japanese Americans were moved inland from strategic areas along the coast in "alien specials." Rumors of enemy submarines lurking offshore became commonplace, especially after one surfaced and fired a shot at the Ellwood oil field on February 23, 1942. This precipitated blackout procedures on mainlines and in yards throughout the Pacific territory. SP employees were urged to "serve in silence" and "keep it dark." Special hoods to shield headlights, signal lights and markers for use along the coast were fabricated in the Bayshore shops. But despite the constant fear of enemy attack, the only SP train to be shelled during the war received its damage from friendly fire. Train No. 99, the westward *Daylight*, was damaged by an errant artillery round during tank maneuvers at Camp Cooke. As the speeding cars passed milepost 293 at Narlon on May 12, 1944, a misdirected shell burst between the tracks and the beach. Dozens of steel fragments riddled the kitchen car, injuring several crewmen and passengers.

Because of the national emergency, little was done in the way of improvements beyond increasing track capacity. In 1941, a new station was built at Salinas and a new 110-foot turntable was installed at Bayshore. Due to unstable ground, work was under-

In keeping with the Coast Line's adopted style, SP opened new stucco and tile depots at Salinas (above) in January, 1942 and at San Luis Obispo (left) on September 5, 1943. The crush of military personnel demanded larger facilities at these locations, but there would be no more such projects for the duration due to government restrictions on scarce materials.

Two photos, Southern Pacific Lines

taken on a line change and the daylighting of tunnel No. 13 near Drake in 1942. And new stations were built at Camp Roberts and San Luis Obispo. The latter station, dedicated on September 5, 1943, would be the last SP would undertake for the duration, due to government restrictions on construction materials.

As the war effort reached its climax, there were other, more sobering, special movements. By 1944, over 8,700 German and Italian prisoners of war were being held at Camp Cooke; all had been brought in by train. And there were trains for the wounded. Most of the hospital trains originated at the Presidio in San Francisco, destined for points throughout the country. More than 360 hospital trains were operated on the SP between July 1944 and December 1945. Some even operated on the Van Nuys Branch with wounded service personnel destined for the Veterans Administration hospital. For these moves, an engine was placed on both ends of each train, as there were no turning facilities on the branch. After the surrender of Japan in August, 1945, the theme became, "Get the boys home for Christmas." Returning troops crowded SP trains that fall to the tune of half a million a month. In just the thirty-day period between October 15 and November 15, 1945, 250 special trains were operated for returning troops.

Along with this incredible burden of war-related traffic, the regular ebb and flow of seasonal freight business continued. There could be little argument that Southern Pacific Coast Line operations reached their zenith in terms of traffic density and manpower during the 1940s. But something else had happened. The Coast Line had matured from a picturesque, predominantly passenger-oriented operation into a vital corridor for commerce and national defense. Operating patterns, physical plant, crew deployment, and motive power usage established during this period were to set the tone for the decades to come. ❏

Steam and the new F3 diesels work side by side at San Luis Obispo in 1949.
Fred Wheeler photo, Jim Orem collection

4

Growth and Prosperity

The Post-War Era on the Coast

THE END OF WORLD WAR II ushered in an era of unprecedented growth and prosperity for California and the Coast Line in particular as returning veterans chose to make their homes in the Golden State. And California industry, already established for war production, geared up for a peace-time economy. The herculean task of "getting the troops home for Christmas" during the 1945 season represented the final rush in war-related traffic along the Coast Line, and by the spring of 1946, Southern Pacific was ready to make service improvements in Coast Line passenger service. Post-war planning had begun early in 1943, and Southern Pacific began implementing these plans on April 14, 1946, when the *Noon Daylight* was restored, leaving both San Francisco and Los Angeles daily at 12:15 PM on a nine-hour 40-minute schedule. At the same time, the *Coaster* was speeded up by one hour and fifty five minutes. Even the *Del Monte* schedule was clipped by forty minutes southward and twenty-five minutes northward. The popular *Suntan Specials* running between San Francisco and the Santa Cruz Boardwalk were restored during the 1949 season, operating every Sunday and weekend holiday during the summer.

Accompanying these improvements was an extensive (and successful) advertising and promotional campaign which, by April 11, 1949, had attracted the ten millionth *Daylight* passenger. The *Morning Daylight* was a resounding success, but the same could not be said for the *Noon Daylight*. The train's mid-day departure failed to attract sufficient patronage to support a full-service streamliner. Conversely, the all-heavyweight *Coaster* was doing well providing overnight coach service. Accordingly, on October 2, 1949, the *Noon Daylight* was "temporarily withdrawn for the winter season," never to return, while a new train, the *Starlight*, utilizing the same equipment and running an hour ahead of the *Lark*, replaced the old *Coaster*.

Along with the varnish, SP restored the popular *Overnight* fast merchandise train service between San Francisco and Los Angeles. These were again operated in conjunction with the feeder network service provided by Pacific Motor Trucking. The trains resumed operation as the *Coast Merchandise West (CMW)* and *Coast Merchandise East (CME)* on April

The *Noon Daylight* rolls past Potrero Tower (**above**) in San Francisco on April 10, 1949. Though part of SP's post-war strategy for the Coast, the train's mid-day departure failed to attract riders, while the heavyweight *Coaster* (**left**), seen departing Santa Susana at dawn, provided well-patronized overnight coach service. That October, the *Starlight* replaced the old *Coaster,* utilizing equipment from the *Noon Daylight* which was discontinued.

Left, Dan Wolf collection; above, John C. Illman

1, 1946, operating under first-class schedules of their own: No. 373 westward (northbound) and No. 374 eastward (south). Regularly assigned power on these runs were the fast and capable Mountain-type 4300's. A 4300 could maintain the demanding schedule on the Coast's undulating territory and handle up to 22 cars unassisted on Cuesta Grade.

At first, cars assigned to this service were distinguished by a white triangle painted on the car door. Then 450 special boxcars equipped with high-speed trucks were delivered in fall, 1946 for the overnight service. The cars were painted entirely black with the usual SP medallion on a yellow background as well as an insignia comprising a yellow circle with a red arrow through it and the word "OVERNIGHT" on the arrow. The *Coast Merchandise* trains were blocked in reverse of standard freight trains, which had the first and subsequent setouts blocked behind the engine. The *CM* trains were blocked with the first setouts ahead of the caboose because the road engine was not cut off on the entire 471-mile run. All switching en route was performed by waiting switch engines which worked from the rear end of the trains.

Railroaders began refering to Nos. 373 and 374 as "Zippers" because they moved so fast. When business was heavy and an advance section was operated, they were called the "Big Zipper" and the "Little Zipper." But in time, and with the advent of piggyback service, an even more romantic name became attached to the trains.

The technology of placing truck trailers on flat cars, or "piggyback," had been around for some time when, in July 1953, Southern Pacific chose the *Coast Merchandise* trains for the first expedited piggyback service on the system. At the outset, PMT's trailers were red and orange, but gleaming new aluminum vans soon replaced them, and at least eight steel cupola cabooses assigned to the service were painted aluminum with red and black lettering to match the trailers. It wasn't long before the piggyback service had all but replaced the old boxcars on the run.

Legend has it that tramps first named the train the "Ghost" when they saw the moonlight reflecting off the sides of the train. The flat cars were little more than low-slung platforms supporting PMT trailers that floated atop them in the night like silver-sheeted ghosts. Even the caboose glowed silver, a spooky sight to behold driving along Highway 101 during a full moon. Coastal fogs and the eerie sight of glowing phosphorescent waves crashing against the rocky shore on a dark night might be enough to incite anyone's imagination. Then again, the rails skirted the "Graveyard of the Pacific" and the district was haunted by tragic wrecks like that of the Shriners'

Special at Honda back in the 'twenties. But for whatever the reason, the name stuck and so did the concept of piggyback.

By 1957, 44,128 vans had operated along the coast, helping to make Southern Pacific the nation's No. 1 piggyback hauler. Even the U.S. mails began diverting to piggyback, starting in December, 1956. As the move to piggyback accelerated, the terminals were moved to provide more room to marshall equipment. In San Francisco, the move was made from the LCL sheds between King and Berry streets (near Third Street station) to Mission Bay yard. In Los Angeles, the old LCL sheds near River Station were abandoned for an entirely new facility built on the site of the former Los Angeles shops (Alhambra roundhouse), dubbed "Piggyville" and now known as the LATC: Los Angeles Transportation Center. Growth in this type of traffic on the Coast Line had increased to such an extent that in the summer of 1955, train Nos. 371 and 372 were placed in the timecard, operating as the *Advance Coast Merchandise East* and *Advance Coast Merchandise West*. Container service was added in 1962.

Freight traffic growth in the post-war era on the Coast Line was not limited to the piggyback business. In 1947, Southern Pacific reported that it handled the largest peacetime volume of freight in its history. The Korean crisis, beginning in June, 1950, as well as a record crop of sugar beets, spurred freight traffic that year. Industrial growth was also a factor. In 1945, General Motors purchased 25 acres at Raymer near Van Nuys in the San Fernando Valley, and SP began construction of trackage to serve a new automobile assembly plant. By the summer of 1947, SP had 29,390 feet of new trackage in place at Raymer, later called Gemco, with the plant expected to be fully operational that fall. With inbound deliveries of auto parts from the east and outgoing shipments of finished vehicles, the new auto plant had a tremendous impact on Coast Line traffic.

During 1945 and 1946, SP expanded industrial trackage in the shed districts at Salinas and an emerging new district at Spreckels Junction. The trackage at Spreckels Junction alone involved 10,625 feet of industrial trackage serving six produce sheds and a cannery. At Oxnard, 43 acres of industrial land adjacent to the SP yards were developed, involving 4,700 feet of new trackage serving vegetable packing sheds and a quick-freeze plant. Similar growth occurred in the San Jose-Santa Clara area, with 18,550 feet of new trackage serving produce sheds, canneries, farm implement manufacturers and food processors.

The impact on Coast traffic was significant. Salinas shipped a whopping 59,000 carloads of perishables east in 1952, over 38,000 of which contained lettuce. During the season, six switching crews operated daily out of busy Salinas, as well as the King City local. Salinas shipped its millionth car of lettuce east on August 20, 1963. The Watsonville district season extended from April through November with mid-season shipments reaching upwards of 300 cars per day. There were other crops besides lettuce, among them strawberries, the most timely and valuable crop on the Coast. Expedited shipments of strawberries out of the valley began each June via Railway Express cars attached to regular trains and within a few weeks solid consists of express cars were wheeling their way east in "Strawberry Specials."

S·P's "Overnights"

THE WEST'S GREATEST
L·C·L
(LESS THAN CARLOAD)
SERVICE

It's 1:20 AM and San Luis Obispo hums with activity as train No. 373, the *Coast Merchandise West*, running one hour ahead of the *Lark*, pauses at San Luis Obispo for a crew change and the addition of a 2-10-2 helper for the Cuesta Grade.
Richard Steinheimer photo, DeGolyer Library, Southern Methodist University

On September 25, 1947, the first section of train No. 97, the *Noon Daylight*, arrived at Santa Barbara, on time at 2:28 PM, but as darkness fell, a total of four trailing section, each composed solely of troop sleepers, rolled into town in quick succession. 2-97 (**right**) was handled by Mountain No. 4302; 3-97 (**below**) was powered by a GS, No. 4438, as were 4th and 5th 97, Nos. 4456 and 4433, respectively (**bottom**). It had been two years since the end of World War II, yet the movement of troops, furloughees and other military traffic continued to be an important factor in Coast Line Operations.

Four photos, Robert McNeel

Santa Fe Extra 228 east rumbles past the depot at Guadalupe on August 2, 1952, twelve days after the disastrous Tehachapi earthquake forced the bulk of both Santa Fe and SP's Valley Line traffic to detour over the Coast Line. During the emergency, which lasted from July 21st through August 15th, the Coast Line handled an average of 24 freight trains a day.
George McCarron

Other perishable shipments handled in 1952 included 6,400 carloads of carrots and 1,900 each of celery and frozen foods. On the southern end of the Coast, the Goleta Lemon Association (the "world's largest" lemon packing association) shipped 1,400 carloads alone in 1959. Oxnard yard was enlarged during May, 1966, to accommodate increased perishable traffic.

Sometimes Coast Line freight traffic was impacted by other factors. At 3:52 AM on July 21, 1952, a major earthquake ripped across central Kern County, knocking out SP's strategic line over Tehachapi Pass. Better than 50 aftershocks a day continued to shake the ground. When the dust settled, it would take over 26 days to rebuild the shattered roadbed and tunnels.

While reconstruction in the Tehachapi was under way, the bulk of both SP and Santa Fe's north-south traffic was diverted over the Coast Line. Westbound trains were routed over the Santa Paula Branch while eastward freights and all passenger trains ran over the main line route via Santa Susana Pass, giving the equivalent of double track between Burbank Junction and Montalvo. Trains were limited to 75 cars or the tonnage equivalent as far north as Watsonville Junction. Train and engine crews were brought in from the San Joaquin, Los Angeles and Rio Grande divisions to operate the influx of trains. During the height of the emergency, the Coast Line handled a daily average of 24 trains compared to eight normally, and 1,702 cars compared to 651. Scheduled freight trains frequently operated in five or more sections.

The peak came on August 10th when 1,886 cars travelled the coast, excluding eight passenger trains, an extra passenger and local freights. Service was restored on Tehachapi on August 15, 1952 and within days traffic on the Coast Line returned to normal.

The immediate post-war era was also characterized by the Southern Pacific's steady conversion from steam to diesel motive power. Alco (American Locomotive Co.) diesel switchers began to invade the Coast about 1950. All industrial switching at Salinas was dieselized about 1951, as were yard operations in Santa Barbara and later Oxnard. Some of the switch engines had been around since before the war, but up to now, there had been no attempt to acquire over-the-road diesel freight units. During 1948, however, the first large orders of EMD F3 freight units were delivered and assigned to Los Angeles. These units were used in the Tehachapi and on Beaumont Hill,

4,500 horsepower Alco-GE gas-turbine No. 101 prepares to depart College Park, San Jose, for Watsonville Junction in May, 1949. Although the unit was subjected to widespread testing on the SP, no orders for gas-turbines were ever placed. The unit was subsequently purchased by the Union Pacific and became UP No. 50.
George McCarron

154

Although E7s lead the southbound *Lark* under the First Street bridge on the last lap into Los Angeles on February 8, 1949 (**bottom**), while another set crosses Castillo Street in Santa Barbara (**right**) that June, these units were normally assigned east out of Los Angeles and it was not until the fall of 1953 and the arrival of E9s, like No. 6046, seen at Glendale (**top**) on No. 98, that Coast Line steam passenger operations were threatened.

Top, James F. Orem; right, Robert McNeel; bottom, Frank J. Peterson

A four-unit set of EMD F7s pauses for a crew change and the addition of a helper at San Luis Obispo in 1961 (**top**). Symbol freight SF, seen here running as No. 921, frequently operated with the day's northbound production from the General Motors auto plant at Gemco.

Top, Ed Workman

When these pictures of EMD and Baldwin diesel switchers were taken in February, 1955, yard operations at Santa Barbara had been dieselized for nearly four years.

Two photos, Robert McNeel

but only made occasional forays up the Coast Line. An alternative to the diesel, an Alco-GE 4,500 horsepower gas turbine, No. 101, tested between Roseville and Watsonville Junction during May, 1949, but no orders were forthcoming. Instead, the period from 1949 through 1952 were peak buying years for the F7s which dieselized large segments of the SP's more arid districts. With batches of up to 112 in an individual order, the "covered wagons" could be seen everywhere, including the Coast. But the newcomers usually were on the hotter trains, working side-by-side with the cab-forwards and other heavy steam power.

It was not until the advent of the EMD GP9 after 1954, that enough diesels were on the property to threaten steam's dominance along the Coast. The first orders of GP9s were received between January and March, 1955, and displaced Mountains and GS series 4-8-4's off the fast merchandise service on the Coast. The following year still more GP9s arrived.

Alco demonstrator No. 1600 (an FA/FB combination aimed to compete with EMD's Fs) tested east on the Coast Line, departing Watsonville Junction

A husky 2-10-2 lends help to a string of EMD F3s as they ascend Cuesta Grade at Chorro in 1952 (**top**). F3s were not common on the Coast Line, as the initial orders of these units were primarily used to dieselize the more arid districts of the Southern Pacific.
Top, Art Laidlaw

A variety of early diesels populates the ready tracks at Watsonville Junction (**center**) in 1957. Baldwin 5207 switches an industry at Ventura (**bottom**) in August, 1952.
Center, Grant Flanders collection; bottom, Robert McNeel

January 1, 1953. While SP never invested in these units, Alco had better luck with its version of the GP9. Demonstrators Nos. 701, 701A and 701B (DL-701 or RS-11), dubbed the "Green Hornets," broke in on the Coast, running west out of Los Angeles on April 27, 1956. Suitably impressed, SP ordered 37 which were delivered during the winter of 1956. These became regulars on the Coast Line, including No. 5721 which had a boiler and dual controls and was occasionally used in commute service. Minority diesel builder Baldwin made its presence known as early as 1952 in yard service based out of Santa Barbara, and with AS-616 road switchers on locals throughout the south end of the Coast Line.

The winter of 1954-55 marked the turning point in the dieselization of the Coast Line passenger service. Even though Southern Pacific had assembled a modest fleet of EMD E7s at Los Angeles for work east on the Golden State and Sunset Routes in the late 'forties, trips up the Coast Line were rare. It was not until the Company began taking delivery of E9s, beginning in October 1953, that the dieselization of SP's premier Coast passenger trains was feasible. A

157

In the fall of 1956, on the eve of total Southern Pacific dieselization, the larger 4-8-2's and 4-8-4's congregated at Third Street station in San Francisco, displacing the lighter 2400-series Pacifics in Peninsula commute service.
Southern Pacific Lines

Retired steamers line tracks 47 and 48 at Bayshore Yard in 1957 prior to scrapping. Steam freight operations on the Coast Line had ceased the previous summer, and passenger operations that January, but a number of engines were stored serviceable here, at Los Angeles, Watsonville Junction and other points in anticipation of the "summer rush." As things turned out, they were never returned to service, but two Consolidations, Nos. 2582 and 2836, stored at Watsonville, were returned to service briefly during fall, 1959, when they were moved to Salinas to provide emergency steam generation at a fire-damaged cannery.
Fred B. Wheeler, James F. Orem collection

set of three of the big EMDs could usually make it over Cuesta unassisted, which cut back significantly on helper usage as well. This was not case for the "Coast Mail," however. Dieselized shortly thereafter with F7s and with usually just two units, the long and heavy Coast Mail usually required help to climb the Cuesta.

At first, diesels were tried on the *Lark* out of Los Angeles and traded for two 4400s at San Luis Obispo, but after enough E9s were on the property, the end came swiftly. On January 7, 1955, through steam passenger operations on the Coast were abolished. On that day, the final engines and the trains they pulled were No. 4458 on train No. 98, the *Daylight*, No. 4459 on train No. 94, the *Starlight*, and No. 4452 on train No. 76, the *Lark*.

By the summer of 1956, remaining steam operations on the Coast found an occasional cab-forward running on the district between San Luis Obispo, Watsonville Junction and San Jose. A notice was posted on July 5, 1956, that there were to be no more steam operations east of Watsonville Junction, but there were exceptions. On July 12th, cab-forward No. 4242 operated as No. 931 from Watsonville Junction to San Jose. On July 25th, No. 73 operated out of San Luis Obispo with Mountain No. 4336 and 23 cars with a three-unit GP9 helper. The same day, Consolidation No. 2849 was used on a "main train" to Camp Roberts. In the last documented working trip over the road, GS No. 4458 ran between Salinas (Fort Ord) and San Luis Obispo on November 6th, in company with GP9 No. 5699 and Fairbanks-Morse "Train Master" No. 4800 pulling a "main train." Though new to the Coast, Train Masters delivered the *coup de grace* to Coast steam operations.

The last stronghold for steam, not only on the Coast Line, but on the entire Southern Pacific system, was the Peninsula commute service. As total dieselization edged ever closer, the commute pool was assigned a seemingly endless succession of Pacifics, Mountains, and Northerns as such power was bumped by diesels on other districts. Then, on September 28, 1953, the first diesel, boiler-equipped EMD SD9 No. 5325, was tried out in commuter service. This was followed in June 1954 with the delivery of four boiler-equipped GP9s, Nos. 5600-5603, which were regulars on the *Del Monte* after it was dieselized in January, 1955. Then came the Train Masters. Originally purchased in 1953-54 for service out of El Paso, the units were found unsuitable for sandy desert work and starting in July 1956, the first of the sixteen Train Masters came west for tests in the commute pool. Proving to be ideally suited for the service, the balance were transferred west. These units, together with four additional boiler-equipped GP9s delivered in April, 1955, provided enough diesels to cover the commute service. Thus the end of steam on the Coast Line, in California and on the system as well was finally at hand. The big steamers held on through the 1956 Christmas season but the inevitable last run occurred on January 22, 1957, when GS No. 4430 left San Francisco on train No. 146 at 5:45 PM for San Jose.

Long lines of stored steamers at Bayshore awaited the call to the torch. A handful of ACs were freshly shopped and stored at Watsonville Junction and elsewhere for another beet season, but they were never used again. The railroad was quick to close steam maintenance facilities along the Coast. Santa Barbara roundhouse was closed first in 1956, then on August 19, 1957, the steam facilities at San Luis Obispo and Watsonville Junction were abandoned. Hostlers' jobs at San Luis Obispo were abolished on October 10, 1957. On February 27, 1960, Mission Bay roundhouse, first opened in 1906, was closed for good. Train Master No. 4812 was the last locomotive to use the facility. Minor repairs were now accomplished at the old coach rip track at 7th and Townsend streets, not far from the San Francisco passenger terminal.

After total dieselization, Coast Line motive power was drawn predominantly from the Los Angeles Division freight pool although there were exceptions. Heavier freight power based at Roseville was often seen at Bayshore and sometimes as far south as Salinas. Another source of power was the Peninsula commute pool, which during steam days was frequently tapped on the weekends for freight service between San Luis Obispo, Salinas and Roseville, especially during the peak perishable season. The tradition continued after dieselization.

The husky F-M Train Masters, having been assigned to the commute pool with a solid freight record already established in New Mexico, were quickly tapped for weekend service, but they were not without their problems. Within days of being

Commute service was a duty in which the F-M Train Masters were unmatched for over a decade. Here they display their imposing bulk at 4th Street, San Francisco (**above**) with gallery commute cars. Weekend trips in freight service down the Coast Line were also common, such as this set (**right**) pulling a strawberry special through Chittenden Pass near Logan in April, 1960. Freight trips were restricted during the summer months, however, due to the F-M's unfortunate tendency to start fires.
Above, J. M. Bunker; right, Don Hansen

assigned to the commute pool, Train Masters Nos. 4807 and 4809 worked No. 1-920 between Watsonville Junction and San Luis Obispo, on July 9, 1956. Another set, Nos. 4804 and 4800, together with helper No. 4818, boosted a 61-car, 4,000-ton beet train east over Cuesta Grade on August 18, 1956, but this train was reported to have started fires at San Ardo. The fires continued each weekend as the Train Masters were pressed into service. Later that August, as the grassy hills turned to a golden brown, Nos. 4814, 4813 and 4801 started some particularly bad fires above Santa Margarita while operating on symbol SF-23. The F-Ms were returned light to San Francisco. On another trip, a fire marshall sidelined them at San Lucas. While possessing more than enough power for heavy freight service it was clear that the Train Masters, with their propensity for emitting sparks while in full throttle, would have to be restricted to districts north of Salinas where the fire hazard was less acute.

The late 1950s and early 1960s were a time of intense development of the diesel locomotive. Extensive testing followed the release of each new "second-generation" model and many of them made test runs on the Coast Line. On September 28, 1960, new EMD GP20s Nos. 7200, 7201 and 7202, on their first run west, operated over the Coast on No. 373 to San Francisco, returning on No. 374 the next night. EMD six-axle SD24 demonstrators operated over the Coast Line October 1, 1960, on the same trains. On January 16, 1961, Alco RS-27 demonstrators Nos. 640-3, -4, and -2 tested on No. 373, returning on No. 374 January 17th. The SP went on to purchase many of these emerging new models. On

COMPARATIVE RATINGS IN TONS FOR THE CUESTA GRADE

CLASS	TYPE	Santa Margarita to San Luis Obispo	San Luis Obispo to Santa Margarita
C-5	2-8-0	1300	1150
F-1	2-10-2	1900	1700
F-3	2-10-2	2100	1900
F-4, 5	2-10-2	2350	1900
AC-4, 5	4-8-8-2	3150	2950
AC-6 to 12	4-8-8-2	3300	3100
MT-1, 3 to 5	4-8-2	1700	1500
MT-2	4-8-2	1800	1600
GS-1, 2	4-8-4	1750	1550
GS-3 to 6	4-8-4	1800	1600
DF-1 to 12	F7	950	950
DF-114, 116 to 118, 120, to 122, 124, 125	SD7, 9	1200	1200
DF-500, 501	H-24-66	1425	1425
DF-602, 603, 605 to 607, 611, 612, 616	GP9	800	800
DF-608 to 610, 613, to 615	RS-11	850	825
DF-618	RS-32	975	975
DF-617, 620	GP20	800	800
DF-619, 622, 624	U25B	975	975
DP-3, 4, 7	E7	625	625
DP-5, 6 to 8	PA	625	625
DP-12	E9	625	625

October 24, 1963, SP posted tonnage ratings for the EMD GP20, Alco RS-32, GE U25B and EMD GP30 over Cuesta Grade between San Luis Obispo and Santa Margarita of 800, 975, 975 and 900 tons, respectively. At the same time the ten-year-old F7s were downgraded from 950 to 750 tons in the same territory. The amount of tonnage a locomotive could drag upgrade was only part of the story, however, as the retarding effort of the the diesel's dynamic brakes was also a significant factor.

In steam days, the setting of retainers was the rule for safely descending all of the Coast Line's major grades. But the diesels had dispensed with all that. The one exception was the sugar beet trains. By far the heaviest trains operated on the Coast Line, the use of retainers on beet trains was relaxed only after a series of braking test runs, operated between August 11th and August 13th, 1959. Each day the beets, operating as train No. 924, were the subject of braking tests with various combinations of power and tonnage: three units with a six-unit helper and 4,929 tons the first day; three units with a six-unit helper and 4,820 tons the second day; and four units with a two-unit helper and 5,870 tons the last day, all without retainers.

The technology of dieselization had allowed for a general speed-up of freight traffic on the Coast Line, effective in December, 1956. And as time went on, freight traffic completely overshadowed the passenger business on the Coast. Emerging technology was applied first to freight-oriented operations. As an example, the SP's first radio telephones were installed on nine switch engines in the San Francisco yards in 1948, enabling terminal supervisors to communicate

The trio of Alco DL-701 (RS-11) demonstrators pauses at San Luis Obispo (**right**) on April 28, 1956. SP ordered 37, all of which were Coast regulars. Some of the later deliveries had "chopped noses," a feature common to most second-generation diesel units from all the builders. Some low-nose RS-11s lead train No. 924 (**top**) into San Luis Obispo in 1962.
*Top, Ed Workman;
right, George McCarron*

After the RS-11, the next advancement from Alco was the RS-32, of which SP ordered ten (Alco only produced 35 of this design). Numbered in the 7300 series, all ten were assigned to the Coast for most of their lives. Here two new 7300s (and a pair of RS-11s) wait for the passenger trains at San Luis Obispo in the summer of 1962.
Ed Workman

162

A string of General Electric U25Bs prepares to depart San Luis Obispo (**above**) on April 21, 1962, with hot train No. 373, the *Coast Merchandise West*. New EMD GP20s (**right**) work a sugar beet drag at Shuman in April, 1961. These and other second-generation locomotives transformed operations on the Coast Line in the mid-'sixties.

Two photos, Don Sims, Southern Pacific Lines collection

with yard crews. Two-way radio was installed on diesel locomotives in freight service between Los Angeles and Watsonville Junction in 1950, long before it was ever installed in passenger diesels.

Having experienced such unprecedented growth since World War II, an optimistic Southern Pacific developed long-range plans for all its major routes, including the Coast Line, and published the results in an internal document dated July 7, 1955. On the Los Angeles Division side of the Coast, the planner anticipated running much larger freight trains through between Los Angeles and San Luis Obispo by 1960, and towards that objective recommended extending sidings to accommodate 125 cars at Carpinteria, Seacliff, Ventura, Oxnard, Leesdale, Camarillo, Moorpark, Strathearn, Santa Susana, Chatsworth, and Northridge. It was anticipated that CTC would be required between Chatsworth and Burbank Junction in the period between 1960 and 1965. In the period 1966-1970, two new 125-car sidings would be needed at Santa Barbara, as well as new diesel servicing facilities at Chatsworth, and double-track, reverse-signal CTC between Chatsworth and Burbank Junction. Between 1971 and 1975 the possibility of extending CTC from Chatsworth to Santa Barbara was mentioned.

On the Coast Division side, 125-car sidings were recommended by 1960 at Capitan, Casmalia-Devon, Guadalupe, Coburn, and Harlem, and line changes at Drake, Jalama, and Honda to get away from seawall erosion problems. Additional line changes were recommended to reduce curvature at Dulah, Callender, Paso Robles, San Miguel, Bradley, Wunpost, and Chittenden to increase freight train speed. Extending the CTC limits west from Santa Margarita to King City was considered a possibility beyond 1970, as was the segment from Lick to Salinas. Reverse-signal CTC was recommended for the Peninsula line between San Francisco and San Jose by 1960-1964, and extension of double track west from Lick to San Jose during 1965-1969. The long-range plan also anticipated modern diesel service facilities being installed at Mission Bay, Bayshore, San Luis Obispo and Watsonville Junction.

Most of these plans never came to pass, but short segments of CTC were installed in 1959 between Corporal and Logan, and between Watsonville Junction and Salinas, to ease congestion.

Operations were becoming more centralized. The CTC machine controlling movements over Cuesta Grade was moved from the station at San Luis Obispo to Coast Division headquarters at Third and Townsend, San Francisco, on November 1, 1957. Slightly less than six hours was needed to move the

As the Coast Line was modernized in the 1950s, the typical small-town station was usually a victim of progress. Those not needed for operational purposes were closed, usually with demolition of the building following soon after. During 1958, the agency was closed at Carpinteria, but the station building itself remained standing. Considered for a time as a possible candidate for a city hall, the Carpinteria station was finally demolished in March 1967.

Roy Graves photo, Bancroft Library collection, University of California, Berkeley

machine (by rail). Along with the move came the consolidation of the entire Coast Line between Santa Barbara and San Francisco under one dispatcher. Two dispatchers had formerly handled the territory, with the dividing line between the two being located at King City.

In the rush to modernize the Coast, the typical small-town agency became the next casualty. With no need for a train order operator, and the agency closed, the following stations were closed for good in 1958: Moorpark, Campbell, Davenport, Camarillo, Los Altos, San Lucas, Carpinteria, Palo Alto/California Ave., Saticoy, Morganhill, Ojai, and Coyote. By July, 1959, Northridge, Menlo Park, Mountain View, and Los Gatos were also closed. By the spring of 1960, Santa Margarita, Gonzales, Soledad, San Ardo, San Miguel, Atascadero, Gaviota, and Chatsworth were all closed. In many cases, demolition of the station building itself soon followed.

Even though freight traffic was up, passenger volume on the Coast Line was disappointing at best. Beginning in the mid-'fifties, the Company began to pursue aggressively the discontinuance of little-used trains. On April 15, 1957, the *Del Monte* was cut back to Monterey, ending service to Pacific Grove and as early as December, 1962, SP was seeking permission to abandon the *Del Monte* entirely. On July 15, 1957, citing a continuing lack of patronage, the *Lark* and the *Starlight* were combined. No *Suntan Specials* were operated after the 1959 season. On May 1, 1959, the Oakland *Daylight* and Oakland *Larks*, train Nos. 73, 74, 250, and 255 made their last runs. The same day Nos. 90 and 91, the Coast Mail, switched terminals from San Francisco to Oakland, but no passengers were carried north of San Jose.

The situation with the commuters was not so clear cut. The year 1955 saw commuter traffic reach a peak of 16,000 daily riders. With trains getting longer, they were beginning to extend beyond the station platforms, so the SP decided to purchase ten "gallery"-type cars which could seat 145. Before the cars were ordered, in January 1954, the SP brought in from Chicago one of the Burlington's new double-deck cars so that Peninsula commuters could evaluate them and make suggestions for improvements. Ten bi-level commute cars were then ordered and placed in service during June and July, 1955. All ten were used on train No. 121 which left San Jose at 6:43 AM weekdays and No. 130 which left San Francisco at 5:14 PM each weeknight. Proving successful, 21 more were ordered in February, 1956. In spite of these improvements, including dieselization, criticism of the service came from the public sector.

Despite rumors of termites in the structure, SP undertook a $21,000 dollar spruce-up of the Third and Townsend terminal building during 1954. The distinctive wood and plaster bell towers were replaced with ones made of light metal, and the concourse was also reroofed. The City of San Francisco scoffed at this "band aid," wanting Southern Pacific to build an entirely new passenger terminal in San Francisco, and even went so far on November 15, 1954, as to threaten legal proceedings to force Southern Pacific into action; little came of it. John M. Peirce, recently appointed general manager of the Bay Area Rapid Transit District (BART), characterized SP's Peninsula commute service in the fall of 1958 as an "antiquated system of the horse-and-buggy days...complete with baggy-pants conductors."

The Coast Mail, here shown crossing the Western Pacific at Magnolia Tower in Oakland in 1960, switched terminals from San Francisco to Oakland on May 1, 1959. The change reflected the increasing dependence on the East Bay hub as the northern terminal of the Coast Line. *Southern Pacific Lines*

165

A San Francisco-Los Gatos passenger train passes a stately oak near Alta Mesa on the Los Altos Branch in 1962. An early victim of plant rationalization, the 6.3-mile Los Altos Branch was abandoned on January 3, 1964. Santa Clara County used the right-of-way to build a highway.
Richard Steinheimer photo, Southern Pacific Lines

Amidst the controversies and seeming success of the service, SP quietly trimmed commute schedules; one round trip on April 26, 1953 and again on September 27, 1953, September 30, 1956 and September 30, 1957 (Nos. 105-144). By the fall of 1957, "Big Game" specials were down to three from San Francisco and two from Berkeley. SP asked to abandon the Los Gatos Branch from Vasona Junction to Los Gatos in July, 1958. And on Friday, January 3, 1964, SP abandoned service entirely on 6.3 miles of the Los Altos Branch between Alta Mesa and Simla so that the county could build an expressway on the right-of-way.

Amid mounting criticism of how the railroad conducted its passenger service, SP demonstrated that it still knew how to run a "first class" train. September 20, 1959, was a big day for the Coast Line when His Excellency Nikita S. Khrushchev, Chairman of the Council of Ministers of the Union of Soviet Socialist Republics, rode a State Department special train from Los Angeles to San Francisco. The special, running as No. 2-99, a second section of the *Daylight*, consisted of 18 cars of primarily *Shasta Daylight* equipment, a four-unit diesel, nine coaches and a dome assigned to the press, one 12-bedroom Pullman, one dome-lounge, two parlor cars and a parlor-observation.

In keeping with the security and priority of the special, train orders were issued that 2-99 was to run 15 minutes behind 1-99 at all stations. Most passengers aboard the *Daylight* were unaware that they were riding a pilot train that would detonate any bombs that might be placed on the tracks for Mr. Khrushchev. The special itself was checked thoroughly for any mechanical problems or hidden bombs. At San Luis Obispo, special agents rousted all hoboes from the yard and all freight cars were moved well away from the mainline tracks. Switches leading into the mainline were spiked. Thirty minutes before 1-99 was scheduled to arrive, all switching ceased. All freights were held in the yards until after the special. Army helicopters heralded the approach of the pilot train and remained overhead over both trains guarding against any sabotage. The helicopters were supplemented by highway patrol cars escorting the train on parallel highways. Krushchev at one point remarked to U.S. host Henry Cabot Lodge, "I'm glad I took the train. This is a fine train and a nice route." For security reasons, the special terminated at Bayshore, nine hours and 45 minutes later–right on schedule–and from there the party motored into downtown San Francisco.

The trip occurred during a period of mounting tension which was to lead to the "Missile Crisis," and as the special sped north along the California coast between Honda and Casmalia, Khrushchev had a chance to observe firsthand U.S. missile activity at Vandenberg Air Force base, located at the old site of Camp Cooke. Deactivated after World War II, Camp Cooke had seen service briefly during the Korean War, but received a new lease on life when, in September 1956, the Air Force acquired it for a new Inter-Continental Ballistic Missile facility. Eventually named Vandenberg Air Force Base after Air Force Chief of Staff Hoyt S. Vandenberg, the facility saw its first intermediate-range ballistic missile launched on December 16, 1958. The first orbiting satellite was launched on a Thor intermediate-range ballistic missile, February 25, 1959.

Lots of activity preceded every launch at Vandenberg and this tended to disrupt SP operations. The question of which had priority, train or missile, came up during Vandenberg's first year of operation. An agreement between the Air Force and Southern Pacific was eventually reached in which Vandenberg would not schedule missile firings to interfere with scheduled train movements. The SP agreed in return that unscheduled freight trains would be delayed on each side of the base during launchings. While trains could be held clear of the area, the same couldn't be said for the station force at Surf. Accordingly, a bomb shelter was dug out of a cliff adjacent to the depot for use by the operator and agent. If this proved too uncomfortable, the Air Force agreed to take the station force into Lompoc for a meal if necessary.

During 1964, the Air Force acquired 19,435 acres at Point Arguello to develop the Pacific Missile Range. During 1966 this was augmented by the acquisition of the Sudden Ranch, with 15 miles of Coast Line, and the Scolari property, to make a total of 98,400 acres. All of this property remains restricted and off limits today–and still largely undeveloped.

As passenger traffic on the Coast Line slid drastically, freight traffic continued to rise proportionately. Symbol freight trains regularly assigned to the Coast Line as of 1962 included these eastward trains: the *CLM* (Coast Line Manifest) between San Francisco-Oakland and Los Angeles; the Advance *CME* (Advance *Coast Merchandise East*) operating as Advance No. 374 between San Francisco and Los Angeles and as Advance No. 336 between Oakland and San Jose making setouts at Raymer and a pick-up at Salinas; No. 374, the *CME*; the *LA* (Los Angeles Manifest) from San Francisco/Oakland to Los Angeles daily; the *WPB* (Watsonville Perishable Block) which operated seasonally out of Watsonville Junction to Los Angeles for connection with the Colton Block; the *SMV* (Santa Maria Vegetable Block, also known as the "Smokey") which operated

Newsmen, officials and Secret Service swarm around Nikita S. Khrushchev, Chairman of the Council of Ministers of the Union of Soviet Socialist Republics, as His Excellency made a short visit to San Luis Obispo on his trip up the Coast Line on September 20, 1959.
Southern Pacific Lines

Southern California photographers often caught the *Daylight* at Chatsworth. In this pair of photos, No. 98 has descended Santa Susana Pass and is accelerating onto the tangent which crosses the San Fernando Valley on August 14, 1954 (**top**), while No. 99 is shown rolling westward at the same location on April 10, 1955 (**center**). The *Daylight* was dieselized in January, 1955.

Top, Jay Bell collection; center, John E. Shaw

A classic perspective of the Coast Line could be achieved, then and now, from a low hill between Ortega and Miramar. Here, No. 99 glides around the curve approaching Fernald Point, with Santa Barbara in the distance, just five miles away. Coastal Highway 101 is a few feet to the right of this view, and parallels the Coast Line and the Pacific Ocean shore for nearly 60 miles between Ventura and Gaviota.

Bottom, Southern Pacific Lines

168

Daylight photography in the diesel era was just as focused on the scenic qualities of the Coast Line as had been the case in steam days. In the publicity photos of the time, someone waving to the train, usually a young woman, was a common feature. Here, the consist of No. 99 is headed by PA-2 No. 6040, just west of Camarillo (**top**). The train's power freely mixed locomotives from EMD and Alco, as illustrated by No. 99 rolling westward within hailing distance of the beach at Carpinteria (**center**). And the passengers' view of the blue Pacific is spectacular for most of two hours, during No. 98's run from Narlon to Ventura (**bottom**).

Three photos, Southern Pacific Lines

February 16, 1963, finds Saugus a busy place as Coast Line freights detour over the Santa Paula Branch from Montalvo due to a disastrous tunnel fire at Santa Susana Pass. Smoke (**left**) can be seen drifting from within tunnel No. 27. During the emergency, No. 374 (**above**), running as an extra, slowly comes off the branch while a Valley Line freight waits in the hole. The Coast was out of service for eight days.

Above, John E. Shaw; left, Southern Pacific Lines

in season from Guadalupe to Los Angeles for connection with Colton or C Blocks.

Westward trains included the *SF* (San Francisco Manifest) for general freight out of Los Angeles destined to San Francisco/Oakland; the *GGM* (Golden Gate Manifest), the work train on the daily Los Angeles-San Francisco/Oakland run with pick-ups at Raymer, Oxnard, Ventura, Santa Barbara, Surf, Guadalupe, San Luis Obispo and Watsonville Jct.; the Advance *CMW* (Advance *Coast Merchandise West*) operating as Advance No. 373 on the Coast Line and Advance No. 335 on the Oakland line; the *CMW* operating as No. 373/335; and the *SV* (Salinas Vegetable Block) which originated at Salinas in up to three sections during the season for operation through to Roseville and a connection with the R Blocks eastward over Donner Pass.

The large number of Coast Line trains terminating at Oakland, or at the dual terminals of Oakland/San Francisco, reflected the decreasing importance of San Francisco as a freight terminal. This was further underscored in the 1964 decision to combine the Western and Coast divisions, with Oakland as the hub of operations. At the same time, the former Coast Line territory between San Luis Obispo and Santa Barbara was absorbed by the Los

Angeles Division. Streamlining of operations on the Coast Line was carried further with the closing of Santa Barbara and San Luis Obispo yards, the latter on February 9, 1970. On February 11, 1972, the framework for future operations was established when interdivisional runs were created between San Luis Obispo and Los Angeles, running through Santa Barbara. The same day, San Jose was eliminated as a terminal, with pool freight crews operating between Oakland and Watsonville Junction.

The heavy rains of January and February, 1969 had a significant affect on Coast Line operations. Rainfall along the Coast that season averaged *nine times* the normal amount. Rain-saturated hillsides began to slip and rain-swollen creeks and rivers went over their banks. Moderate to severe damage occurred over a 60-mile stretch between Salinas and San Luis Obispo. Near Capitan, a slipout caused train No. 373 to derail at speed. Several locomotives and 19 cars derailed including many tri-level auto racks which erupted in flames from leaking auto fuel. More than 13 inches of rain fell in the Santa Ynez drainage within a nine-day period ending January 28, 1969. More than four miles of SP's branch line were under water near Lompoc. The flood-swollen Santa Ynez River hit the steel bridge at Surf hard; it was mangled beyond repair and eventually had to be knocked out of the way by explosives so that reconstruction could commence. The 46-mile Santa Paula Branch was also severely damaged. Ten bridges and trestles were either lost or damaged and hardly a mile of track was unaffected by slides, washouts, and mud and debris on the right-of-way. Over $350,000 damage was done to the Ojai Branch.

Repairs to the Coast Line took weeks but virtually all was restored, the diminutive Ojai Branch being the only casualty. Considering its light traffic base and the extent of damage, plans were made to abandon the line. The branch's single shipper, the Ojai Orange Association, which shipped about 400 cars annually, objected. Eventually a deal was struck whereby SP would buy the old packing house for $550,000 and the Ojai Growers would join the Tapo Citrus Association, which had just completed a plant at Somis, to be operated as the Ojai-Tapo Citrus Association. Finally, on December 31, 1969, with this one objection overcome, the upper 9.4 miles of the Ojai branch between Ojai and Canet was abandoned.

On the passenger front, Southern Pacific continued to pursue energetically the abandonment of unneeded and unprofitable trains. Little was done in the way of capital improvement. An exception to this was the Peninsula commute service. A new San Bruno depot, midway between the San Bruno depot and Lomita Park stops, was built in the summer of 1963. But by February, 1964, Southern Pacific was claiming a $650,000 loss annually on the commuter runs. In order to trim costs, SP argued, it would be necessary to eliminate five trains by turning some at Belmont, as well ask for a 30 percent fare increase. Even though resistance to fare increases was encountered, SP continued to invest in the service. An additional order of 15 commute cars arrived in 1968, allowing for the retirement of some labor-intensive heavyweight suburban cars.

The Coast Mail, trains Nos. 90 and 91, assumed San Francisco-San Jose local Nos. 151-154 in June 1964, as the power and crews began going through to San Luis Obispo. The change was short-lived, however, because on April 30, 1965, the California PUC (Public Utilities Commission), recognizing SP's claims of operating losses in excess of $628,200 annually, finally authorized the discontinuance of the trains. SP claimed that the trains were losing mail to trucks and carried a pathetic four to eight passengers daily who were willing to brave the 16-hour trip between San Francisco and Los Angeles.

While the PUC was willing to let the Coast Mail go with little opposition, the contest for the discontinuance of the *Lark* was protracted and bitter. For it was not only the *Lark* that was at stake, but in a larger view, the future of the Coast Line, and its long heritage as a premier passenger hauler. That there was a long history of declining patronage of the *Lark* was never questioned; it was only "why" that stirred the debate.

Suffice it to say, by 1959, the number of Pullman cars on the *Lark* had declined to seven. On May 2, 1960, the *Oakland Lark* was discontinued in favor of trans-Bay buses. By 1966, the consist was down to three Pullmans, two coaches, dining and lounge cars and two head-end cars. On February 2, 1966, Southern Pacific asked to suspend the *Lark*. With an

Crews work the mail and express while the engine crew changes out on the Coast Mail at San Luis Obispo, just prior to its discontinuance on April 30, 1965. For years the Coast Mail, affectionately known as "Sad Sam," had plied the Coast Line. But by the mid-'sixties, SP was claiming an operating loss in excess of $628,000 annually. The Post Office was gradually shifting its operations to trucks and there was little revenue in the handful of riders brave enough to make the 16-hour trip.

Four photos, Ed Workman

The consist of the first section of the *Lark* stretches out past 4th St. Tower as it prepares to get under way at San Francisco in 1961. The once-popular overnight train became the subject of a bitter discontinuance fight in the mid-'sixties. Citing increased air passenger traffic between Los Angeles and San Francisco, Southern Pacific argued that the money-losing *Lark* ("the bird that couldn't fly") had outlived its usefulness. SP's critics countered that the railroad had worked to discourage riders. In the end, loss of the postal contract doomed the train. Indeed, the second section of the *Lark* this night was the *Advance CME* carrying piggyback vans of mail for Los Angeles.

Two photos, Bob Morris

average of just 95 passengers a night, SP claimed a $993,683 out-of-pocket loss for the first 11 months of 1965 on the *Lark*, and blamed the fast and frequent air travel in the same corridor as the cause. SP's critics held another view.

With a headline blaring "the train your 'Friendly Railroad' is so enthusiastically measuring for a casket," Maitland Zane, reporting in the San Francisco *Chronicle* on June 20, 1966, described the *Lark* as "clean but antiquated. The coaches are uncomfortable, and the food is mediocre and overpriced. It is operated by old men afraid for their jobs and ashamed of their work." Allegation surfaced in the press that the *Lark* was "routinely held out of Los Angeles to miss connections to San Diego–an average of five days out of seven." SP President Donald J. Russell was quoted in the April, 1966 issue of *Newsweek* that "Passengers are just not in the cards."

But the California PUC did not agree and denied the application, citing "evidence that SP had not promoted these trains and in fact had made specific efforts to divert passengers."

Following the news that the U.S. Post Office would discontinue RPO service on the *Lark* effective September 29, 1967, Southern Pacific reapplied on September 2, 1967 to discontinue the *Lark*. Henceforth first class mail would fly up the coast or take piggyback freight trains. To bolster its argument, Southern Pacific cited a 551 percent growth in air passenger traffic between Los Angeles and San Francisco in the years 1951-1966. During September, 1967, there were 82 daily northbound flights and 78 southbound flights between the two cities. But it was the private automobile that was the predominant passenger carrier in the corridor, surpassing all other modes combined. This time, after hearings and heat-

The *Del Monte* prepares to depart Monterey on April 3, 1971 (**left**). Nationalization of passenger service is less than a month away and despite arguments that the train was a commuter run and not subject to the Amtrak agreement, the *Del Monte* would not be among those trains operating after May 1, 1971. Interestingly enough, it was the consist of No. 126, the eastbound *Del Monte*, deadheading home from Monterey, that was the last non-commuter passenger run operated by SP on the eve of Amtrak.

Left, Dick Dorn

Train No. 141, the *Del Monte*, eases to a stop on the branch main at Castroville (**above**) while the conductor performs the time-honored ritual of signing the register. The date is April 8, 1971, and three weeks from now there will be no more trains to list on the weathered arrival and departure board.

Three photos, Dick Dorn

Train No. 98, the eastward *Daylight*, pauses at San Luis Obispo on April 6, 1971. In the twilight of its 34-year career, spring break has swollen the consist of this, the last remaining passenger train on the Coast Line. Normally a single SDP45 could handle the skimpy consist of what the press now dubbed "the lonesome train."
Dick Dorn

ed debate, SP was allowed to discontinue the *Lark*, effective Sunday, April 7, 1968. The decision hadn't been unanimous. Following the 3-2 decision of the California PUC on March 12, 1968, commissioners Bennett and Mitchell, in casting their dissenting votes, charged that "Southern Pacific has consistently ignored the needs of the traveling public of California. It has failed to advertise (in direct opposition to a PUC order), it has downgraded service, it has ignored schedules...based upon the greed for profit at the expense of the people and upon an ignorance of the needs of the State of California."

Opposition to the *Lark* abandonment was particulary vocal. The San Luis Obispo County *Telegram-Tribune* of April 21, 1966 interviewed a number of affected employees and passengers. "The Company does all it can to discourage passengers on the train," said railroader Al Mazza; "...the ticket men are told to tell customers that the train is full and they can't get a seat for days." A passenger complained that she was told that the train was filled up for three weeks in advance. "But when the ticket seller found out I was related to a railroader, and knew the score, I quickly got a ticket–ocean side–and in the middle of the train." Passengers were often surprised to find that their baggage didn't accompany them aboard the *Lark*, but was shipped by PMT truck, often arriving three days later and in a disheveled condition.

As the time came for the final runs of the *Lark*, Southern Pacific made special arrangements to send the train into history in a grand manner. The final trains consisted of 16 cars each way: a baggage car, five Pullmans, a lounge, a diner, four coaches, a diner, and three coaches in that order. Passengers were given a special "Farewell to the *Lark*" booklet and a special stamp was prepared to authenticate materials used on the last run. Excited crowds gathered on the platform at San Francisco to send the train off, while at Palo Alto, crowds lined the tracks and sang "Auld Lang Syne." The bulk of the passengers were railfans. As the *Lark* sped south, members of the Davis Railroad Club argued late into the night about who was ultimately at fault over the demise of the passenger train.

The last run out of Los Angeles went out in grand style as well. A total of 177 passengers boarded the *Lark* for her last trip north. The scene in the lounge car, as the *Lark* rolled north, was frenetic. According to the Los Angeles *Times*, "excited women bumped into each other spilling drinks. An era was ending and they were determined to make the best of it. As the evening wore on, the atmosphere grew wilder in the lounge. Ruth Schacket, a Shell Oil analyst from Menlo Park, gleefully allowed her arms and legs to be stamped 'Last Run-*Lark*.' Then, grabbing the special stamp, she attempted to brand discomfited railroad assistant superintendent Robert Thruston of Los Angeles. Back in the coaches, railfans, parents and children were fitfully trying to sleep. Others stared moodily out at the bright moon and silvery Pacific."

The demise of the *Lark* left the Coast Line with but one through passenger train, the *Coast Daylight*, to which further economies were now directed. To cut down on maintenance costs, *Sunset Limited* equipment began running through to San Francisco on the *Daylight* during the spring of 1968 with the result that the northbound run of the *Daylight* was frequently quite late due to late connections from the East. Also in 1968, diners were discontinued in favor of "coffee shop-automat" cars. Pressure was placed on the PUC to reduce remaining trips to tri-weekly. Ridership was awful. By the fall of 1970, the Ventura *Free Press* characterized the *Coast Daylight* as the "lonesome train." With fewer than 85 passengers per trip, "San Francisco cabbies do not go out of their way to meet the *Daylight*." Passengers agreed that the ride was superb in a scenic sense, but a bore in comfort and convenience. The trip "drags on" for nearly ten hours between Los Angeles and San Francisco and the lack of a dining car made the trip "in the late-1930s vintage cars with their yellowed, torn and faded pictures tedious."

The situation regarding passenger traffic on the Coast Line was not unique. Lack of riders was endemic throughout the country, and train removals were affecting every Class 1 railroad. With the total demise of the long-distance passenger train looming on the horizon, Congress took steps to salvage a basic national system. John Volpe, secretary of transportation, announced November 30, 1970, that the Transportation Department had selected 16 routes to be preserved in a stripped-down National Rail Passenger Network. In the scheme, Chicago would serve as a hub for long-distance routes radiating out across the country, and the coast run between San Francisco and Los Angeles would not be among them. While this situation was regarded favorably by the Southern Pacific, there were many who objected.

In the early spring of 1971, as the day for Amtrak takeover was rapidly approaching, Volpe reversed his decision regarding the Coast Line, under pressure from the ICC and the National Association for Railroad Passengers. Thus, on May 1, 1971, when Amtak took over responsibility for most of the nation's long-distance passenger service, a new Seattle-San Diego train, dubbed the *Coast Starlight*, was to usher in the modern era on the Coast Line. ❑

Located beyond the Third Street station, which was mile post 0, the Beale Street team track, shown after modernization in 1957, must have been less than zero as it was as close as one could get to the General Office and still be on SP rails.
Southern Pacific Lines

Discounting rumors in the press of termites, SP undertook a modest sprucing-up of the venerable Mission Revival station at Third and Townsend streets, San Francisco, during 1954. Eleven years later, when these views were taken, the structure was still there and looking good at 50. Ten thousand commuters still passed through its stucco archways twice daily, some of whom no doubt paused at "Ricky's Rendezvous Room" (at far left, **above**) for a toddy before taking the train down the Peninsula.

Two photos, Southern Pacific Lines

SAN FRANCISCO SUBDIVISION

EASTWARD

Timetable No. 162
September 28, 1952

FIRST CLASS

Capacity of sidings in car lengths	114 Passenger Leave Daily Ex. Sunday and Holidays	164 Passenger Leave Sunday and Holidays only	112 Passenger Leave Daily	98 Morning Daylight Leave Daily	250 Passenger Leave Daily	162 Passenger Leave Sat.,Sun.and Holidays only	110 Passenger Leave Daily Ex.Sat.,Sun. and Holidays	108 Passenger Leave Daily Ex.Sat.,Sun. and Holidays	106 Passenger Leave Daily	Mile Post Location	STATIONS	Distance from San Francisco
BKWOITYP	AM 11.00	AM 11.00	AM 8.20	AM 8.15		AM 7.05	AM 6.50	AM 5.45	AM 12.30	0.0	TO-R SAN FRANCISCO	0.0
		f				s 7.09	s 6.54		s 12.34	1.9	1.9 23rd STREET	1.9
P										3.1	1.2 NEWCOMB AVE.	3.1
										4.1	1.0 PAUL AVE.	4.1
BKWOITP			s 8.29			s 7.15	s 7.00	s 5.55	s 12.40	5.2	1.1 BAYSHORE	5.2
KIP	11.10	11.10	8.31	8.25		7.17	7.02	5.57	12.42	6.9	R 1.7 VISITACION	6.9
P			f				s 7.04			8.6	1.7 BUTLER ROAD	8.6
PK	s 11.14	s 11.15	s 8.36			s 7.20	s 7.07	s 6.01	s 12.46	9.3	0.7 SO. SAN FRANCISCO	9.3
YP	s 11.18	s 11.19	s 8.40			s 7.24	s 7.11	s 6.06	s 12.49	11.0	1.7 SAN BRUNO	11.0
						f	f	s 6.08	f	12.1	1.1 LOMITA PARK	12.1
M 44 P	s 11.24	f	s 8.45			s 7.28	s 7.15	s 6.11	f	13.7	1.6 MILLBRAE	13.7
P	s 11.27	s 11.26	s 8.49			s 7.32	s 7.19	s 6.14	s 12.57	15.2	1.5 BROADWAY	15.2
P	s 11.33	s 11.29	s 8.52	8.35		s 7.35	s 7.22	s 6.19	s 1.01	16.3	1.1 BURLINGAME	16.3
M 80 WP	s 11.39	s 11.33	s 8.56			s 7.39	s 7.26	s 6.24	s 1.05	17.9	1.6 SAN MATEO	17.9
		f						s 6.26	f	18.9	1.0 HAYWARD PARK	18.9
P	s 11.43	s 11.37	s 9.01			s 7.43	s 7.32	s 6.28	s 1.09	20.3	1.4 HILLSDALE	20.3
P	s 11.48	s 11.40	s 9.04			s 7.45	s 7.35	s 6.31	f	21.9	1.6 BELMONT	21.9
M 43 P	s 11.52	s 11.43	s 9.07			s 7.48	s 7.38	s 6.34	s 1.14	23.2	1.3 SAN CARLOS	23.2
Yd.Lmts. P	AM s 11.59	s 11.47	s 9.11			s 7.52	s 7.42	s 6.40	s 1.18	25.4	2.2 REDWOOD CITY	25.4
WIYP	PM 12.01	11.48	9.12	8.46		7.53	7.43	6.41	1.19	26.2	R 0.8 REDWOOD JCT.	26.2
		s 11.51	s 9.14			s 7.45	s 6.43		f	27.8	1.6 ATHERTON	27.8
P	s 12.06	s 11.54	s 9.17			s 7.58	s 7.48	s 6.47	s 1.23	28.9	1.1 MENLO PARK	28.9
M 44 P	s 12.17	AM s 11.57	s 9.20			s 8.02	s 7.54	s 6.55	s 1.26	30.1	1.2 PALO ALTO	30.1
M 44 WYP	s 12.20	PM s 12.01	s 9.23			s 8.06	s 7.59	s 6.58	s 1.29	31.8	R 1.7 CALIFORNIA AVE.	31.8
										34.8	3.0 CASTRO	34.8
M 42 P	s 12.28	s 12.08	s 9.31			s 8.13	s 8.06	s 7.06	s 1.49	36.1	1.3 MOUNTAIN VIEW	36.1
P	s 12.36	s 12.13	s 9.36		Via Newark	s 8.18	s 8.11	s 7.13	s 1.55	38.8	2.7 SUNNYVALE	38.8
KIP	s 12.44	s 12.19	s 9.43	9.02	AM 8.44	s 8.24	s 8.18	s 7.20	f 2.02	44.3	R 5.5 SANTA CLARA	44.3
BKWP										45.2	0.9 SAN JOSE YARD	45.2
IP		f					f			45.7	0.5 COLLEGE PARK	45.7
BKWOITYP	s 12.50 PM	s 12.25 PM	s 9.50 AM	s 9.08 AM	s 8.50 AM	s 8.30 AM	s 8.25 AM	s 7.28 AM	s 2.10 AM	46.9	TO-R 1.2 SAN JOSE	46.9
	Arrive Daily Ex. Sunday and Holidays	Arrive Sunday and Holidays only	Arrive Daily	Arrive Daily	Arrive Daily	Arrive Daily Sat.,Sun.and Holidays only	Arrive Daily Ex.Sat.,Sun. and Holidays	Arrive Daily Ex.Sat.,Sun. and Holidays	Arrive Daily		(46.9)	

Automatic Block Signal System — Double Track

San Francisco
Third & Townsend streets
CIRCA 1950

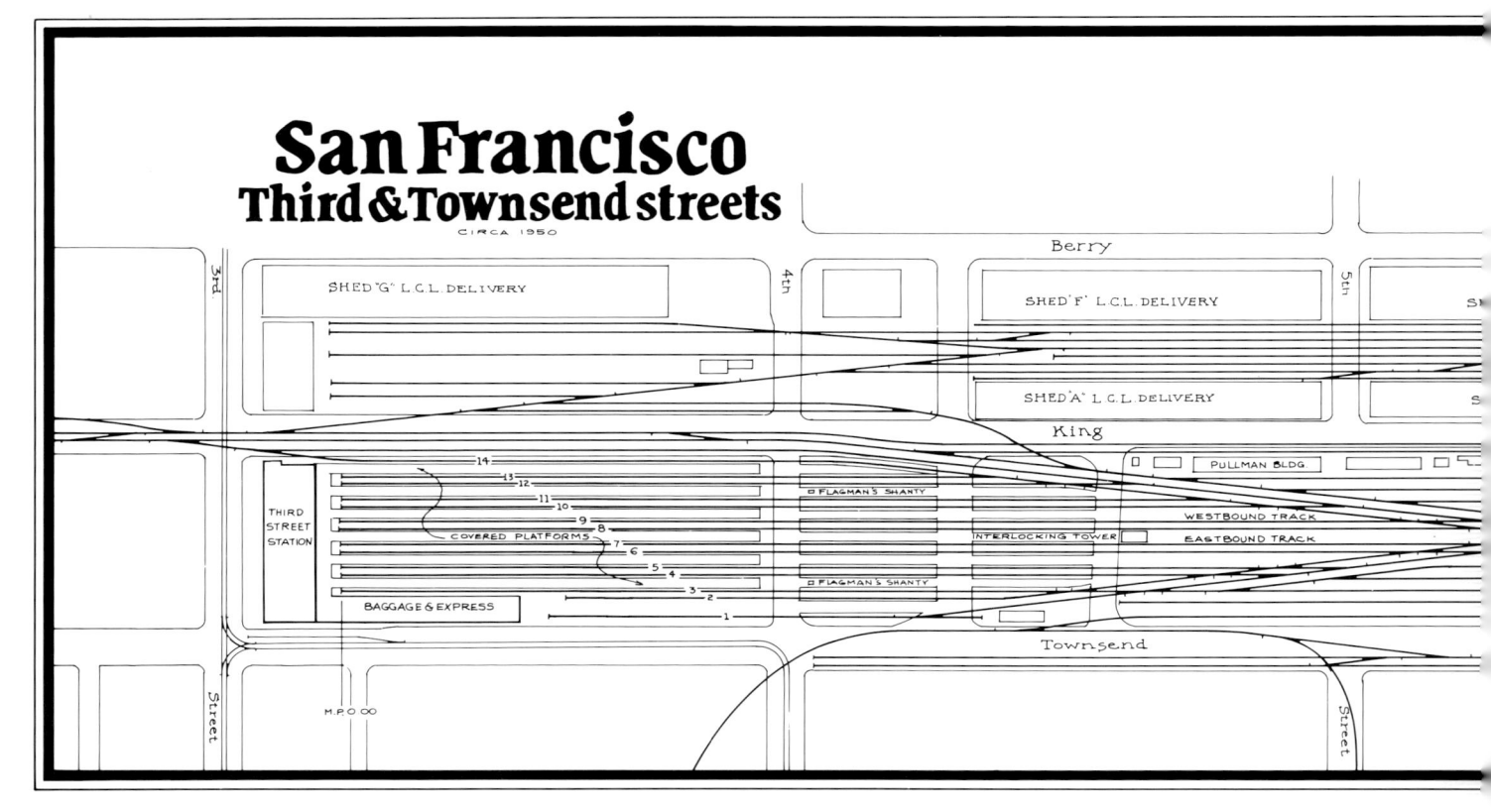

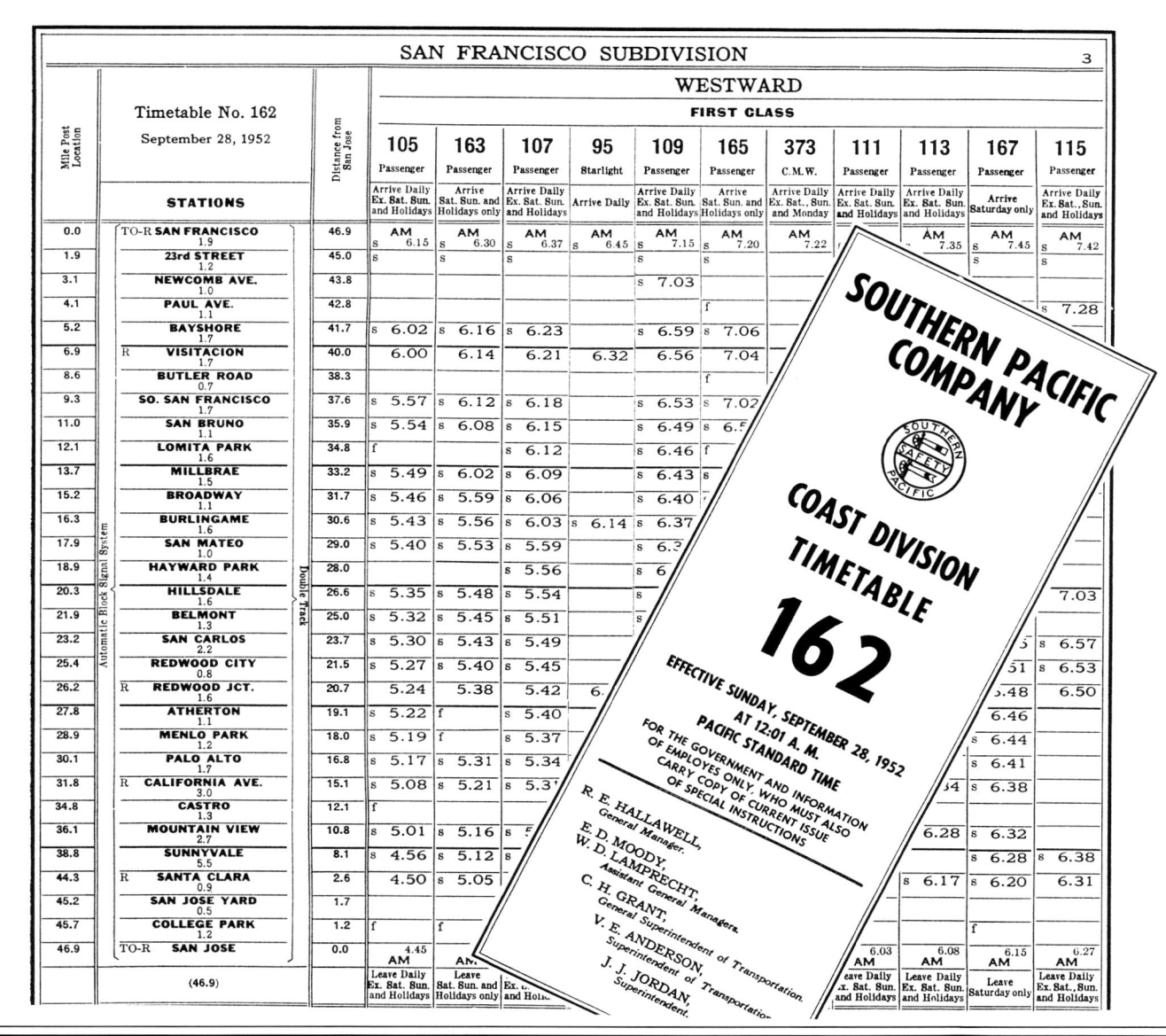

SAN FRANCISCO SUBDIVISION

WESTWARD — FIRST CLASS

Timetable No. 162 — September 28, 1952

Mile Post Location	Stations	Distance from San Jose	105 Passenger Arrive Daily Ex. Sat. Sun. and Holidays	163 Passenger Arrive Sat. Sun. and Holidays only	107 Passenger Arrive Daily Ex. Sat. Sun. and Holidays	95 Starlight Arrive Daily	109 Passenger Arrive Daily Ex. Sat. Sun. and Holidays	165 Passenger Arrive Sat. Sun. and Holidays only	373 C.M.W. Arrive Daily Ex. Sat., Sun. and Monday	111 Passenger Arrive Daily Ex. Sat. Sun. and Holidays	113 Passenger Arrive Daily Ex. Sat. Sun. and Holidays	167 Passenger Arrive Saturday only	115 Passenger Arrive Daily Ex. Sat., Sun. and Holidays
0.0	TO-R SAN FRANCISCO	46.9	AM s 6.15	AM s 6.30	AM s 6.37	AM 6.45	AM s 7.15	AM s 7.20	AM 7.22	AM	AM s 7.35	AM s 7.45	AM s 7.42
1.9	23rd STREET	45.0	s	s	s		s	s					s
3.1	NEWCOMB AVE.	43.8					s 7.03						
4.1	PAUL AVE.	42.8					f						s 7.28
5.2	BAYSHORE	41.7	s 6.02	s 6.16	s 6.23		s 6.59	s 7.06					
6.9	R VISITACION	40.0	6.00	6.14	6.21	6.32	6.56	7.04					
8.6	BUTLER ROAD	38.3					f						
9.3	SO. SAN FRANCISCO	37.6	s 5.57	s 6.12	s 6.18		s 6.53	s 7.02					
11.0	SAN BRUNO	35.9	s 5.54	s 6.08	s 6.15		s 6.49	s 6.5					
12.1	LOMITA PARK	34.8	f		s 6.12		s 6.46	f					
13.7	MILLBRAE	33.2	s 5.49	s 6.02	s 6.09		s 6.43						
15.2	BROADWAY	31.7	s 5.46	s 5.59	s 6.06		s 6.40						
16.3	BURLINGAME	30.6	s 5.43	s 5.56	s 6.03	s 6.14	s 6.37						
17.9	SAN MATEO	29.0	s 5.40	s 5.53	s 5.59		s 6.3						
18.9	HAYWARD PARK	28.0			s 5.56		s 6						
20.3	HILLSDALE	26.6	s 5.35	s 5.48	s 5.54		s						7.03
21.9	BELMONT	25.0	s 5.32	s 5.45	s 5.51								
23.2	SAN CARLOS	23.7	s 5.30	s 5.43	s 5.49							s 6.57	
25.4	REDWOOD CITY	21.5	s 5.27	s 5.40	s 5.45							:51	s 6.53
26.2	R REDWOOD JCT.	20.7	5.24	5.38	5.42	6.						:48	6.50
27.8	ATHERTON	19.1	s 5.22	f	s 5.40							6.46	
28.9	MENLO PARK	18.0	s 5.19	f	s 5.37							s 6.44	
30.1	PALO ALTO	16.8	s 5.17	s 5.31	s 5.34							s 6.41	
31.8	R CALIFORNIA AVE.	15.1	s 5.08	s 5.21	s 5.3					:4		6.38	
34.8	CASTRO	12.1	f										
36.1	MOUNTAIN VIEW	10.8	s 5.01	s 5.16	s 5.						6.28	s 6.32	
38.8	SUNNYVALE	8.1	s 4.56	s 5.12	s							s 6.28	s 6.38
44.3	R SANTA CLARA	2.6	4.50	5.05							s 6.17	s 6.20	6.31
45.2	SAN JOSE YARD	1.7											
45.7	COLLEGE PARK	1.2	f	f							f		
46.9	TO-R SAN JOSE	0.0	4.45 AM Leave Daily Ex. Sat. Sun. and Holidays	AM Leave Sat. Sun. and Holidays only	Ex. and Hol		6.03 AM eave Daily x. Sat. Sun. and Holidays	6.08 AM Leave Daily Ex. Sat. Sun. and Holidays	6.15 AM Leave Saturday only	6.27 AM Leave Daily Ex. Sat. Sun. and Holidays			

(46.9)

Automatic Block Signal System — Double Track

SOUTHERN PACIFIC COMPANY

COAST DIVISION TIMETABLE

162

EFFECTIVE SUNDAY, SEPTEMBER 28, 1952 AT 12:01 A.M. PACIFIC STANDARD TIME

FOR THE GOVERNMENT AND INFORMATION OF EMPLOYEES ONLY, WHO MUST ALSO CARRY COPY OF CURRENT ISSUE OF SPECIAL INSTRUCTIONS

R. E. HALLAWELL, General Manager.
E. D. MOODY,
W. D. LAMPRECHT, Assistant General Managers.
C. H. GRANT, General Superintendent of Transportation.
V. E. ANDERSON, Superintendent of Transportation.
J. J. JORDAN, Superintendent.

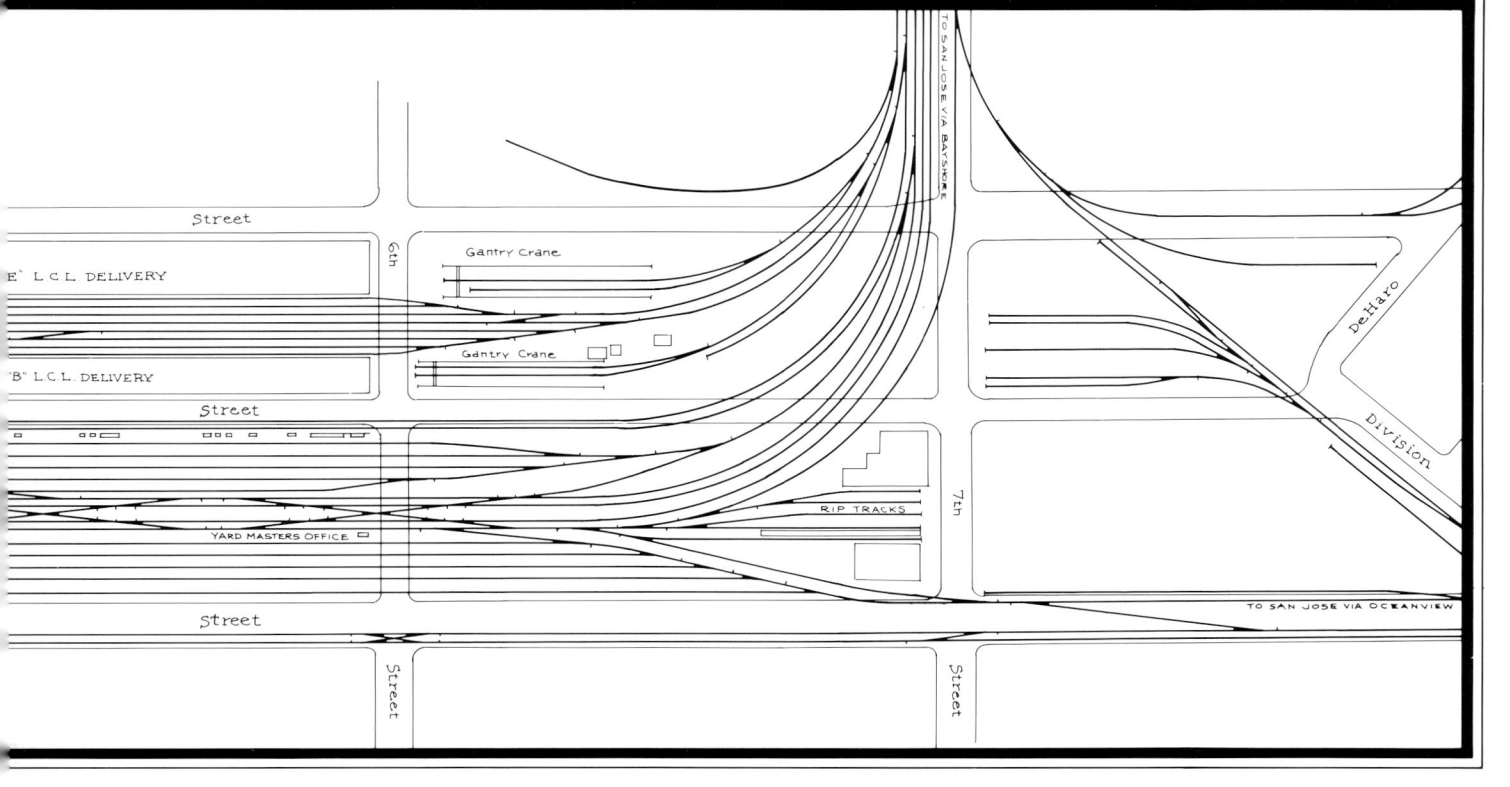

On a Sunday afternoon all is deceptively quiet on the concourse and in the waiting room (**top**) at Third and Townsend station. A lone train (**above**) rolls in from San Jose, stirring the pigeons. But come Monday, the place will once again come alive with activity as the morning "fleet" arrives from the suburbs.
Top, Fred B. Wheeler, Jim Orem collection;
above, Bob Morris

Upstairs in the south wing of the building, unseen by most, the 2nd trick Coast dispatcher goes about his duties in 1959. Primarily a "train order" job, there were some small segments of CTC to deal with. The box on the right controlled the segment between Corporal and Logan. Other controls out of sight handled Watsonville Junction to Salinas. The Cuesta CTC machine was moved to this office in November, 1957.
Bob Morris

The line-up of suburban trains at Third and Townsend terminal in San Francisco, as viewed from 4th Street Tower, was certainly impressive. It was the summer of 1952, a time when 70 regular arrivals and departures were scheduled daily through the interlocking plant and a listing of all these trains took the first nine pages of the Coast Division operating timetable.
Two photos, Southern Pacific Lines

Fog has settled over "Bagdad by the Bay" as the afternoon "fleet" prepares to depart Third and Townsend in December 1963.
Southern Pacific Lines

After February 1960, minor servicing of Coast passenger power was accomplished at 7th and Townsend, not far from the San Francisco passenger terminal. Here Alco PAs called for the Coast Mail prepare to back down to track No. 3 (**left**), while an interesting assortment of power clusters at 7th Street on a rainy afternoon in 1967 (**right**).
Left, Bob Morris; right, Richard E. Buike

182

The silver sides of piggyback trailers gleam in the yard lights (**above**) as a switcher finishes putting the *Coast Merchandise East* together at Mission Bay ramp in March, 1959. Soon the GP9 road power is on (**right**) and the air is tested. Promptly at 7:35 PM, the "highball" is given and engineer W.W. Lewis (**below**) cracks the throttle and another "Zipper" departs San Francisco for a dash down the Coast.

Three photos, Southern Pacific Lines

183

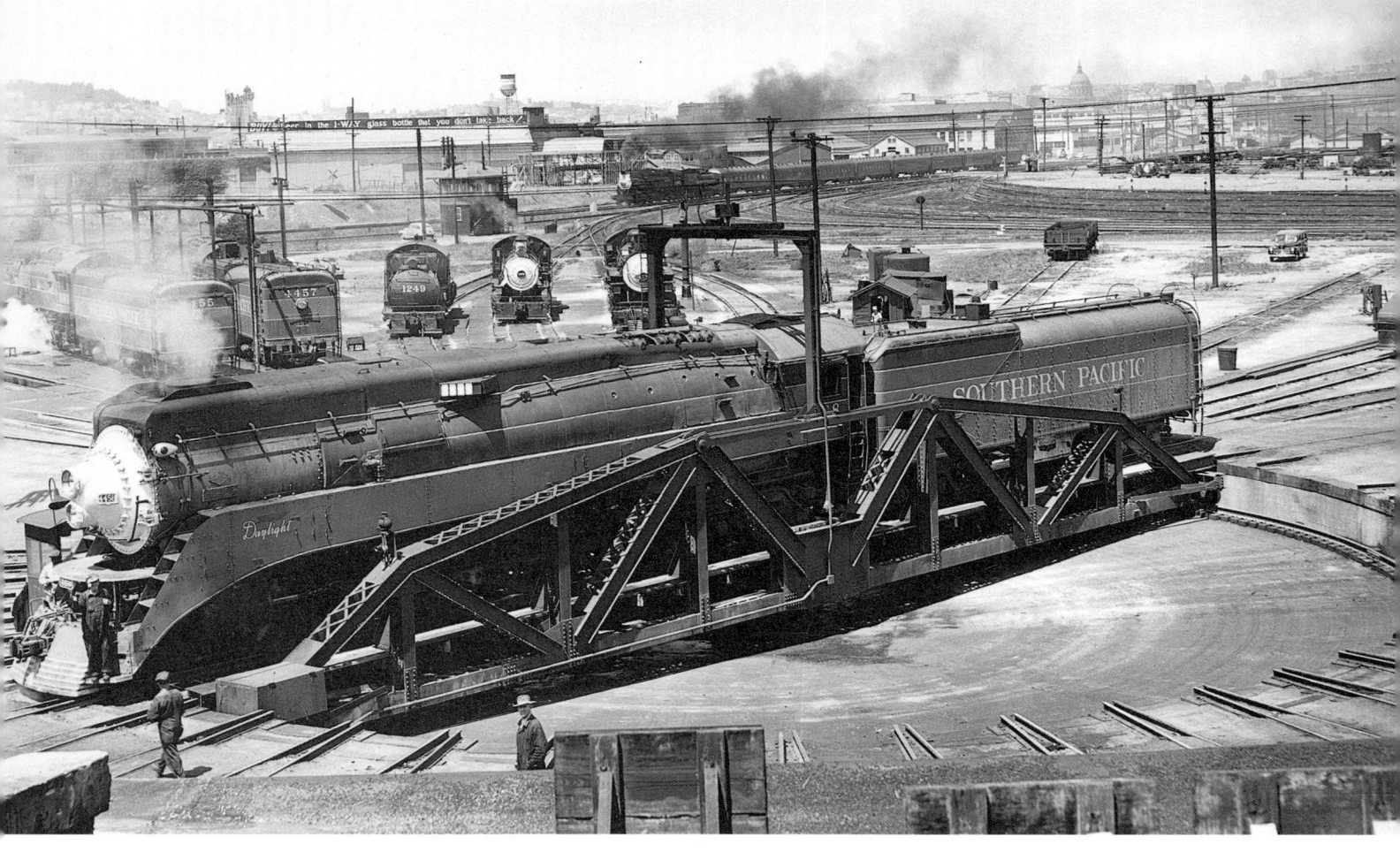

GS-4 No. 4458 takes a spin on the turntable at Mission Bay (**top**) as an outbound train steams past Potrero Tower in the distance. Opened in 1906, the Mission Bay roundhouse was closed on February 27, 1960. Fred Delves (**left**), for many years the roundhouse foreman at Mission Bay, compares time with dapper Road Foreman of Engines Lance Proudfit. The two were on hand (**above**) as engineer Chas. E. Hoppe brought in 1-75 for his last run on June 26, 1950. The man on the right is fireman Harry Price. Stories abound about Proudfit, who was evidently quite the ladies' man; he had a propensity for snapping waitresses' garters–but supposedly he could get away with it!

*Top, Southern Pacific Lines, courtesy Lee Barnett;
above and left, George McCarron collection*

The yards at Mission Bay were developed between 1903 and 1910 in conjunction with the Bayshore Cutoff to service San Francisco's bustling wharves and industrial district. During World War II (**above**) and even as late as 1958 (**right**), the yard hummed with activity. But by 1961, when the *Advance CME* was seen departing south from Mission Bay (**below**), the industrial activity that San Francisco had enjoyed was in decline.

Above, Jim Orem; left and below, Southern Pacific Lines

185

An inbound commuter train clips past the freighter *Aristotelis* (**above**) at the old copra docks on Islais Creek in 1961. A few years earlier, a steam-powered *Lark*, 1-75, rounds the big curve at Sierra Point (**left**) with the gantries and smokestacks of Bethlehem Steel's bridge division forming a backdrop of industrial prosperity. Within a few years, the steel mills would be gone and San Francisco's magnificent wharfage would go unused in reponse to intense competitive pressure from the Port of Oakland and other progressive West Coast shipping centers that were embracing the new technology of containerization.

Above, Bob Morris;
left, Southern Pacific Lines

The Coast Division yard at Bayshore in the post-war era was also a busy place. This view of the west end taken in 1964 from the vantage point of tunnel No. 4 (**above**) gives a general idea of the layout of the Bayshore interlocking, including hand-thrown "puzzle" switches in the center and car and locomotive shops in the right distance. The Bayshore depot was eventually removed and became a shanty for switchmen. The views from the east end (**right**) near Visitacion Cut and of Bayshore roundhouse (**below**) were taken in 1950.

Above, Fred B. Wheeler, Jim Orem collection; right, Southern Pacific Lines; below, Doug Richter

The *Daylight* consist often extended to 4th St. Tower and beyond (**top**), as in this Feb. 9, 1952 photo. The Train Masters from Fairbanks-Morse were synonymous with Peninsula commute service for over 15 years, as exemplified here by No. 3022 heading north out of Palo Alto with train No. 147, just leaving San Francisquito Creek past Palo Alto's namesake tree (**center**).

Top, Jack Whitmeyer; center, John Kirchner

Even before the Train Masters arrived, some Peninsula trains were powered by "passenger" GP9s with steam generators, dual cab controls, pilots, and Mars signal lights. Nos. 5603 and 5601 power train No. 130 on Sept. 15, 1957 (**bottom**), while 5603 and 5602 power a piggyback extra on the Peninsula (**opposite page**) for publicity photos. Note the double-ended "black widow" paint on the passenger Geeps. Eight cabooses (and 300 box cars) were painted in 1956 to complement the PMT trailer paint and lettering.

Bottom, J. Bell collection; opposite page, two photos, Southern Pacific Lines

188

SOUTHERN PACIFIC
5603
SOUTHERN PACIFIC
5602

SOUTHERN PACIFIC
1097
TRAILER-FLATCAR SERVICE
SOUTHERN PACIFIC
TRUCK SERVICE

On April 1, 1946, the old *Overnights* resumed operations, but for scheduling purposes they were now operated as the *Coast Merchandise West* (*CMW*), No. 373, and *Coast Merchandise East* (*CME*), No. 374, between Los Angeles and San Francisco. Here the *CMW* is seen racing up the Peninsula double track near Broadway with 4-8-4 No. 4437 and 23 high-speed merchandise cars in tow (**top**). The merchandise business was a vital part of Coast Line traffic in the post-war era. In 1953, SP introduced piggyback to the Coast Line (initially for PMT trailers only) and the service expanded rapidly. By the summer of 1955, it was necessary to inaugurate the regular run of an advance section of these merchandise trains, running as Nos. 371 and 372. Train No. 372, the *Advance CME*, rounds the curve at Visitacion (**left**) in August, 1955, not long after the inception of service.

Two photos, Southern Pacific Lines

Train No. 69, the *Coaster*, gets underway at Burlingame during the winter of 1948, just prior to its discontinuance, as another train (presumably No. 165) waits in the distance. It's a cold, damp morning and condensation dripping from the stately row of eucalyptus trees adjacent to the main line has deposited oil on the rails, causing the big 4-8-4 to slip. Under the same conditions, speeding southbound commuter trains with scheduled stops at Burlingame have been known to slide on past the station with brakes fully applied.
Southern Pacific Lines

A trainman appears in the vestibule of the rear chair car as train No. 149 approaches Burlingame (**left**) in 1959. While the Peninsula is best known as a high-density passenger corridor, historically it was also for many years the highest-density freight line, in terms of ton-miles, on the SP system. Even in the early 1960s, with the industrial might of San Francisco in sharp decline, a number of freight trains still plied the Peninsula's double track. Here an eastward train moves through Millbrae (**top**) with a long string of rock cars in tow.

Two photos, Bob Morris

192

Darkness has descended on San Jose during a busy weeknight in 1959. The commute fleet power has all been serviced, turned and placed on the ready track (**right**) for the morning call to service. Units needing a bit more attention than fuel and water have been shunted to the six-stall Lenzen Ave. roundhouse (**above**), while out on the running track at Newhall yard in nearby Santa Clara (**below**) the "Zipper" has arrived and is picking up its Oakland fill (cars from the East Bay section of the train).

Three photos, Richard Steinheimer, Southern Pacific Lines

GILROY SUBDIVISION

14 — **EASTWARD** — Timetable No. 162, September 28, 1952

FIRST CLASS

Capacity of sidings in car lengths		76 Lark	374 C. M. E.	94 Starlight	78 Del Monte	98 Morning Daylight	72 Passenger (e)	Mile Post Location	STATIONS	Distance from San Jose
		Leave Daily	Lv. Daily Ex. Fri. Sat. Sun.	Leave Daily	Leave Daily	Leave Daily	Leave Daily			
San Jose yard BKWOITYP	Interlocking	PM 10.15	PM 9.20	PM 8.56	PM 5.06	AM 9.12	AM 1.30	46.9	TO-R SAN JOSE	0.0
	I							49.1	2.2 WPRR Crossing	2.2
	P	10.22	9.27	9.02	5.12	9.18	1.36	51.4 / 55.3	2.3 LICK	4.5
M90	WP	10.31	9.36	9.10	5.20	9.26	c 1.45	63.1	TO 7.8 COYOTE	12.3
125	P	10.36						66.3	3.2 PERRY	15.5
	P						c	69.2	2.9 MADRONE	18.4
121	P	10.41	9.46	9.18	5.28	9.34	s 1.56	70.8	TO 1.6 MORGANHILL	20.0
126	P	10.45				c	2.00	74.6	3.8 SAN MARTIN	23.8
125	P	10.48					2.03	77.0	2.4 RUCKER	26.2
Yard Limits M94	KWTP	10.52	9.57	9.28	s 5.40	9.44	s 2.20	80.7	TO-R 3.7 GILROY	29.9
	P							83.2	2.5 CARNADERO	32.4
	P	10.58	10.07	9.34	5.47	9.50	2.27	86.4	3.2 CORPORAL	35.6
124	WP							87.1	0.7 SARGENT	36.3
123	P						2.36	91.9	4.8 CHITTENDEN	41.1
	P	11.10	10.19	9.45	5.58	10.01	2.39	93.2	1.3 LOGAN	42.4
	P							94.6	TO 1.4 AROMAS	43.8
Watsonville Jct. yard BKWOTYPD		s 11.20 PM	10.29 PM	s 9.56 PM	s 6.08 PM	10.10 AM	s 2.50 AM	100.4	TO-R 5.8 WATSONVILLE JCT. (49.6)	49.6
		Arrive Daily	Ar. Daily Ex. Fri. Sat. Sun.	Arrive Daily	Arrive Daily	Arrive Daily	Arrive Daily			
		(1.05) 45.78	(1.09) 43.13	(1.00) 49.60	(1.02) 48.00	(0.58) 51.31	(1.20) 37.20		Time over District Average Speed per Hour	

Automatic Block Signal System

A passenger extra, powered by Pacific No. 2454, rounds a curve on the Monterey Branch near Pacific Grove on July 13, 1947.
Will Whittaker

GILROY SUBDIVISION

WESTWARD — FIRST CLASS

Timetable No. 162 — September 28, 1952

Mile Post Location	Stations	Distance from Watsonville Jct.	373 C.M.W. Ar. Daily Ex. Sat.Sun.Mon.	95 Starlight Arrive Daily	75 Lark Arrive Daily	77 Del Monte Arrive Daily	71 Passenger (c) Arrive Daily	99 Morning Daylight Arrive Daily
46.9	TO-R SAN JOSE	49.6	AM 5.06	AM s 5.24	AM s 7.20	AM s 9.25	PM s 3.20	PM s 4.58
49.1	WPRR Crossing 2.2	47.4						
51.4 / 55.3	LICK 2.3 / 7.8	45.1	4.58	5.16	7.12	9.18	3.12	4.49
63.1	TO COYOTE 3.2	37.3	4.50	5.08	7.04	9.09	c 3.04	4.42
66.3	PERRY 2.9	34.1	4.46		7.01		3.00	
69.2	MADRONE 1.6	31.2					c	
70.8	TO MORGANHILL 3.8	29.6	4.41	5.01	6.56	9.01	s 2.55	4.35
74.6	SAN MARTIN 2.4	25.8	4.37		6.52		c 2.48	
77.0	RUCKER 3.7	23.4	4.34		6.49		2.45	
80.7	TO-R GILROY 2.5	19.7	4.30	4.51	6.45	s 8.51	s 2.41	4.25
83.2	CARNADERO 3.2	17.2						
86.4	CORPORAL 0.7	14.0	4.23	4.45	6.37	8.44	2.30	4.19
87.1	SARGENT 4.8	13.3						
91.9	CHITTENDEN 1.3	8.5	4.14		6.29			
93.2	LOGAN 1.4	7.2	4.11	4.33	6.26	8.33	2.19	4.08
94.6	TO AROMAS 5.8	5.8					f	
100.4	TO-R WATSONVILLE JCT.	0.0	4.01 AM	4.24 AM	6.15 AM	8.23 AM	2.08 PM	4.00 PM
	(49.6)		Lv. Daily Ex. Sat.Sun.Mon.	Leave Daily	Leave Daily	Leave Daily	Leave Daily	Leave Daily
	Time over District / Average Speed per Hour		(1.05) 45.78	(1.00) 49.60	(1.05) 45.78	(1.02) 48.00	(1.12) 41.33	(0.58) 51.31

RULE 5. Schedule time and train-orders apply at the end of double track at Lick, Coyote, Gilroy, and Logan, except that of eastward trains at Gilroy will apply at train-order signal.

RULE S-72. Exception: No. 98 is superior to Nos. 71, 75, 373, 95 and 77.

RULE 93. First-class trains enter and leave San Jose passenger station on yard tracks between MP 45.91 and MP 47.29.

Timetable No. 162 — September 28, 1952 — Hollister Branch

Capacity of sidings in car lengths	EASTWARD Mile Post Location	STATIONS
P	83.2	CARNADERO
12 WP	94.9	11.7 HOLLISTER
		(11.7)

Train No. 91, the Coast Mail, roars through Chittenden Pass near Logan on August 13, 1960. Up front are five express cars filled with strawberries picked up at Salinas.
Don Hansen

No. 91 pauses at Gilroy to work the mail in 1959 (**top**). Few trains operating on the Coast Line in later years garnered as much nostalgia and genuine affection as Nos. 90 and 91, nicknamed "Sad Sam." The views on this and the opposite page depict this Coast legend on a typical run, June 7, 1956. Departing track No. 3 at Third and Townsend at 12:20 AM, train No. 90 is under the skillful control of engineer John Pospich (**below, left**). Although capable of 70 mph, nearly half of No. 90's sixteen hour and ten minute schedule is spent standing at stations loading or unloading mail. The first stop is 35 minutes at San Jose (**right**) where cars from Oakland are added by a steam switcher. Once underway again, conductor Clyde Davis (**below, right**) has time to enjoy a donut and a cup of coffee.

Top, Bob Morris; all others, Southern Pacific Lines

Rear brakeman Joe Quinlan lines behind at Coyote (**top**) as No. 90 takes the center siding for No. 371, the *Advance Coast Merchandise West*. Inside the head-end cars, TBM (train baggage man) Pat Ryan (**center, left**) works company mail, while Ed Sheehy (**center, right**) handles cans of milk and cream. No. 90 is running a bit behind its scheduled time of 3:50 AM at Watsonville (**bottom**) as men work the head-end cars in the pink coolness of pre-dawn. Ahead lay 375 miles of railroad and another twelve hours before No. 90 would reach the end of its run.

All, Southern Pacific Lines

No. 98, the *Morning Daylight*, steams across the Pajaro River bridge (**above**) in Chittenden Pass just west of Logan in April, 1945. Fifteen years later, a diesel-powered *Coast Daylight* (**left**) is not doing as well. While stabbed for a freight train "in emergency" up ahead, conductor C.E. Jones confers with fireman Charlie Stumi at Logan on April 13, 1960. The previous July, a block of empty "OK" reefers destined for Salinas Valley packing sheds (**below**) rolls past the Granite Rock quarry complex at Logan, powered by a single SD9.

Above, Southern Pacific Lines;
left and below, Don Hansen

On this page are views of Salinas Valley beet harvesting activities during the 1948 campaign. A 2-10-2 assigned to a beet "hauler" steams north (**top**), trailing a mixed consist of new composite gondolas and older flat cars fitted with wooden "racks." Even though the gondolas soon completely replaced the "beet racks," the name stuck for cars assigned to the service. The same job works Union Sugar's beet "dump" at Cooper (**right** and **below**), near Salinas, one of many strung out along the Coast Line. In the valley, during the beet season between August and October, "haulers" were operated out of Salinas to Camphora/King City and out of Watsonville Junction to San Jose and Gilroy.

All, Southern Pacific Lines

SANTA MARGARITA SUBDIVISION

EASTWARD

Timetable No. 162 — September 28, 1952

Capacity of sidings in car lengths		SECOND CLASS 922 Freight Leave Daily	SECOND CLASS 920 Freight Leave Daily	SECOND CLASS 924 Freight Leave Daily	FIRST CLASS 374 C.M.E. Lv. Daily Ex. Fri. Sat. Sun.	FIRST CLASS 94 Starlight Leave Daily	FIRST CLASS 98 Morning Daylight Leave Daily	FIRST CLASS 72 Passenger (c) Leave Daily	FIRST CLASS 76 Lark Leave Daily	Mile Post Location	STATIONS	Distance from King City
108 Yard Limits	KWOP	PM 4.40	AM 7.45	AM 1.10	PM 11.59	PM 11.20	AM 11.20	AM 5.25	AM 12.50	163.7	TO-R **KING CITY**	0.0
71	P									167.1	3.4 **WELBY**	3.4
101	P	4.52	7.57	1.22	AM 12.09	11.29	11.28	s 5.35	12.59	172.4	5.3 TO **SAN LUCAS**	8.7
40	P									177.7	5.3 **DOCAS**	14.0
118	WP	5.06	8.11	1.36	12.20	11.38	11.37	s 5.58	1.11	182.9	5.2 TO **SAN ARDO**	19.2
40	P						11.40			186.4	3.5 **GETTY**	22.7
103	P	5.15	8.20	2.00	12.27	11.45	11.44	6.08	1.19	189.7	3.3 **WUNPOST**	26.0
105	P	5.24	8.29	2.09	12.35	PM 11.54	11.52	s 6.18	1.28	195.9	6.2 **BRADLEY**	32.2
64	P									201.4	5.5 **NACIMIENTO**	37.7
No.1-102 No.2-77	P	5.34	8.39	2.22	12.44	AM 12.02	NOON 12.00	6.27	1.43	203.8	2.4 **McKAY**	40.1
33	WP	5.38	8.43	2.26				s 6.35		207.0	3.2 TO **SAN MIGUEL**	43.3
97	P	5.43	8.48	2.31	12.52	12.10	PM 12.07	6.41	1.57	210.9	3.9 **WELLSONA**	47.2
54	P	5.50	8.55	2.38	12.58	c 12.19		s 7.00	2.04	216.3	5.4 TO **PASO ROBLES**	52.6
96	P	5.57	9.02	2.45	1.04	12.27	12.19	s 7.10	2.10	221.8	5.5 **TEMPLETON**	58.1
28	P									224.9	3.1 **ASUNCION**	61.2
	P							s 7.18		226.7	1.8 TO **ATASCADERO**	63.0
114	P	6.05	9.10	2.53	1.16	12.35	12.26	7.20	2.19	228.0	1.3 **HENRY**	64.3
64	P	6.08	9.13	2.56						230.3	2.3 **EAGLET**	66.6
121	P	6.12	9.17	3.00	1.25	12.42	12.33	7.27	2.26	233.4	3.1 **CUSHING**	69.7
No.1-115 Yard Limits No.2-126	BKWYP	6.25	9.30	3.21	1.30	12.46	12.36	s 7.32	2.31	235.5	2.1 **SANTA MARGARITA**	71.8
127	P									238.9	3.4 **CUESTA**	75.2
171	WP							c		243.4	4.5 **SERRANO**	79.7
104	P									246.3	2.9 **CHORRO**	82.6
36	YP									248.0	1.7 **GOLDTREE**	84.3
S.L.O. yard 99	P									250.6	2.6 **HATHAWAY**	86.9
	BKWOTYP	7.25 PM	10.30 AM	4.00 AM	2.30 AM	s 1.27 AM	s 1.17 PM	s 8.15 AM	s 3.12 AM	252.1	1.5 TO-R **SAN LUIS OBISPO**	88.4
		Arrive Daily	Arrive Daily	Arrive Daily	Ar. Daily Ex. Sat. Sun. Mon.	Arrive Daily	Arrive Daily	Arrive Daily	Arrive Daily		(88.4)	
		(2.45) 32.15	(2.45) 32.15	(2.50) 31.20	(2.31) 35.13	(2.07) 44.20	(1.57) 45.33	(2.55) 30.31	(2.22) 37.33		Time over District / Average Speed per Hour	

Automatic Block Signal System / Centralized Traffic Control

The Southern Pacific station at Paso Robles, completed in January 1887, is holding up well at 52 in this October, 1939 view. As of this writing, the station still stands and is used as a maintenance-of-way base.
Robert H. McFarland photo, Arnold S. Menke collection

SANTA MARGARITA SUBDIVISION

WESTWARD

Mile Post Location	Timetable No. 162 September 28, 1952 STATIONS	Station Number	Distance from San Luis Obispo	FIRST CLASS 373 C.M.W. Ar. Daily Ex. Sat.Sun.Mon.	95 Starlight Arrive Daily	75 Lark Arrive Daily	71 Passenger (e) Arrive Daily	99 Morning Daylight Arrive Daily		THIRD CLASS 919 Freight Arrive Daily	921 Freight Arrive Daily	923 Freight Arrive Daily
163.7	TO-R KING CITY 3.4	160	88.4	AM 2.29	AM 3.05	AM c 4.45	PM s 12.17	PM 2.48		AM 6.25	PM 1.40	PM 9.34
167.1	WELBY 5.3	163	85.0				12.12					
172.4	TO SAN LUCAS 5.3	169	79.7	2.19	2.56	4.34	s 12.05 PM	2.40		6.11	1.27	9.15
177.7	DOCAS 5.2	174	74.4									
182.9	TO SAN ARDO 3.5	179	69.2	2.08	2.47	4.23	s 11.50 AM	2.31		5.58	1.14	9.02
186.4	GETTY 3.3	183	65.7				11.40					
189.7	WUNPOST 6.2	186	62.4	2.00	2.39	4.16	11.25	2.24		5.48	1.04	8.52
195.9	BRADLEY 5.5	192	56.2	1.52	2.31	4.08	s 11.17	2.17		5.38	12.54	8.43
201.4	NACIMIENTO 2.4	198	50.7									
203.8	McKAY 3.2	200	48.3	1.43	2.22	3.59	11.05	2.08		5.28	12.44	8.33
207.0	TO SAN MIGUEL 3.9	203	45.1			3.55	s 11.00			5.23	12.39	8.28
210.9	WELLSONA 5.4	207	41.2	1.35	2.14	3.51	10.52	2.01		5.18	12.34	8.23
216.3	TO PASO ROBLES 5.5	212	35.8	1.29	c 2.04	3.45	s 10.46			5.11	12.27	8.16
221.8	TEMPLETON 3.1	218	30.3	1.23	1.48	3.38	s 10.36	1.50		5.03	12.19	8.08
224.9	ASUNCION 1.8	221	27.2									
226.7	TO ATASCADERO 1.3	223	25.4				s 10.29					
228.0	HENRY 2.3	224	24.1	1.16	1.40	3.32	10.23	1.43		4.55	12.11	8.00
230.3	EAGLET 3.1	226	21.8			3.28	10.20			4.52	12.08	7.57
233.4	CUSHING 2.1	230	18.7	1.10	1.33	3.24	10.16	1.37		4.47	12.03 PM	7.52
235.5	TO SANTA MARGARITA 3.4	232	16.6	1.07	1.30	3.21	s 10.13	1.34		4.42	11.58 AM	7.47
238.9	CUESTA 4.5	235	13.2									
243.4	SERRANO 2.9	240	8.7				c					
246.3	CHORRO 1.7	242	5.8				c					
248.0	GOLDTREE 2.6	244	4.1									
250.6	HATHAWAY 1.5	247	1.5									
252.1	TO-R SAN LUIS OBISPO	248	0.0	12.20 AM	12.45 AM	2.35 AM	9.30 AM	12.53 PM		3.30 AM	10.45 AM	6.35 PM
	(88.4)			Lv. Daily Ex. Sat.Sun.Mon.	Leave Daily	Leave Daily	Leave Daily	Leave Daily		Leave Daily	Leave Daily	Leave Daily
	Time over District Average Speed per Hour			(2.09) 41.22	(2.20) 37.89	(2.10) 40.80	(2.47) 31.76	(1.55) 46.12		(2.55) 30.31	(2.55) 30.31	(2.59) 29.63

RULE 5. Schedule time and train-orders apply at McKay at No. 1 siding, and at San Miguel westward at crossover west of station building.

Schedule time and train-orders for westward trains at Santa Margarita apply at west switch, No. 2 siding, and for eastward trains at station building.

RULE S-72. Exception: No. 98 is superior to Nos. 71, 75, 373, 95 and 99.

GUADALUPE SUBDIVISION

EASTWARD Capacity of sidings in car lengths	Mile Post Location	Timetable No. 162 September 28, 1952 Lompoc and White Hills Branches STATIONS	Station Number	Distance from White Hills	WESTWARD THIRD CLASS 925 Freight Arrive Daily
Yard Limits WOYP	302.7	TO SURF 1.1	299	14.0	AM 10.30
26	303.8	BARODA 3.8	1301	12.9	
17	307.6	POST 2.2	1305	9.1	
5	309.8	ACORN 2.6	1307	6.9	
BKWP	312.4	TO-R LOMPOC 0.5	1310	4.3	10.00 AM
	312.9	WHITE HILLS JCT. 3.8	1311	3.8	
Yd.Lmts.	316.7	WHITE HILLS (14.0)	1314	0.0	Leave Daily

As these Santa Margarita Subdivision timetable pages illustrate, there were a number of scheduled freight trains in the early 1950s, listed either as second or third class. Additional tonnage usually moved as sections of these scheduled trains, or sometimes as extras. At some terminals such as San Luis Obispo, a scheduled freight would terminate. This meant that its cars would be distributed among subsequent schedules and local trains (which ran extra).

The Golden Gate Manifest or *GGM*, running as 1-915, rolls through the upper Salinas Valley (**top**) between San Lucas and San Ardo on a warm summer day on 1955. Displaying green flags for the following section is a rather worn-looking GS-4. Bumped from the varnish, the Coast Line was the last stand for SP's most modern steam locomotives.

Top, Fred Wheeler, Jim Orem collection

The *WCP*, the "West (northbound) Coast Peddler," pauses for water at the San Miguel tanks (**center**) in July, 1953. In a few short years, the steam engine, the tanks and the importance of San Miguel itself would fade into history. But further up the line, Paso Robles continued to serve as an important point for Coast Line operations. Here the East Coast Peddler or *ECP* rolls through town on August 16, 1962 behind a dusty string of first-generation diesel hood units (**bottom**).

Center, Jack Williams photo, George McCarron collection; bottom, Don Hansen

On April 30, 1950, a manifest train operating as 1-915 and powered by AC No. 4184 pauses to take on water at Santa Margarita (**top**) after surmounting Cuesta Grade. Its pops blowing, the 2-10-2 which helped 1-915 over Cuesta has already turned on the wye in the distance. The train order signal has one blade, for westward movement only, as eastward territory is controlled by the CTC dispatcher. Before CTC came in 1942, there were two blades (**right**). A few years later, in December, 1954, four EMD F7s are about to uncouple from the northbound *Daylight* at Santa Margarita after helping the still steam-powered streamliner over the grade (**bottom**). Diesels powered all *Daylights* after January 7, 1955.

Top, Al Phelps; right, Robert H. McFarland, Arnold S. Menke collection; below, Art Laidlaw

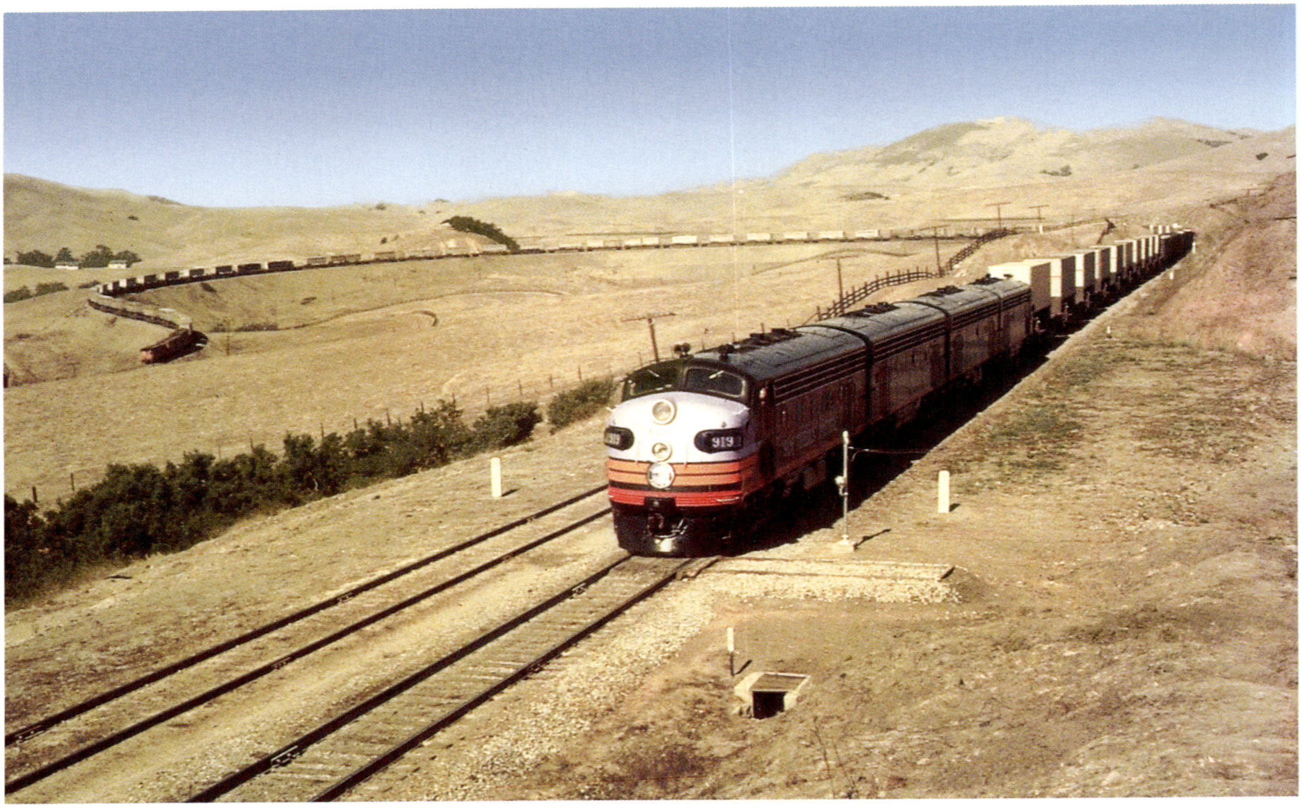

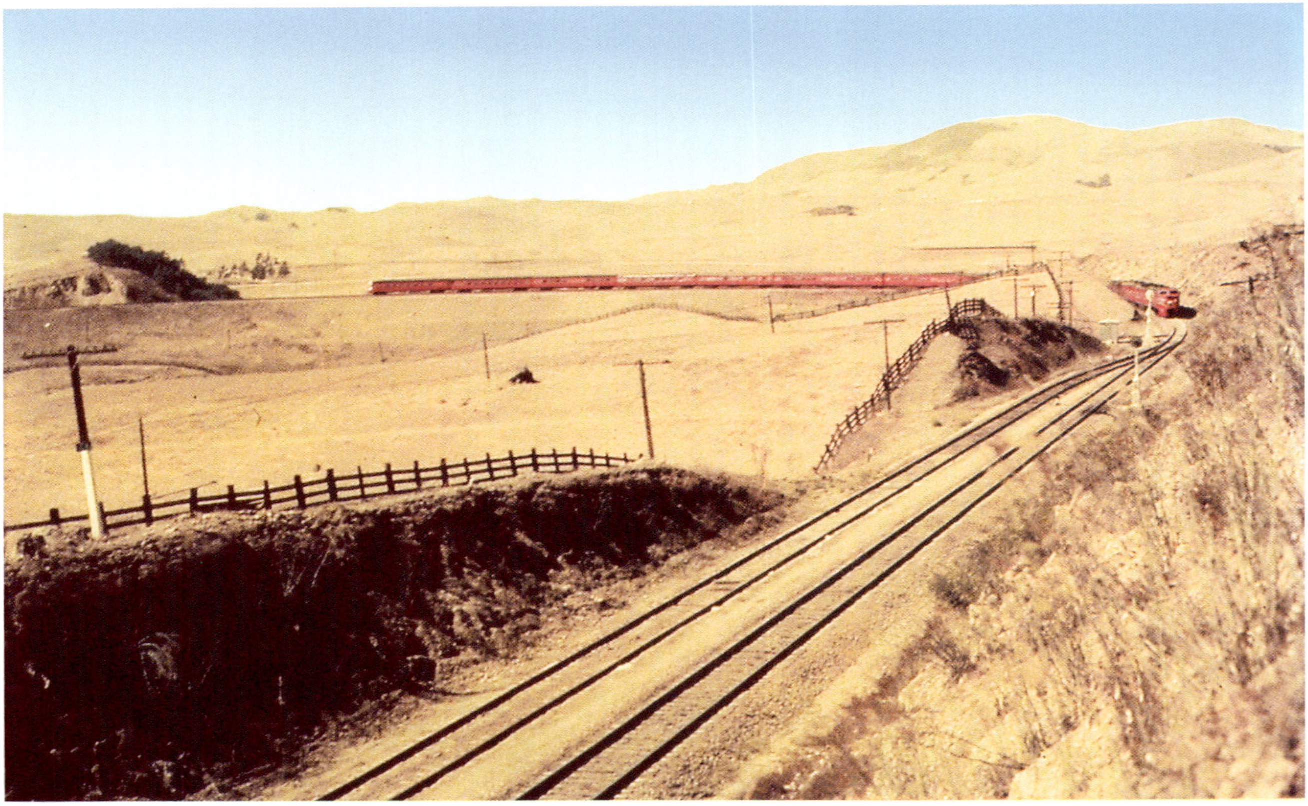

Included on these pages are parts of a series of photos made in 1957 by a company photographer, taken at Chorro siding above Horseshoe Curve. The first train seen is No. 919, led by EMD F3 No. 6146, with a solid consist of PMT trailers on flat cars (**opposite, top**), assembled for publicity purposes. A bit later, No. 99, the *Daylight*, moves up the hill behind Alco PAs (**opposite, bottom**). Next, an eastward beet train behind GP9s takes the siding, and the reason is soon obvious (**above**): opposing train No. 2-921, nearly filled with PFE refrigerator cars, is moving westward, also pulled by GP9s. As the reefers pass, the beet train's Geeps rev up under a cloud of smoke (**right**), ready to move into San Luis Obispo on their way to Betteravia.

All, negative series N-4072 and N-5319, Southern Pacific Lines

Twelve years later, all is dieselized as train 2-920 approaches the west portal of tunnel No. 6 at Cuesta on March 31, 1962. Despite the impressive string of six Alco RS-11s up front, the second section of 920 still required a two-unit helper to achieve the summit this day (**left**).
Left, Don Hansen

From the vantage point of an open vestibule door, one could watch train No. 98 slip downgrade (**below**) through Serrano in December, 1953, with GS No. 4457 and a three-unit point helper.
Below, Jack Seeback

As seen from the siding at Chorro, train No. 99 charges upgrade over the Stenner Creek Viaduct (**above**) in March, 1953. A few moments later, the train takes the siding at Chorro (**right**) for its southbound counterpart. Being in CTC territory, this was not a scheduled meet, but the two trains frequently met on the Cuesta Grade, and more often than not at Chorro.

Two photos, Art Laidlaw

Helpers are added to the point of No. 71 during the 30-minute station stop at San Luis Obispo (**top**) in 1953, as perennial San Luis Obispo Consolidation No. 2829 switches the yard. The mail train didn't attract much of a crowd at the depot (**left**), as this view from 1962 would demonstrate. But for those interested in railway operations, the west end of San Luis Obispo was a fascinating place to spend some time. Here Alco S-4 switcher No. 1466 pulls a cut of cars, including the ever-present PFE reefers, in 1955 (**bottom**).

Top, Richard Steinheimer photo, DeGolyer Library collection; left, Ed Workman; below, Southern Pacific Lines

During the early 1950s, the Coast Mail trains were scheduled to arrive at San Luis Obispo in the early morning. No. 71, here receiving F7 helpers (**above**), was due at 9:10 AM, and No. 72 an hour earlier. But on a morning when No. 72 was running an hour and a half late (**right**), No. 71 was ready to depart as soon as No. 72 cleared the west switch.

*Above, Art Laidlaw;
right, Donald Duke*

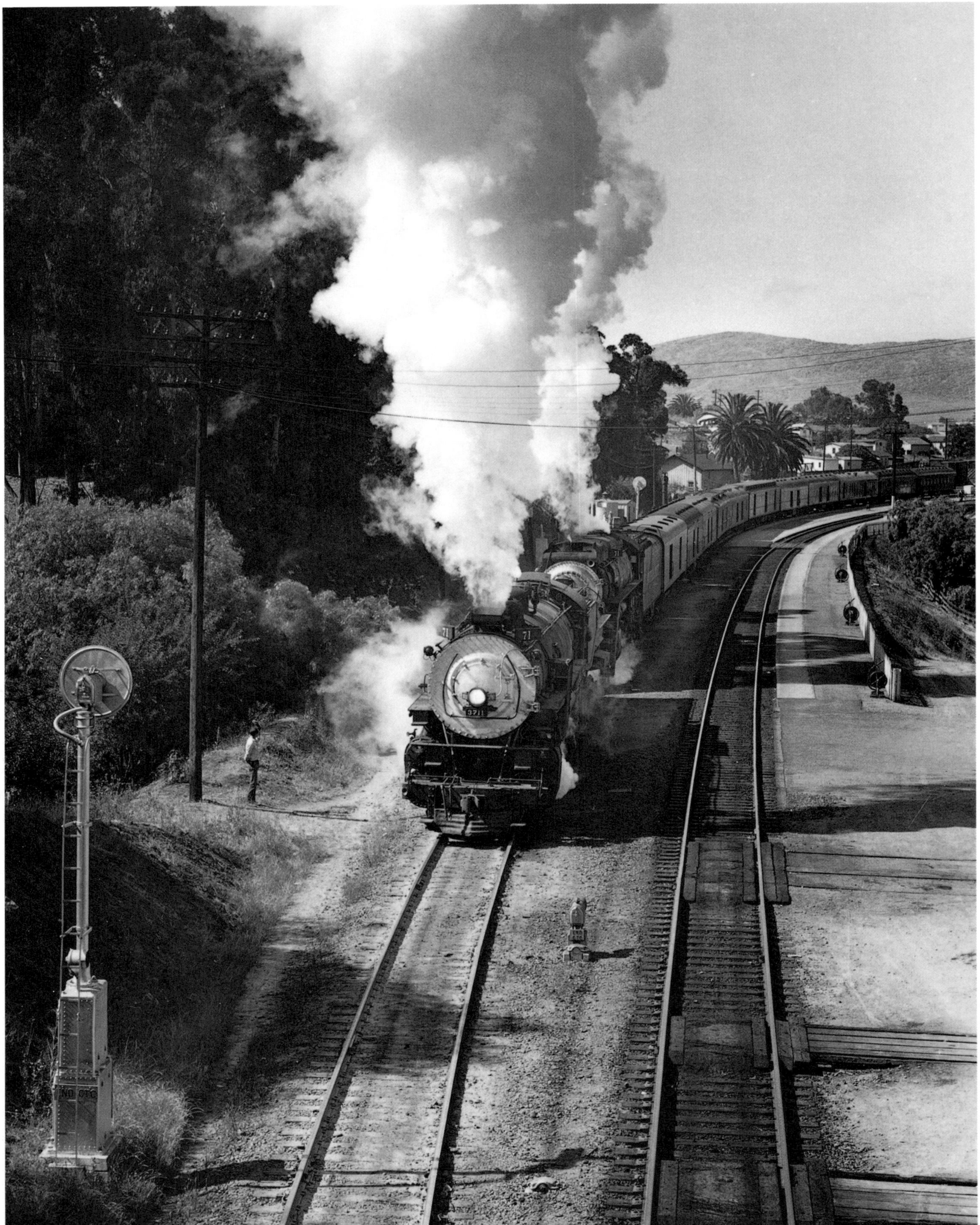
71
71

With its counterpart in the clear, No. 71 charges out of town (**left** and **above**), under a canopy of steam condensing in the cool marine air. The year is 1954, and the end of steam is near. By 1962, all is dieselized and the departure of a westward manifest from the east switch at Hathaway (**right**) is marked by an even more impressive cloud of diesel exhaust. Fairbanks-Morse locomotives, such as this goat (**below**) assigned to San Luis Obispo in 1962, were also known for excessive smoke.

Above and left, Donald Duke;
right and below, Ed Workman

216

For many years, Osos Street passed directly through the San Luis Obispo yards just south of the express office. Though not common on the Coast, F3 diesels congregate at Osos Street (**top left, top right**) in 1951. The other two photos on these pages depict activity at Osos Street crossing in the summer of 1953. In a view taken from the caboose track, freight 919 behind AC No. 4280 is about to precede the King City Local, behind 2-8-2 No. 3251 at the far left of the photo, out of San Luis Obispo (**bottom, left**). Long-time Coast engineer and historian George McCarron held this King City job for years and had a special whistle fitted to this engine and on alternate 2-8-2 No. 3264. Another departing King City Local behind Consolidation No. 2824 and 2-10-2 helper No. 3711 (**bottom, right**) passes yard goat No. 1491, a Fairbanks-Morse H-12-44. Osos Street crossing was closed to through traffic on June 12, 1956.

Top left and right, Fred Wheeler photos, collection Jim Orem; bottom left and right, Malcolm Gaddis

217

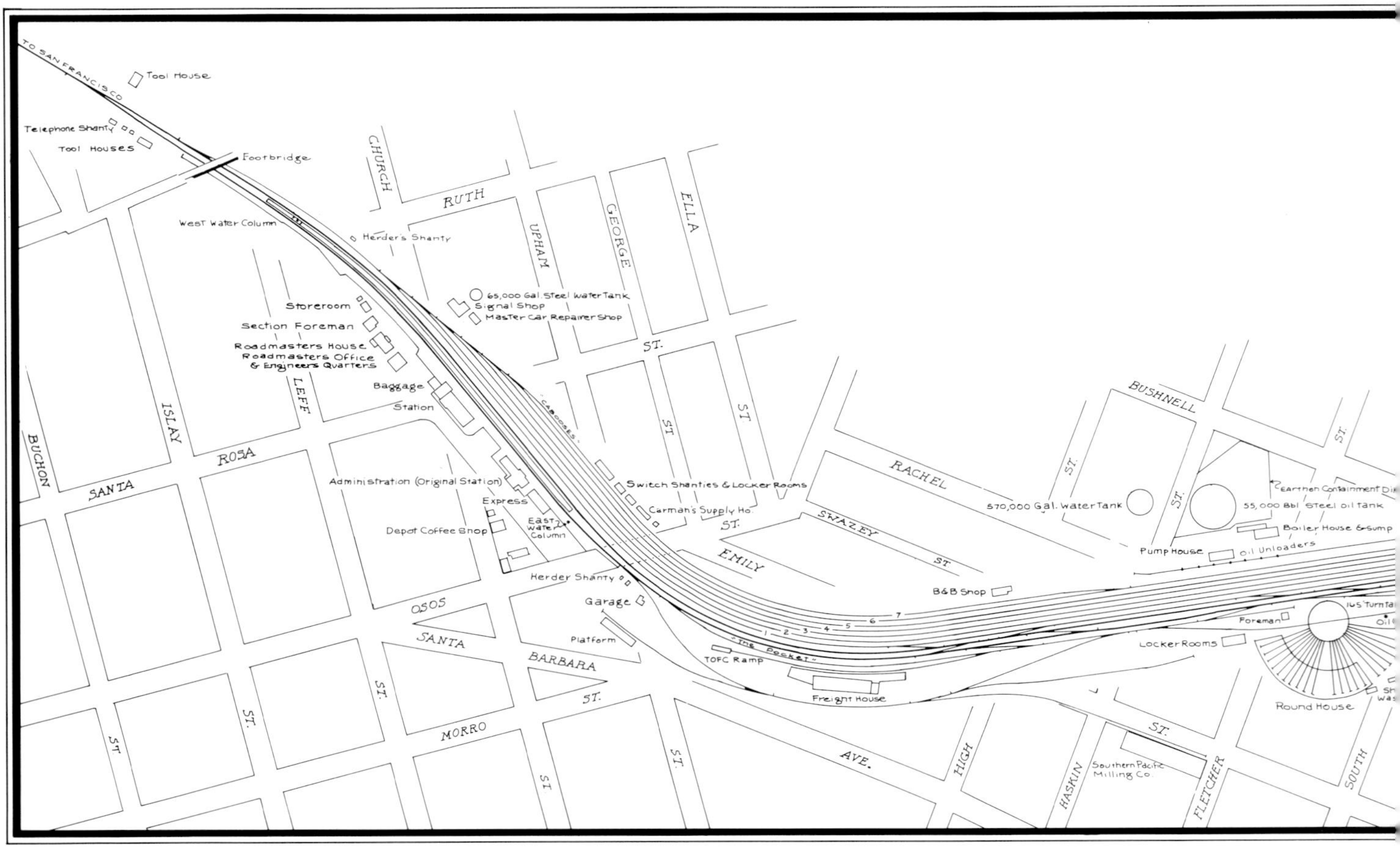
TO SAN FRANCISCO
Tool House
Telephone Shanty
Tool Houses
Footbridge
CHURCH
RUTH
UPHAM
GEORGE
ELLA
West Water Column
Herder's Shanty
65,000 Gal. Steel Water Tank
Signal Shop
Master Car Repairer Shop
Storeroom
Section Foreman
Roadmasters House
Roadmasters Office
& Engineers Quarters
Baggage
Station
ISLAY
LEFF
ST.
CABOOSES
BUCHON
SANTA
ROSA
Administration (Original Station)
Express
Depot Coffee Shop
East Water Column
Switch Shanties & Locker Rooms
Carman's Supply Ho.
EMILY
SWAZEY
RACHEL
BUSHNELL
570,000 Gal. Water Tank
Earthen Containment Dike
55,000 Bbl Steel oil tank
Boiler House & Sump
Pump House
Oil Unloaders
B&B Shop
Herder Shanty
Garage
OSOS
SANTA
BARBARA
Platform
The Pocket
TOFC Ramp
Freight House
Foreman
Locker Rooms
Round House
MORRO
AVE.
HIGH
HASKIN
Southern Pacific
Milling Co.
FLETCHER
SOUTH
1
2
3
4
5
6
7

On an overcast day in 1955, Art Laidlaw ascended Terrace Hill to record these views of San Luis Obispo on the eve of total dieselization. The section quarters are in the foreground as a yard engine weighs cars on the scale track and a handful of steam engines populate the engine facilities in the distance (**left**). Huge black fuel tanks dominate the view to the northwest, as an AC moves west toward three EMD E units near the freight house (**above**).

Two photos, Art Laidlaw

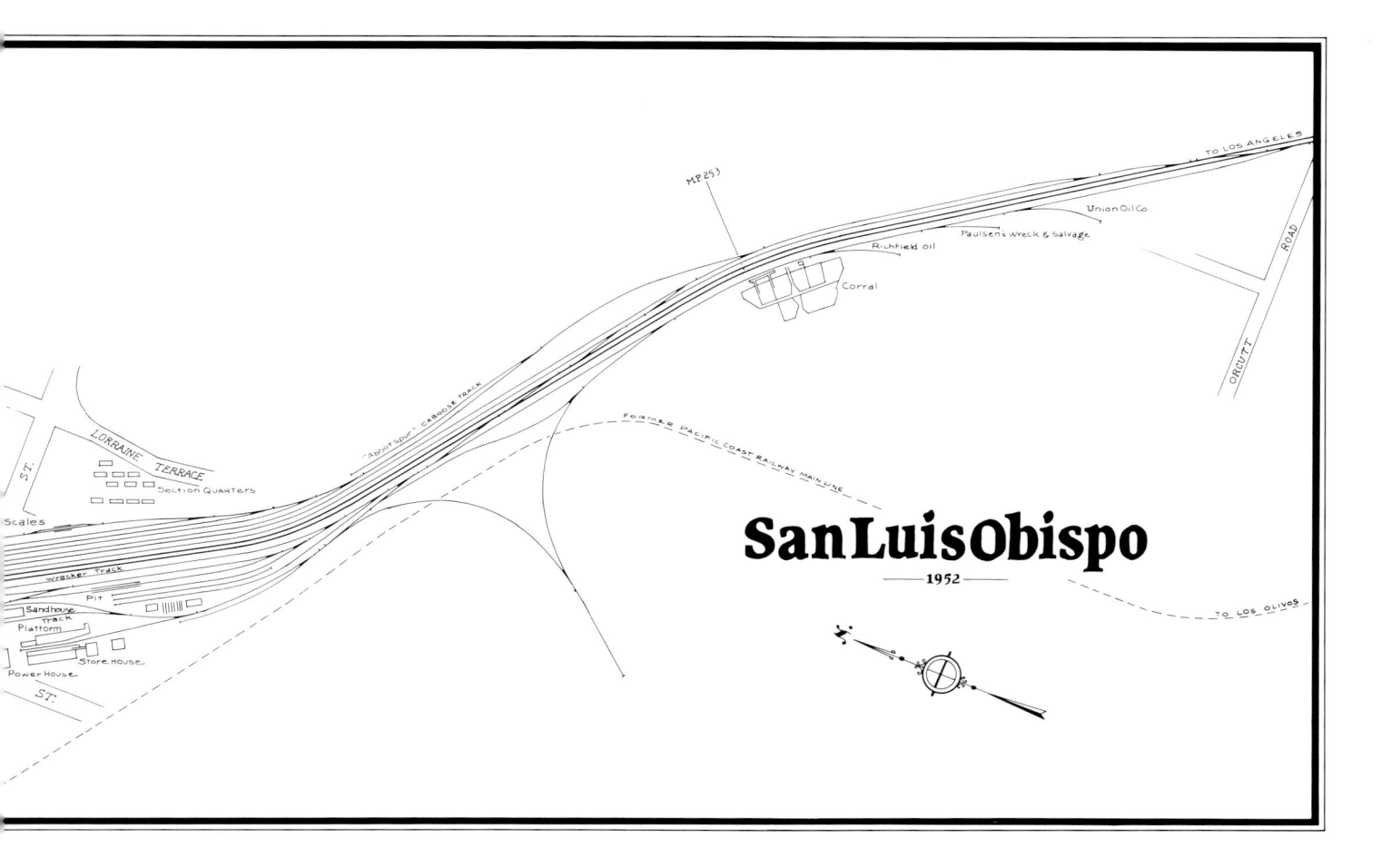

During 1953, when diesels were spreading over other divisions on a large scale, steam still ruled the Coast Line. That year, Ten Wheeler No. 2344 (**top**) rests quietly in the roundhouse at San Luis Obispo, while outside (**center**), on November 16, 1953, steam is still king.
*Top, George McCarron;
below, Malcolm Gaddis*

Not only was steam still king on the Coast, but locomotives formerly assigned to other districts, like the massive AC cab-forwards, now came to the Coast in unprecedented numbers. Witness this AC No. 4282 (**left**) moving onto the turntable at San Luis Obispo in 1954, while in the distance two more ACs steam quietly. Too long for the San Luis turntable, the ACs turned at the wye (**opposite, below**) which was built at east San Luis Obispo to accommodate the Mallet Moguls during their assignment to the Coast Line (see p. 118).
Left, Richard Steinheimer photo, DeGolyer Library; opposite below, Art Laidlaw

220

For a short time in 1953, EMD E7s assigned to the *Sunset Limited* would run up the Coast at night with the *Lark*. Once in San Luis, the E7s were traded for two GS engines which would continue north, and the EMDs would return to Los Angeles on No. 76 in time to depart on the *Sunset Limited* or the *Golden State*. Timing was critical to this plan, however, and incidents like this derailment (**top**) on August 24th, affected not only the *Larks* but Sunset Route schedules as well. The practice was soon discontinued. EMD SD7 No. 5289 (**right**), less than four months old in February 1953, and twin 5288 were ballasted by the builder with 15 extra tons of concrete in the frames for Cuesta helper service. It made little difference in practice.

Top and right, Malcolm Gaddis

221

Making a run for Casmalia Hill, the *Coast Daylight* thunders through Guadalupe (**top**) at full speed in 1958. Though an important operating point on the Coast Line, and gateway to the beet sugar refinery at Betteravia served by the Santa Maria Valley Railroad, Guadalupe was not important enough for the *Daylight* to stop. EMD E units were commonly assigned to Nos. 98 and 99, but Alco PA units (often, as here, with E7-Bs) were sometimes used. This view of the Guadalupe combination station building (**right**) dates from June 20, 1938.

Top, Jim Orem; right, Southern Pacific Lines photo, collection Benny Romano

Two views of Casmalia Hill ten years apart depict a troop train operating as a second section of No. 99 (**top**) during the summer of 1954, and No. 99 itself (**right**) rounding a curve at Casmalia in 1964. It was after passing this point that the Coast Line threaded Schumann Canyon (though SP's station was named Shuman) and first emerged on the sand dunes above the Pacific Ocean at Narlon, to began its uninterrupted 107-mile run down the coast of Santa Barbara and Ventura counties.

Both, Richard Steinheimer, Southern Pacific Lines collection

223

GUADALUPE SUBDIVISION

EASTWARD

Timetable No. 162 — September 28, 1952

Capacity of sidings in car lengths	918 Freight	916 Freight	914 Freight	912 Freight	98 Morning Daylight	72 Passenger (c)	76 Lark	374 C. M. E.	94 Starlight	Mile Post Location	STATIONS	Distance from San Luis Obispo
	Leave Daily	Leave Daily	Leave Daily	Leave Daily	Leave Daily	Leave Daily	Leave Daily	Lv. Daily Ex. Sat.Sun.Mon.	Leave Daily			
S. L. Obispo yard BKWOTYP	PM 10.10	PM 3.30	AM 10.30	AM 3.30	PM 1.20	AM 8.35	AM 3.25	AM 2.50	AM 1.35	252.1	TO-R SAN LUIS OBISPO	0.0
P	10.25	3.45	10.45	3.45	1.32	8.54	3.37	3.05	1.47	259.1	7.0 HADLEY	7.0
121 P	10.35	3.55	10.55	3.55	1.39	9.02	3.45	3.13	1.55	264.2	5.1 GROVER	12.1
32 P						s 9.09				265.9	1.7 TO OCEANO	13.8
94 P	10.43	4.03	11.03	4.03	1.46	9.14	3.52	3.19	2.01	269.9	4.0 CALLENDER	17.8
38 P						9.17				272.4	2.5 BROMELA	20.3
Yard Limits 104 BKWP	10.51	4.11	11.11	4.11	1.52	s 9.35	c 4.00	3.27	2.08	276.5	4.1 TO GUADALUPE	24.4
73 P	10.58	4.18	11.18	4.18	1.57	9.41	4.06	3.33	2.13	280.7	4.2 WALDORF	28.6
42 P						ʌ				284.8	4.1 SHUMAN	32.7
83 P	11.06	4.26	11.26	4.26	2.04	9.48	4.14	3.41	2.20	286.5	1.7 DEVON	34.4
36 P						s 9.51				287.5	1.0 CASMALIA	35.4
70 P	11.11	4.31	11.31	4.31		9.55	4.18	3.45	2.24	290.0	2.5 ANTONIO	37.9
124 P	11.16	4.36	11.36	4.36	2.12	10.00	4.22	3.49	2.28	293.2	3.2 NARLON	41.1
No. 1-71 No. 2-109 YP	11.21	4.41	11.41	4.41	2.17	10.05	4.27	3.54	2.33	297.2	4.0 TANGAIR	45.1
Yard Limits 113 WOYP	11.31	4.48	AM 11.49	4.48	2.23	s 10.21	c 4.35	3.59	2.38	302.7	5.5 TO SURF	50.6
133 P	PM 11.43	5.00	PM 12.01	5.00	2.28	10.28	4.41	4.08	2.46	307.9	5.2 HONDA	55.8
P						f				310.5	2.6 ARLIGHT	58.4
40 P						10.43		4.21		317.3	6.8 SUDDEN	65.2
81 P	AM 12.03	5.20	12.20	5.20	2.41	10.49	4.55	4.26	3.00	320.8	3.5 JALAMA	68.7
No. 1-121 No. 2-48 P	12.10	5.27	12.28	5.27	2.46	f 10.56	5.01	4.33	3.06	325.3	4.5 TO CONCEPCION	73.2
40 P										329.8	4.5 GATO	77.7
101 P	12.26	5.41	12.45	5.41	2.56	11.15	5.11	4.44	3.17	334.8	5.0 SACATE	82.7
74 WP	12.39	5.49	12.53	5.49	3.01	s 11.30	5.16	4.50	3.22	339.4	4.6 TO GAVIOTA	87.3
40 P										342.6	3.2 LENTO	90.5
42 P										345.7	3.1 TAJIGUAS	93.6
98 P	12.57	6.07	1.07	6.15	3.12	11.44	5.27	5.03	3.33	349.9	4.2 CAPITAN	97.8
No. 1-78 No. 2-36 P	1.06	6.16	1.16	6.24	3.17	11.52	5.32	5.09	3.38	355.0	5.1 NAPLES	102.9
43 P						AM 11.57				358.9	3.9 ELLWOOD	106.8
P										361.7	2.8 LA PATERA	109.6
115 P	1.16	6.26	1.26	6.34	3.25	PM f 12.04	5.40	5.21	3.47	362.8	1.1 TO GOLETA	110.7
35 P										366.5	3.7 HOPE RANCH	114.4
P	1.24	6.34	1.34	6.44		12.12	5.47	5.27	3.53	368.5	2.0 WEST SANTA BARBARA	116.4
Santa Barbara yard BKWOTP	1.35 AM	6.45 PM	1.45 PM	6.55 AM	s 3.37 PM	s 12.20 PM	s 5.58 AM	5.35 AM	s 4.00 AM	370.7	2.2 TO-R SANTA BARBARA	118.6
	Arrive Daily	Arrive Daily	Arrive Daily	Arrive Daily	Arrive Daily	Arrive Daily	Arrive Daily	Ar. Daily Ex. Sat.Sun.Mon.	Arrive Daily		(118.6)	
	(3.25) 34.71	(3.15) 36.49	(3.15) 36.49	(3.25) 34.71	(2.17) 51.94	(3.45) 31.63	(2.33) 46.51	(2.45) 43.13	(2.25) 49.06		Time over District Average Speed per Hour	

RULE 5. Schedule time and train-orders at Concepcion and Naples apply at No. 1 siding.
Schedule time and train-orders at Tangair for eastward trains apply at No. 1 siding, and for westward trains at No. 2 siding.

GUADALUPE SUBDIVISION

WESTWARD

Timetable No. 162 — September 28, 1952

Mile Post Location	Stations	Station Number	Distance from Santa Barbara	71 Passenger (c) Arrive Daily	99 Morning Daylight Arrive Daily	373 C. M. W. Ar. Daily Ex. Sat. Sun. Mon.	95 Starlight Arrive Daily	75 Lark Arrive Daily	911 Freight Arrive Daily	913 Freight Arrive Daily	915 Freight Arrive Daily	917 Freight Arrive Daily
252.1	TO-R SAN LUIS OBISPO / 7.0	248	118.6	AM s 9.10	PM s 12.50	AM 12.05	AM s 12.35	AM s 2.20	AM 9.40	PM 5.10	PM 8.50	AM 2.50
259.1	HADLEY / 5.1	255	111.6	8.54	12.38	11.49 PM	12.24	2.05	9.22	4.52	8.32	2.33
264.2	GROVER / 1.7	260	106.5	8.45	12.31	11.41	12.15	1.55	9.12	4.42	8.21	2.23
265.9	TO OCEANO / 4.0	262	104.8	s 8.43		11.39			9.09			
269.9	CALLENDER / 2.5	266	100.8	8.33	12.25	11.34	12.08	1.47	9.03	4.34	8.13	2.16
272.4	BROMELA / 4.1	269	98.3	8.30								
276.5	TO GUADALUPE / 4.2	273	94.2	s 8.25	12.19	11.27	12.02 AM	s 1.38	8.54	4.25	8.04	2.08
280.7	WALDORF / 4.1	277	90.0	8.00	12.14	11.22	11.57 PM	1.30	8.48	4.18	7.57	1.57
284.8	SHUMAN / 1.7	281	85.9									
286.5	DEVON / 1.0	283	84.2	7.53	12.07	11.15	11.50	1.24	8.39	4.04	7.49	1.49
287.5	CASMALIA / 2.5	284	83.2	s 7.50								
290.0	ANTONIO / 3.2	286	80.7	7.45	12.03 PM	11.11	11.46	1.20	8.34	3.57	7.44	1.44
293.2	NARLON / 4.0	289	77.5	7.41	11.59 AM	11.07	11.41	1.16	8.30	3.53	7.40	1.40
297.2	TANGAIR / 5.5	293	73.5	7.36	11.55	11.03	11.37	1.11	8.24	3.47	7.34	1.34
302.7	TO SURF / 5.2	299	68.0	s 7.29	11.49	10.55	11.31	s 1.03	8.16	3.37	7.26	1.26
307.9	HONDA / 2.6	304	62.8	7.11	11.43	10.48	11.24	12.55	8.09	3.30	7.19	1.19
310.5	ARLIGHT / 6.8	307	60.2	f								
317.3	SUDDEN / 3.5	313	53.4									
320.8	JALAMA / 4.5	317	49.9	6.54	11.30	10.32	11.10	12.42	7.53	3.14	7.03	1.03
325.3	TO CONCEPCION / 4.5	321	45.4	f 6.48	11.25	10.26	11.05	12.36	7.47	3.08	6.57	12.57
329.8	GATO / 5.0	326	40.9									
334.8	SACATE / 4.6	331	35.9	6.35	11.15	10.15	10.55	12.26	7.35	2.56	6.45	12.45
339.4	TO GAVIOTA / 3.2	336	31.3	s 6.29	11.10	10.10	10.50	12.21	7.29	2.50	6.39	12.39
342.6	LENTO / 3.1	339	28.1									
345.7	TAJIGUAS / 4.2	342	25.0	6.20	11.04	10.03			7.19	2.40	6.29	12.30
349.9	CAPITAN / 5.1	346	20.8	6.15	10.59	9.58	10.39	12.10	7.13	2.34	6.23	12.24
355.0	NAPLES / 3.9	351	15.7	6.09		9.52		12.05 AM	7.06	2.25	6.16	12.16
358.9	ELLWOOD / 2.8	355	11.8	6.03								
361.7	LA PATERA / 1.1	358	9.0									
362.8	TO GOLETA / 3.7	359	7.9	f 5.57	10.48	9.44	10.28	11.57 PM	6.57	2.16	6.07	12.07 AM
366.5	HOPE RANCH / 2.0	363	4.2									
368.5	WEST SANTA BARBARA / 2.2	365	2.2	5.47	10.42	9.37	10.22	11.51	6.50	2.09	6.00	11.59 PM
370.7	TO-R SANTA BARBARA	367	0.0	5.40 AM	10.35 AM	9.30 PM	10.15 PM	11.44 PM	6.40 AM	2.00 PM	5.50 PM	11.50 PM
	(118.6)			Leave Daily	Leave Daily	Lv. Daily Ex. Fri. Sat. Sun.	Leave Daily	Leave Daily	Leave Daily	Leave Daily	Leave Daily	Leave Daily
	Time over District			(3.30)	(2.15)	(2.35)	(2.20)	(2.36)	(3.00)	(3.10)	(3.00)	(3.00)
	Average Speed per Hour			33.89	52.71	45.91	50.83	45.62	39.53	37.45	39.53	39.53

RULE 5. Schedule time and train-orders at Concepcion and Naples apply at No. 1 Siding. Schedule time and train-orders at Tangair for eastward trains apply at No. 1 Siding, and for westward trains at No. 2 Siding.

ADDITIONAL STATIONS

Station Number	Name	Mile Post	Capacity
	Guadalupe Subdivision		
255	Edna .... (Spur)	257.9	5 P
256	Tiber	260.0	..
259	Pismo	262.8	..
327	San Augustine ... (Spur)	331.0	19
330	Drake .... (Spur)	334.2	14 P
356	Coromar .... (Spur)	360.2	6

During February of 1956, Richard Steinheimer went north from Glendale to the Point Conception area, shooting the Coast Line. He rented a plane in Santa Maria and, despite strong winds, captured No. 98 on film as it rolled through Surf with a matched set of PAs (**top**) on its way to Honda and Point Arguello. In the same vicinity, the Surf Local, led by Baldwin AS-616 No. 5267, approaches the east portal of tunnel No. 12 (**right**) at a point called "the Espada" near Sudden in January, 1955. Tunnel No. 12 was "daylighted" in September, 1956.

Above, Richard Steinheimer, DeGolyer Library, Southern Methodist University; right, Southern Pacific Lines

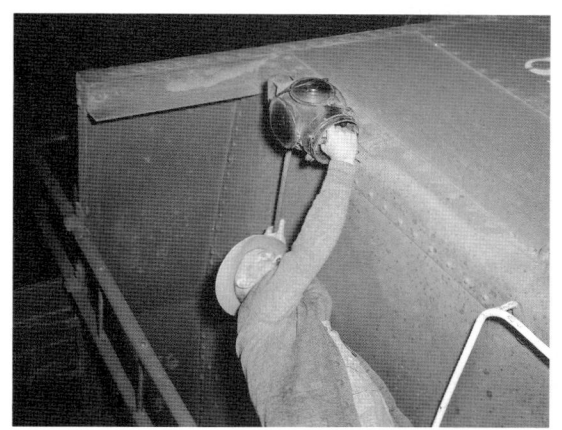

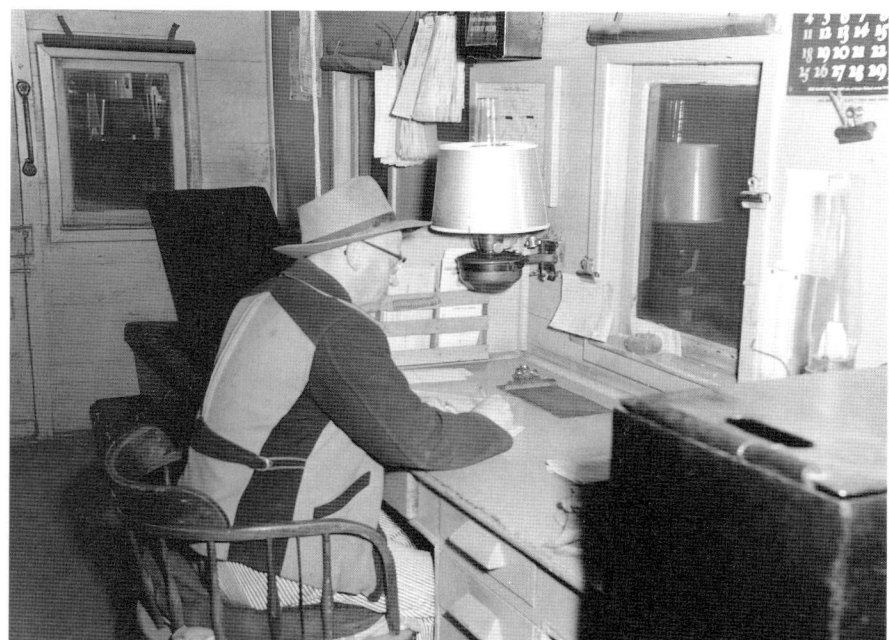

The Surf Local was, judging by the seniority of its crew, a very desirable job. Originating early in the morning at Santa Barbara, daily except Sunday (**top, left**), the Surf Local peddled cars west, including a tank car of water every second day to the station at Gaviota. Conductor on the job was "Shorty" Wardle (**top, right**); he and his crew were a hardy bunch of Coast veterans. Pausing for "coffee" (**right**), the train crew consisted of, from left, Johnny Renner, John Johnson, "Shorty," and Harry Heckman. The hoghead, in the cab of Baldwin No. 5270 (**below**), was Bill Shifflette, while the fireman was Dick Proudfit, son of the popular Road Foreman. It took all day for the Surf Local to do its work, including the run to Lompoc and staying out of the way of the "varnish." But Shorty always managed to tie up in "15:59."

All, Southern Pacific Lines

228

Behind its typical late-'fifties power, a quartet of GP9s, *CME* No. 374 nears the end of the run, passing Taylor Yard and Dayton Ave. Tower on the way to the trailer facility at Alhambra (**right**). In an early 'sixties view, train No. 913 heads up the coast at Refugio State Beach behind three GP9s led by No. 5817 (**below**).

Two photos, Southern Pacific Lines

Facing Page: Well after most steam was gone from the Coast Line, GS engines continued to power the Coast Mail. Here No. 4415, a product of the first GS order from Lima, heads No. 72 near Ventura on April 10, 1955 (**opposite, top**). Morning shadows are shortening on June 14, 1958, as No. 99 begins her trip behind E8 No. 6018, passing Taylor Yard and Baldwin goat No. 5209 (**opposite, bottom**). The powerful but slow Baldwins were gradually demoted in the late 'fifties from road service to heavy yard and transfer work.

Opposite page, two photos, John E. Shaw

229

The 37-mile stretch between Surf and Gaviota provides the most dramatic interaction between the Coast Line and the Pacific Ocean along the entire route. No. 926 pauses at Sacate (**above**) with a string of newly-delivered EMD F3s in February 1949. Two years later, a string of F7s rumbles across the Gaviota Trestle (**opposite, top**) with eastward tonnage. It was not the F units that finally dieselized the Coast Line, but it was EMD E units which dieselized the Coast passenger trains. By 1955, the *Coast Daylight* was handled exclusively by diesels, as attested by these views of No. 99, approaching Sacate (**left**) from the south behind SP's only E8, No. 6018, and racing through Gaviota (**opposite, below**). Power in these photos is a mixture of EMD E and Alco PA units.

*Opposite top, John C. Illman;
all others, Southern Pacific Lines*

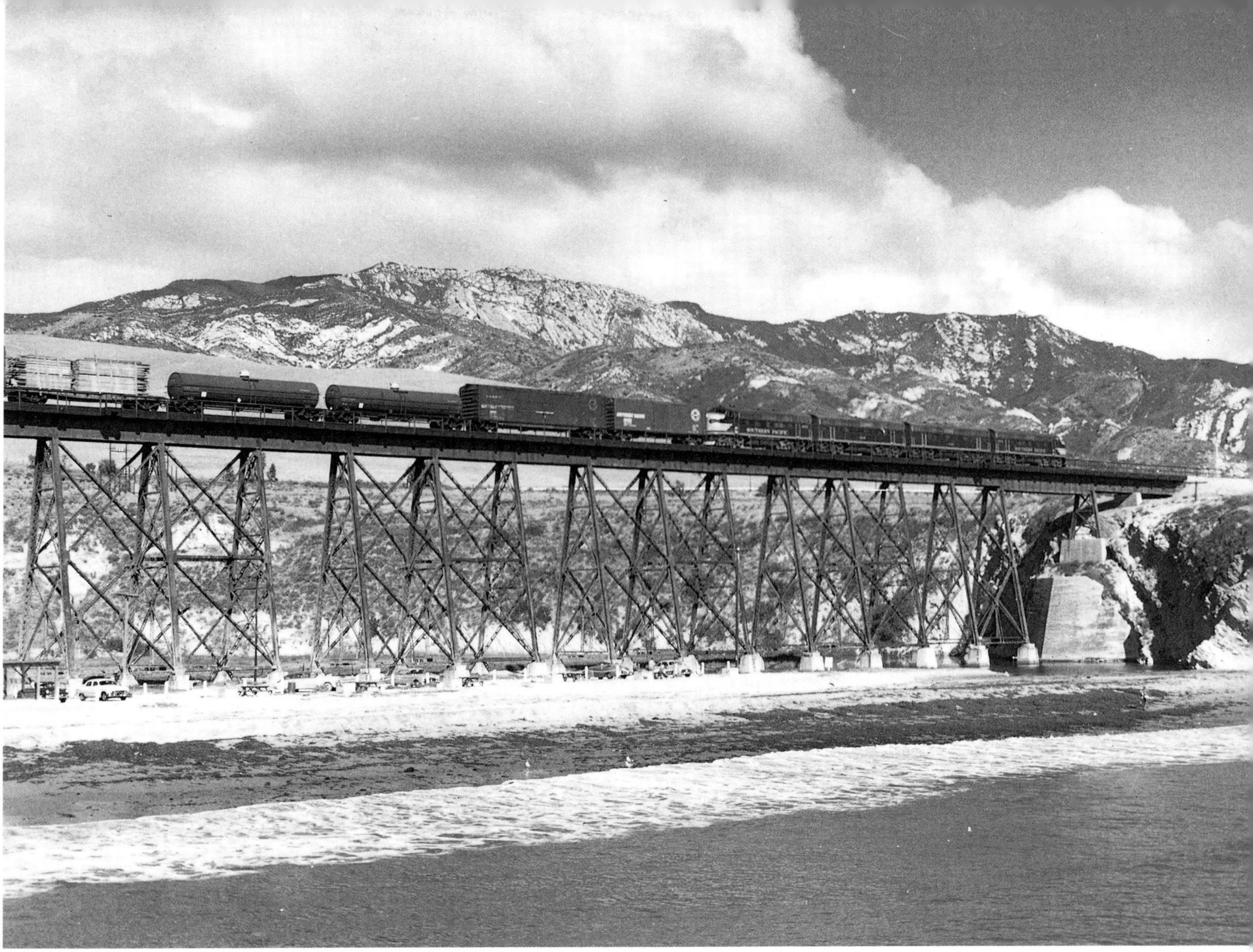

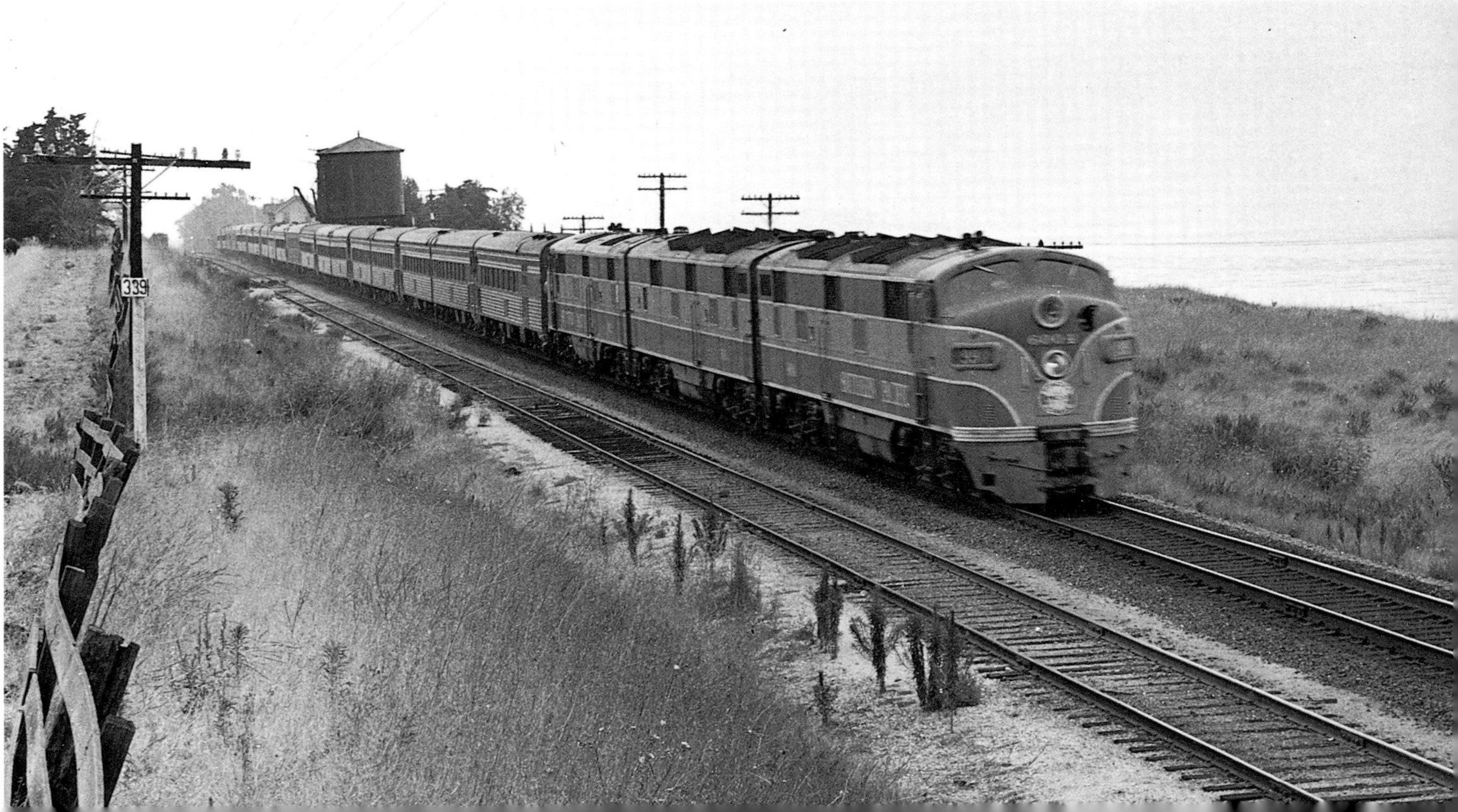
339

In a stunning scene (**above**), the *Morning Daylight* clips through Tajiguas, 25 miles west of Santa Barbara, at 65 miles per hour on a December day in 1947. It's just after three in the afternoon, and the winter sun is low on the horizon, casting deep shadows on the Santa Ynez Mountains in the background. As the speeding train receded into the distance, photographer Orem wheeled around to snap this shot (**left**) of the peaceful section quarters.

Two photos, Jim Orem

No. 98 steams south along the rocky bluffs at Rincon Point between Carpinteria and Dulah, near Ventura (**above**). "Rincón" is Spanish for "corner," referring to the shape of the point.

Above, Art Laidlaw

OVERLEAF: Brand-new EMD F3s pose with train No. 913 for the publicity camera at Honda in February, 1949.
Southern Pacific Lines

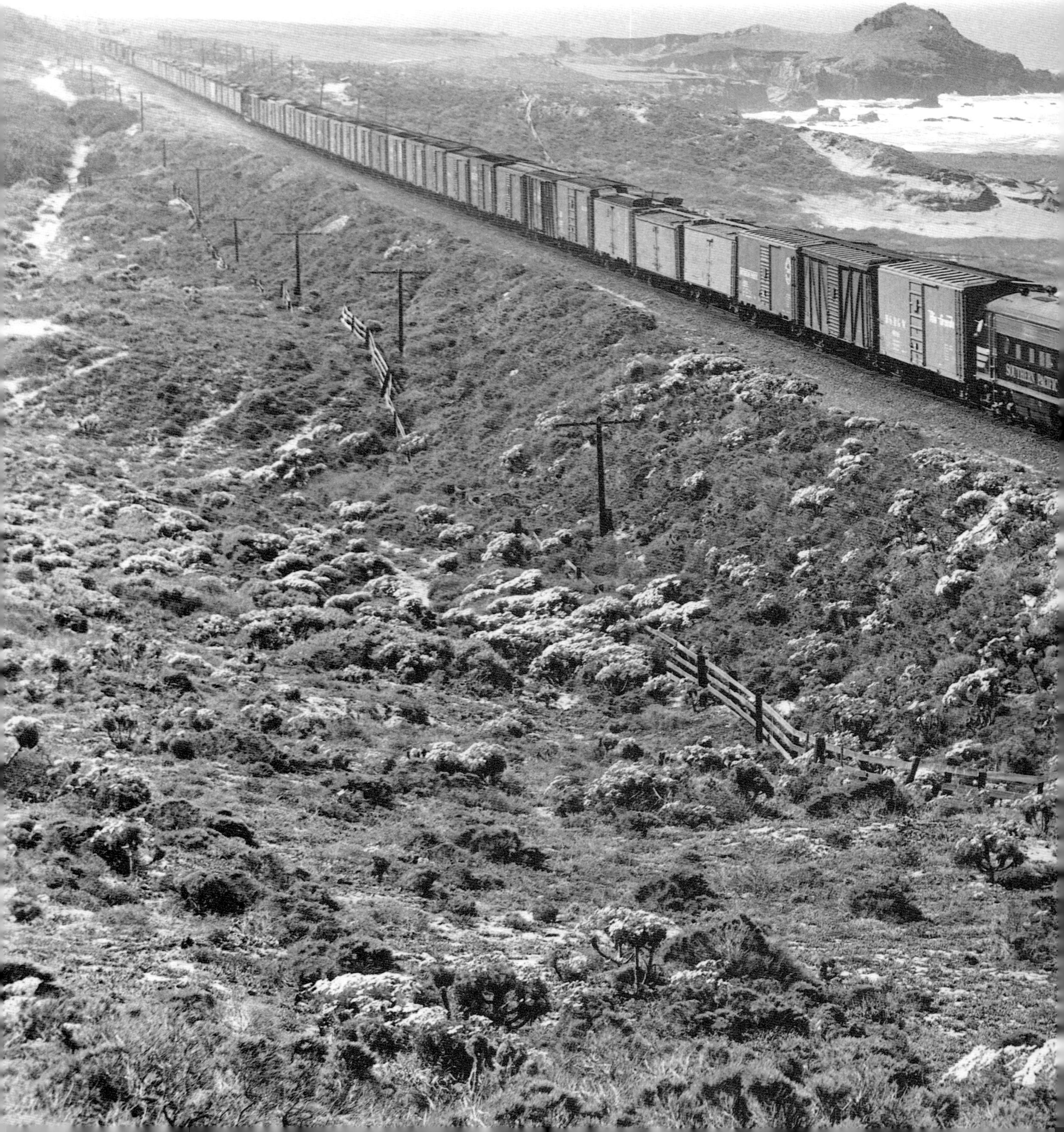

HONDA

AC No. 4201 prepares to depart Santa Barbara yard (**above**) westward with train No. 913 on November 10, 1952. On June 22, 1962, a string of new General Electric U25Bs rolls into Santa Barbara for a crew change (**left**) with the first section of No. 915. What a difference ten years can make!

Above, John C. Illman;
left, Don Sims, Southern Pacific Lines collection

An EMD NW2 diesel switcher works a string of reefers at Oxnard (**top**) in 1957, while more diesels wait for assignments on the engine track. The center of an expanding Ventura County economy, Oxnard was the scene of much post-war development, including 4,700 feet of new trackage to serve vegetable packing sheds and a quick-freeze plant. In addition, Oxnard received a new depot (**right**) in 1956.

Top and right, Southern Pacific Lines

The eastward Coast Mail hugs the shore near Seacliff (**below**) in 1950.

Stan Kistler

VENTURA SUBDIVISION

EASTWARD

Timetable No. 198 — September 28, 1952

Capacity of sidings		52 San Joaquin Daylight	98 Morning Daylight	72 Passenger (c)	58 Owl	76 Lark	60 West Coast	374 C. M. E.	94 Starlight	56 Passenger	Mile Post Location	STATIONS	Distance from Santa Barbara
		Leave Daily	Leave Daily	Leave Daily	Leave Daily	Leave Daily	Leave Daily	Lv. Daily Ex. Sat. Sun. Mon.	Leave Daily	Leave Daily			
Santa Barbara yard	BKWOTP		PM 3.42	PM 12.35		AM 6.10		AM 5.45	AM 4.07		370.7	TO-R SANTA BARBARA	0.0
			3.46	12.39		6.15		5.49	4.11		371.9	1.2 EAST SANTA BARBARA	1.2
102	P		3.54	12.47		6.23		5.57	4.19		377.3	5.4 ORTEGA	6.6
36	P		3.59	s 12.56		6.28		6.02	4.24		381.2	3.9 TO CARPINTERIA	10.5
36	P										383.4	2.2 WAVE	12.7
35	P								4.30		385.7	2.3 PUNTA	15.0
101	P		4.09	f 1.08		6.40		6.12	4.34		388.6	2.9 SEACLIFF	17.9
25	P										392.9	4.3 DULAH	22.2
Yd. Lmts.	P										397.3	4.4 VENTURA JCT.	26.6
119	WP		4.21	s 1.40		s 6.56		6.24	s 4.51		398.2	0.9 TO VENTURA	27.5
36	YP			f 1.47		7.04		6.29	4.57		403.2	5.0 MONTALVO	32.5
Yard Limits 103	BKWOP		4.32	s 2.05		7.12		6.35	s 5.07		407.8	4.6 TO OXNARD	37.1
62	P		4.37	2.11		7.17		6.40	5.13		412.1	4.3 LEESDALE	41.4
113	P		4.41	s 2.21		7.22		6.45	5.17		416.6	4.5 TO CAMARILLO	45.9
39	P			c 2.26		7.26					419.8	3.2 SOMIS	49.1
61	P			2.31		7.30		6.52	5.24		422.9	3.1 LAGOL	52.2
99	WP		4.52	f 2.40		7.36		6.57	5.30		427.1	4.2 TO MOORPARK	56.4
65	P			2.48		7.44		7.04	5.37		432.2	5.1 STRATHEARN	61.5
101	P		5.04	f 3.00		7.52		7.12	5.44		437.5	5.3 TO SANTA SUSANA	66.8
68	P		5.09	3.07		7.58		7.17	5.48		441.0	3.5 HASSON	70.3
81	WYP		5.16	f 3.15		8.06		7.24	5.55		445.5	4.5 TO CHATSWORTH	74.8
E 52 W 52	P		5.20	s 3.25		8.12		7.29	6.00		449.9	4.4 TO NORTHRIDGE	79.2
E 34 W 40	TP			3.30		8.18		7.34	6.04		454.1	4.2 RAYMER	83.4
99	P		5.27	3.35		8.24		7.39	6.08		458.4	4.3 HEWITT	87.7
100	IP		PM 6.51	5.32	3.40	AM 10.09	8.30	AM 8.13	7.45	6.13	AM 5.25	462.7 471.6	4.3 BURBANK JCT.	92.0
	YP				f		c					472.1	0.5 BURBANK	92.5
	P		s 7.01	s 5.42	s 3.55	s 10.25	s 8.42	s 8.27		s 6.25	s 5.37	477.1	5.0 GLENDALE	97.5
	I											477.3	0.2 GLENDALE TOWER	97.7
Los Angeles yard	BKWOYP											479.7	2.4 TO-R LOS ANGELES YARD	100.1
	I		7.10	5.49	4.04	10.33	8.49	8.35	8.10 AM	6.32	5.47	480.6	0.9 DAYTON AVE. TOWER	101.0
			7.14	5.53	4.08	10.37	8.53	8.39		6.36	5.51	481.9	1.3 EAST BANK JCT.	102.3
	I		7.15	5.55	4.10	10.39	8.54	8.41		6.38	5.52	482.1	0.2 MISSION TOWER	102.5
	BKWIYP		s 7.20 PM	s 6.00 PM	s 4.15 PM	s 10.45 AM	s 9.00 AM	s 8.50 AM	Ar. Daily Ex. Sat. Sun. Mon.	s 6.45 AM	s 6.00 AM	482.8	0.7 TO-R LOS ANGELES	103.2
			Arrive Daily	Arrive Daily	Arrive Daily	Arrive Daily	Arrive Daily	Arrive Daily		Arrive Daily	Arrive Daily		(103.2)	
			(0.29) 23.17	(2.18) 44.81	(3.40) 28.14	(0.36) 18.36	(2.50) 36.40	(0.37) 17.87	(2.25) 41.79	(2.38) 39.19	(0.35) 19.20		Time over District. Average Speed per Hour	

On this and preceding pages in this chapter (pp. 178, 194, 200, 204, 224) are samples from employee timetables for the Coast Line. These schedules give a snapshot of operations, though for the San Francisco Subdivision, just two pages–including the *Daylight*, *Starlight*, and *CMW*–have to represent some nine pages of schedules. Preceding examples are drawn from timetable No. 162, issued Sept. 28, 1952, with J.J. Jordan still serving as division superintendent. However, the southernmost subdivision of the Coast Line, the Ventura Subdivision, was part of the Los Angeles Division, thus these two pages are from L.A. Division employee timetable No. 198, issued Sept. 28, 1952. It thus matches in date the preceding timetable pages in this chapter.

VENTURA SUBDIVISION

Timetable No. 198 — September 28, 1952

WESTWARD — FIRST CLASS

Mile Post Location	Stations	Dist. from L.A.	71 Passenger (e) Arrive Daily	51 San Joaquin Daylight Arrive Daily	99 Morning Daylight Arrive Daily	57 Owl Arrive Daily	373 C.M.W. Ar. Daily Ex. Fri. Sat. Sun.	59 West Coast Arrive Daily	95 Starlight Arrive Daily	75 Lark Arrive Daily	55 Passenger Arrive Daily
370.7	TO-R SANTA BARBARA — 1.2	103.2	AM s 5.15		AM s 10.30		PM 9.15		PM s 10.10	PM s 11.37	
371.9	EAST SANTA BARBARA — 5.4	102.0	5.09		10.26		9.12		10.06	11.32	
377.3	ORTEGA — 3.9	96.6	4.56		10.18		9.03		9.58	11.24	
381.2	TO CARPINTERIA — 2.2	92.7	s 4.50		10.13		8.57		9.53	11.19	
383.4	WAVE — 2.3	90.5									
385.7	PUNTA — 2.9	88.2	4.30								
388.6	SEACLIFF — 4.3	85.3	4.17		10.03		8.47		9.43	11.08	
392.9	DULAH — 4.4	81.0									
397.3	VENTURA JCT. — 0.9	76.6									
398.2	TO VENTURA — 5.0	75.7	s 4.05		9.51		8.34		s 9.31	s 10.55	
403.2	MONTALVO — 4.6	70.7	f 3.44				8.27		9.21	10.45	
407.8	TO OXNARD — 4.3	66.1	s 3.37		9.40		8.21		s 9.15	10.39	
412.1	LEESDALE — 4.5	61.8	3.19		9.35		8.15		9.06	10.33	
416.6	TO CAMARILLO — 3.2	57.3	s 3.13		9.31		8.10		9.02	10.28	
419.8	SOMIS — 3.1	54.1	s 2.57								
422.9	LAGOL — 4.2	51.0	2.52		9.25				8.56	10.20	
427.1	TO MOORPARK — 5.1	46.8	s 2.46		9.21		7.59		8.52	10.15	
432.2	STRATHEARN — 5.3	41.7	2.35		9.16		7.53		8.47	10.10	
437.5	TO SANTA SUSANA — 3.5	36.4	s 2.23		9.11		7.47		8.42	10.04	
441.0	HASSON — 4.5	32.9	f 2.14		9.07		7.43		8.38	9.59	
445.5	TO CHATSWORTH — 4.4	28.4	s 2.05		9.00		7.35		8.31	9.53	
449.9	TO NORTHRIDGE — 4.2	24.0	f 1.55		8.55		7.30		8.26	9.48	
454.1	RAYMER — 4.3	19.8	1.45				7.25		8.22	9.43	
458.4	HEWITT — 4.3	15.5	1.40		8.48		7.20		8.18	9.38	
462.7 / 471.6	TO BURBANK JCT. — 0.5	11.2	1.35	AM 7.47	8.43	PM 6.10	7.15	PM 8.00	8.13	9.33	PM 9.50
472.1	BURBANK — 5.0	10.7				c					
477.1	GLENDALE — 0.2	5.7	s 1.25	s 7.38	s 8.33	s 6.00		s 7.50	s 8.04	s 9.25	s 9.40
477.3	GLENDALE TOWER — 2.4	5.5									
479.7	TO-R LOS ANGELES YARD — 0.9	3.1									
480.6	DAYTON AVE. TOWER — 1.3	2.2	1.11	7.29	8.24	5.50	6.55 PM	7.39	7.54	9.10	9.20
481.9	EAST BANK JCT. — 0.2	0.9	1.07	7.25	8.20	5.46		7.35	7.50	9.06	9.15
482.1	MISSION TOWER — 0.7	0.7	1.05	7.24	8.19	5.44		7.34	7.49	9.05	9.14
482.8	TO-R LOS ANGELES	0.0	1.00 AM	7.20 AM	8.15 AM	5.40 PM		7.30 PM	7.45 PM	9.00 PM	9.10 PM
	(103.2)		Leave Daily	Leave Daily	Leave Daily	Leave Daily	Lv. Daily Ex. Fri. Sat. Sun.	Leave Daily	Leave Daily	Leave Daily	Leave Daily
	Time over District		(4.15)	(0.27)	(2.15)	(0.30)	(2.20)	(0.30)	(2.25)	(2.37)	(0.40)
	Average Speed per Hour		24.28	24.80	45.86	22.40	43.28	22.40	42.70	39.48	16.80

Between Mission Tower and Dayton Ave. Tower, via East Bank Jct., trains or engines may use main tracks, in either direction, being governed by signal indication.

Trains or engines stopped by interlocking signals at signal bridges 3, 4 or 6 will, if signal does not clear, call signal operator on telephone located on signal bridge.

RULE 5. Schedule time and train-order time at Burbank Jct. apply at end of double track.

RULE 93. Trains and engines entering and leaving Los Angeles Union Passenger Terminal operate on tracks of that company.

The north end of the San Fernando Valley was still largely rural in 1954 when train No. 98, with no scheduled stop, roared through Chatsworth (**top**) as it accelerated down the long tangent towards Burbank Junction. Following the streamliner minutes later, this string of new EMD F7s (**right**) appeared on scheduled freight No. 632. The diesels remained in dynamic, however, as the rear of the train was still strung out on Santa Susana Pass.

Two photos, Donald Duke

A Bakersfield-bound freight behind a quartet of EMD SD9s departs Taylor Yard at Los Angeles (**above**) about 1960. Taylor, developed in the 1920s, was used by both Coast Line and Valley Line trains. And Valley and Coast trains also shared the double track from Taylor to Burbank Junction, where the Coast mainline diverged westward. Here the Coast Mail rounds the curve at Burbank Junction (**right**) on its last lap into Los Angeles.

Above, Jim Orem;
right, Bob Morris

Amtrak train No. 13, the *Coast Starlight*, moves up the Coast Line at milepost 329.5, formerly the west end of Gato, on March 20, 1986. The *Coast Starlight*, since its inception, has been Amtrak's most popular long-distance passenger train.
Tim Zukas

5

Decline & Rebirth

Recent Coast Line Operations

SOUTHERN PACIFIC'S cooperation was deemed essential if Amtrak were to provide any service on key corridors on the west coast and in the southwest. In spite of protests from every quarter, the railroad ultimately joined the Amtrak agreement and April 30, 1971 saw the last runs of SP-operated passenger trains, including the *Coast Daylight* and the *Del Monte*. In fact the *Del Monte* held the honor of being the last SP passenger movement not connected with Amtrak when the cars were dead-headed back from Monterey the night of April 30th. Only SP's Peninsula commuter service remained. This was despite a last-ditch effort by the California PUC to save the *Del Monte*. Hearings were set May 12th as the ICC had earlier ruled that the *Del Monte* might in fact be a commuter run and not subject to abandonment under Amtrak legislation. The effort failed.

As Amtrak assumed the Coast Line run on May 1, 1971, things were not the same. Train Nos. 98 and 99, the *Coast Daylight*, continued to operate, but the northern terminus was changed from San Francisco to Oakland. Further, Nos. 98 and 99 only operated on Monday, Wednesday, Thursday and Saturday while unnamed trains "11" and "12" operated Tuesday, Friday and Sunday through from Seattle to San Diego on the same schedule. Eliminated as stops were not only San Francisco, but also Palo Alto (because of the re-route) and Glendale. The latter was reinstated as a stop on September 25, 1971. That fall more changes were made to the Coast Line schedules. Effective November 14th, the *Cascade* was renumbered Nos. 11 and 14 and became the *Coast Starlight* operating through to San Diego tri-weekly while the *Coast Daylight* was renumbered train Nos. 12 and 13 and extended to San Diego on the days the *Starlight* did not operate. Service was slow. Running time between Oakland and Los Angeles approximated the most recent schedule of the SP *Coast Daylight*, ten hours and 20 minutes if the trains were not delayed, and they frequently were.

Joseph Vranich, executive director of the Washington-based National Association of Railroad Passengers, a longtime adversary of the SP, charged in August, 1972 that the Southern Pacific was "sabotaging" Amtrak. Vranich said that SP was "philosophically opposed" to government trains running over its private lines and interfering with its freight

Train No. 98, the *Coast Daylight*, races through King City on September 19, 1971, five months after the Amtrak takeover. While the train's consist had changed dramatically, SP SDP45s continued to be used as power.
John C. Illman

The venerable Mission-style depot at 3rd and Townsend Streets, San Francisco, succumbs to the wrecker's ball in July, 1975.
Bob Morris

operations. "This is the worst record for any railroad participating in Amtrak," commented Vranich, citing the fact that between June 30 and August 16, 1972, the *Coast Starlight* was on time only 36 percent of the time. Vranich went on to express concern that SP's top executive, B.F. Biaggini, was lobbying the Nixon administration to abolish Amtrak.

With the elimination of through passenger service to San Francisco under Amtrak, the Mission-style passenger station at Third and Townsend Streets was the next target. Built in 1914, the sprawling facility, which once served as headquarters for the Coast Division and served a variety of through trains as well as the commute fleet, had in SP's view, "simply outlived its usefulness." The fact that the real estate upon which it stood was becoming more valuable, or that it seemed to be in the path of a planned freeway extension, didn't help matters. The subject came up in the spring of 1971, when SP proposed to eliminate the building in favor of a more modest facility at Fourth and Townsend.

The approval process was swift and in September of the same year, the Planning Commission of the City of San Francisco approved plans to tear down the 57-year old structure and replace it with a

$200,000 one-story, pre-cast concrete building with a waffle-type slab roof at Fourth and Townsend Streets. Work proceeded slowly as there were a great many alterations to the track layout and interlocking plant required before actual construction could commence. But finally, on June 21, 1975, the new station was officially opened with a "Grand Opening" slated for June 23rd. Demolition of the old station, built for the Panama-Pacific Exposition of 1915, came swiftly and before long, the freeway offramp was completed. The remainder of the site was developed as a recreational vehicle park.

Despite the prospect of a new "user friendly" terminal in San Francisco, and other improvements including a new San Mateo station, opened on July 28, 1975, the Peninsula commute service continued to be the subject of controversy. Prior to 1968, the SP strategy had consistently been to chip away at the timecard, eliminating many off-hour schedules and the service via the Vasona Branch. After 1968, the SP had petitioned successfully for five fare increases with a cumulative increase of 43 percent. But on August 23, 1974, SP startled the community by asking the California PUC for a whopping 111 percent increase in fares, claiming that during 1973, the service took in $4.3 million while costing $9.1 million to operate. The requested increase would bring the service to break-even level under present conditions, SP said.

Assemblyman Louis Pappan chaired subcommittee hearings investigating the request and came to the conclusion, in no uncertain terms, that the increase should be denied. During the hearings it came out that the SP had commissioned a secret consultant's study which showed that ridership would decrease if the proposed increase were adopted. Cost figures supplied by the SP were then challenged. SP claimed to have spent $9,247,775 in operating the service in 1973. The Auditor General reviewed $6,496,002 of those expenses and found that approximately 40 percent of them were inadequately supported or incorrectly charged. Pappan further stated that he was considering forwarding copies of the Auditor General's report to district attorneys and grand juries in San Mateo, Santa Clara and San Francisco counties to consider possible perjury charges. "There is no question that at least half the numbers are way off, but it's the intent that determines whether or not criminal perjury was committed." No prosecution on such charges materialized.

At a meeting of the Metropolitan Transportation Commission in Oakland, December 17, 1975, SP Vice President-Operations D. K. McNear offered to sell a portion of the railroad's Peninsula right-of-way, stations, locomotives, cars and "other lands" to an as-yet non-existent government agency for "less than $200 million." Readers of the fine print noted that the railroad proposed only to sell the west track of its double-track line and then only from San Jose to San Bruno. The SP would retain all of the Bayshore Cutoff and would sell instead the San Bruno Branch so that the trains could reach "the area" of the Daly City BART station.

During the fall of 1976, with daily commute ridership hovering at 8,000, Southern Pacific announced an even more unusual proposal in which the railroad would purchase up to 1,000 8-passenger vans and would aid in the formation of van pools. "...most people consider time and personal convenience paramount," commented SP Vice President Alan DeMoss. "That's why so many of our commuters over the years have chosen to drive to work on the fine freeways." Southern Pacific, for its part, would have to be allowed to discontinue entirely its commute service before delivering the vans. If not, the Company would seek a 96 percent fare increase. None of these proposals were seriously considered, nor acted upon by any of the governing bodies.

Using SP's own advertising, the concept of "Van Pools" was satirized by the avant-garde Bay Area railfan publication *Everywhere West* in October, 1976.
Everywhere West

Morning commuters pour onto the platform at 3rd and Townsend station (**above**) in July, 1973. The power mixture included (**left**) SDP45 No. 3205. The previous summer (**below**) the FM Train Masters were still solidly in command of the commute service, but by September 1974, all but three had been displaced by SDPs bumped from mainline passenger runs by deliveries of new Amtrak power. In January 1975, only one, No. 3031, was still operating and it was soon gone. In July 1978, SP leased 15 Amtrak P30CHs for the commute service, releasing the SDP45s for freight service.

Above, Ted Benson; left, Bob Morris; below, Tim Zukas

FACING PAGE: The two views on the opposite page depict the general layout of the San Francisco passenger terminal in November, 1972. Looking north (**top**), outbound No. 130 departs at left while a goat works the coach yard. Turning in the opposite direction, No. 133 rolls in from San Jose (**bottom**) while the power from the morning commute gathers at the 7th Street engine track.

Top, Bob Morris; bottom, Tim Zukas

247

In July of 1980, the State of California assumed operation of the Peninsula commuter line. SP cars and locomotives continued in service for some time after. But during the late spring of 1985, the service was entirely outfitted with new push-pull train sets powered by EMD F40s. Painted in the distinctive "Caltrain" color scheme, each locomotive also was named for a city along the route. No. 902 (**above**) was named *San Mateo*. Train No. 59 (**left**) passes Santa Clara Tower on the shove to San Francisco on June 12, 1985.

Above, Bob Morris; left, Ted Benson

Finally, in May, 1977, Southern Pacific, now citing a $10 million annual loss, asked the PUC for authority to discontinue the commute trains entirely. Ridership had declined to less than 7,500 a day since August, 1973 and inflation had driven up costs 58 percent. In the "1,000 days" of regulatory stagnation and governmental indifference, the deficit had grown and SP was determined to spark some sort of governmental action, whatever the cost. Evidently, the strategy worked.

Following protracted negotiations with the state, San Francisco, San Mateo and Santa Clara counties, an agreement was finally reached, providing at least $250 million to underwrite SP's deficit and upgrade the service. On July 1, 1980, Southern Pacific's commute service was formally turned over to the State of California, with actual operation of the service conducted by Caltrans on a ten-year renewable contract. Under the agreement, Caltrans set the overall policies for the passenger service, including maintenance and performance standards, fares, scheduling and train consists, while Southern Pacific remained responsible for implementation of policies in management and operation of the commute service, guaranteeing Caltrans a minimum of 90% on-time train performance.

At startup, the new service, dubbed "Caltrain," leased SP locomotives and cars although the new operators planned to eventually acquire new cars and locomotives. SP train and engine crews also continued to staff the trains. As part of the deal, provisions were made for increasing the existing 44 trains a day to 52. Although the idea was met with resistance, there was talk of bringing the commuter trains closer to the financial district in San Francisco over State Belt Railway street trackage to the Ferry Building.

On July 7, 1980, the SP and Caltrans celebrated state takeover by operating a special train from San Francisco to San Jose and return. Aboard the train were Governor Jerry Brown and Secretary of Transportation Adriana Gianturco. For a time, the commuter trains continued to run as they always had, looking for all the world like SP trains, from the indicators up front to the last chair car. But changes did come. October 24, 1981, was the last day of three-digit, SP-numbered commuter trains and, due to differences of opinion over the value of gallery cars, Caltrans in the spring of 1982 began entertaining thoughts of new push-pull equipment with "cab cars." This idea came to fruition in the spring of 1985 when the service was entirely outfitted with new "push-pull" rolling stock with cab cars and nine new F40 locomotives, all in the distinctive Caltrain color scheme. The end had finally come for any SP passenger operations on the Coast Line.

Empowered by the seeming success of Caltrain and other state-supported service in the San Joaquin and San Diego corridors, the Brown administration moved forward with a bold plan for additional passenger service on the Coast Line. Overnight service between Los Angeles and Sacramento via Oakland was slated to start October 25, 1982. With joint funding by Amtrak and the State of California, resistance by Southern Pacific was limited. Even though pre-inaugural publicity indicated that the new trains would be called the "Californian," the new trains, operating on the Coast Line as Nos. 16 and 17, commenced service carrying no name. A "name the train" contest was sponsored by Caltrans and Amtrak, but some wags, alluding to the agricultural pest then creating a stir in the news, started calling the train the "Med Fly"–a sort of 'eighties version of the *Lark*. After due and careful consideration, the name *Spirit of California* was selected for the new overnight train. But the press had by now picked up on the name "Med Fly" and it stuck. After much fanfare, the first westbound train out of Sacramento was delayed an hour and five minutes at San Jose due to a bomb threat but the future looked good for the new train. Even then, optimistic studies were under way to

Caltrain No. 102, one of the ill-fated Oxnard Commuter runs, approaches Los Angeles Union Passenger Terminal near Broadway on December 24, 1982. The controversial service was in operation for just five months. *Clifford Prather*

extend *Spirit of California* service to Reno and Indio.

While there was little public comment from Southern Pacific regarding the *Spirit of California*, the proposed "Oxnard Commuter" train was another matter. The railroad, fearing interference with switching operations at the huge General Motors assembly plant at Gemco, resisted the concept bitterly. After a lengthy battle worthy of a television soap opera, the PUC ordered Southern Pacific to provide commuter train service for a pair of Caltrains between Oxnard and Los Angeles, starting October 18, 1982. SP was adamantly opposed to the idea from its inception, but the battle between SP and the state heated up significantly in September of 1982, when Governor Jerry Brown publicly placed his support behind the project. Caltrans sought and won permission to enter onto SP property and to build platforms and parking lots at Simi Valley and "Panorama City." Additional stations were built at Moorpark and Burbank Airport. The SP was to be paid $10 million to provide the service for one year, and trains were to be turned at Montalvo during the night.

Three days after start-up of service, SP filed suit in Sacramento Superior Court against Caltrans and its chief, Adriana Gianturco; the California Transportation Commission; and the Department of Finance and its director Mary Ann Graves, seeking to prevent the spending of future taxpayers' money on the service. On February 4, 1983, while this matter was being litigated, SP abruptly discontinued service because Caltrans had not yet paid them for running the train. Caltrans on the other hand, had loudly protested the SP's charges of $588,000 per month to operate the trains. After the discontinuance, a lawsuit was filed in Federal Court to have the service resumed and SP was ordered by the court to resume service, which it did on February 9th. After another month of struggle, the Oxnard Commuter trains died a quiet death on March 10, 1983, a victim of too few riders, too high fares and excessive fees demanded by the operator of the service. The final blow was a washout at Moorpark that caused operations to be suspended and then finally cancelled.

But perhaps the most decisive factor in the demise of the Oxnard Commuter was a new Republican governor. In the face of a large budget deficit, California's new Governor Dukemejian took a long, hard look at state-supported passenger service. It was only through persistent lobbying that the *San Joaquin* and *San Diegan* service was spared. The *Spirit of California* was the last casualty. In the face of weak ridership, funding for the *Spirit of California* was withdrawn and the trains made their last runs on September 30, 1983.

With the loss of these passenger trains on the Coast Line, Southern Pacific could concentrate on running its freight trains with only "minor" interference from the *Coast Starlight*. Since the advent of Amtrak in the spring of 1971, freight activity along the Coast had remained constant, with a tendency towards longer and heavier trains, although much was done to consolidate and streamline operations. All yard jobs (switchmen) were abolished at Santa Barbara and San Luis Obispo in 1970, the latter on February 9th. Traditional crew changes remained in place but during the spring of 1972, the freight crew changes at San Jose and Santa Barbara were abolished and the freight runs lengthened. Crews now operated between Los Angeles (Taylor Yard) and San Luis Obispo on an inter-divisional run-through, while on the north end, crews operated between Oakland and Watsonville Junction, bypassing San Jose. The run between Watsonville Junction and San Luis Obispo was unaffected.

Trains operating on the Coast during the fall of 1972 included a mixture of symbols. There were old standbys Nos. 373 and 374, the *Coast Merchandise*; the *ECP* or East Coast Peddler operating as No. 920; the *GGM* (Golden Gate Manifest); the *SF* (the San Francisco Expediter); the *SMV* (the Santa Maria Vegetable) and sugar beet trains, "the beets." But there were a few new ones: the *BAWC* (Bay Area West Colton), the new name for the old *LA*, carrying Oakland traffic destined for the new yard at West

Train No. 16, the *Spirit of California*, arrives at Glendale on its last run, October 1, 1983.
Clifford Prather

Crews still changed out on the "Zipper" at San Luis Obispo on a warm night in August, 1972. But during spring, 1972, the Santa Barbara and San Jose crew changes were replaced with new inter-divisional "run-throughs."
Tim Zukas

Symbol freight *LAOAT* (train symbols are defined on p. 260) departs Watsonville Junction (**above**) in 1976 while another westbound moves up in the distance. In another view (**right**), crews change on the curve in front of the depot. Oregon lumber train *CZLAT* (Crown Zellerbach) rolls between Welby and San Lucas (**below**) in 1987. During the mid-1970s and continuing into the early 1980s, the Coast Line experienced an increase in heavy freight traffic, much of it run-through in nature.

Above and right, Grant Flanders; below, Ted Benson

Running 50 minutes late, Amtrak train No. 12, the *Coast Starlight*, approaches the west switch at Harlem (**above**) in the upper Salinas Valley on December 24, 1975. The Hollister local arrives at Watsonville Junction (**left**) the same year. In both views, the agricultural richness of the valleys the Coast Line traverses is apparent.

Above, Tim Zukas;
left, Grant Flanders

During the dark days of the Coast Line's closure between September 1987 and August 1990, often the only action to be seen was the daily passage of Amtrak and–during the season–the beet trains. On this page "the beets" are seen at speed between Bradley and McKay (**top**), meeting No. 13 at Harlem (**left**) and No. 13 again at Sargent (**bottom**), all in 1987.

All, Ted Benson

253

254

In the panorama across these pages (**top**), the *LABAF* negotiates the "Little Horseshoe" curve near Serrano on Cuesta Grade, August 28, 1990. On April 9th of that year, beet loads drift downgrade (**above**) approaching Chorro. With the trend towards longer and heavier train, helpers were still a vital part of railroading over the Santa Lucia Range. After helping the *SF* over the hill, this three-unit helper (**left**) drops back downgrade over the Stenner Creek viaduct on August 14, 1973. The Cerro Romualdo lends a striking backdrop.

Top and above, Ed Workman; left, Tim Zukas

During the immediate pre-dawn hours of September 25, 1969, a five-unit helper operating light towards San Luis Obispo left the rails just east of tunnel No. 7 (**right**), killing three men. In recent times, tragedies such as this have been few.

Right, Southern Pacific Lines

Extra 7415 west wraps itself around the Horseshoe Curve between Goldtree and Chorro on April 5, 1990, with a solid train of empty beet racks (**top**). By now the wood-sided GS gondolas are approaching 45 years of age and considered classics by the railfan fraternity. Train crews, however, find no pleasure in the cars' friction bearings and outmoded braking systems. Conductor Elmer White (**left**) keeps a watchful eye for signs of a derailed car or dragging equipment, as he gazes at the ties receding into the distance behind the train.

Two photos, Ted Benson

A 10,716-ton sugar beet drag charges upgrade (**above**) at milepost 268.5 near Callender on April 27, 1983. Earlier in the day, the train had departed Santa Margarita with three units on the point, a six-unit "swing" helper cut in behind 50 cars, and three more units ahead of the caboose. The rear helper was cut out at San Luis Obispo, but the "swing" helper continued on to Guadalupe in order to get this monster over Callender Hill. A few years earlier, in August 1976, No. 13 zips through rows of towering eucalyptus trees (**right**) west of Callender. The groves are the legacy of C.R. Callender, who promoted eucalyptus growing on the Nipomo Mesa in the 1890s.

Two photos, Tim Zukas

Located nearly midway on the 115-mile run between Santa Barbara and San Luis Obispo, Surf continued into the early 1980s as a key operating point on the central coast. Manned 24 hours a day as late as 1985, the familiar implements of a train order office (**below, right**) were much in evidence.

All, John Roskoski

Amtrak No. 13 kicks up a cloud of dust and sand as it blasts through Surf during March, 1985. Second-trick telegrapher Glenn Trussell "rolls by" the speeding streamliner although Surf had been discontinued as a train order office March 13th: note the burlap sack covering the train order signal.

Right and below, John Roskoski

With the monument erected to commemorate the Honda Naval tragedy of 1923 (p. 64) in the foreground, the Surf Turn passes the South Vandenberg facility of the Pacific Missile Range at Honda. Though the activities at Vandenberg have, as yet, not suffered as disastrous a tragedy as that which befell the flotilla of destroyers so many years before, there have been some failures. The most recent, as of this writing, occurred June 15, 1993, when an off-course Minuteman 1 was aborted at 1,500 feet altitude, dropping debris and causing brush fires along the right-of-way.

John Roskoski

Colton in Southern California, and the *SF/I* (San Francisco/Indio), the hottest train on the Coast other than Nos. 373 and 374, which consisted of Bay Area traffic pulled from Sunset Route hotshots *Blue Streak Merchandise*, *GS* (Gold Streak) and *MTS* (a hotshot symbol operated in partnership with the Missouri Pacific, Texas and Pacific, and SP) at Indio. Trains were getting heavy enough that Cuesta helpers were sometimes run east to Oceano, milepost 265.9, where they were cut into westward trains for assistance up the one percent Price Canyon grade. By January, 1974, the *SF* was running in three sections, with the first section originating at West Colton, and the second and third sections operating out of Taylor Yard in Los Angeles.

On May 1, 1974, Southern Pacific released Condensed Perishable Merchandise and Manifest Train Schedule No. 28, which presented major changes in the way freight was to be handled on the Coast Line. A new computer-oriented symbol reference was adopted for each train, indicating its origin and destination as well as its makeup: "M" for manifest, "T" for TOFC, "F" for freight forwarder, "P" for perishable, etc. The old *CME*, No. 374, now became the *OALAT*, operating Oakland to Los Angeles daily except Saturday, Sunday and holidays with merchandise and TOFC. The *SMV* became the *GUWCP* originating at Guadalupe (cab hop from San Luis Obispo) and operating through Los Angeles to West Colton with perishables for connection with the C or Colton block, the solid-perishable train scheduled east over the Sunset Route from Colton. The *OAWCZ* handled general traffic from the Bay Area destined to Los Angeles, West Colton and beyond. The *WJLAP*, in essence the old *ECP*, operated from Watsonville Junction to Los Angeles, handling per-

Duplicating a classic 1937 *Daylight* publicity view (p. 126), the Surf local moves north along the Coast Line (**above**) at milepost 329.5 near the former siding of Gato in March, 1986. In another fine view, train No. 13, the *Coast Starlight*, approaches Gaviota in February, 1989. It is timeless, unspoiled vistas such as these that continue to capture the imagination of the traveling public.

*Above, Tim Zukas;
right, Bonnie Adams*

ishables for connection with the C block, while the *WJRVP* handled perishables from the Salinas Valley through to Roseville for connection with the R block, the Overland route perishable schedule. The *LAOAF* originated in Los Angeles destined to Oakland/San Francisco with forwarder and manifest traffic including the "Coast Hot Block" off the *BSMFF* (the Blue Streak fast freight from Chicago) connection at Los Angeles. The *LAOAT* was the new name for the *Coast Merchandise West* and handled TOFC from Los Angeles to Oakland daily except Saturday and Sunday. The *LAWJY* was in essence the "West Coast Peddler" operating out of Los Angeles to Watsonville Junction, with manifest traffic destined to Coast locations up to and including Watsonville Junction.

Not included in this list were a host of trains that originated or terminated at Bayshore or Mission Bay, San Francisco. These included Overland Route "hot shots" off the Union Pacific, like the *UPSFF* and *UPSFT* which took the Dumbarton Cutoff from Oakland and terminated at Mission Bay, and several trains that were assembled routinely at Bayshore Yard in order to relieve congestion at West Oakland. These included the *SFOAY*, *SFOGY* (Ogden), the *SFRVY*, and the *SFEUY* (Eugene), plus the Hayward Turn and the Pleasanton Turn. All of these trains also took the Dumbarton Cutoff for the East Bay. Strictly Coast trains originating at Bayshore included the Permanente Turn and the Watsonville Turn. Locals made up at Watsonville Junction included the Santa Cruz, Monterey, Hollister, San Jose, and Welby (King City) Turns, and two Salinas Turns.

The recession of 1975-1976 impacted Coast Line operations. A general slackening of business combined with management efforts to control costs resulted in fewer, larger trains. The downgrading and eventual elimination of the long-running *Coast Merchandise* trains occurred in this period. Trains Nos. 373 and 374, running as *LAOAT* and *OALAT*, were discontinued on September 4, 1975. Actually, No. 374 still continued to run for a time as far as San Luis Obispo where it became the "Coast Peddler" for the remainder of its journey to Los Angeles. The TOFC traffic continued on to Los Angeles on the *WJLAP*. No. 373 was eliminated entirely, its traffic handled by the *WCOAF*. Thus ended a service dating back to 1935 when the "Zipper" was inaugurated.

The beginning of the end for these trains could be traced back to the end of direct San Francisco service about 1971. Following World War II, the importance of San Francisco as a manufacturing center and seaport began a long decline. Most of its factories and mills were old and cramped for space, and when faced with rebuilding and expansion, many companies left the City for locations where there was more room to grow. In many cases this was the East Bay. Indeed, the Port of Oakland was perhaps the ultimate undoing of San Francisco's once-great waterfront. The Port of Oakland, learning from its experience as the primary Port Of Embarkation for the Vietnam War, had early on embraced the concept of containerization and, as this concept swept the shipping industry, had succeeded in garnering the lion's share of the ocean-going traffic.

With the diminished importance of San Francisco as a terminal, the "Zipper" which had previously been split (or joined, depending on direction) at San Jose into San Francisco and Oakland sections now served only the Port of Oakland. Any trailers destined to San Francisco were simply detrained at Oakland and trucked across the Bay Bridge. With the marketplace changing, the importance of these trains declined. Their time schedules were unreliable and frequently they were annulled between Oakland and San Jose so that they could switch the General Motors plant at Warm Springs.

Description of these new symbol trains to handle Coast Line perishable traffic should not conceal the reality that SP had suffered a steady decline in perishable carloadings since trucks began to make serious inroads into the business about 1960. The completion of the 56,000-mile federal Interstate Highway system dealt a serious blow to the railroads. An independent trucker could load right in the field and deliver the product to Chicago in 56-$\frac{1}{2}$ hours as opposed to the railroad's three days plus transloading to a packing house. Pacific Fruit Express (SP and partner Union Pacific's perishable shipping subsidiary) countered with refrigerated trailers of their own for shipping aboard trains. But the PFE trailers were narrower than highway ones, and gave shippers little incentive to divert from trucks. Before long, the situation had deteriorated to the point that if the price of lettuce fell, it went to the trains, if it rose, it went to trucks.

The year 1974 saw a tremendous burst in the productivity of the Salinas Valley. Where for years an

Empty PFE reefers roll through Oceano (**above**) in July, 1972, while a switcher works fully-spotted shed trackage in the distance. Howard Cissner (**right**) leans out the cab window during switching operations amongst the lettuce fields at Watsonville Junction in 1976. The same year, the second section of perishable hauler *WJRVP* departs Watsonville Junction (**below**) behind commute SDPs borrowed for the weekend. Despite vigorous attempts to retain the business, and the deregulation of perishable traffic in 1979, the bulk of the Coast Line's once-profitable perishable haul has been lost to trucks.

Above, Tim Zukas; right and below, Grant Flanders

In the 1980s and beyond, railroading on the Coast retained many of its historic features. On the Cuesta, the age-old meets at Chorro still took place, as shown by this train behind rebuilt SD9 No. 4350, in the hole for a westward extra in October, 1984 (**top**). The long-lived SD9s continued to serve as Cuesta helpers during the 1980s. In San Luis Obispo crews still changed (**center**), as in this scene from July, 1987 with Roseville-based EMD SD45T-2 No. 9344, and a helper set in the background. And as long as "the beets" used the old wood-sheathed general-service gondolas with side extensions, one could still catch scenes like this westward train at Waldorf in 1992, with the Betteravia plant's steam plume in the distance (**bottom**). But today the veteran beet gons are finally retired.

Top, Jay Bell; center, Anthony Thompson; bottom, John Roskoski

Scenery along the Pacific shore remains a quintessential Coast Line feature. With GP40-2M No. 7137 on the point in new lettering, merchandise freight WSWCM rolls past wildflowers in bloom at Dulah along the Ventura coast on April 20, 1992 (**above**). As Amtrak took charge in 1971, most trains were at first little altered in appearance. Here four ex-SP F units lead No. 98 eastward over Gaviota Trestle (**right**). Twenty years later, spring green covers the hills as engine No. 286 and the westward *Coast Starlight* leave Gaviota Trestle on April 11, 1991 (**below**).

Above and below, Bonnie Adams; right, Southern Pacific Lines

A work train lays fiber-optic communication cable along the main line at Seacliff in March, 1989. In an increasingly urbanized California, new uses have been found for the Coast Line and its 482-mile unbroken right-of-way between San Francisco and Los Angeles.
Bonnie Adams

With real estate prices skyrocketing, some underutilized railroad yards in urban areas on the Coast Line were targeted for redevelopment. In recent times, Taylor Yard in Los Angeles and Bayshore and Mission Bay Yards in San Francisco have all been considered prime areas for development. This model depicts the project proposed for the as-yet unbuilt Mission Bay site, as it was initially visualized in August, 1983.
Southern Pacific Lines

acre had produced about 200 cartons of lettuce, now with improved irrigation, fertilizer and seeds, the same field might yield between 800 and 1,000 cartons per acre. But despite this bounty, the railroad's share of the business had fallen off markedly after 1973 and fell further during the 1975 recession, until dedicated perishable trains were discontinued entirely. It was difficult to compete with independent truckers who charged whatever it took to get the traffic, while the railroad had to stay within published tariffs.

Determined to compete for the lucrative Coast perishable traffic, Southern Pacific placed in service a new experimental perishable schedule, dubbed the "Salad Bowl Express," on May 12th, 1976. The recession had ended and perishable counts increased in the Salinas Valley, averaging by mid-summer from 160 to 225 cars a day and with the *WJRVP* running in three sections most days. But following seasons were discouraging, with truckers rallying for the business and a new competitor, Santa Fe, trucking lettuce out of the valley for the ramp at Calwa Yard in Fresno to be loaded on Santa Fe's hotshots bound for Chicago. On May 28, 1979, the ICC removed regulations governing rail transportation of fresh produce. SP responded quickly by re-establishing the "Salad Bowl Express" and over the summer SP's volume of lettuce shipments out of the Salinas Valley tripled over the previous year. But despite deregulation, the bulk of the Coast perishable business was still being handled by truck and today, a number of factors combine to limit SP's perishable movement to a mere shadow of its former self.

All was not bleak, however. In the midst of the decline in perishable business SP found itself at the forefront of the boom in intermodal shipments. Trailers and international containers comprised the bulk of the traffic to be handled on a new SP Coast Line symbol called the *LAOAC* and *OALAC*. Established on June 13, 1980, the new hotshots sported specially assigned motive power consisting of two sets of four units apiece, made up of GP40Xs and GP40-2s. To save on fuel, the trailing units were set up with remote devices which allowed them to remain at idle, only kicking in where needed to maintain speed.

With the rapid decline in rail perishable shipments, Watsonville Junction suffered. During November 1976, SP razed the old Watsonville

Junction yard office, comprising the original 1875 Pajaro station and various additions, and further trimmed the yard's ability to clean and precool reefers. But Watsonville Junction was not the only Coast terminal in this period to suffer cutbacks.

In the spring of 1979, Bayshore Yard was phased out, with Newhall Yard in San Jose picking up the slack. Over the next several years, Bayshore was slowly dismantled while SP pondered what to do with all that prime real estate. San Francisco's other major yard, Mission Bay, was the first to fall to the developers. On August 2, 1983, Southern Pacific and the City of San Francisco announced a plan to develop the former Mission Bay Yards site into 7,577 residential units, 4.1 million square feet of office space, 2.6 million square feet of research and development facilities and 200,000 square feet of retail space, all in buildings not higher than eight stories. All SP freight operations on the north end of the Peninsula, as modest as they had become, were eventually switched from what remained of Bayshore Yard to South San Francisco on November 17, 1988.

Further cutbacks to the physical plant in the Bay Area were to follow. During May, 1982, the SP closed the Dumbarton Bridge line—and this less than five years after a million-dollar program had replaced miles of post and pile trestle with modern concrete bents and decks. Redwood Junction Tower, opened in 1909 to issue orders to the Dumbarton line, remained open after the closure but only two trains a day used interlocking crossovers: the Broadway Local, switching the Ravenswood district of Menlo Park, and the San Carlos Turn switching the area around the Redwood City Port. Eventually, in December, 1986, the tower was closed as well. It was finally destroyed by fire on March 12, 1987.

Plant rationalization was not confined to just the north end of the Coast Line. A series of brutal storms that ravaged California in late February and early March, 1983 closed the Coast Line for more than a week and would eventually lead to the abandonment of part of the Santa Paula Branch. Record amounts of rain had fallen during the last half of January, saturating the ground and setting the stage for disaster. The next series of storms began pounding California on February 24th and by the morning of March 1st, both the Coast and Tehachapi lines were out. Amtrak was annulled until further notice. A washout, 125 feet long by 35 feet deep, occurred at Moorpark and 2,500 feet of track at Seacliff was lost to the pounding surf. Maintenance-of-way inspectors found riprap thrown up on the track near Carpinteria. Some of the boulders weighed upwards of 900 pounds. The 549-foot bridge at the Santa Ynez River near Surf suffered severe damage which took seven days to repair. The trouble at Moorpark was cleared up on the 3rd but it took until 2:50 AM, March 9th, for the Santa Ynez River bridge to be repaired. The *RVWCY*-06, a train normally operated over the Tehachapi, was the first train over the rebuilt bridge and the start of an anticipated ten trains each way in 16 hours. Temporary train order offices were set up at Santa Susana and Gaviota in trailers. Two days later, at 11:05 AM on March 10, the Tehachapi line was finally opened.

Also damaged in the '83 storm was the Santa Paula Branch; in fact, it was dealt a fatal blow. Once the main line into Los Angeles, the Santa Paula line had been relegated to secondary status since 1904. Nevertheless, it had been used in a pinch as a detour on numerous occasions. The most recent detours had taken place in the fall of 1972. Due to lowering the tunnel floor in tunnel No. 26, the main line over Santa Susana Pass was out of service for seven days, effective 5:30 AM, October 2, 1972. Trains No. 12 and 13 terminated at Oxnard with bus connections between Oxnard and Los Angeles. All other traffic was rerouted over the Santa Paula Branch. Due to a lack of passing tracks, trains were fleeted first westward (373, *GGM* and *WCP*) then east (*SMW*, 374, *OLA*). On October 7th, the *OLA* with 130 cars required the services of the Saugus switcher to boost the train up to Tunnel from Fillmore. The huge train broke in two, dramatically underscoring the difficulties of the route. The following year there was a hasty Amtrak detour, but the line was not being maintained up to standard. A violent storm over Labor Day weekend, 1976, dubbed "Hurricane Kathleen," took out the Santa Clara River bridge west of Saugus as well as the smaller span over San Francisquito Creek near Castaic, and these bridges were not replaced. The additional damage sustained during the 1983 storm was widespread enough to merit abandonment. Since the 1976 storm, the east end of the branch had been plugged with stored cars. On June 25, 1983, the last group of these cars was retrieved and late in July,

Due to the demands of increased traffic, a temporary train order office, utilizing a caboose, was established at the west end of Santa Margarita during the spring of 1982.
John R. Signor

The "Tracy Beets" works the Santa Maria Valley interchange at Guadalupe in April, 1988, while the Guadalupe switcher holds the main. Rising prominently in the foreground are the Direct Traffic Control signs designating the line between the Guadalupe and Waldorf blocks. The implementation of DTC on the Coast Line in late 1985 and early 1986 resulted in the closure of all remaining train order offices on the line.
Ted Benson

the Santa Paula Branch between Piru and Saugus was formally abandoned.

The temporary train order office, established at Gaviota during the 1983 storms, was resurrected the following year, on May 25th, 1984, with business mounting on the Coast. An additional office, housed in a former caboose, had been set up at the west end of Santa Margarita during the spring of 1982. But these offices, as well as all other train order offices on the Coast Line, were on short time. With the widespread use and reliability of radio, Southern Pacific began adopting a new form of traffic control in former train order territory. Direct Traffic Control or DTC was implemented on the Coast Line between Salinas and Santa Margarita on November 20, 1985. Burbank Junction to San Luis Obispo was cut over to the new system on March 1, 1986. Under DTC, the railroad was divided up into a series of "blocks," each with a passing track, and operations were conducted by radio, with the dispatcher authorizing trains to advance in blocks and train crews releasing blocks behind them. Meets were accomplished by simply notifying a train by radio to "take siding." With no further need for train order operators, the remaining stations along the Coast were closed one by one. Surf was closed for good August 30, 1985; Santa Barbara on September 14, 1985; and Guadalupe, Oxnard, and Paso Robles all suffered similar fates.

Cabooseless operations, another trend of the modern era, came to the Coast Line late in the spring of 1986.

During the summer months, when the grass-covered slopes turn a golden brown, the fire danger rises dramatically. For years, fire cars were assigned to Cuesta Grade and located at Cuesta siding in season. Serious fires had closed the Coast Line on September 6, 1955, near Gaviota. The principal damage was to the pole lines, with some 70 miles of wire having to be replaced. A particularly devastating wildfire developed in the mountains ringing San Luis Obispo on July 8, 1985. The Cuesta fire train was hastily assembled and made a pass between Santa Margarita and San Luis Obispo, hosing down the interiors of the two remaining wood-lined tunnels on the grade. After soaking down the right-of-way and ties, SP crews then proceeded to attack the head of the advancing flames. A spokesman for the California Division of Forestry later said that several homes would have undoubtedly been lost without the intervention of the fire train.

It was a fire on the Cuesta Grade less than two years later that proved to be a turning point in the history of the Coast Line. Just after midnight, on April 29, 1987, a westbound train passing through tunnel No. 7 reported a fire in the 1,354-foot long, partly concrete-lined, partly wooden-beam bore. The fire burned for two days before finally being extinguished by SP specialists brought in from Eugene, Oregon. But the fire managed to get into some of the old wooden timbers behind the concrete-lined construction and flared up again on May 3rd. Part of the tunnel collapsed 400 feet from the east portal. When the smoke finally cleared for the second time, SP was faced with rebuilding over 1,100 feet of the tunnel. The fire and reconstruction effort closed the Coast Line for a total of 13 days, forcing the re-routing of all freight trains to the San Joaquin Valley Line. Amtrak was annulled for the duration. At last the tunnel was reopened on May 11, 1987, at a total cost of $1.9 million.

After the Coast Line was reopened, only Amtrak, the *LABAF*, the *OALAT* and the tri-weekly Coast Peddler were allowed to pass through the tunnel "to allow maintenance-of-way personnel time to complete repairs." As the summer wore on, no additional trains were routed on the Coast Line; then, without prior notice, Southern Pacific closed down the Coast Line to through freight operation on September 29, 1987. Henceforth, the railroad announced, the only through trains scheduled to operate were the Amtrak *Coast Starlights*. The rerouting of all Coast freight traffic during the fire had gone more smoothly than anticipated, and a cost-conscious SP had conducted a secret study over the summer, evaluating the economics of closing the Coast Line entirely to through traffic. Unit sugar beet trains to Guadalupe were now handled as turns, as were the weekly unit coke trains operating out of Callender. Locals continued to service the line as before.

The closing of the Coast Line hit the hardest at San Luis Obispo, where employees were handed termination notices on September 28th. Before the closure there were 18 clerks, 107 trainmen and 41 engineers at San Luis Obispo; now just six trainmen and four engineers remained. Forty-eight picketers marched in front of the SP office building at One Market Plaza (formerly 65 Market Street), San Francisco, on October 19, 1987, to protest the closure of the Coast Line and the elimination of San Luis Obispo as a terminal. The big crash of the stock market that day apparently had something to do with the sparse media coverage for the event.

Following the closure, local service was provided by a Guadalupe-based road switcher that worked the territory between San Luis Obispo and Surf, and Oxnard-Surf turns operating out of Oxnard. Watsonville Junction was eliminated as a crew change also. Crews from Oakland or San Jose now turned at Salinas. Coast sidings were filled with stored cars. Seacliff, Narlon, Gaviota and Sudden, after being filled with out-of-service cars, actually had the switches removed to prevent entry of the cars onto the mainline.

A year after the closure, despite rumors of impending new reduced-crew "Sprint" intermodal train service, the Coast Line was strangely quiet. Only an occasional detour disturbed the daily passage of the Amtrak train. (The *LABAF* operated over the Coast Line on April 12, 1988, due to a derailment in the Tehachapi.) A more consistent pattern of detours started January 7, 1989. Due to rail replacement in the Tehachapi which was supposed to last 30 days, it was planned to run as many trains as possible on the Coast, but operations were thwarted by a shortage of crews, most notably at San Luis Obispo. The detours continued on and off through May 8, 1989. By this time, San Luis Obispo yard had been completely dismantled except for No. 1 track, and the double track main line.

By the summer of 1989, the future of the Coast Line looked bleak indeed, but there was a change in the wind. Southern Pacific, which had suffered in the 1980s due to the failed merger attempts with arch-rival Santa Fe, was acquired by billionaire Denver oil man Philip Anschutz on October 13, 1988. Immediately upon assuming control of the SP, Anschutz announced the reopening of the recently closed Modoc Line in northern California and Nevada. Hopes were raised about a possible Coast Line reopening as well, and Anschutz had indeed promised three trains a day each way if, and when, the brotherhoods would sign "favorable agreements." This referred to the industry trend towards operating freight trains with a conductor and engineer only.

As promised, following the implementation of two-man crews, through freights resumed regular operation over the Coast Line on August 1, 1990, after a lapse of some three years. Things were different, though. San Luis Obispo was no longer an originating terminal. The reduced crews now operated between Oakland and San Luis Obispo and Los Angeles and San Luis Obispo, laying over only at the former division point.

Anschutz control of the Southern Pacific had brought back the freight trains to the Coast Line, but perhaps even more significantly, the SP under new management now held a more enlightened view towards government-subsidized passenger service operating over its rail lines–including the Coast Line. This attitude, together with the passage of several state rail transit bond issues and mounting pressures to solve the transportation problems of an increasingly urbanized California, pointed the way towards a re-emergence of the Coast Line as a premier rail passenger corridor, something it was made for but hadn't been since the late 1940s.

The popularity of the Coast Line as a passenger route was already underscored by the phenomenal success of the *Coast Starlight*, the most popular long-distance train in the Amtrak system. Capitalizing on this success, the *California Sun Express*, a service offered by Princess Rail Tours, began inaugural runs out of Oakland and Los Angeles on April 1, 1990. Princess Rail Tours was an offshoot of the Princess Cruises ship operation. The cars employed in the service, full-length "super" domes touted in travel literature as "originally used on the Milwaukee Road's *Olympian Hiawatha* and the Canadian Pacific," were entirely refurbished for about $1.5 million and had recently been used on the company's successful "Tour Alaska" excursions.

In operation, the cars were simply attached to the rear of the *Coast Starlight*, providing exclusive and deluxe accommodations completely separate from the rest of the train. The daily excursions were packaged with side trips to San Simeon and Hearst Castle, Cambria and Morro Bay. A full deluxe one-way fare topped out at $399 (double occupancy), with various other options including partial trips terminating at San Luis Obispo and basic "no-meal service" priced accordingly.

The Princess Rail Tours operation rotated three cars in the *California Sun Express* service in order to provide adequate maintenance, but there were maddening equipment failures, most notably air conditioning, forcing patrons to complete their journeys by bus or in the regular part of the train. Ridership was soft. By the beginning of July, Princess Tours announced that "it has become clear that public demand will not achieve levels necessary to make the *California Sun Express* an economically viable operation." The deluxe service was discontinued on July 31, 1990, with 37 boarding at Oakland for the final run; another 30 got on at San Luis Obispo.

With the country in the midst of a recession, the timing wasn't right for a deluxe service on the Coast, but the economies of rail travel for the masses were more relevant than ever. Caltrans, having recovered ground from the disappointments of the early 1980s, initiated its first Santa Barbara extension of *San Diegan* service on June 26, 1988. Not intended as a commuter, the service was scheduled as a morning departure from Santa Barbara, and assumed a mid-morning southbound *San Diegan* schedule out of Los Angeles. The return trip was an extension of the late

During the spring of 1990, Princess Tours began offering a deluxe railcar service on the Coast Line, dubbed *The California Sun Express*. In operation, a specially outfitted dome car was added to the rear of the *Coast Starlight* between Oakland and Los Angeles. Under-patronized from the start, the service was discontinued on July 31, 1990. Here the Princess Tours car brings up the rear of No. 13 at Chatsworth the day before discontinuance.
Bruce Veary

San Diegan No. 771 skirts the Pacific on March 18, 1992 at the Coast Line classic location near Ortega (see pp. 55 and 168). Extension of *San Diegan* service to Santa Barbara began during summer, 1988 with a single round trip. Currently there are two. *Bonnie Adams*

afternoon departure from San Diego, returning to Santa Barbara late in the evening.

The new Santa Barbara service used the existing Amtrak stops of Glendale and Oxnard, but also stopped at the ill-fated Oxnard Commuter platforms at Chatsworth, Van Nuys-Panorama City and Burbank Airport. A new stop was planned for Ventura. A second train was added on October 28, 1990 and at the same time, an additional stop, Simi Valley (first opened October 26, 1986), was added to the service. Proposals were under consideration to add a third and fourth train to the Santa Barbara service as well as to extend rail service to San Luis Obispo and also San Francisco-Monterey (connecting buses were already in place). Even a revival of the ill-fated Sacramento-Los Angeles overnight service via the Coast Line was not out of the question.

There was renewed optimism regarding the future of rail passenger service in California, but it took something distinctively Californian to drive the point home that rail service wasn't necessarily a luxury, but could become a necessity. Earthquakes are nothing new to the Coast Line. Coast Line rails were destroyed in the great San Francisco quake and fire of 1906, the Santa Barbara quake of 1925, and in more recent memory, on Sunday, August 13, 1978. On that day at 3:55 PM, an earthquake registering 5.6 on the Richter scale shook the Santa Barbara area. At 4:08 PM, the Extra 7605 West (01-*LAOAY*-13) was rolling past milepost 357, just west of Ellwood, when the train encountered shifted roadbed and warped rail. The locomotives made it through without incident but 31 trailing cars were derailed. The line was closed for 24 hours, but impact on highway transportation was minimal.

Then came Tuesday, October 17, 1989. A major earthquake registering 7.1 on the Richter scale hit northern California at the worst possible time, during the afternoon rush hour. The epicenter of the quake was nine miles northeast of Santa Cruz, causing widespread damage in Santa Cruz, Los Gatos and Watsonville, but the quake also hit hard in the

Marina District in San Francisco, the industrial section of West Oakland, and even collapsed a span of the strategic Oakland-San Francisco Bay Bridge. When the dust had settled, the "Loma Prieta" quake had accounted for 62 deaths and over $6 billion in damage.

The quake knocked out the computer mainframes and did considerable damage to the exterior of the Southern Pacific general office at One Market Plaza. Out on the line, the force of the quake ripped a three-foot twist in the Coast Line at Sargent and shifted the Pajaro River Bridge near Logan. A landslide and compression of the subgrade took out the Santa Cruz Branch. The computers were back up by 8:45 PM, Tuesday the 17th, and all major rail routes inspected and approved for reopening of service by 6:00 AM, Wednesday, October 18th. "From literally moments after the earthquake until shortly before 10 PM, our maintenance crews inspected the four tunnels in San Francisco and both mainline tracks between the City and San Jose," said SP President Mike Mohan. "There was no damage but the trains traveled at restricted speeds because power outages knocked out signals and crossing gates at intersections along the route."

The Coast Line was relatively undamaged, but the same could not be said for the Bay Area's complex network of highways. Not only did the strategic Bay Bridge suffer damage and closure, but whole stretches of the double-deck Interstate 880 freeway in West Oakland collapsed, killing a number of motorists. Because of this failure, double-deck portions of both I-280 in San Francisco and the Embarcadero Freeway were closed, and the latter was eventually dismantled.

With major highway arteries in shambles, public transit, including rail, picked up the slack. On Monday, October 23rd, in an effort to ease the commuter crunch, the Peninsula service was extended with a single daily round trip between San Jose and Salinas. This was cancelled on November 10, 1989 as things began to settle back to normal. But to alleviate traffic congestion resulting from the closure of earthquake-damaged I-280 in San Francisco, Caltrans implemented two reverse-peak trains for a one-year period effective April 1, 1991. Ridership rose dramatically, 11.4 percent in the first four months following the quake. All other rail service in the area experienced markedly increased ridership. This rekindled interest in rail commuter transit in California as a whole and, more importantly, resulted in the passing of critical funding legislation.

Those expanding rail passenger operations benefiting from this funding, and most directly affecting the Coast Line were the Peninsula commute operation and those operations planned by the Los Angeles County Transportation Commission, for separate and different reasons.

Several years before the Loma Prieta Quake, in July, 1987, representatives of the city and county of San Francisco, along with the counties of Santa Clara and San Mateo, formed the Peninsula Corridor Joint Powers Board or JPB for the express purpose of saving SP's Peninsula commuter operation from being abandoned.

Shortly before the original operating contract between Caltrans and SP expired on June 30, 1990, a new agreement was reached to ensure continued commute service into 1991. The new agreement provided for an increase in frequency of up to 66 trains per day and the operation of up to 15 special trains per year (up from 12).

In January, 1991, the Joint Powers Board approved a letter of intent to purchase 52.4 miles of SP Coast Line right-of-way between San Francisco and San Jose for $242.3 million. The agreement also provided for future acquisition of the eleven-mile Dumbarton line, an 8.4-mile section of the Vasona Branch and trackage rights for an additional 25 miles to Gilroy.

State Senator Quentin Kopp, I-San Francisco, charged in mid-June 1991 that SP had "bamboozled" the negotiators and that the property should be taken over by eminent domain at a far lower price—about $20 million. But with Caltrain's future in question as a result of the state budget crisis, Peninsula rail boosters feared Kopp could inadvertently torpedo the deal. SP Vice Chairman Robert F. Starzel countered that the SP was in a "very precarious financial position" and that the Peninsula line was now carrying so little freight that it "already meets ICC freight guidelines for abandonment." Starzel warned that unless the deal was allowed to continue, the railroad would have no choice but to file for abandonment of the line, putting 22,000 daily commuters onto the region's already congested highways and crippling the Port of San Francisco's expansion plans.

The Joint Powers Board control of Peninsula commute service brought many changes, including service south of San Jose to Tamien (**above, left**), and the consolidation of control from old interlocking towers like College Park (**above, right**), closed during April 1993, into a new operations center near the Cahill Station. Tamien comprises little more than a passage beneath the railroad and an underground ticket booth, with stairs to overhead platforms of both the San Jose light rail and Peninsula heavy rail services. Automobile parking and bus service complete the facility.

Above left, Anthony Thompson; above right, Bruce Veary

Despite these threats, the state Transportation Commission, chaired by Kopp, spent four months criticizing the deal, but finally on October 18, 1991, voted 6-1 with "grave reservations" to go ahead with the deal. SP had also agreed to contribute $10 million toward building a $66 million maintenance shop in San Jose. The deal was consummated December 27, 1991, ending the Company's 127-year ownership of the Peninsula passenger service.

Southern Pacific continued to contract with the state to operate the service, but on July 1, 1992, Amtrak, the successful bidder for the operating contract, assumed operations and under direction from the JPB, immediately expanded Caltrain service from 54 to 60 weekday trains. In addition, two morning and two evening round trips were established to Gilroy. The service cutover was not without its problems, but there was a renewed sense of optimism.

Elaborate plans were laid for the revitalized Peninsula service in which San Jose would take a major role. Both Amtrak and the Peninsula commute equipment would share a proposed centralized maintenance facility at the site of the former Lick Quarry south of the city. Major changes and improvements were also slated for San Jose Terminal itself. The old SP station on Cahill Street was to be rehabilitated and parking increased to accommodate 880 vehicles.

In addition, an entirely new terminal was to be built at West Alma Avenue, about two miles south of the existing station on Cahill Street. The new terminal, called Tamien after the Indian village and burial ground discovered at the site, provides a direct interface with the Guadalupe Corridor of San Jose's expanding light rail transit system and with city buses, as well as parking for over 400 vehicles.

Traffic control functions, once handled by a series of interlocking towers strung out along the Peninsula, were at first planned to be consolidated in the San Francisco terminal tower. But plans were changed and all functions were eventually cut over to the SCO (Supervisor Commute Operations), located a block from Cahill Street station. As the SCO came on line, functions handled by the remaining towers were consolidated, and one by one the towers were closed: San Jose Telegraph first, then Fourth Street Tower in San Francisco, College Park during April 1993, and finally Santa Clara in July 1993.

Looking into the future, Caltrain planners considered service extensions to downtown San Francisco, as well as the extension of service to Gilroy and over the Dumbarton Bridge. Draft improvement plans recommended such bold concepts as line electrification in the years 1993-95; San Francisco Terminal relocation in the years 1993-96; and Peninsula CTC by 1996.

By the fall of 1993, some of these plans were coming to fruition. CTC was being extended to Gilroy as part of an overall program in progress designed to accommodate increased Caltrain commuter operations between Oakland and Gilroy. As part of this project, a new CTC siding was being installed at Morgan Hill (still called Morganhill by SP), and extensive modifications and additions were being made to the track layout at Gilroy.

Meanwhile, a different scenario was unfolding in southern California. Southern Pacific and the newly formed Los Angeles County Transportation Commission (LACTC) announced on October 12, 1990, that they had agreed on the sale of "certain rights-of-way plus 150 acres of land for stations and shops [which included 65 acres at the old Taylor Yard site] for $450 million." The LACTC, empowered by the passage of rail passenger bond issues, was embarking on an ambitious plan to create a Southern California rail passenger network based on the use of conventional technology and existing right-of-way. That the SP was in total support of the idea was demonstrated by the Company running a "Proposition C Special" on November 1st, with business cars *Stanford*, *Sunset* and *Utah*, from San Fernando out to Pomona and back. The SP deal included the Burbank Branch and trackage rights–for $50 million–over 46 miles of Coast Line from Los Angeles Union Passenger Terminal to Moorpark, as well as a forty-foot strip of land adjacent to the mainline for a future commuter rail system. Without releasing many details, service start-up was projected for 1992, with four round trips operating between Moorpark (Ventura County) and Los Angeles.

Funding for the track, signals, facilities and equipment was to come from a combination of Amtrak, LACTC, state and local funds. During the summer of 1991, the LACTC service was designated as "Metro Link," and all Southern California rail transit agencies were joined under one umbrella as the Southern California Regional Rail Authority with LACTC acting as lead agency. SP's former Taylor Yard was selected as the site for run-through car and locomotive shops and the mid-day layover point for LACTC runs up the Coast, to Santa Clarita (Saugus Line) and San Bernardino. The Moorpark-Los Angeles run was designated the "West Line."

LACTC ordered 40 bi-level commuter cars from Canadian car builder UTDC (similar to Toronto GO transit coaches) and 17 General Motors F59PH locomotives for Metro Link, with delivery anticipated for

A new Metro Link commuter train, No. 101, approaches Santa Susana on May 28, 1993. The inauguration of Metro Link service over the route between Moorpark and Los Angeles took place on October 26, 1992, with four trains a day each way. As of this writing, service is up to six a day each way.
Bruce Veary

February through July, 1992. In addition, Caltrans ordered 88 bilevel "California Cars" (24 of them cab cars) of stainless steel construction from Morrison-Knudsen of Boise, Idaho, 48 of which were to be used evenly between the Caltrain Peninsula Corridor and Metro Link.

Because of this unique mix of local, regional, state and federal funding of rail projects in California, the state took the lead in overall coordinating of the various projects under way, and published the results of their study. "The California Rail Passenger Development Plan for 1991-1996 Fiscal Years," published by Caltrans in July, 1991, targeted the Coast Line for a sweeping plan of betterments to be funded under the state Intercity Rail Program. For the fiscal years 1991-92, funding was already available to acquire and upgrade the Burbank, Glendale, Ventura and Van Nuys stations as well as provide double-track CTC from Burbank Junction to Raymer, reverse signal CTC from the Allen Ave. crossovers in Burbank to Dayton Tower in Los Angeles, and to upgrade the Chatsworth and Moorpark sidings and construct a four-track layover yard at Moorpark

Southern Pacific engineers were contracted by the LACTC to do the design work for the CTC improvements on the Coast Line between Burbank Junction and Moorpark. During 1992-93, the plan envisioned extending Camarillo siding, installing CTC from Moorpark to Goleta, and constructing a new siding at Carpinteria. During 1993-94, numerous improvements to the Santa Barbara station facilities were planned, including reverse running on the Santa Barbara double track, upgrading Seacliff and Ventura sidings for faster running, installing a new siding at East Simi Valley, improving the new Simi Valley Station, and constructing double track from Northridge to Raymer. During 1994-95, plans were in place to extend the double track from Northridge to the south portal of tunnel No. 28. And during 1995-96, plans were to extend service to Goleta as well as fund studies to extend service to San Luis Obispo, with connecting buses as far as Paso Robles, San Francisco and Monterey.

Once under way, the pace of change to the southern end of the Coast Line increased. On February 14, 1992, a groundbreaking ceremony was held for a new Amtrak/Metro Link commuter station at Simi Valley.

A press run for the new *San Diegan* service to Santa Barbara moves out from the newly completed Oxnard "Transportation Center" in shove mode on June 25, 1988. *Clifford Prather*

The historic Burbank depot burned before renovation could be undertaken, but it was to be replaced with a new "Community Transportation Center." An entirely new station was planned for Chatsworth, patterned after the original Southern Pacific building which was demolished in December, 1962.

Once enough power and cars had been delivered, and most of the track improvements completed, a series of timing runs were conducted between LAUPT and Moorpark during early September, 1992 to develop schedules. Finally, on October 26th, revenue service commenced with four trains running each way. The initial trains were as follows: departing Moorpark, No. 100 at 5:06 AM, No. 102 at 5:51 AM, No. 104 at 6:31 AM and No. 106 at 7:16 AM; departing Los Angeles, No. 101 at 4:10 PM, No. 103 at 4:45 PM, No. 105 at 5:30 PM and No. 107 at 6:20 PM. Trains were normally in "push" mode inbound into Los Angeles. By the following summer, an additional train each way, Nos. 108 and 109, were on the timecard.

These trains, combined with the four daily Amtrak Santa Barbara trains and the daily *Coast Starlight*, totaling 16 passenger trains a day on the Coast Line between Burbank Junction and Moorpark, have created a passenger train density in the area not seen since the late 'twenties! ❏

Epilogue

AS THIS IS WRITTEN, demand for more rail passenger service along the Coast Line is enormous and growing. Existing trains like the *Coast Starlight* are booked weeks and months in advance, even during the winter months. Bus systems set up to divert passenger traffic to the less popular *San Joaquin* rail route are spectacular successes. In contrast, freight service on the Coast line has dwindled to the point that the Southern Pacific has determined that the cost of maintaining the right-of-way for the current level of Amtrak trains that use the route exceed the freight revenues and Amtrak reimbursement. Consequently if there is to be increased rail passenger service along the coast, the SP has argued that a public agency or a consortium of public agencies would have to come together to acquire the right-of-way and assume the financial responsibilities for upgrading the track and improving signaling.

The concept of selling strategic right-of-way to public agencies had already been demonstrated as feasible in Southern California and the Bay Area, with participation by all three western transcontinental ralroads serving California. Consequently, Southern Pacific began to explore ways to market its 380-mile Coast Line between Gilroy (the line north of Gilroy was already owned by the JPB) and Los Angeles. A major thrust of SP's plans included use of the route as a "high-speed" corridor. A study was conducted during the summer of 1992, which determined that schedules of 6.25 hours could be achieved between Burbank Junction and San Jose with conventional rolling stock (and five hours with "tilt-trains") without major engineering work to eliminate Cuesta Grade. About 60% of the route could be re-engineered to support 80 mph for conventional rolling stock and at least 100 mph for tilt-trains. SP concluded that elapsed times of six to seven hours between San Francisco and Los Angeles were possible, and even more if a tunnel under Cuesta Grade were added to the list of engineering improvements.

On September 30, 1992, Southern Pacific announced that it had granted a one-year option on the Coast Line to the Los Angeles County Transportation Commission with assignability by LACTC to other interested county transit agencies along the 424-mile route.

"We were approached by LACTC as to the possibility of such an agreement," said Tom Matthews, vice president-administration for SP, "and we have cooperated fully with the Commission staff in the discussions that led to this announcement." Matthews predicted that the Coast Line could provide "fast train" service as early as 1994 between Los Angeles and the Bay Area, and in addition sufficient right-of-way existed to allow commuter or tourist service between the cities of San Jose, Salinas, Santa Cruz, Monterey/Carmel, San Luis Obispo, Santa Barbara and Ventura/Oxnard.

But there were clouds on the horizon. The federal Department of Transportation, in December 1992, selected the San Diego-Los Angeles-Oakland corridor as one of five routes to be studied for possible upgrading to 110-mph passenger speeds. A $1.2-million federal grant was provided, enabling Caltrans to continue feasibility studies of the 655-mile route: but via the San Joaquin Valley. The San Joaquin Route, however, would require extensive tunneling to reduce grades in the Techachapi Mountains, as well as much

The look of the future? Amtrak and Southern Pacific sponsored the Bay Area–Los Angeles segment of the American tour by the X2000 Swedish-built tilt-train in mid-July, 1993. The exotic-looking train descends Cuesta Grade below Serrano (**above**) on July 13th. The same day, the X2000 pauses for the publicity cameras (**left**) near Honda.
Above, John R. Signor; left, Phil Gosney

entirely new right-of-way, grading, and track.

The question as to whether high-speed rail in California is developed via the Coast or San Joaquin routes—or at all—is still open for speculation. But Southern Pacific, for its part, sponsored the Bay Area-Los Angeles segment of Amtrak's X2000 Swedish tilt-train American tour. Departing Oakland on July 13, 1993, the sleek six-unit electrified train (pushed by conventional diesels) made a two-day whistle stop tour down the Coast Line touting the merits of both the tilt-train technology and the Coast Line as the only existing, and therefore most cost effective, route for linking Los Angeles and the Bay Area with high-speed trains.

As the Coast Line's age approaches the century mark, this historic route is on the threshold of regaining its former glory, emerging as a vital passenger corridor linking the two principal metropolitan centers of California with fast frequent train service...a function for which it was originally designed. ❑

South San Francisco depot (**above, left**) as it appeared on August 23, 1909, during the construction of the Bayshore Cutoff. Restored *Daylight* steam locomotive No. 4449 races past the depot at Gonzales (**above, right**) on May 3, 1989. The Gonzales depot was burned down by the local fire department as a training excercise on December 29, 1990. Menlo Park station (**left**), as it appeared about 1909. Southern Pacific Peninsula commuter No. 151 rolls to a stop at Santa Clara (**below**) in 1961. Still standing today, Santa Clara depot, built about 1877, is the oldest existing station on the Coast Line.

Above left, C.M. Kurtz photo, Southern Pacific Line collection; above right, Ted Benson; left, Roger Titus collection; below, Bob Morris

278

Station List
SOUTHERN PACIFIC COAST LINE

"A Southern Pacific timetable reads like a Litany to the Saints." - Charles Warren Stoddard

Compiled by L. D. Farrar

The following station list was compiled using Southern Pacific's "List of Officers, Agencies and Stations," first issued in 1877, and published more or less annually thereafter until August, 1973. The list covers the main line from San Francisco to Los Angeles via the Bayshore and Montalvo Cutoffs from 1877 through 1969. The "Northern Division" between San Francisco and Soledad was not a part of these lists until June 1, 1887, hence many points, although considerably older, are first listed as 6/1/87. Mileposts were historically determined by the distance from San Francisco and, as the Coast Line evolved, a given station's milepost number might change several times. For instance, prior to the completion of the Coast Line in 1901, stations distances south of Ellwood were measured via the San Joaquin Valley Line. The notations on place name origins comes from a variety of sources including Southern Pacific records, county recording offices, *California Place Names* by Erwin G. Gudde and *Spanish Place Names in California: Their Meaning and Their Romance* by Nellie Van de Grift Sanchez.

Mile Post	Station Name and origin if available	Active from	Notes

SAN FRANCISCO Padre Junípero Serra, president of the Franciscans in California, established a mission here in the autumn of 1776 and bestowed upon it and the town the name San Francisco in honor of St. Francis of Assisi.

Mile Post	Station Name	Active from	Notes
0	San Francisco, Drumm St.	1/1/12 - 1/1/59	Dropped from list
0	San Francisco	6/1/87 - 1966	
0.0	San Francisco, 4th & King Sts.	1/1/96 - 1/1/19	Name changed
0.0	San Francisco, 3rd & Townsend Sts.	1/1/19 -	
	San Francisco, 4th & Berry Sts.	1/1/19 - 1969	Dropped from list
	Stock Yards	1/1/04 - 1/1/07	Dropped from list
0	Grocer's Terminal	1/1/24 - 1/1/59	Dropped from list
1.9	San Francisco, 23rd St.	7/1/08 - '32-'36	
2	San Francisco, 23rd St.	'32-'36 - '68-'69	
1.9	San Francisco, 23rd St.	'68-'69 -	
2.2	San Francisco, Army St.	7/1/08 - 1936	Dropped from list
3	San Francisco, 14th Ave. South	7/1/08 - 12/15/41	Name changed
3	San Francisco, Newcomb Ave.	12/15/41 - 7/1/54	Dropped from list
4.1	San Francisco, Paul Ave.	1/1/29 -	

BAYSHORE A fanciful name developed with the construction of the Bayshore (originally "Bay Shore") Cutoff. The station itself was later moved to become a "herder's shanty" at Visitacion.

5	Bayshore	7/1/08 - '68-'69	
5.2	Bayshore	'68-'69 -	

VISITACION Named for Visitacion Point, a prominent headland through which the railway made a great cut in 1904. "Visitacion" is Spanish and alludes to an "encounter with angels."

5	Visitacion	1/1/08 - 7/1/08	
7	Visitacion	7/1/08 - 3/1/20	
6.5	Visitacion	3/1/20 - 3/1/47	
6.9	Visitacion Tower	1/1/22 - 3/1/47	
6.9	Visitacion	3/1/47 -	

Bayshore station on July 24, 1908.
C. M. Kurtz photo, Southern Pacific Lines

BRISBANE Named for the journalist Arthur Brisbane, who built one of the first houses here.

7	Brisbane	'62-'66 - '68-'69	
6.9	Brisbane	'68-'69 -	

BUTLER ROAD
8.6	Butler Road	'32-'36 -

SOUTH SAN FRANCISCO
--	South San Francisco	1/1/94 - 1/1/07
13	South San Francisco	1/1/07 - '32-'36
9.3	South San Francisco	'32-'36 -

SAN BRUNO The name of this station, announced in the itinerary of the San Francisco & San Jose Rail Road, dated October 16, 1863, was drawn from the nearby mountain and stream. The name was apparently applied by Palóu in 1774 and honors San Bruno, a German saint of the 11th century, founder of the Carthusian Order.

14.0	San Bruno	6/1/87 - 3/1/91
14	San Bruno	3/1/91 - 1/1/98
15	San Bruno	1/1/98 - 3/1/20
13.6	San Bruno	3/1/20 - '32-'36
11.6	San Bruno	'32-'36 -

San Bruno, circa 1939.
Robert H. McFarland photo, Arnold S. Menke collection

LOMITA PARK Fanciful name of real estate promoters.
15.8	Lomita Park	7/1/12 - 3/1/20
12.1	Lomita Park	3/1/20 - '62-'66

Dropped from list

AQUA The Latin word for "water," presumably a well site.
16.6	Aqua (spur)	1/1/99 - 1/1/00
16.6	Aqua	1/1/00 - 3/1/20
12.9	Aqua	3/1/20 - 7/1/49

Dropped from list

MILLBRAE The town is laid out over the former estate of "bonanza king" Darius Ogden Mills and was named for him.
16.7	Millbrae	6/1/87 - 3/1/91
17	Millbrae	3/1/91 - 3/1/20
14	Millbrae	3/1/20 - '68-'69
13.7	Millbrae	'68-'69 -

Millbrae, circa 1939.
Robert H. McFarland photo, Arnold S. Menke collection

BROADWAY Named for a principal thoroughfare in north Burlingame.
19	Haufe	9/18/03 - 1/1/07

Dropped from list
19	Easton	7/1/07 - 1/1/18

Name change
19	Broadway	1/1/18 - 3/1/20
15	Broadway	3/1/20 - '68-'69
15.2	Broadway	'68-'69 -

Broadway, circa 1930.
Southern Pacific Lines

BURLINGAME A product of banker William C. Ralston's ambitious dream of a colony of summer homes for the San Francisco elite. Named after the Honorable Anson Burlingame, High Minister Plenipotentiary and Envoy Extraordinary to the Court of Pekin, a Ralston supporter.

19.0	Oak Grove	6/1/87 - 3/1/91	
19	Oak Grove	3/1/91 - 6/10/94	
20	Burlingame	6/10/94 - 3/1/20	Name change
16.3	Burlingame, North and South Lanes	3/1/20 - '37-'40	
16.3	Burlingame	7/1/59 -	
16.5	Burlingame, Howard Ave. and Myrtle Road	'37-'40 - 7/1/59	Dropped from list

HOWEST
21	Howest	1/1/10 - 3/1/20
16.8	Howest	3/1/20 -

SAN MATEO Named after the apostle St. Matthew.
20.9	San Mateo	6/1/87 - 3/1/91
21	San Mateo	3/1/91 - 1/1/98
22	San Mateo	1/1/98 - 3/1/20
17.9	San Mateo	3/1/20 -

DONALDS
22	Donalds	1/1/94 - 1/1/98

Dropped from list

HAYWARD PARK
23	Leslie	1/1/02 - 7/1/11
22.6	Leslie	7/1/11 - 3/1/20
18.9	Leslie	3/1/20 - '32-'36
18.9	Hayward Park	'32-'36 -

Name changed

ROMAC
23	Romac	7/1/11 - 3/1/20
19.7	Romac	3/1/20 -

PANSY
23	Pansy	6/25/97 - 1/1/98	
23.6	Pansy	1/1/98 - 1/1/99	
23.8	Pansy	1/1/99 - 1/1/02	Dropped from list

BAY MEADOWS Station stop named and provided for adjacent Bay Meadows Race Track.
20	Bay Meadows	'32-'36 - 10/1/67	Dropped from list

HILLSDALE
23.5	Laurel Creek	6/1/87 - 3/1/91	
24	Laurel Creek	3/1/91 - 1/1/97	
24	Beresford	1/1/97 - 3/1/20	Name change
20	Beresford	3/1/20 - '32-'36	
20.3	Beresford	'32-'36 - 12/15/41	
20.3	Hillsdale	12/15/41 -	Name change

BELMONT Station and later the town developed around the hotel built in 1850-51 by Steinburger & Beard.
24.9	Belmont	6/1/87 - 3/1/91
25	Belmont	3/1/91 - 1/1/98
26	Belmont	1/1/98 - 3/1/20
21.9	Belmont	3/1/20 -

PUMORK A contraction of Pumping Works, its original name.
25.7	Pumping Works	6/1/90 - 1/1/98	
26.4	Pumping Works	1/1/98 - 1/1/99	
26.5	Pumping Works	1/1/99 - 1/1/09	
26.5	Pumork	1/1/09 - 7/1/10	Name change
26.4	Pumork	7/1/10 - 3/1/20	
22.7	Pumork	3/1/20 - '37-'40	Dropped from list

SAN CARLOS Accounts vary; possibly named for Lt. Manuel de Ayala's ship *San Carlos*, the first vessel to enter the Golden Gate.
26.2	San Carlos	6/1/90 - 3/1/91
26	San Carlos	3/1/91 - 1/1/98
27	San Carlos	1/1/98 - 3/1/20
23	San Carlos	3/1/20 - '68-'69
23.2	San Carlos	'68-'69 -

SARDOC A contraction of Standard Oil Co.
28.4	Standard Oil Co. Spur	1/1/98 - 1/1/00	
28.4	Standard Oil Co.	1/1/00 - 1/1/07	
28	Standard Oil Co.	1/1/07 - 1/1/09	
28	Sardoc	1/1/09 - 1/1/11	Name changed, then dropped from list

San Mateo in 1910.
Roger Titus collection

REDWOOD CITY This section, once surrounded by redwoods which were the subject of large-scale commercial exploitation, was known as Redwood City as early as 1860.

28.3	Redwood	6/1/87 - 3/1/91
28	Redwood	3/1/91 - 1/1/98
29	Redwood	1/1/98 - 7/1/14
29	Redwood City	7/1/14 - 3/1/20
Name change		
25	Redwood City	3/1/20 - 1/1/28
25.4	Redwood City	1/1/28 - '32-'36
25	Redwood City	'32-'36 - '68-'69
25.4	Redwood City	'68-'69 -

STAUFFER SPUR

29.9	Stauffer Spur	7/1/15 - 3/1/20
26.1	Stauffer Spur	3/1/20 - 1/1/28
27.3	Stauffer (Spur)	1/1/28 -

THETIS (SPUR)

30	Thetis (Spur)	1/1/99 - 1/1/10	Dropped from list

REDWOOD JUNCTION Junction with the Dumbarton Cutoff line across the bay to Newark.

30	Redwood Jct.	1/1/11 - 3/1/20
26.2	Redwood Jct.	3/1/20 - 1/1/28
26.2	Redwood Junction	1/1/28 - '32-'36
26	Redwood Junction	'32-'36 - '62-'66
26.2	Redwood Jct.	'62-'66 - '68-'69

REDWOOD HARBOR (SPUR)

28.7	Redwood Harbor (Spur)	1/1/25 - 1/1/28
28.7	Redwood Harbor (Spur)	1/1/28 -

Redwood City, 1916.
Southern Pacific Lines

ATHERTON The first estate in this vicinity was Faxon Dean Atherton's mile-square Valparaiso Park, laid out in 1860. Station was originally named Fair Oaks.

30.9	Fair Oaks	6/1/87 - 6/1/88
30.6	Fair Oaks	6/1/88 - 3/1/91
31	Fair Oaks	3/1/91 - 1/1/98
32	Fair Oaks	1/1/98 - 1/1/00
31	Fair Oaks	1/1/00 - 1/1/04
32	Fair Oaks	1/1/04 - 7/1/12
32	Atherton	7/1/12 - 3/1/20
Name change		
27.8	Atherton	3/1/20 -

MENLO PARK This community grew up with the advent of the railroad in 1863 around an estate named by D.J. Oliver and D.C. McGlynn for their home in Ireland. Initially named Big Trees station, the name was changed to Menlo Park by the time Southern Pacific was publishing its station lists. Menlo Park agency was closed on June 9, 1959.

31.9	Menlo Park	6/1/87 - 3/1/91
32	Menlo Park	3/1/91 - 1/1/98
33	Menlo Park	1/1/98 - 3/1/20
29	Menlo Park	3/1/20 - 1/1/25
28.9	Menlo Park	1/1/25 -

Menlo Park as it appeared in 1957.
Southern Pacific Lines

FREMONT

29.3	Fremont	1/1/25 - '32-'36	Dropped from list

CAMP FREMONT

33.2	Camp Fremont	1/1/18 - 3/1/20	Established for a short time during World War I.

CATHOLIC COLLEGE

| 34a | Catholic College | 1/1/97 - 1/1/99 | Dropped from list |

PALO ALTO Spanish for "high tree," named after a redwood whose branches shaded Portolá's camp in November, 1769. Leland Stanford gave the name to his estates here. The tree still stands by the railroad bridge over San Francisquito Creek near the station.

33	Palo Alto	3/1/91 - 1/1/97	
34	Palo Alto	1/1/97 - 3/1/20	
30	Palo Alto	3/1/20 - 1/1/25	
30.1	Palo Alto	1/1/25 - 1/1/46	
30.1	Palo Alto (University Ave.)	1/1/46 - '62-'66	
30.1	Palo Alto	'62-'66 -	
31.8	Palo Alto (California Ave.)	5/1/48 - 1/1/59	See Mayfield

BONAIR

34	Bonair	3/1/93 - 1/1/98	
35	Bonair	1/1/98 - 1/1/99	
35	Bonair (Spur)	1/1/99 - 1/1/00	
35	Bonair	1/1/00 - 1/1/10	Dropped from list

MAYFIELD (Later **PALO ALTO, CALIFORNIA AVE.**) In 1853, Elisha O. Crosby bought a tract of land here which he called "Mayfield Farm." The name was applied to the railway station in 1863. The Palo Alto (California Ave). agency was closed September 15, 1958.

34.7	Mayfield	6/1/87 - 3/1/91
35	Mayfield	3/1/91 - 1/1/98
35.4	Mayfield	1/1/98 - 7/1/10
36	Mayfield	7/1/10 - 3/1/20
32	Mayfield	3/1/20 - 12/15/41
32	California Ave.	12/15/41 - 5/1/48
31.8	Palo Alto (California Ave.)	5/1/48 - 1/1/59

Dropped from list

Mayfield in March, 1923.
Benny Romano collection

CASTRO Located on the Los Animas Rancho, granted in August, 1802 to Jose Mariano Castro, who provided an easement for the railroad and for whom the station is named.

37.7	Castros	6/1/87 - 3/1/91
38	Castro	3/1/91 - 1/1/00
38	Castro	1/1/00 - 3/1/20
35	Castro	3/1/20 - '68-'69
34.8	Castro	'68-'69 -

MOUNTAIN VIEW Before the railroad arrived in 1864, the Mountain View House was a main stop for the four-horse Concord coaches on the San Francisco-San Jose stage line. Agency was closed on July 10, 1959.

39.1	Mountain View	6/1/87 - 3/1/91
39	Mountain View	3/1/91 - 1/1/98
40	Mountain View	1/1/98 - 3/1/20
36	Mountain View	3/1/20 - '68-'69
36.1	Mountain View	'68-'69 -

BRICKYARD SPUR

| 39.6 | Brickyard Spur | 6/1/87 - 3/1/91 | Dropped from list |

ENDOR

| 41 | Endor | 1/1/01 - 1/1/11 | Dropped from list |

SUNNYVALE Name applied by W.E. Crossman in 1900 to a subdivision of the Pastoria de las Borregas grant.

41.9	Murphy's	6/1/87 - 3/1/91	
42	Murphy's	3/1/91 - 1/1/98	
43	Murphy's	1/1/98 - 1/1/00	
43	Murphy	1/1/00 - 1/1/01	
43	Sunnyvale	1/1/01 - 3/1/20	Name change
39	Sunnyvale	3/1/20 - '68-'69	
38.8	Sunnyvale	'68-'69 -	

LAWRENCE Lawrence tract, Lawrence Station Road.
43.7	Lawrence's	6/1/87 - 3/1/91
44	Lawrence's	3/1/91 - 1/1/00
44	Lawrence	1/1/00 - 7/1/10
45	Lawrence	7/1/10 - 3/1/20
41	Lawrence	3/1/20 - 7/1/54

Dropped from list

SANTA CLARA Named after nearby Mission Santa Clara de Asís, dedicated to the founder of an order of Franciscan nuns noted for their strict lives.
47.3	Santa Clara	6/1/87 - 3/1/91
47	Santa Clara	3/1/91 - 1/1/98
48	Santa Clara	1/1/98 - 3/1/20
44.3	Santa Clara	3/1/20 - '37-'40
44	Santa Clara	'37-'40 - '68-'69
44.3	Santa Clara	'68-'69 -

Lawrence, 1911.
Benny Romano collection

SAN JOSE YARD Also informally called "Newhall," for nearby Newhall Street.
45	San Jose Yard	1/1/52 - '68-'69
45.2	San Jose Yard	'68-'69 -

PACMANCO A contraction name created from Pacific Manufacturing Company.
48.5	Pacific M'f'g. Co.	1/1/04 - 7/1/09	Dropped from list
48.4	Pacmanco	7/1/15 - 3/1/20	Reinstated with name change
44.7	Pacmanco	3/1/20 - '37-'40	Dropped from list

COLLEGE PARK Adjacent to the University of Santa Clara. This, the oldest institution of higher learning in the West, was founded by the Franciscan padres in 1777. The Old Mission School was succeeded by the college, which later developed into the University. Initially the station was named Polhemus for the adjacent real estate tract.
49.0	Polhemus	6/1/87 - 6/1/90	
49.0	College Park	6/1/90 - 1/1/98	Name change
49.6	College Park	1/1/98 - 1/1/07	
50	College Park	1/1/07 - 7/1/10	
49	College Park	7/1/10 - 3/1/20	
46	College Park	3/1/20 - '68-'69	
45.7	College Park	'68-'69 -	

SAN JOSE Named after St. Joseph, husband of the Virgin Mary, and was the site of the first colony of white settlers in California. The pueblo was founded in 1777, and the mission in 1797.
50.0	San Jose	6/1/87 - 3/1/91
50	San Jose	3/1/91 - 1/1/98
51	San Jose	1/1/98 - 3/1/20
47	San Jose	3/1/20 - '37-'40
46.8	San Jose, San Pedro and Basset Sts.	'37-'40 - '68-'69

Dropped from List
46.9	San Jose, 65 Cahill St.	'37-'40 - '68-'69
46.9	San Jose	'68-'69 -

Name change
50.8	Gas Switch, San Jose	6/1/87 - 1/1/96

Dropped from list
51.1	Fourth Street, San Jose	6/1/87 - 3/1/91
51	Fourth Street, San Jose	3/1/91 - 1/1/98
52	Fourth Street, San Jose	1/1/98 - 1/1/00
52	4th St. San Jose	1/1/00 - 7/1/08
52	San Jose (4th St.)	7/1/08 - 3/1/20
48	San Jose (4th St.)	3/1/20 - '32-'36	Dropped from list

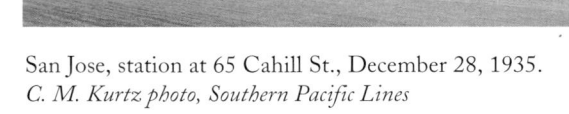

San Jose, station at 65 Cahill St., December 28, 1935.
C. M. Kurtz photo, Southern Pacific Lines

MAYBURY (SPUR)
47.1	Maybury (Spur)	'37-'40 - 5/1/48	Dropped from list

LUTHER JUNCTION
49.3   Luther Junction   5/1/48 -

LICK Lick was named in honor of James Lick, eccentric millionaire real estate speculator whose body lies under one of the supporting pillars of the telescope at Lick Observatory on nearby Mt. Hamilton, a short distance east from this station.
54.8   Hillsdale   6/1/87 - 3/1/91
55   Hillsdale   3/1/91 - 1/1/98
56   Hillsdale   1/1/98 - 7/1/14
56   Lick   7/1/14 - 1/1/24   Name change; Hillsdale moved to MP 20.3
55.5   Lick   1/1/24 - '32-'36
51.4   Lick   '32-'36 -

EDENVALE
56.9   Eden Vale   6/1/87 - 3/1/91
57   Eden Vale   3/1/91 - 1/1/98
58   Eden Vale   1/1/98 - 1/1/05   Name change
58   Edenvale   1/1/05 - 7/1/10
57   Edenvale   7/1/10 - '68-'69
57.4   Edenvale   '68-'69 -

SPARROW
58   Sparrow   1/1/18 - 1/1/30   Dropped from list

OAK GROVE
59   Oak Grove   10/1/57 -

POMAR
60   Pomar   7/18/03 - 1/1/31   Dropped from list

HONK
61   Honk   1/1/18 - 1/1/23   Dropped from list

COYOTE GRAVEL PIT
62.6   Coyote Gravel Pit   1/1/97 - 1/1/98
62.9   Coyote Gravel Pit   1/1/98 - 7/1/08
Dropped from list

COYOTE The Coyote River is nearby, named for the native wolf of California, whose name in turn comes from the Aztec word "coyotl." The SP agency here was closed on December 10, 1958.
62.6   Coyote   6/1/87 - 3/1/91
63   Coyote   3/1/91 - '68-'69
63.1   Coyote   '68-'69 -

PERRY Named for local rancher J.F.Perry.
65.6   Perry's   6/1/87 - 3/1/91
66   Perry's   3/1/91 - 1/1/00
66   Perry   1/1/00 - '68-'69
66.3   Perry   '68-'69 -

MADRONE The common name for the beautiful evergreen tree that is indigenous to California and grew in abundance in this area, from the Spanish "madroño."
68.6   Madrone   6/1/87 - 3/1/91
69   Madrone   3/1/91 - 7/1/61
Dropped from list

MORGANHILL This settlement was named about 1892 after Morgan Hill, owner of the adjacent Morgan Hill Ranch. Unlike the geographic name, the railroad name has been all one word since 1899. Morganhill agency was closed November 20, 1958.
70   Huntington   7/25/92 - 1/5/93
70   Morgan Hill   1/5/93 - 1/1/98

Coyote station, 1955.
Southern Pacific Lines

Morganhill, 1955.
Southern Pacific Lines

71	Morgan Hill	1/1/98 - 1/1/99	
71	Morganhill	1/1/99 - '68-'69	
70.8	Morganhill	'68-'69	

TENNANT

72	Tennant	1/1/00 - '37-'40	
Dropped from list			

DURNEY

74	Durney	1/1/10 - 12/15/41	
Dropped from list			

SAN MARTIN   Named by the land owner Martin Murphy, a devout Roman Catholic, after his patron saint, St. Martin.

74.1	San Martine	6/1/87 - 3/1/91	
74	San Martine	3/1/91 - 1/1/96	
Name change			
74	San Martin	1/1/96 - 1/1/98	
75	San Martin	1/1/98 - '68-'69	
74.6	San Martin	'68-'69 -	

RUCKER   Named for local land owner and rancher R.T. Rucker.

77	Rucker	1/5/93 - 1/1/31	
Dropped from list			
77	Rucker	'37-'40 - '68-'69	
Reinstated			
77.0	Rucker	'68-'69 -	

ANIMAS   Railroad crossed the Animas Rancho at this point.

79	Animas	1/1/07 -7/1/16	
79	Lonoke	7/1/16 - '68-'69	
Name change			
79.1	Lonoke	'68-'69	

GILROY   Owes its name to California's first English-speaking settler, the Scotsman John Cameron, who took the name Gilroy when he jumped ship at Monterey in 1814. He settled here, acquiring Rancho San Ysidro by marrying Ygnacio Ortega's daughter.

80.1	Gilroy	6/1/87 - 3/1/91	
80	Gilroy	3/1/91 - 1/1/98	
81	Gilroy	1/1/98 - '68-'69	
80.7	Gilroy	'68-'69 -	

CARNADERO   The word, Spanish in origin and probably meaning "butchering place," is recorded as a name for this place as early as 1784.

82.5	Carnadero	6/1/87 - 3/1/91	
83	Carnadero	3/1/91 - '68-'69	
83.2	Carnadero	'68-'69 -	

NEMA   Originally called Miller's (Spur) for landowner Henry Miller who acquired large tracts from the former Animas Rancho.

83.9	Miller's	6/1/87 - 3/1/91		
84	Miller's	3/1/91 - 1/1/99		
84.2	Miller's Spur	1/1/99 - 1/1/00		
84.2	Nema	1/1/00 - 1/1/07	Name change	
84	Nema	1/1/07 - 12/15/41	Dropped from list	

San Martin, 1915.
Southern Pacific Lines

Gilroy, 1915.
Southern Pacific Lines

New Gilroy station, circa 1921.
Southern Pacific Lines

SARGENT Named for J.P. Sargent, one-time Governor of California, who once owned a ranch one mile north of this station.

86.5	Sargent's	6/1/87 - 3/1/91
87	Sargent's	3/1/91 - 1/1/00
87	Sargent	1/1/00 - '68-'69
87.1	Sargent	'68-'69 -

BETABEL

| 88 | Betabel | 1/1/97 - 1/1/98 |
| 89 | Betabel | 1/1/98 - '43-'44 |

Dropped from list

NEWRIA

| 90 | Newria | 1/1/05 - 1/1/08 |

Dropped from list

Sargent, during the 1930s.
R.H. McFarland photo, Arnold S. Menke collection

CHITTENDEN Named for Capt. Hiram M. Chittenden, at one time a brigadier general in the Army Corps of Engineers.

91.4	Chittenden's	6/1/87 - 3/1/91	
91	Chittenden's	3/1/91 - 1/1/98	
92	Chittenden's	1/1/98 - 1/1/00	
92	Chittenden	1/1/00 - '43-'44	Dropped from list
92	Chittenden	5/1/48 - 7/1/59	Reinstated, then dropped from list

LOGAN Granite Rock Co. quarry located here on a portion of the former Judge Logan Ranch.

92.1	Logan	6/1/90 - 3/1/91
92	Logan	3/1/91 - 1/1/98
93	Logan	1/1/98 - '68-'69
93.2	Logan	'68-'69 -

AROMAS Originally known as Sand Cut because of the large cut built by the Southern Pacific here in the 1870s. The present name is derived from the land grant Aromitas y Agua Caliente, "little odors and warm water," all referring to the odors of the nearby sulfur spring.

94.2	Sand Cut	6/1/87 - 3/1/91	
94	Sand Cut	3/1/91 - 1/1/95	
94	Aromas	1/1/95 - 1/1/98	Name change
95	Aromas	1/1/98 - '68-'69	
94.6	Aromas	'68-'69 -	

EATON Originally named Vega, Spanish for "flat lowland," a term that accurately describes the surrounding Pajaro Valley adjacent to this place. Renamed Eaton after vegetable packing shed built here.

96.5	Vega	6/1/87 - 3/1/91	
97	Vega	3/1/91 - 12/15/41	
97	Eaton	12/15/41 - '68-'69	Name change
97.1	Eaton	'68-'69 -	

WATSONVILLE JUNCTION The junction for the Santa Cruz Branch. Originally named Pajaro for the adjacent river, whose name is attributed to the soldiers of Portolá's expedition of 1769. Pajaro is Spanish for "bird" and it was at this location that the soldiers saw a bird "which the heathen had killed and stuffed with straw." The town proper, just across the river, was laid out in 1852 by D.S. Gregory and Judge John H. Watson, and named for the latter.

99.4	Pajaro	6/1/87 - 3/1/91
99	Pajaro	3/1/91 - 1/1/98
100	Pajaro	1/1/98 - 7/1/13
100	Watsonville Jct.	7/1/13 - '68-'69

Name change

| 100.4 | Watsonville Jct. | '68-'69 - |
| 98.6 | Pajaro | 1/1/46 - 5/1/48 |

Name briefly reinstated at different location

Watsonville Jct. yard office, circa 1969. Left side of structure was the original Pajaro depot.
Dick Dorn

287

LYDA
104	Lyda	7/1/16 - '37-'40	Dropped from list

ELKHORN Named after Elkhorn Slough, which the line crosses at this point.
106.5	Elkhorn	6/1/87 - 3/1/91
107	Elkhorn	3/1/91 - 1/1/00
106	Elkhorn	1/1/00 - '68-'69
105.8	Elkhorn	'68-'69 -

MOSS LANDING
108	Moss Landing	7/1/49 - '68-'69
107.7	Moss Landing	'68-'69 -

CASTROVILLE Named for settlement founded in 1864 by Juan B. Castro.
109.7	Castroville	6/1/87 - 3/1/91	
110	Castroville	3/1/91 - 7/1/13	
110	Del Monte Jct.	7/1/13 - '32-'36	Name change
110	Castroville	'32-'36 - '68-'69	Name change
110.4	Castroville	'68-'69 -	
110.1	Jct. Monterey Br.	'70-'73 -	Additional point

COOPER Captain John B.R. Cooper, an early Anglo resident of Monterey County, deeded a right-of-way to the railroad across his ranch in this vicinity.
113.2	Cooper's	6/1/87 - 3/1/91
113	Cooper's	3/1/91 - 1/1/98
114	Cooper's	1/1/98 - 1/1/00
114	Cooper	1/1/00 - '68-'69
113.9	Cooper	'68-'69 -

GRAVES
115	Graves	1/1/96 - 1/1/98	
116	Graves	1/1/98 - 1/1/55	Dropped from list

SALINAS Was first reached by the Portolá expedition of 1769 and took its name from a series of salt marshes near the mouth of the Salinas River. The name is Spanish for "salt works."
117.6	Salinas	6/1/87 - 3/1/91
118	Salinas	3/1/91 - '68-'69
118.2	Salinas	'68-'69 -

SPRECKELS JUNCTION The junction for the short branch to Spreckels, location of a huge beet sugar refinery built in 1899 by German-born industrialist Claus Spreckels.
120	Spreckels' Junc	1/1/98 - 1/1/00	
121	Spreckels Junc	1/1/00 - 7/1/10	
120	Spreckels Junc	7/1/10 - 1/1/26	
120	Spreckels Junction	1/1/26 - '62-'66	
120	Spreckels Jct.	'62-'66 - '68-'69	
120.3	Spreckels Jct.	'68-'69 -	
123.3	Spreckels (Spur)	1/1/99 - 1/1/00	
123	Spreckels	1/1/00 - 5/1/48	In list as Spreckels Branch

Salinas, 1930.
Southern Pacific Lines

SPENCE Name applied in 1872 by the SP, commemorating David Spence, grantee of the Encinal y Buena Esperanza grant on which this station was built.
124.6	Spence's	6/1/87 - 3/1/91	
125	Spence's	3/1/91 - 1/1/00	
125	Spence	1/1/00 - '68-'69	Name change
125.3	Spence	'68-'69 -	

CHUALAR Was named by the Spaniards after the pig weed or goose foot ("chual"), which abounds in the area. The Spanish term means "place where chual grows." The Rancho Santa Rosa de Chualar is nearby.

128.5	Chualar	6/1/87 - 3/1/91
129	Chualar	3/1/91 - '68-'69
129.1	Chualar	'68-'69 -

GABILAN

131	Gabilan	7/1/15 - 10/1/41

Dropped from list

PENVIR

132	Penvir	1/1/05 - '68-'69
131.9	Penvir	'68-'69 -

DEAN

134	Dean	7/1/15 - 1/1/24

Dropped from list

GONZALES Teodoro Gonzales was granted Rincon de la Punta del Monte de la Soledad on which the station is located. But it may have been named for Alfredo and Mariano Gonzales who were prominently associated with the Monterey and Salinas Railroad.

134.5	Gonzales	6/1/87 - 3/1/91
135	Gonzales	3/1/91 - '68-'69
135.1	Gonzales	'68-'69 -

RACK

137	Rack	1/1/18 - '34-'44

Dropped from list

MOLUS

139	Molus	1/1/11 - '68-'69
138.8	Molus	'68-'69 -

CAMPHORA

140.2	Gravel Pit	6/1/87 - 3/1/91	
140	Vincente	3/1/91 - 1/1/94	Name change
140	Camphora	1/1/94 - 1/1/98	Name change
141	Camphora	1/1/98 - '68-'69	
140.6	Camphora	'68-'69 -	

SOLEDAD Literally "solitude," so named by the Spanish because of the dry plains in this district. These plains, however, upon cultivation proved to be exceedingly fertile.

142.9	Soledad	6/1/87 - 3/1/91
143	Soledad	3/1/91 - 1/1/98
144	Soledad	1/1/98 - 3/1/20
143.6	Soledad	3/1/20 -

DOUD

145.1	Siding No.1	6/1/87 - 3/1/91	

Name change

145	Doud	3/1/91 - 1/1/98	
146	Doud	1/1/98 - 1/1/99	
146	Doud (Spur)	1/1/99 - 1/1/00	Name change
146	Doud	1/1/00 - 1/1/02	Name change, moved to MP 138
138	Doud	1/1/02 - 1/1/23	Dropped from list

Chualar, 1915.
Southern Pacific Lines, courtesy Steve Donaldson

Gonzales, 1955.
Southern Pacific Lines

Soledad, 1955.
Southern Pacific Lines

289

HARLEM
147.2	Siding No.2	6/1/87 - 3/1/91	
147	Riverbank	3/1/91 - 1/1/98	Name change
148	Riverbank	1/1/98 - 1/1/12	
148.7	Harlem	1/1/12 - '68-'69	Name change
148.3	Harlem	'68-'69 -	

METZ Originally Chalone, after Chalone Peaks (now The Pinnacles). But it was renamed in 1891 for W.H.H. Metz, a local stock raiser and first postmaster of the community.
151.7	Cholone	6/1/87 - 3/1/91	
152	Metz	3/1/91 - '68-'69	Name change
152.3	Metz	'68-'69 -	

COBURN
158.2	Coburn's	6/1/87 - 3/1/91
158	Coburn's	3/1/91 - 1/1/98
159	Coburn's	1/1/98 - 1/1/00
159	Coburn	1/1/00 - '68-'69
158.9	Coburn	'68-'69 -

ELSA
161	Elsa	1/1/02 - '68-'69
161.0	Elsa	'68-'69 -

KING CITY Named for Charles H. King, who laid out the town on his Rancho San Lorenzo when the Southern Pacific was extended to this place in 1886.
163.2	King's City	6/1/87 - 3/1/91
163	King's City	3/1/91 - 1/1/98
164	King's City	1/1/98 - 7/1/12

Name change
164	King City	7/1/12 - '68-'69
163.7	King City	'68-'69 -

ARGUS
165	Argus	1/1/18 - 1/1/29

Dropped from list

WELBY
167	Welby	1/1/01 - '68-'69
167.1	Welby	'68-'69 -

SAN LUCAS The Spanish name for St. Luke the Evangelist was applied to the land grant in 1842 and given to the station by SP in 1886, although the station is outside of the grant boundaries. San Lucas agency was closed on June 13, 1958.
171.9	San Lucas	6/1/87 - 3/1/91
172	San Lucas	3/1/91 - 1/1/98
173	San Lucas	1/1/98 - 7/1/10
172	San Lucas	7/1/10 - '68-'69
172.4	San Lucas	'68-'69 -

DOCAS
178	Upland	1/1/01 - 7/1/08
178	Docas	7/1/08 - 10/1/57

Name changed, then eventually dropped from list

SAN ARDO M.J. Brandenstein, who had bought the San Bernardo Rancho, wanted the name San Bernardo. But the Post Office objected to the name because of possible confusion with San Bernardino, so a new saint name was created by lopping off "Bern."
182.4	San Ardo	6/1/87 - 3/1/91

King City, 1915.
Southern Pacific Lines

San Lucas, 1955 (**above**); San Ardo, 1936 (**below**).
Above, Southern Pacific Lines; below, Benny Romano collection

| 182 | San Ardo | 3/1/91 - 1/1/98 |
| 183 | San Ardo | 1/1/98 - '68-'69 |

GETTY A siding in a rich oil-producing district, named for George F. Getty, a developer of oil lands.

| 187 | Getty | 1/1/05 - 7/1/10 | |
| 186 | Getty | 7/1/10 - 7/1/60 | Dropped from list |

WUNPOST A name supposedly chosen to convey the emptiness of the upper Salinas Valley.

189.1	Siding No. 3	6/1/87 - 3/1/91	
189	Wunpost	3/1/91 - 1/1/98	Name change
190	Wunpost	1/1/98 - '68-'69	
189.7	Wunpost	'68-'69 -	

BRADLEY Named by Southern Pacific for the owner of the land, Bradley V. Sargent, State senator, 1887-1889.

195.5	Bradley	6/1/87 - 3/1/91
196	Bradley	3/1/87 - '68-'69
195.9	Bradley	'68-'69 -

BUCKSPUR

| 198 | Buckspur | 1/1/01 - 1/1/05 | Dropped from list |

NACIMIENTO This siding was named after the adjacent river in 1905. The origin of the name is attributed to Father Crespi, who camped on the river in September, 1769, calling it "a very large river whose source (*nacimiento*)...was not far off." In 1776, however, de Anza assumed that the previous expedition had named this river after the "Nativity," another meaning of the word.

202	Flint	1/1/97 - 1/1/99	
202	Nacimiento	1/1/99 - 7/1/10	Name change
201	Nacimiento	7/1/10 - 7/1/59	Dropped from list

CAMP ROBERTS This Army training camp was originally to be named Camp Nacimiento, but when opened, it was named after Corporal Harold D. Roberts, a World War I Congressional Medal of Honor winner. It was the first Army camp in the United States named for an enlisted man.

| 203 | Camp Roberts | 12/15/41 - 5/1/48 | Dropped from list |

McKAY The siding at which the coal-hauling Stone Canyon Railroad once connected. At one time named Watkins, for the developer of the Stone Canyon coal mine. Renamed for J.A. Chanslor, who took over the property, and later for contractor Pat McKay, who figured in "closing The Gap," and in building additional sidings such as this, once the through line was in operation.

204	Watkins	7/1/08 - 1/1/09	
204	Chanslor	1/1/09 - 1/1/10	Name change
204	McKay	1/1/10 - '68-'69	Name change
203.8	McKay	'68-'69 -	

SAN MIGUEL Named for nearby Mission San Miguel, built in 1797, and dedicated to Saint Michael. Southern Pacific applied the name to the station in 1886.

206.8	San Miguel	6/1/87 - 3/1/91
207	San Miguel	3/1/91 - 1/1/98
208	San Miguel	1/1/98 - 7/1/10
207	San Miguel	7/1/10 - '68-'69
207.0	San Miguel	'68-'69 -

WELLSONA

210.8	Wells Siding	6/1/87 - 3/1/91
211	Wells Siding	3/1/91 - 7/25/92
211	Wellsona	7/25/92 - 1/1/98

Name change

212	Wellsona	1/1/98 - 7/1/10
211	Wellsona	7/1/10 - '68-'69
210.9	Wellsona	'68-'69 -

EOCENE A geological term for one of the early epochs of the Tertiary period. The term is significant to the geologist because much of California's oil and gas production has been obtained from rock strata laid down in that epoch.

San Miguel, 1936.
Alzora Snyder collection

| 215 | Eocene | | 7/1/12 - 3/1/20 | Dropped from list |

PASO ROBLES Originally, Paso de Robles, so named by Father Crespi for the great number of oaks with which this part of the Salinas Valley was populated. "Paso de robles" means "pass of the oaks."

216.1	Paso Robles	6/1/87 - 3/1/91	
216	Paso Robles	3/1/91 - 1/1/98	
217	Paso Robles	1/1/98 - 7/1/10	
216	Paso Robles	7/1/10 - '68-'69	
216.3	Paso Robles	'68-'69 -	
216a	Paso Robles Gravel Pit	1/1/97 - 1/1/02	Dropped from list

TEMPLETON Laid out by the West Coast Land Company with the coming of the railroad in 1886, and named Crocker. Because the name was changed shortly thereafter, it has been assumed the town was named for Templeton Crocker, a grandson of Charles Crocker.

221.6	Templeton	6/1/87 - 3/1/91
222	Templeton	3/1/91 - '68-'69
221.8	Templeton	'68-'69 -

ASUNCION Spanish for "ascension." Pedro Font, diarist of the de Anza expedition of 1776, named this place for the Ascension of the Virgin Mary. The siding took its name from the land grant.

224.8	Asuncion	6/1/90 - 3/3/91
225	Asuncion	3/3/91 - 1/1/98
226	Asuncion	1/1/98 - 7/1/10
225	Asuncion	7/1/10 - 7/1/59
Dropped from list		
225	Asuncion Gravel Pit	1/1/98 - 7/1/08
Dropped from list		

Templeton, 1939.
Robert H. McFarland photo, Arnold S. Menke collection

ATASCADERO Was applied to the provisional land grant by Americans who possibly did not know that the name meant "boggy ground, quagmire or deep miry place." The community, originally known as Atascadero Colony, was founded by E. G. Lewis in 1913.

228.0	Atascadero	6/1/90 - 3/1/91
228	Atascadero	3/1/91 - 1/1/98
229	Atascadero	1/1/98 - 7/1/10
228	Atascadero	7/1/10 - 7/1/15
226	Atascadero	7/1/15 - 1/1/23
Location change, possibly due to colony		
226.7	Atascadero	1/1/23 -

HENRY Named for J. H. Henry, owner of the Asuncion Ranch when the railroad was built through this area.

| 228 | Henry | 7/1/15 - '68-'69 |
| 228.0 | Henry | '68-'69 - |

EAGLET Named for the Eagle Ranch, Baron von Schroeder's ranch, southwest of Atascadero.

230	Havel	1/1/99 - 1/1/00	
231	Havel	1/1/00 - 1/1/07	
231	Eaglet	1/1/07 - 7/1/10	Name change
230	Eaglet	7/1/10 - '68-'69	
230.3	Eaglet	'68-'69 -	
230	Havel	7/1/08 - 7/1/10	Name reused in different location
229	Havel	7/1/10 - 1/1/23	Dropped from list

Atascadero, circa 1939.
Robert H. McFarland photo, Arnold S. Menke collection

PALOMA

| 230.3 | Paloma | 6/6/90 - 3/1/91 | |
| 230 | Paloma | 3/1/91 - 1/1/99 | Dropped from list |

CUSHING

| 233 | Cushing | 1/1/24 - '62-'66 | Dropped from list |

SANTA MARGARITA Originally mentioned in de Anza's diary of 1776; Mission San Luis Obispo operated the Asistencia of Santa Margarita on the site, so named for Margaret of Cortona. The name was carried over to the land grant and to the railway station.

235.6	Santa Margarita	6/1/90 - 3/3/91	
236	Santa Margarita	3/3/91 - '68-'69	
235.5	Santa Margarita	'68-'69 -	

CUESTA Spanish for "slope" or "grade" (thus conventional usage, "Cuesta Grade," is redundant). The nearby pass was named Cañada de la Cuesta in 1842. Station located just west of the summit of the grade over the Santa Lucia Range.

240	Cuesta (Summit)	4/11/94* - 1/1/97	*From memo dated 5/15/95
240	Cuesta	1/1/97 - 7/1/10	Name change
239	Cuesta	7/1/10 - '68-'69	
238.9	Cuesta	'68-'69 -	

THYLE Site of a railroad construction camp during the building of the Cuesta tunnels. It was probably named for the Thyle family, whose son, Irvine, worked for the Southern Pacific and lost an arm in a switching accident at Paso Robles.

241	Thyle	1/1/04 - 7/1/10	
240	Thyle	7/1/10 - 7/1/61	Dropped from list

NOVA

243	Nova	7/1/10 - '37-'40	Dropped from list

SERRANO While this is the Spanish term for "mountain or highland," and certainly appropriate for this station as it is located high in the Santa Lucia Range on the Cuesta Grade, the station was in fact named by the Southern Pacific for Miguel Serrano, from whom the right-of-way was obtained in 1893. Serrano was a son-in-law of Estevan Quintana, who acquired the property in the 1820s.

244	Serrano (Water Station)	4/11/94* - 1/1/97	*From memo dated 5/15/95
244	Serrano	1/1/97 - '68-'69	Name change
243.4	Serrano	'68-'69 -	

CHORRO The name, corresponding to the American term "rapids," was applied to a creek, and to the adjacent land grants, Arroyo del Chorro and Cañada del Chorro.

246	Chorro	7/1/07 - '68-'69	
246.3	Chorro	'68-'69 -	

GOLDTREE Named after the Goldtree brothers, Nathan, Isaac and Morris, San Luis Obispo merchants and land holders who supported the railway.

249	Goldtree	4/11/94* - 7/1/10	*From memo dated 5/15/95
248	Goldtree	7/1/10 - '68-'69	
248.0	Goldtree	'68-'69 -	

HATHAWAY Named after a Dr. Hathaway, over whose estate the railway was constructed into San Luis Obispo in 1894.

252	Hathaway Ave.	4/11/94* - 1/1/18	*From memo dated 5/15/95
251	Hathaway	1/1/18 - '68-'69	Name change
250.6	Hathaway	'68-'69 -	

RAMONA HOTEL Named for a large resort hotel that once stood adjacent to this site. The depot still exists and has been moved to the grounds of the Dallidet Adobe in San Luis Obispo.

252.3	Ramona Hotel	4/11/94* - 1/1/09	*From memo dated 5/15/95, dropped from list

SAN LUIS OBISPO Or "St. Louis the Bishop," named by the Portolá expedition after the Bishop of Toulouse of the same name, a minor saint, but considered patron saint of the monastery in Majorca, Spain, from which Father Serra, Father Crespi and many other of the early Franciscan missionaries had come. Name was applied to the mission, and the town which grew up around it.

253	San Luis Obispo	4/11/94* - 1/1/98	*From memo dated 5/15/95
254	San Luis Obispo	1/1/98 - 1/1/99	
253	San Luis Obispo	1/1/99 - 7/1/10	
252	San Luis Obispo	7/1/10 - '37-'40	
252.1	San Luis Obispo, Osos and Upham Sts.	'37-'40 - 7/1/59	Name change
252.1	San Luis Obispo	7/1/59 -	
252.3	San Luis Obispo, Santa Barbara Ave.	'37-'40 - 7/1/59	Dropped from list
255	East San Luis Obispo	1/1/59 - '68-'69	
254.8	East San Luis Obispo	'68-'69 -	

EDNA Named for the post office established in 1887 and later, the settlement laid out by Lynferd Maxwell. Who Edna was has never been fully established, but Maxwell's first grandaughter was named Edna.
259	Edna	5/15/95• - 7/1/09	*From memo dated 5/15/95
258	Edna	7/1/09 - 7/1/60	Dropped from list

HADLEY
259	Hadley	7/1/09 - 1/1/22

Dropped from list
259	Hadley Tower	1/1/23 - '43-'44

Name change
259	Hadley	'43-'44 - 1/1/59

Name change, dropped from list

P.I. CO. QUARRY SPUR
260	P.I. Co. Quarry Spur	1/1/97 - 1/1/02

Dropped from list

TIBER Probably named for the adjacent Tiber Oil Fields.
260	Tiber	1/1/08 - 7/1/53

Dropped from list

Edna depot, October 5, 1958.
George McCarron collection

PISMO Laid out by the Southern Pacific as a potential townsite in 1891, Pismo was not developed until much later and derived its name from its position on the Ranch El Pismo land grant. The name is attributed to the Chumash Indian word "pismu," meaning "asphalt" or "tar."
263	Pizmo	1/1/07 - 7/1/16	
263	Pismo	7/1/16 - '68-'69	Name change
262.8	Pismo	'68-'69 -	

GROVER Originally founded in 1887 in anticipation of the coming of the railroad. When the railroad failed to arrive within the year, the subdivision passed from promoter to promoter until eventually it began to grow in the late 1930s. Named for Dwight W. Grover, the original founder of the community.
265	Grover	5/15/95* - 7/1/10	*From memo dated 5/15/95
264	Grover	7/1/10 - '68-'69	
264.2	Grover	'68-'69 -	

OCEANO This name, Spanish for "ocean," reflects the location near the shore of the Pacific Ocean.
267	Oceano	5/15/95* - 7/1/10	*From memo dated 5/15/95
266	Oceano	7/1/10 - '68-'69	
265.9	Oceano	'68-'69 -	

OCEAN BEACH SPUR
267a	Ocean Beach Spur	1/1/97 - 1/1/00
267a	Ocean Beach	1/1/00 - 7/1/09

Dropped from list

CALLENDER Named for C.R. Callender, who was involved with promoting eucalyptus growing on the Nipomo Mesa. He also subdivided and promoted the town of Los Berros.
271	Callender	5/15/95* - 7/1/10

*From memo dated 5/15/95
270	Callender	7/1/10 - '68-'69
269.9	Callender	'68-'69

BROMELA
273	Bromela	5/15/95* - 7/1/10

*From memo dated 5/15/95
272	Bromela	7/1/10 - '68-'69
272.4	Bromela	'68-'69 -

Oceano depot, 1915.
Southern Pacific collection

GUADALUPE The name appears as early as 1830 and refers to the Virgin of Guadalupe (the patron saint of Mexico). The name was applied to a land grant in this area and later, in 1872, to the post office here.

| 277 | Guadalupe | 5/15/95* - '68-'69 | *From memo dated 5/15/95 |
| 276.5 | Guadalupe | '68-'69 - | |

WALDORF
282	Waldorf	1/1/97 - 7/1/10
281	Waldorf	7/1/10 - '68-'69
280.7	Waldorf	'68-'69 -

SHUMAN Named for John L. Shuman, local businessman and land owner. Here the Coast Line threads Schumann Canyon as it winds its way to the coast. It is not known why the geographic name, "Schumann," does not correctly spell Mr. Shuman's name.
286	Schumann	1/1/97 - 7/1/10
285	Shuman	7/1/10 - '68-'69
284.8	Shuman	'68-'69 -

DEVON
287	Oil Spur	1/1/08 - 1/1/09	
287	Ek	1/1/09 - 7/1/09	Name change
287	Devon	7/1/09 - 7/1/10	Name change
286	Devon	7/1/10 - '32-'36	Dropped from list
287	Devon	12/15/41 - '68-'69	Name reinstated
286.5	Devon	'68-'69 -	

CASMALIA The name is apparently the Spanish rendition of a Chumash Indian word, "kasmali," which means "the last" or "last place." It dates back to 1837 and is applied to the land grant, town and surrounding hills.
288	Someo	1/1/97 - 1/1/99
288	Casmalia	1/1/99 - '68-'69
287.5	Casmalia	'68-'69 -

ANTONIO The name appears on the local Spanish land grant, Todos Santos y San Antonio, and presumably refers to St. Anthony of Padua.
| 291 | Casmalia | 1/1/97 - 1/1/99 |
| 291 | Antonio | 1/1/99 - 7/1/10 |

Name change
| 290 | Antonio | 7/1/10 - '68-'69 |

Dropped from list

NARLON
294	Narlon	1/1/97 - 7/1/10
293	Narlon	7/1/10 - '68-'69
293.2	Narlon	'68-'69 -

MARSHALL (SPUR)
| 295.5a | Marshall (Spur) | 1/1/31 - 12/15/41 | Dropped from list |

TANGAIR
298	Tangair	1/1/97 - 7/1/10
297	Tangair	7/1/10 - '68-'69
297.2	Tangair	'68-'69 -

AJAX
| 301 | Ajax | 7/1/16 - 12/15/41 |

Dropped from list

SANTA YNEZ RIVER
| 302 | Santa Ynez River | 1/1/97 - 1/1/98 |

Dropped from list

SURF Doubtlessly named for the heavy, crashing surf that pounds the coast at this location.
| 304 | Surf | 1/1/97 - 7/1/10 |
| 303 | Surf | 7/1/10 - 7/1/15 |

Casmalia depot, 1915.
Southern Pacific collection

Surf depot, 1915.
Southern Pacific collection

303	Lompoc Jct.	7/1/15 - 3/1/20	Name change
303	Surf	3/1/20 - '68-'69	Name change
302.7	Surf	'68-'69 -	

BURR Probably a construction camp of short duration.
| 304.2 | Burr | 1/1/01 - 1/1/02 | Dropped from list |

WESER
| 305 | Weser | 1/1/02 - 1/1/08 | Dropped from list |

HONDA Spanish for "deep." The Coast Line passes over Cañada Honda Creek at this point on a long steel trestle.
309	Honda	1/1/01 - 7/1/10	
308	Honda	7/1/10 - '68-'69	
307.9	Honda	'68-'69 -	

SOUTH VANDENBERG A spur serving the adjacent Vandenberg Pacific Missile Range. The base was named after Air Force Chief of Staff Hoyt S. Vandenberg in 1956.
| 309 | South Vandenberg | 10/1/67 -'68-'68 | |
| 309.2 | South Vandenberg | '68-'69 - | |

ARLIGHT A contraction of "Arguello Light." The historic lighthouse is located a stone's throw from the right-of-way at this location.
| 311 | Arlight | 1/1/12 - 7/1/61 | Dropped from list |

ARGUELLO Named for the nearby point. The British explorer, George Vancouver, named this point in 1792 for Jose Dario Arguello, at that time comandante at Monterey.
| 313 | Arguello | 1/1/01 - 7/1/49 | Dropped from list |

SUDDEN Located on Robert Sudden's Espada Ranch.
318	Sudden	1/1/01 - 7/1/10	
317	Sudden	7/1/10 - '68-'69	
317.3	Sudden	'68-'69 -	

JALAMA The name is of Chumash origin, from "khalam," which means "bundle." Mention of a Chumash rancheria of the same name, part of Mission La Purísima Concepción, dates from 1791.
| 321 | Jalama | 1/1/01 - 7/1/59 |
Dropped from list

CONCEPCION The station is located on the neck of Point Concepcion as it juts into the sea, with the lighthouse nearby. The point was named by Vizcaíno, who reached it on Dec. 8, the day of the "immaculate conception" of the Virgin Mary, in 1602.
326	Concepcion	1/1/01 - 7/1/10	
325	Concepcion	7/1/10 - '68-'69	
325.3	Concepcion	'68-'69 -	

ANACAPA Named for the easternmost islands in the Santa Barbara Channel, from the Chumash word "anyapakh," meaning "mirage," a good name for these low-lying islands which are often obscured by haze.
| 329 | Anacapa | 7/1/14 - '37-'40 |
Dropped from list

GATO Spanish for "cat." Station named for Gato Canyon, spanned by a large steel trestle at this point.
| 331 | Gato | 1/1/01 - 7/1/10 | |
| 330 | Gato | 7/1/10 - 1/1/59 | |
Dropped from list

SAN AUGUSTINE For the nearby arroyo. The name probably refers to Saint Augustine, Bishop of Hippo.
| 332 | San Augustine | 1/1/01 - 7/1/10 | |
| 331 | San Augustine | 7/1/10 - '68-'69 | |

Sudden depot, 1915.
Southern Pacific collection

Concepcion depot, 1915.
Southern Pacific collection

DRAKE   Possibly for Grover C. Drake, for many years the district agent at Santa Barbara, although the name was applied in 1907, early for his tenure; or for the English navigator Sir Francis Drake, who landed in California in 1579 (though nowhere near this area).

335	Santa Anita	1/1/01 - 1/1/07	
335	Drake	1/1/07 - 7/1/10	Name change
334	Drake	7/1/10 - 7/1/61	Dropped from list

SACATE   The name of a nearby canyon. Sacate is Spanish for "hay."

336	Sacate	1/1/01 - 7/1/10
335	Sacate	7/1/10 - '68-'69
334.8	Sacate	'68-'69 -

GAVIOTA   Spanish for "sea gull." Father Crespi noted in his diary that at this point one of Portolá's soldiers killed a seagull.

340	Gaviota	1/1/01 - 7/1/10
339	Gaviota	7/1/10 - '68-'69
339.4	Gaviota	'68-'69 -

SEAGIRT

| 340 | Seagirt | 1/1/19 - '32-'36 |

Dropped from list

LENTO   Spanish for "sluggish" or "heavy."

| 343 | Lento | 1/1/07 - 10/1/42 |

Dropped from list

TAJIGUAS   After Tajiguas Creek. The name evidently was derived from that of a Chumash village.

347	Tajiguas	1/1/01 - 7/1/10
346	Tajiguas	7/1/10 - '68-'69
345.7	Tajiguas	'68-'69 -

Gaviota depot, 1940, with the Surf local headed eastward.
Bancroft Library, University of California, Berkeley

ORELLA   Named for Bruno Orella, a local ranch owner.

| 349 | Orella | 1/1/01 - 10/1/42 | Dropped from list |

CAPITAN   For the nearby arroyo, which is mentioned as early as 1804. The name may commemorate El Capitan Jose Francisco Ortega, holder of a local grant.

351	Capitan	1/1/01 - 7/1/10
350	Capitan	7/1/10 - '68-'69
349.9	Capitan	'68-'69 -

VERAS

| 354 | Veras | 1/1/03 - 7/1/10 | |
| 353 | Veras | 7/1/10 - 1/1/25 | Dropped from list |

NAPLES

356	Naples	1/1/01 - 7/1/10
355	Naples	7/1/10 - '68-'69
355.0	Naples	'68-'69 -

VILO

| 357 | Vilo | 1/1/07 - 10/1/42 | Dropped from list |

ELLWOOD   Named for pioneer orchardist Elwood Cooper whose olives, olive oil, persimmons and lemons were famous the world over. On most maps, the geographic name correctly reflects his name, "Elwood;" the railroad has persisted in "Ellwood" since 1911.

541	Elwood	3/1/88 - 3/1/91	(On Ventura Division)
543	Elwood	3/1/91 - 1/1/01	(On Ventura Division)
360	Elwood	1/1/01 - 7/1/10	Changed to Coast Division milepost
359	Elwood	7/1/10 - 7/1/11	
359	Ellwood	7/1/11 - '68-'69	Name change
358.9	Ellwood	'68-'69 -	

COROMAR

| 361 | Coromar | 1/1/02 - 7/1/10 |
| 360 | Coromar | 7/1/10 - '68-'69 |

| 360.2 | Coromar | '68-'69 | |

LA PATERA Spanish for "place where ducks congregate." The name appeared as early as 1842 and was commonly applied to the marshes to the west of this location.

539	La Patera	3/1/88 - 3/1/91	(On Ventura Division)
540	La Patera	3/1/91 - 1/1/01	(On Ventura Division)
363	La Patera	1/1/01 - 7/1/10	Changed to Coast Division milepost
362	La Patera	7/1/10 - '68-'69	
361.7	La Patera	'68-'69 -	

GOLETA Spanish for "schooner," the name was applied to the land grant and later to the townsite in 1875. The name originated with an American schooner that stranded in the estuary and lay there for many years.

537	Goleta	3/1/88 - 3/1/91	(On Ventura Division)
539	Goleta	3/1/91 - 1/1/01	(On Ventura Division)
364	Goleta	1/1/01 - 7/1/10	Changed to Coast Division milepost
363	Goleta	7/1/10 - '68-'69	
362.8	Goleta	'68-'69 -	

HOPE RANCH Originally Hopevale, after Thomas W. Hope, who granted a right-of-way across his ranch, a portion of the old Cañada de Calera land grant. The later name dates from the subdivision by his heirs.

534	Hopevale	3/1/88 - 3/1/91	(On Ventura Division)
536	Hopevale	3/1/91 - 1/1/01	(On Ventura Division) Dropped from list
367	Irma	1/1/02 - 1/1/10	Name change, Coast Division milepost
367	Hope Ranch	1/1/10 - '68-'69	
366.5	Hope Ranch	'68-'69 -	

OLIVE

| 368 | Olive | 1/1/18 - '68-'69 | Dropped from list |

SANTA BARBARA The name was applied to the passage between the mainland and what are now the Channel Islands by Vizcaíno on December 4, 1602, the feast day of the Roman maiden who was beheaded by her father because she had become a Christian. The mission was founded in 1786, and the town incorporated in 1850.

369	West Santa Barbara	1/1/18 - '68-'69	
368.5	West Santa Barbara	'68-'69 -	
530	Victoria St., Santa Barbara	3/1/88 - 3/1/91	(On Ventura Division)
532	Victoria St., Santa Barbara	3/1/91 - 1/1/01	(On Ventura Division)
532	Victoria St.	1/1/01 - 1/1/02	Dropped from list
528	Santa Barbara	3/1/88 - 3/1/91	(On Ventura Division)

Santa Barbara depot, 1911.
Southern Pacific collection

529	Santa Barbara	3/1/91 - 1/1/01	(On Ventura Division)
373	Santa Barbara	1/1/01 - 1/1/02	Changed to Coast Division milepost
370	Santa Barbara	1/1/02 - 7/1/07	
371	Santa Barbara	7/1/07 - '68-'69	
370.7	Santa Barbara	'68-'69 -	
372	East Santa Barbara	7/1/50 - 5/1/69	
371.9	East Santa Barbara	5/1/69 -	
529	Mason St.	1/1/02 - 1/1/07	(On Ventura Division)
373	Mason St.	1/1/07 - 7/1/07	Changed to Coast Line milepost, dropped from list.

COUNTRY CLUB

374	Ames	1/1/07 - 7/1/09	
374	Country Club	7/1/09 - 7/1/10	Name change
373	Country Club	7/1/10 - 1/1/28	
373	Biltmore	1/1/28 - 1/1/29	Name change
374	Biltmore	1/1/29 - 12/15/41	Exchanged mileposts with and renamed Montecito

MONTECITO The origin of the name, which is mentioned as early as 1783, is unresolved. Some attribute the name to the Spanish word for "little woods," and others say it means "little mountains."

525	Montecito	3/1/88 - 3/1/91	(On Ventura Division)
527	Montecito	3/1/91 - 1/1/07	(On Ventura Division)
374.3	Montecito	1/1/07 - 7/1/10	Changed to Coast Line milepost
374	Montecito	7/1/10 - 1/1/29	
373	Montecito	1/1/29 - 12/15/41	Exchanged mileposts with Biltmore, dropped from list (see Miramar)

MIRAMAR Spanish for "behold the sea."

| 526.8 | Miramar | 1/5/93 - 1/1/07 | |
(On Ventura Division)
375	Miramar	1/1/07 - 1/1/57	Changed to Coast Line milepost
375	Montecito	1/1/57 - 5/1/69	Name change, reviving Montecito
374.6	Montecito	5/1/69 -	

AJAX

| 524.3 | Williams Spur | 1/1/95 - 1/1/00 | |
(On Ventura Division)
| 524.3 | Ajax | 1/1/00 - 1/1/07 | |
(On Ventura Division) Name change
| 377a | Ajax | 1/1/07 - 7/1/09 | |
Changed to Coast Line milepost, dropped from list

SUMMERLAND So named in 1889 when J.L. Williams formed his spiritualist colony on the Ortega Ranch.

| 522 | Summerland | 6/1/90 - 3/1/91 | |
(On Ventura Division)
| 524 | Summerland | 3/1/91 - 1/1/07 | |
(On Ventura Division)
| 377 | Summerland | 1/1/07 - 7/1/10 | |
Changed to Coast Line milepost, dropped from list
| 376 | Summerland | 7/1/10 - 5/1/69 | |
| 376.2 | Summerland | 5/1/69 - | |

Miramar depot, 1916.
Roger Titus collection

ORTEGA Siding and townsite were located on the Ortega Ranch.

521	Ortega	3/1/88 - 3/1/91	(On Ventura Division)
523	Ortega	3/1/91 - 1/1/07	(On Ventura Division)
378	Ortega	1/1/07 - 7/1/10	Changed to Coast Line milepost
377	Ortega	7/1/10 - 5/1/69	
377.3	Ortega	5/1/69 -	

SERENA Spanish for "calm" or "serene." Also known unofficially as Carpinteria Landing.

520	Smith's Wharf Spur	6/1/90 - 3/1/91	(On Ventura Division)
522	Smith's Wharf Spur	3/1/91 - 7/25/92	(On Ventura Division)
522	Serena	7/25/92 - 1/1/07	Name change

| 379 | Serena | 1/1/07 - 7/1/10 | Changed to Coast Line milepost |
| 378 | Serena | 7/1/10 - 1/1/26 | Dropped from list |

CARPINTERIA Spanish for "carpenter shop," named in August, 1769, by Father Crespi and his companions of the Portolá expedition, who found Chumash Indians making canoes. The Southern Pacific agency was closed on September 18, 1958.

517	Carpinteria	3/1/88 - 3/1/91	(On Ventura Division)
519	Carpinteria	3/1/91 - 1/1/07	(On Ventura Division)
382	Carpinteria	1/1/07 - 7/1/10	Changed to Coast Line milepost
381	Carpinteria	7/1/10 - 5/1/69	
381.2	Carpinteria	5/1/69 -	

SEAROAD At this point, the old coast highway once dropped down onto the beach.

| 382 | Searoad | 7/1/12 - 1/1/27 | |
| Dropped from list | | | |

WAVE

| 383 | Wave | 1/1/11 - 5/1/69 | |
| 383.4 | Wave | 5/1/69 - | |

SEA WALL SPUR

| 516 | Sea Wall Spur | 6/1/90 - 3/1/91 | |
(On Ventura Division), dropped from list

BENHAM

| 515 | Rincon | 6/1/90 - 3/1/91 | |
(On Ventura Division)
| 516 | Rincon | 3/1/91 - 1/1/95 | |
(On Ventura Division)
| 516 | Benham | 1/1/95 - 1/1/07 | Name change |
| 385 | Benham | 1/1/07 - 12/15/41 | Changed to Coast Line milepost, dropped from list |

Carpinteria depot, 1915.
Southern Pacific Lines

PUNTA An abbreviation of Punta Gorda, a prominent headland near this siding. "Gorda" is Spanish for "broad" or "big."

515	Punta Gorda Spur	3/1/91 - 1/1/00	(On Ventura Division)
515	Punta Gorda	1/1/00 - 1/1/07	(On Ventura Division), name change
386	Punta	1/1/07 - 5/1/69	Changed to Coast Line milepost, name change
385.7	Punta	5/1/69 -	

SEACLIFF

510	Sea Cliff	3/1/88 - 3/1/91	(On Ventura Division)
512	Sea Cliff	3/1/91 - 1/1/07	(On Ventura Division)
389	Sea Cliff	1/1/07 - 5/1/69	Changed to Coast Line milepost
388.6	Sea Cliff	5/1/69 -	

DULAH

507	Dulah	1/1/02 - 1/1/07	(On old Ventura Division)
393	Dulah	1/1/07 - 5/1/69	Changed to Coast Line milepost
392.9	Dulah	5/1/69 -	

BITUMA Probably so named for the tar or bitumen deposits found near here.

| 503 | Bituma | 3/1/88 - 3/1/91 | (On old Ventura Division) |
| 505 | Bituma | 3/1/91 - 1/1/01 | (On old Ventura Division), dropped from list |

VENTURA Abridged from the name of nearby Mission San Buenaventura, completed in 1782 and named for Saint Bonaventure.

503	Ventura Junc.	1/1/99 - 1/1/07	(On old Ventura Division)
398	Ventura Junc.	1/1/07 - 7/1/10	Changed to Coast Line milepost
397	Ventura Junc.	7/1/10 - 7/1/11	
397	Ventura Jct.	7/1/11 - 1/1/26	Name change
397	Ventura Junction	1/1/26 - 5/1/69	Name change
397.3	Ventura Jct.	5/1/69 -	Name change
500	San Buena Ventura	6/1/87 - 3/1/91	(On old Ventura Division)

502	San Buena Ventura	3/1/91 - 1/1/07	
(On old Ventura Division)			
399	San Buena Ventura	1/1/07 - 7/1/08	
Changed to Coast Line milepost			
399	Ventura	7/1/08 - 7/1/10	
Name change			
398	Ventura	7/1/10 -5/1/69	
398.2	Ventura	5/1/69 -	

ABSCO
399	Absco	1/1/19 - 12/15/41
Dropped from list		

LEMON
400	Lemon	1/1/19 - 5/1/69
400.2	Lemon	5/1/69 -

EDFU
499	Edfu	1/1/00 - 1/1/07	
(On Ventura Division)			
402	Edfu	1/1/07 - 7/1/10	Changed to Coast Line milepost
401	Edfu	7/1/10 - '37-'40	Dropped from list

Ventura depot in 1905, decorated for President Theodore Roosevelt's tour of that year (sign on depot reads, "OUR TEDDY"). *Ventura County Museum of Art & History*

MONTALVO The name was applied to the station when the railroad reached this point in 1887. Ordoñez de Montalvo is thought to be the author of the novel *Las Sergas de Esplandián*, in which the name "California" appears for the first time. Montalvo is also the name of James Phelan's estate in Santa Clara County.

495	Conejo	6/1/87 - 3/1/88	(Milepost via Saugus)
495	Montalvo	3/1/88 - 3/1/91	(Milepost via Saugus), name change
497	Montalvo	3/1/91 - 1/1/07	(Milepost via Saugus)
404	Montalvo	1/1/07 - 7/1/10	Changed to Coast Line milepost
403	Montalvo	7/1/10 - 5/1/69	
403.2	Montalvo	5/1/69 -	

EL RIO The town was founded in 1875 and called New Jerusalem. About 1895 the name was changed to El Rio.
406	El Rio	1/1/07 - 5/1/69
405.6	El Rio	5/1/69 -

OXNARD Named for industrialists Henry, James, Robert and Benjamin Oxnard, who incorporated the American Beet Sugar Company and built a beet sugar mill at this place in 1898.
501	Oxnard	1/1/99 - 1/1/07	(Milepost via Saugus)
408	Oxnard	1/1/07 -5/1/69	Changed to Coast Line milepost
407.8	Oxnard	5/1/69 -	

LENNOX
410	Lennox	7/1/11 -1/1/30	Beet Spur, dropped from list

ARNEZ
411	Arnez	7/1/11 - 1/1/27	Dropped from list

TODD (SPUR)
411	Todd (Spur)	1/1/30 - 1/1/46	Dropped from list

LEESDALE
506	Leesdale	1/1/00 - 1/1/07	(Milepost via Saugus)
413	Leesdale	1/1/07 - 7/1/10	Changed to Coast Line milepost
412	Leesdale	7/1/10 - 5/1/69	
412.1	Leesdale	5/1/69 -	

SUCROSA Name coined by the railroad. This siding was in the midst of fields of sugar beets, a source for sucrose sugar.
507	Sucrosa	1/1/00 - 1/1/07	(Milepost via Saugus)
414	Sucrosa	1/1/07 - 12/14/41	Changed to Coast Line milepost, dropped from list

CAMARILLO Established on September 29, 1899, the station site rests on the old Rancho Calleguas and commemorates one of its owners, Juan Camarillo. Southern Pacific's Camarillo agency was closed on April 28, 1958.

510	Camarillo	1/1/00 - 1/1/07	(Milepost via Saugus)
417	Camarillo	1/1/07 - 5/1/69	Changed to Coast Line milepost
416.6	Camarillo	5/1/69 -	

SOMIS A rancheria named "somes" is mentioned as early as 1795. The new spelling was adopted in 1899 when Southern Pacific built through the area.

513	Somis	1/1/00 - 1/1/07	(Milepost via Saugus)
420	Somis	1/1/07 - 5/1/69	Changed to Coast Line milepost
419.8	Somis	5/1/69 -	

LAGOL

516	Lagol	1/1/01 - 1/1/07	(Milepost via Saugus)
423	Lagol	1/1/07 - 5/1/69	Changed to Coast Line milepost
422.9	Lagol	5/1/69 -	

TERNEZ

518	Ternez	1/1/01 - 1/1/07	(Milepost via Saugus)
425	Ternez	1/1/07 - 7/1/10	Changed to Coast Line milepost
424	Ternez	7/1/10 - 1/1/24	Dropped from list

MOORPARK Founded in 1900, the town was named for the well-known English variety of apricot. The Southern Pacific agency at Moorpark was closed February 12, 1958.

521	Moorpark	1/1/01 - 1/1/07	(Milepost via Saugus)
428	Moorpark	1/1/07 - 7/1/10	Changed to Coast Line milepost
427	Moorpark	7/1/10 - 5/1/69	
427.1	Moorpark	5/1/69 -	

STRATHEARN

| 526 | Strathearn | 1/1/01 - 1/1/07 | |

(Milepost via Saugus)

| 433 | Strathearn | 1/1/07 - 7/1/10 | |

Changed to Coast Line milepost

| 432 | Strathearn | 7/1/10 - 5/1/69 | |
| 432.2 | Strathearn | 5/1/69 - | |

SIMI The name, attributed to the Chumash word "shimiyi," for "a place or village," appears as a land grant name as early as 1795, and was applied to the rancho, pass and creek. For the first six months of its existence the SP station bore the impressive name Simiopolis. The present name dates from July, 1899.

| 434 | Simi | 1/1/08 - 5/1/69 | |
| 433.5 | Simi | 5/1/69 - | |

Moorpark after a fire, November 28, 1933.
Southern Pacific Lines

SANTA SUSANA The name, which honors Saint Susana, the Roman virgin and martyr of the third century, appears in the area as early as 1804, and was applied to the mountains between the San Fernando and Simi valleys. The railroad adopted the name in 1902.

531	Santa Susana	1/1/01 - 1/1/07	(Milepost via Saugus)
438	Santa Susana	1/1/07 - 7/1/10	Changed to Coast Line milepost
437	Santa Susana	7/1/10 - 5/1/69	
437.5	Santa Susana	5/1/69 -	

DILLON

| 441 | Dillon | 1/1/07 - 7/1/10 | |
| 440 | Dillon | 7/1/10 - 3/1/20 | Dropped from list |

HASSON Reportedly the name derives from the nearby Hasson Brothers ranch.

534	Hasson	1/1/04 - 1/1/07	(Milepost via Saugus)
442	Hasson	1/1/07 - 7/1/10	Changed to Coast Line milepost
441	Hasson	7/1/10 - 5/1/69	
441.0	Hasson	5/1/69 -	

CHATSWORTH The place was named in the boom year of 1887, after Chatsworth, England.

495	Chatsworth Park	1/1/94 - 1/1/05	
On Burbank Branch			
539	Chatsworth	1/1/05 - 1/1/07	(Milepost via Saugus), name change
446	Chatsworth	1/1/07 - 7/1/15	Changed to Coast Line milepost
445.5	Chatsworth	7/1/15 -	
446.1	Chatsworth Jct.	7/1/15 - 1/1/21	
445.9	Chatsworth Jct.	1/1/21 - 1/1/27	
446.1	Chatsworth Jct.	1/1/27 - 1/1/31	
446.1	Chatsworth Junction	1/1/31 - 5/1/48	Dropped from list

WARDLAW

| 448 | Wardlaw | 7/1/16 - 1/1/25 | Dropped from list |

NORTHRIDGE Originally known as Zelzah, the station was renamed North Los Angeles after 1928. It became Northridge during the Depression. The Northridge Southern Pacific agency was closed April 30, 1959.

543	Govan	1/1/04 - 1/1/05	On Burbank Branch
543	Zelzah	1/1/05 - 1/1/07	On Burbank Branch, name change
450	Zelzah	1/1/07 - 1/1/31	Changed to Coast Line milepost
450	North Los Angeles	1/1/31 - '37-'40	Name change
450	Northridge	'37-'40 - 5/1/69	Name change
449.9	Northridge	5/1/69 -	

No. 374, the "Zipper," races past Northridge depot on April 11, 1940.
Frank J. Peterson photo, Robert McNeel collection

LA METRO

| 453 | La Metro | 1/1/31 - 5/1/69 |
| 452.5 | La Metro | 5/1/69 - |

RAYMER

548	Raymer	1/1/04 - 1/1/07	
On old Burbank Branch			
455	Raymer	1/1/07 - 7/1/10	Changed to Coast Line milepost
454	Raymer	7/1/10 - 5/1/69	
454.1	Raymer	5/1/69 -	

GEMCO An abbreviation of General Motors Corporation, which built a major automobile assembly plant here in 1948.

| 456 | Gemco | 7/1/53 - 5/1/69 |
| 456.1 | Gemco | 5/1/69 - |

HEWITT Named for E.E. Hewitt, an early-day Southern Pacific official who held various positions on the Los Angeles Division in the 1880s and 1890s, including those of assistant superintendent and superintendent.

552	Hewitt	1/1/04 - 1/1/07	On old Burbank Junction
459	Hewitt	1/1/07 - 7/1/10	Changed to Coast Line milepost
458	Hewitt	7/1/10 - 5/1/69	
458.4	Hewitt	5/1/69 -	

VEGA Spanish for "flat lowland," a name used until 1941 at milepost 97 on the Coast Line.
| 461 | Vega | 12/15/41 - 5/1/69 |
| 460.5 | Vega | 5/1/69 - |

BURBANK The city was laid out in 1887 and named for one of the subdividers, Dr. David Burbank, a Los Angeles dentist. The name is sometimes incorrectly assumed to honor botanist Luther Burbank, whose work was carried out in Sonoma County.
473	Burbank	6/1/87 - 7/1/11	Milepost via Tehachapi
472	Burbank	7/1/11 - 1/1/31	Dropped from list
471.6	Burbank Jct.	1/1/23 - '62-'66	
462.7 (via Coast) 471.6 Burbank Jct.		'62-'66 - 5/1/69	
471.6	Burbank Jct.	5/1/69 -	

SEPULVEDA Name applied in 1873, probably for Fernando Sepulveda whose adobe was near the base of the Verdugo Mountains.
462	Sepulveda	3/1/79 - 6/1/87	Milepost via Tehachapi
474	Sepulveda	6/1/87 - 3/1/91	
475	Sepulveda	3/1/91 - 7/1/11	
474	Sepulveda	7/1/11 - 7/1/51	Dropped from list

GLENDALE When founded about 1880, the town was named Riverdale, but changed soon after to avoid confusion with a Riverdale in Fresno County. Tropico was the name for the south side of Glendale.
| -- | Tropico | 6/1/87 - 3/1/88 |
| 476 | Tropico | 3/1/88 - 3/1/91 |

Milepost via Tehachapi
478	Tropico	3/1/91 - 7/1/11
477	Tropico	7/1/11 - 1/1/19
477	Glendale	1/1/19 - 5/1/69

Name change
| 477.1 | Glendale | 5/1/69 - |

INDUSTRIAL
477.9	Industrial	1/1/23 - '37-'40
478	Industrial	'37-'40 - 5/1/69
477.9	Industrial	5/1/69 -

Glendale station, circa 1960.
Bob Morris

ARROYO JUNCTION
| 478.5 | Arroyo Junction | '37-'40 - 7/1/61 | Dropped from list |

SQUAB
| 481 | Squab | 1/1/07 - 7/1/09 | Dropped from list |

TAYLOR Named for the original owner of the property on which much of the yard lies.
481.5	Taylor	7/1/09 - 7/1/11
480.5	Taylor	7/1/11 - 3/1/20
479.3	Taylor	3/1/20 - '37-'40
479	Taylor	'37-'40 - 7/1/61	Dropped from list

LOS ANGELES YARD
479.7	Los Angeles Yard	1/1/26 - 7/1/61
478.5	Los Angeles Yard	7/1/61 - 5/1/69
478.5	Los Angeles-Taylor Yard	5/1/69 -
"	-Local Yard	
"	-B Yard	
"	-C Yard	
"	-Rip	

DAYTON AVE. TOWER
| 480.7 | Dayton Ave. Tower | '37-'40 - | Improvements in place with opening of LAUPT |

EAST BANK JUNCTION
481.9	East Bank Junction	'37-'40 -	Improvements in place with opening of LAUPT

MISSION TOWER
482.2	Mission Tower	'37-'40 -	Improvements in place with opening of LAUPT

MISSION JUNCTION
482.3	Mission Junction	'37-'40 -	Improvements in place with opening of LAUPT

LOS ANGELES The name had its origins on August 2, 1769, when Portolá named the river here (now called the Los Angeles River) El Rio de Nuestra Señora la Reina de los Angeles de Porciúncula (Our Lady Queen of the Angels of Portiúncula), whose feast day it was. The Portiúncula chapel, the cradel of the Franciscan order, is in the basilica of "Our Lady of the Angels" near Assisi, Italy. The same name was applied by Neve in 1777 to the Pueblo which was founded here, nearly a century before the arrival of the railroad. The name, soon shortened to Pueblo de Los Angeles and officially to Los Angeles in 1850, has, in any case, perhaps more charm than the Gabrieleño Indian name for the place, Yang-na.

482.8	Los Angeles (LAUPT)	'37-'40 -	
481.7	West yard	1/1/02 - 7/1/11	
481	Westyard	7/1/11 - 1/1/18	Dropped from list
482	San Fernando St.	3/1/91 - 1/1/94	Dropped from list
471	Los Angeles	3/1/79 - 6/1/87	
482	Los Angeles	6/1/87 - 1/1/26	
482	Los Angeles	1/1/26 - 1/1/28	Dropped from list
---	Los Angeles Freight Depot		
	San Fernando St.	6/1/90 - 3/1/91	
	Los Angeles Frt. Depot	3/1/91 - 1/1/94	Name change
	Los Angeles River Station	1/1/94 - 1/1/25	Dropped from list
	Los Angeles Freight Depot	1/1/94 - 7/1/10	
483	Los Angeles Freight Depot	7/1/10 - 7/1/11	
482	Los Angeles Freight Depot	7/1/11 - '37-'40	Dropped from list
483	Naud Junction	6/1/90 - 3/1/91	
482.9	Naud Junction	3/1/91 - 7/1/10	Dropped from list
482.5	Naud Junction	7/1/15 -	Name reinstated, milepost change
483	Commercial St.		
	Arcade Depot (5th St.)	6/1/90 - 3/1/91	Moved
483.3	Commercial St.	3/1/91 - 7/1/08	Name change
483.3	Los Angeles (Commercial St.)	7/1/08 - 7/1/10	Name change
483.9	Los Angeles (Commercial St.)	7/1/10 - 1/1/11	Dropped from list
483.6	First Street	1/1/95 - 1/1/07	Dropped from list
484	Arcade Depot (5th St.)	3/1/91 - 7/1/08	Moved
484	Los Angeles (Arcade Depot, 5th St.)	7/1/08 - 7/1/10	
484.7	Los Angeles (Arcade Depot, 5th St.)	7/1/10 - 7/1/11	
484	Los Angeles (Passenger Station, 5th St.)	7/1/11 - '37-'40	

Central Station, Los Angeles, 1926.
Union Pacific Railroad Museum

A new depot was built at Monterey, on the Monterey Branch rather than on the main Coast Line, because of the great growth in traffic at nearby Fort Ord in World War II. Shown here are views of both sides of the old depot, taken during September of 1942 (**top** and **center**), and a photo of the track side of the new stucco depot in December, 1943 (**bottom**).

All, Benny Romano collection

Bibliography

BOOKS

Best, Gerald M., and David Joslyn, *Locomotives of the Southern Pacific Company*, Bulletin 94, The Railway and Locomotive Historical Society, Boston, Mass., 1956.
Church, Dr. Robert J., *The 4300 4-8-2s*, Central Valley Railroad Publications, Wilton, Cal., 1980.
_____, *Cab Forward*, Kratville, Omaha, Nebr., 1968; revised edition, Central Valley Railroad Publications, Wilton, Cal., 1982.
_____, *Those Daylight 4-8-4s*, Kratville, Omaha, Nebr., 1976.
Coombs, Gary B., *Goleta Depot*, Institute For American Research, Goleta, Cal., 1988.
Coombs, Gary B. and Phyllis J. Olsen, *Sentinal at Ellwood*, Institute For American Research, Goleta, Cal., 1985.
Diller, J. S., and others, *Guide Book of the Western United States, Part D, Shasta Route and Coast Route*, United States Geological Survey Bulletin 614, Department of the Interior, U.S. Government Printing Office, Washington, DC, 1915.
Gudde, Erwin G., *California Place Names*, University of California Press, Berkeley and Los Angeles, Cal., 1959.
Hamman, Rick, *California Central Coast Railways*, Pruett Publishing Co., Boulder, Colo., 1980.
Johnston, Robert B., *Salinas 1875-1950, From Village to City*, Fidelity Savings and Loan Assoc., Salinas, Cal., 1950.
Kennan, George, *E. H. Harriman* (two volumes), Houghton Mifflin Co., Boston, Mass., 1922.
Lockwood, Charles A. and Hans Christian Adamson, *Tragedy at Honda*, Valley Publishers, Fresno, Cal., 1974.
Limerick, Jeffrey, Nancy Ferguson, and Richard Oliver, *America's Grand Resort Hotels*, Pantheon Books, New York, NY, 1979.
Nicholson, Loren, *Rails Across the Ranchos*, Valley Publishers, Fresno, Cal., 1980.
Outland, Charles F., *Man-Made Disaster, the Story of St. Francis Dam*, Arthur H. Clark, Glendale, Cal., 1977.
Ryan, Dennis and Joseph Shine, *Southern Pacific Passenger Trains. Vol. 1, Night Trains of the Coast*, Four Ways West, La Mirada, Cal., 1986.
Sanchez, Nellie Van de Grift, *Spanish Place Names in California: Their Meaning and Their Romance*, A.M. Robertson, San Francisco, Cal., 1917.
Teague, Charles C., *Fifty Years A Rancher*, California Fruit Growers Exchange, Los Angeles, Cal., 1944.
Thompson, Anthony W., Robert J. Church and Bruce H. Jones, *Pacific Fruit Express*, Central Valley Railroad Publications, Wilton, Cal., 1992.
Taylor, Frank and Earl M. Welty, *Black Bonanza*, Whittlesen House, McGraw-Hill, New York, NY, 1950.
Wood, Stanley, *Over The Range to the Golden Gate*, R.R. Donnelley and Sons, Chicago, Ill., 1912.
WPA Federal Writers Project, *California, A Guide to the Golden State*, Hastings House, New York, NY, 1939.

PERIODICALS

"A Farewell to the Lark," *Wheel Clicks*, Vol. 32, No. 3, June, 1968.
Ahern, T., "Following in the Footsteps of the Padres—a History of the Coast Division," *Southern Pacific Bulletin* (Coast Division Number), November, 1920, pp. 11-15.
"Bayshore Cut-Off of the Southern Pacific," *Railroad Gazette*, Vol. 42, No. 11, March 15, 1907, pp. 328-331.
"Bayshore and Dumbarton Cut-Offs of the Southern Pacific," *Railroad Gazette*, Vol. 44, No. 6, Feb. 15, 1909, pp. 176-177.
Brotherhood of Locomotive Firemen Magazine.
Charlton, Robert, "The Story of a Great Tunnel," *Sunset*, May, 1904, pp. 219-224.
Didion, Joan, "The Golden Land," *The New York Review*, August 21, 1993, pp. 85-94.
Ditzel, Paul C., "The Ghost Train of Espee," *Westways*, May, 1958, pp. 20-21.
Everywhere West, Berkeley, Cal.
E. J. Elbury's Big 4 Railroad Record, Vol. 14, 1926, Coast Division.
Fabing, Horace W., "Granite Rock Co.," *Western Railroader*, Vol. 39, issue 429, March, 1976.
——, "Monterey & Pacific Grove Railway," *Western Railroader*, Vol. 22, No. 10, Issue 238, September, 1959.
——, "Southern Pacific Hollister Branch, the Tres Pinos Line," *Western Railroader*, Vol. 36, Issue 398, June, 1973.
——, "Salinas Railway," *Western Railroader*.
Flimsies, Orange, Cal.
Guthohrlein, Adolf, "Santa Maria Valley Railroad," *Western Railroader*, Vol. 25, No. 4, issue 268, April 1962.
Hunkins, Harrison James, "Earthquake," *Railroad*, Vol. 28, No.5, October, 1940, pp. 116-120.
Lawler, Nan, "Closing the Gap," *Railroad History*, Bulletin 145, R&LHS, 1981, pp. 87-105.
Maguire, Joseph F., "The Boomer of Ventura County, with Apologies to Eddie Sands," *Ventura County Historical Society Quarterly*, Vol. XV, No. 2, February, 1970, pp. 6-13.
——, "The Ventura County Railway," *Ventura County Historical Society Quarterly*, Vol. VI, No. 3, May, 1961, pp 2-24.
McNeel, Robert R., "The Last Days of Steam, Recollections of the Santa Paula Branch; Memories of the Ojai Branch." *Ventura County Historical Society Quarterly*, Vol. XXV, No. 1, Fall, 1979.
Morgan, William T., "The Ventura County Railway, Part 1," *Pacific News*, January, 1985, pp. 10-15.
——, "The Ventura County Railway, Part 2," *Pacific News*, February, 1985, pp. 11-16.
Myrick, David F., "Santa Barbara County Railroads, a Centennial History." *Noticias*, Vol. XXXIII, Nos. 2 and 3, Summer/Fall, 1987.
——, "Ventura County Railroads, a Centennial History, Vol. 1," *Ventura County Historical Society Quarterly*, Vol. 33, No. 1, Fall 1987.

———, "Ventura County Railroads, a Centennial History, Vol. 2," *Ventura County Historical Society Quarterly*, Vol. 33, Nos. 2&3, Winter/Spring, 1988.
"New Bayshore Yard of the Southern Pacific at San Francisco," *Railroad Gazette*, Vol. 42, No. 1, January 4, 1907, pp. 12-13.
"Notes on the Market Street Railway, San Francisco," *Street Railway Journal*, Vol. 17, No. 5, May, 1901, pp. 346-352
"Lompoc Centennial, Our City's First 100 Years 1888-1988," Lompoc *Record*, 1988.
"Pacific Coast Railway," *Western Railroader*, Vol. 45, Issue 500, 1982.
Parker, Jim, and Kitty Dill, "The Lonesome Train," Ventura *Star-Free Press*, December 27, 1970, pp. 7-11.
Pruess, Theodore C., "Stone Canyon R.R.," *Western Railroader*, Vol. 30, No. 8, Issue 340, August, 1967.
Railway Age, New York and Chicago.
Souvenir Railroad Edition, San Luis Obispo *Tribune*, May 5, 1894.
Southern Pacific Bulletin, San Francisco.
Stindt, Fred A., "Peninsula Service–the Story of the Southern Pacific Commuter Trains," *Western Railroader*, Vol. 20, No. 9, Issue No. 213, June, 1957.
"The Railways and the California Expositions," *Railroad Age Gazette*, Vol. 59, Nos. 11 and 12, September 10 and 17, 1915, pp. 460-464 and 499-501.
Whalen, W. H., "Southland Grows as Rails are Laid–a History of the Los Angeles Division," *Southern Pacific Bulletin* (Los Angeles Division Number), July, 1921, pp. 3-10.
Woodson, Weldon D., "Eucalyptus Boom and Bust," *Railroad*, Vol. 53, No. 1, October, 1950, pp. 74-79

DOCUMENTS, REPORTS AND STUDIES

"California Rail Passenger Development Plan, 1991-96 Fiscal Years," Caltrans, Sacramento, Cal., 1991.
Interstate Commerce Commission Investigation No. 2543, The Southern Pacific Co., Report in re Accident Near Hasson, Calif., November 19, 1941.
Southern Pacific Coast Line Analysis, Wilber Smith Associates, June 26, 1992.
Oil Field Review, Geologic Formations & Economic Development of the Oil and Gas Fields of California, California Division of Mines, Ferry Building, San Francisco, Cal., 1943.
Sanford, W. E. "Bud," Day Books while Coast Division Road Foreman of Engines, 1952-1963.
Southern Pacific Company, *Annual Reports*, 1899-1966.
———, *List of Officers, Agencies, Stations, Etc.*, Circular 4/Form 70, 1874-1974.
———, Division Maps, Pacific System, Compiled by Valuation Department, San Francisco, Cal., June 30, 1916.
———, Files of the Bureau of News, San Francisco, Cal.
———, Files of the Chief Engineer, San Francisco, Cal.
———, Files of the General Manager, San Francisco, Cal.
———, Long Range Planning Program Item No. 5, Coast Route, July 7, 1955.
———, Memorandum of Agreement Between Southern Pacific Transportation Company, Western Lines, and its Engineers Represented by Brotherhood of Locomotive Engineers, January 25, 1990.
———, Resume of Special Notices and Circulars, Coast Division, 1957.
———, *Road of a Thousand Wonders*, San Francisco, Cal., 1908.
———, *Through Manifest; Merchandise and Perishable Freight Schedules Between Principal Points*, Office of the General Superintendent of Transportation, San Francisco, 1956, 1962, 1968.
———, Timetables, Operating and Public, 1879-1993.
Souvenir Folder, 1936 Streamlined Convention, Rexall Drug Co.
The Future of Rail Passenger Traffic in the West, Stanford Research Institute, Menlo Park, Cal., March, 1965.
U.S. Surveyor General's Office, Report of the Commissioners, San Francisco & San Jose RR, February 9, 1866.

NEWSPAPERS

Burbank *Leader*, Burbank, Cal.
Enquirer Bulletin, San Carlos, Belmont, Cal.
Lompoc *Record*, Lompoc, Cal.
Los Angeles *Express*, Los Angeles.
Los Angeles *Star*, Los Angeles.
Los Angeles *Times*, Los Angeles.
Salinas *Daily Index*, Salinas, Cal.
San Francisco *Chronicle*, San Francisco.
San Francisco *Examiner*, San Francisco.
San Luis Obispo County *Telegram-Tribune*, San Luis Obispo, Cal.
San Luis Obispo *Tribune*, San Luis Obispo, Cal.
San Luis Obispo *Daily Telegram*, San Luis Obispo, Cal.
Santa Barbara *News-Press*, Santa Barbara, Cal.
Ventura *Star-Free Press*, Ventura, Cal.

Index

Almaden, 39, 40
Almaden Branch, 39
American Beet Sugar Co., 20, 25, 46, 299
American Locomotive Co. (Alco), 154, 156, 157, 160-162, 199, 210, 215
Amtrak, 174, 176, 242-244, 246, 249, 252, 257, 259, 261, 265, 267, 269-271, 273-277
Anschutz, Philip, 269, 270
Antonio, 17, 295
Arguello, 134 (*see also* Point Arguello)
Aromas, 57, 58, 92, 143, 287
Arroyo Hondo, 21
Atascadero, 52, 54, 165, 292
Atchison, Topeka and Santa Fe Ry. (AT&SF), 43, 105, 106, 108, 154, 266, 269
Atherton, 282
Automobiles, shipping, 151
Bakersfield, 39, 112, 241
Baldwin diesels, 156, 157, 226, 227, 229
Bay Area Rapid Transit District (BART), 165, 245
Bay Meadows, 281
Bayshore (Bay Shore) Cutoff, x, 28, 31-35, 37, 53, 58, 68, 112, 185, 245, 278, 279
Bayshore Shops, 34, 35, 49, 146, 187
Bayshore Yard, 33-35, 48, 49, 70, 146, 158, 159, 164, 167, 187, 262, 267, 279
Beaumont Hill, 118, 156
Belmont, 6, 171, 281
Betteravia, 19, 20, 46, 137, 209, 222, 264
Betteravia Branch, 19, 20
Bradley, 116, 164, 251, 290
Branches, *see* individual branch names
Bridgeport, 17, 18
Brisbane, 279
Burbank, Burbank Branch, 20, 22, 23, 25, 48, 54, 249, 271, 274, 275, 303
Burbank Jct., 25, 154, 164, 240, 241, 275, 276, 303
Burlingame, 6, 26, 52, 54, 69, 104, 191, 192, 280
Business cars, 85, 88, 274
California Fun Express, 268
Callender, 61, 134, 164, 255, 267, 292
Caltrain, 248, 249, 272-275
Caltrans (Calif. Dept. of Transportation), 248-250, 271-273, 275, 276
Camarillo, 47, 143, 164, 165, 169, 275, 301
Camp, military, *see* Military facilities
Camphora, 43, 289
Cañada de Alegria, 99
Cañada Honda, 17, 18, 64, 295
Capitan, 18, 21, 164, 171, 297
Carmel, 10, 51

Carnadero, 286
Carpinteria, 1, 11, 58, 108, 164, 165, 233, 267, 275, 300
Carrots, 151
Cascade, 243
Casmalia, 17, 164, 167, 222, 223, 295
Castaic, 1, 59, 268
Castro, 283
Castroville, 39, 78, 85, 174, 288
Cauliflower, 112
Celery, 112, 151
Celite Co., 46, 47
Cementario Canyon, 21
Central Pacific Railroad, 4, 7
Chatsworth, 21, 23, 25, 100, 139-141, 143, 164, 165, 168, 240, 270, 271, 275, 303
Chicago, Burlington & Quincy Railroad, 146, 165
Chittenden, Chittenden Pass, 7, 58, 84, 85, 160, 164, 195, 198, 287
Chorro, 14, 76, 96, 117, 145, 157, 209, 211, 255, 256, 264, 293
Chualar, 289
City of Los Angeles, 86
Coast, business car, 85, 88
Coast Daylight, see *Daylight*
Coaster, 50, 57, 60, 65, 74, 88, 93, 104, 149, 150, 191
Coast Line Limited, 49
Coast Line closure, 269
"Coast Mail," 159, 165, 171, 172, 182, 195-197, 212, 213-215, 229, 237, 241
Coast Merchandise, 150, 152, 163, 190, 197, 229, 262
  Advance section, 151, 185, 190
  piggyback, 150, 151, 183, 189, 190, 229
"Coast Peddler," 206, 250, 260, 262, 269
Coast Starlight, 176, 242-244, 250, 252, 257, 259, 261, 265, 270, 275, 276
Commuter trains, 67, 68, 104, 158, 159, 165, 166, 171, 181, 182, 188, 191-193, 243, 245-250, 272-276, 278
  gallery cars, 165, 247
Concepcion, 18, 61-63, 108 (*see also* Point Conception)
Containers, 151, 262, 266
Cooper, 203, 288
Counties
  Los Angeles, 4
  Monterey, 4
  San Diego, 4
  San Francisco, 3, 4, 245, 248, 272
  San Luis Obispo, 4, 13, 19
  San Mateo, 3, 39, 245, 248, 272
  Santa Barbara, 13, 19, 38, 46, 47, 59, 71, 223, 237
  Santa Clara, 3, 4, 166, 245, 248, 272
  Tulare, 4
  Ventura, 17, 23, 46, 47, 59, 71, 223, 237, 274

Coyote, 84, 165, 285
Crespi, Juan, 1, 291-293, 297, 300
CTC, 105, 109, 143, 146, 164, 180, 207, 211, 274, 275
Cuesta, Cuesta Grade, 12-14, 43, 56, 60, 61, 70, 73-77, 87, 93, 95, 109, 118-123, 140, 141, 150, 152, 159-161, 164, 180, 207-211, 254, 255, 264, 268, 269, 276, 277, 293
    Horseshoe Curve, 14, 15, 75, 78, 91, 95, 120, 140, 209, 256
    Stenner Creek, 14-16, 74, 96, 120, 211, 254, 255
Davenport, 111, 112, 165
Daylight, 75, 82, 91-99, 104, 107, 108, 117, 126, 132, 139, 145, 146, 149, 150, 159, 165, 166, 168, 169, 175, 176, 198, 199, 207, 208, 210, 211, 222, 223, 228-233, 240, 243, 261, 278
    christening, 93
    Daylight Limited, 66
    gray color, 91
    GS-class locomotives, 93-99, 120, 134, 139, 153, 156, 159
    new trains, 82, 91, 107
    Morning Daylight, 107, 149
    Noon Daylight, 107, 117, 141, 143, 149, 150, 153
    shellfire damage, 146
de Havilland, Olivia, 93
Del Monte, 29, 78, 104, 149, 159, 165, 174, 243
Del Monte Hotel, 8, 10, 50-52
Depression, the, 85-87, 100
"Devil's Jaw," 63, 64
Dieselization, 154-59
Direct Traffic Control (DTC), 268
Divisions, subdivisions
    Coast Division, 40-42, 58, 109, 112, 131, 164, 165, 170, 244
    Gilroy Subdivision, 194, 195
    Guadalupe Subdivision, 112, 224, 225
    Los Angeles Division, 42, 112, 131, 154, 159, 170, 238
    Northern Division, 39, 40, 51, 279
    Rio Grande Division, 154
    Salinas Subdivision, 112, 200, 201
    Salt Lake Division, 119
    San Francisco Subdivision, 112, 178, 179
    San Joaquin Division, 39, 42, 43, 112, 137, 154
    Santa Barbara Subdivision, 112
    Santa Margarita Subdivision, 204, 205
    Ventura Division, 11, 39, 58, 112
    Ventura Subdivision, 238, 239
    Western Division, 170
Drake, 147, 164, 297
Dulah, 47, 164, 233, 265, 300
Dumbarton Cutoff, 36, 37, 48, 66-68, 69, 262, 267, 274
Earthquakes, 35, 37, 57, 58, 84, 154, 271
    San Francisco, 1906, 35, 37, 57, 58
Edna, 294
El Camino Real, 1, 3, 51
Electrification, Peninsula, 68, 69, 274
Electromotive Division (EMD) of GM, 154-157, 159-161, 163, 207, 215, 221, 230, 231, 237
Elkhorn, Elkhorn Slough, 58, 85, 199, 288
Ellwood, 11, 12, 17-19, 21, 22, 25, 27, 39, 46, 47, 137, 146, 271, 279, 297
Fairbanks-Morse, 159, 160, 215
Ferry Building, 4, 58, 249
Fillmore, 11, 47, 59, 134, 137, 267
Fires, 43, 160, 170, 268, 269
    fire trains, 269
Floods, 58, 59, 107, 108, 171, 267, 268
Freight tonnage, 48, 87, 143, 151
Freight train symbols, *see* Symbols
Frozen food, 151
"Gap, The," 12, 13, 17-19, 21-23
Gas turbine engine, 154, 156
Gato, 18, 242, 261, 296
Gaviota, 1, 18, 21, 98, 126, 127, 134, 165, 168, 227-229, 261, 265, 267-269, 296
Gaviota Pass, 2, 3, 12
Gemco, 151, 156, 249, 303
General Electric, 154, 161, 163, 236
"Ghost," 150, 151
Gilroy, 4, 7, 54, 84, 112, 196, 203, 272-274, 276, 286
Gilroy Hot Springs, 51
Glendale, 54, 93, 100, 154, 155, 243, 250, 271, 275, 304
Golden State, 221
Goldtree, 91, 120, 140, 256, 293
Goleta, 87, 275, 298
Goleta Lemon Association, 154
Gonzales, 43, 56, 165, 278, 289
Guadalupe, 1, 2, 17, 19, 20, 61, 63, 70, 83, 128, 129, 132, 134, 137, 154, 164, 167, 170, 222, 257, 260, 268, 269, 294
Hadley, 47, 294
Harlem, 43, 164, 252, 253, 290
Harriman, E.H., 25, 33, 35, 37, 68
Harrison St., San Francisco, 4, 28-32
Hasson, 25, 137, 140, 143
Hathaway, 74, 215, 293
Helpers, 87, 96, 118-123, 125, 131, 143, 152, 156, 157, 207, 212, 221, 254, 255, 257, 264
Hewitt, 108, 303
Highway competition, 87, 262, 266
Hillsdale, 39, 281
Hollister, 4, 7, 51, 111, 112, 252, 262
Holly Sugar, 137
Honda, 18, 56, 57, 61-65, 129, 164, 167, 226, 234, 235, 260, 277, 296
Hood, William, 12, 14, 21
Hope Ranch, 11, 134, 136
Huntington, Collis P., 4, 12, 21, 23, 25, 35
Huntington, Henry, 21
Islais Creek, 35, 186
Jalama, 18, 134, 164, 296
Johns-Manville, 47
Joint Powers Board (JPB), Peninsula, 272, 273, 276
Jordan, J.J., 85, 88, 91
King City, 1, 11, 43, 111, 117, 143, 154, 164, 165, 200, 244, 262, 290

Khrushchev, Nikita S., 166, 167
Lark, 50, 56, 65-67, 100, 104, 107, 108, 139, 140, 149, 152, 154, 159, 165, 171, 173, 175, 176, 221
   last run, 175, 176
   two-tone gray, 107
LCL freight, 88
Lemons, 47, 59, 132, 134, 154
Lento, 61, 62
Lettuce, 83, 112, 115, 151, 154, 266
Lick, 84, 100, 105, 143, 164, 273, 285
Lick Observatory, 50, 51, 285
Line improvements, 23-25, 31-35, 84, 85, 100, 101, 164
Logan, 46, 57, 58, 84, 85, 112, 160, 164, 180, 195, 198, 272, 287
Loma Prieta Branch, 39, 40
Lomita Park, 280
Lompoc, 19, 21, 46, 63-65, 70, 167, 171, 229
Lompoc Branch, 18, 19, 70
Los Altos, 165
Los Altos Branch, 67, 166
Los Angeles, 1, 2, 7, 21-23, 39, 42, 54, 66, 67, 88, 93, 105, 107, 108, 112, 154, 155, 157, 158, 171, 243, 249, 250, 260, 262, 270, 271, 274, 276, 277, 304, 305
   Central Station, 69, 105, 107, 305
   Dayton Ave., 107, 229, 275, 304
   Taylor Yard, 90, 229, 243, 250, 274, 304
   Union Passenger Terminal, 105, 106, 249, 274, 305
Los Angeles County Transportation Commission (LACTC), 272, 274, 276
Los Gatos, 165, 166, 272
Los Olivos, 18
Madrone, 285
"Main trains," *see* Military trains
Mayfield, 67, 283
McCarron, George A., v, vi
McDonald, A.D., 93
McKay, 116, 142, 253, 291
"Med Fly," 249
Menlo Park, 3, 32, 39, 165, 267, 278, 282
Merchandise freight, 87-91, 262
Metro Link, 273, 274
Metz, 56, 100, 107, 290
Midwinter Exhibition, 40, 42, 43
Millbrae, 66, 192, 280
Military facilities
   Camp Clayton, 142
   Camp Cooke, 143, 146, 147, 167
   Camp McQuaide, 142
   Camp Roberts, 142, 143, 147, 159, 291
   Camp San Luis Obispo, 140, 145
   Fort Lewis, 142
   Fort Ord, 142, 159, 306
   Pacific Missile Range, 167, 260, 296
   Port Hueneme, 142
   Vandenberg Air Force Base, 167, 260, 296
Military trains, 142-147, 153, 223
   hospital trains, 147
Miramar, 38, 44, 55, 168, 271, 299
Mission Bay, 48, 159, 164, 184, 185, 262, 266, 267
Mission Revival style, 26, 27, 51-54, 177
Missions, 1, 44, 50, 51, 66, 71, 93
Monterey and Salinas Valley Rail Road Co., 9
Montalvo, 20, 23, 25, 27, 59, 93, 100, 108, 134, 137, 154, 170, 249, 301
Montalvo Cutoff, 20, 23-25, 27
Montecito, 44, 97, 300
Monterey, 9, 10, 21, 61, 78, 79, 83, 88, 111, 142, 174, 243, 271, 275, 276, 306
Monterey Bay, 1, 2, 112
Monterey Branch, 20, 39, 78, 79, 112, 194, 306
Morganhill (Morgan Hill), 118, 165, 274, 285
Moorpark, 47, 164, 165, 249, 250, 267, 274, 275, 302
Morro Bay, 1
Moss Landing, 85, 94, 288
Mountain View, 283
Nacimiento, 291
Naples, 18, 47, 134, 142, 297
Narlon, 17, 61, 223, 269, 295
National Asssociation of Railroad Passengers (NARP), 243
Nevada Central Railroad, 9
Newark, 36, 37
Niles, 37, 40
Nipomo, 2, 257
Northridge, 164, 165, 275, 303
Nursery, plants, 87
Oakland, 35, 37, 58, 66, 67, 80, 91, 165, 167, 170, 171, 186, 193, 196, 243, 249, 250, 260, 262, 269, 270, 272, 274, 276, 277
Oceano, 17, 65, 134, 137, 263, 294
Oceanview, 31, 32, 37
Oil production, *see* Petroleum
Ojai, 21, 47, 165, 171
Ojai Valley Branch, 21, 59, 71, 134, 171
Ortega, 143, 168, 271, 299
Overnight, 88-91, 109, 133, 143, 149-151, 190
   boxcars, 89-91, 133, 150
   loading, 89
Owensmouth, 21, 25
Oxnard, 20, 25, 46, 59, 61, 71, 134, 137, 142, 143, 151, 154, 164, 170, 237, 249, 250, 267-269, 271, 275, 276, 301
Pacheco Pass, 4, 7
Pacific Coast Railway, 11, 18, 47-48
Pacific Fruit Express, PFE, 112, 113, 202, 209, 212, 262, 263
Pacific Grove, 10, 78, 79, 88, 194
Pacific Improvement Co., 7-10, 13
Pacific Motor Transport, 87, 91
Pacific Motor Trucking, PMT, 87-91, 133, 149-151, 175, 188, 209
Pacific Railroad Reports, 12, 23
Pacific Southwestern Railroad, 47
Padre, 66, 87
Pajaro, 7, 10, 109, 265, 287

Pajaro River, Pajaro Valley, 2, 7, 58, 83, 84, 85, 107, 112, 198, 272, 287
Pajaro Valley Consolidated Railroad, 113
Palo Alto, 3, 32, 67-69, 105, 175, 188, 243, 283
Panama-Pacific Exposition, 43, 53, 54, 56, 245
Paraiso Springs, 51
Parke, Lt. John G., 2, 12, 23
Paso Robles, 10, 44, 51, 164, 204, 205, 268, 275, 292
Passenger trains
    discontinuance, 165, 171-176
    specials, 66, 67, 166, 167
    tour packages, 270
Peninsula line purchase, 272, 273
Perishable shipping, 48, 83, 84, 112, 151, 202, 262, 263, 266, 267
Petroleum, 37, 47
Pickwick Stage Lines, 91
Piggyback, 150, 151, 188, 189, 229, 262, 266
    terminals, 151
Piru, 11, 47, 59, 268
Pismo, Pismo Beach, 17, 61, 294
Point Arguello, 2, 12, 55, 143, 167, 226, 296
Point Conception (Concepcion), 1-3, 11, 12, 226, 296
Point Purisima, 2, 63
"Port Los Angeles," 23
Portolá, Gaspar de, 1, 283, 287, 288, 293, 297, 300, 305
Potrero Tower, 48,
Princess Tours, 270
Prisoners of war, 147
Profile, Coast Line, 118, 119
Public Utility Commission (PUC), California, 171, 173, 175, 243, 245, 248
Pullman Co., 91, 106
Punta Gorda, 58, 300
Raymer, 151, 167, 170, 275, 303
Redwood City, 28, 37, 68, 70, 282
Redwood Junction, 36, 48, 49, 143, 267, 282
Refugio, 132, 229
Retainers, 119, 161
Rexall Co. train, 86
Rincon Point, 11, 44, 58, 71, 233
Roseville, 159, 262
Sacate, 18, 62, 99, 230, 297
Sacramento, 4, 90, 91, 249, 271
Sacramento Valley Rail Road Co., 4
Saint Francis Dam failure, 59
"Salad Bowl Express," 266
Salinas, 1, 7-9, 20-22, 40, 42, 46, 70, 83, 88, 93, 100, 111-117, 147, 151, 154, 159, 160, 164, 167, 170, 171, 180, 195, 199, 202, 262, 269, 272, 276, 288
Salinas River, Salinas Valley, 1, 9, 17, 39, 40, 56, 58, 83, 85, 107, 143, 203, 206, 252, 260, 266, 288
San Andreas fault, 58, 70, 84
San Ardo, 17, 116, 160, 165, 206, 290
San Bruno, 22, 28, 32, 33, 68, 171, 245, 280

San Carlos, 281
San Diegan, 250, 271, 275
San Diego, 54, 65, 243, 271, 276
San Fernando, San Fernando Valley, 2, 20, 22, 23, 151, 274
San Francisco, 1-5, 16, 21, 22, 27-30, 32-37, 39, 40, 42, 51, 54, 56, 66, 67, 88, 91, 94, 109, 112, 141, 158, 164, 165, 167, 170, 173, 175-183, 185, 186, 192, 243, 246, 247, 249, 262, 271-275, 279
    Fourth St. Tower, 54, 181, 188, 274
    station, Third and Townsend, 4, 5, 40, 53, 54, 68, 158, 177, 180-182, 244-247
    terminals, 48, 49
San Francisco & San Jose Railroad Co., 3-7, 30, 280
San Joaquin, 250, 276
San Joaquin Valley, 4, 7, 21, 42, 60, 108, 137, 241, 279
San Jose, 1-4, 22, 27, 32, 37, 39, 46, 48, 51, 56, 68, 80, 81, 84, 85, 91, 93, 100-103, 105, 109, 151, 165, 171, 180, 193, 196, 245, 249, 250, 262, 269, 272-274, 276, 284
    Cahill St. station, 100, 101, 103, 105, 273, 284
    College Park, Tower and Yard, 80, 81, 84, 105, 154, 273, 284
    Fourth St. Tower, 80
    Lenzen Ave. roundhouse, 81, 102, 193
    Market St. station, 68, 80, 81, 101
    Newhall Yard, 84, 267, 284
    Tamien, 273
San Jose Line Change, 84, 85, 100-103
San Lucas, 160, 165, 206, 251, 290
San Luis Obispo, 1, 7, 11-14, 16, 18, 21, 40, 42, 43, 48, 51, 57-61, 65, 72-77, 83, 85, 88, 92, 93, 95, 96, 100, 109, 112, 118-125, 128, 129, 141, 143-148, 152, 156, 159-164, 167, 170-172, 175, 180, 200, 207, 209, 212-221, 250, 255, 257, 258, 260, 262, 264, 268-271, 275, 276, 293
    new depot, 147
    roundhouse, 73, 124, 125, 220
San Martin, 286
San Mateo, 28, 39, 69, 104, 245, 281
San Miguel, 2, 7, 10, 11, 50, 51, 116, 118, 164, 165, 291
Santa Barbara, 1, 2, 7, 11-13, 18, 21-23, 25-27, 39, 42, 44, 47, 48, 51, 54, 57-59, 70, 93, 97, 100, 108, 109, 112, 128-131, 134-137, 139, 146, 154-156, 159, 164, 165, 168, 170, 171, 227, 236, 258, 268, 271, 275, 276, 298
    roundhouse, 130, 159, 218, 220, 221
Santa Barbara Passenger, 21
Santa Clara, 51, 69, 70, 81, 84, 151, 193, 248, 274, 278, 284
Santa Clara and Pajaro Valley Rail Road Co., 4, 7
Santa Clara River, Santa Clara Valley (in Santa Clara County), 4, 7, 39, 40, 46, 101, 105
Santa Clara River, Santa Clara Valley (in Ventura County), 1, 2, 11, 20, 22, 23, 58, 59, 71, 83, 108, 267
Santa Cruz, 10, 51, 83, 88, 104, 111, 262, 272, 276
Santa Cruz Branch, 10, 39, 40, 100, 109, 112, 272, 287
Santa Cruz Railroad Co., 10
Santa Fe, *see* Atchison, Topeka and Santa Fe Ry.
Santa Lucia Mountains, 12, 14, 70, 73, 77, 293
Santa Margarita, 2, 12-14, 22, 56, 60, 76, 77, 83, 100, 116, 118,

119, 143, 160, 161, 164, 165, 200, 207, 257, 268, 269, 293
Santa Maria, 47, 61, 83, 132
Santa Maria River, Santa Maria Valley, 17, 19
Santa Maria Valley Railroad, 19, 222, 268
Santa Monica, 23
Santa Paula, 11, 23, 24, 47, 58, 59, 134
Santa Paula Branch, 42, 47, 59, 137, 154, 170, 171, 267, 268
Santa Susana, Santa Susana Pass, 20, 23-25, 56, 95, 108, 131, 137-139, 154, 164, 168, 240, 267, 302
Santa Ynez River, Santa Ynez Valley, 17-19, 58, 63, 70, 83, 171, 267
Santa Ynez Mountains, 47, 97, 232
Sargent, 43, 58, 70, 84, 107, 253, 272, 287
Saticoy, 11, 20, 59, 134, 165
Saugus, 11, 22, 39, 42, 137, 170, 267, 268, 274
Scheduled freights, 61, 109, 143, 144, 154, 205, 250, 260, 262
Seacliff, 47, 58, 164, 237, 266, 267, 269, 275, 300
Seashore Express, 50, 56, 65, 66
Second-generation diesels, 160-163
Serra, Junípero, 1, 26, 279, 291
Serrano, 70, 76, 119, 121, 141, 210, 255, 277, 293
Sespe, 11, 47
Shore Line Limited, 38, 50, 55, 66, 74, 76, 77, 87
Shuman, 134, 163, 223, 295
Sierra Point, 33, 35, 186
Simi, Simi Valley, 23, 47, 137, 249, 271, 275, 302
"Smokey," 134, 137, 167
Soledad, 2, 7, 10, 40, 51, 114, 118, 165, 289
Somis, 25, 171, 302
South Pacific Coast Railroad, 100
South San Francisco, 48, 278, 280
Speed boards, yellow, 100
Spence, 43, 288
Spirit of California, 249, 250
Spreckels, Spreckels Junction, 20, 39, 46, 116, 151, 202, 288
Spreckels Sugar Co., 20, 46
Spring Valley Branch, 40
Sproule, William, 68, 69
Stanford football trains, 67, 68, 166
Stanford, Leland, 3, 4
Starlight, 149, 150, 159, 165
Stations, *see* individual place names
"Stormy end," 134
Strathearn, 25, 164, 302
Strawberries, 112, 151, 195
Sudden, 18, 62, 226, 269, 296
Sugar beets, 19, 20, 43, 46, 112, 118, 137, 151, 160, 161, 202, 203, 209, 253, 256, 257, 264, 268, 269, 301
  beet gondolas, 203, 256, 257, 264
Summerland, 108, 299
Sunkist, 132
Sunset Express, 21, 49, 58, 60, 66, 69
Sunset Limited, 49, 66, 67, 87, 93, 104, 105, 108, 139, 141, 143, 176, 221
Sunset magazine, 22, 51

"Sunset Manifest," 110
Sunnyvale, 283
"Suntan Specials," 149, 165
Surf, 17-19, 55, 57, 61, 63, 65, 70, 128, 129, 134, 143, 167, 170, 171, 226, 227, 258, 259, 267-269, 295
Symbols, freight trains, 167, 170, 250, 260
Tajiguas, 62, 87, 232, 297
Tangair, 17, 63, 134, 143, 295
Tapo, 47, 137, 171
Tehachapi, 14, 42, 43, 154, 156, 267, 269, 276
  earthquake (1952), 154
Templeton, 10, 11, 12, 39, 292
Ten Commandments, 61, 63
Thyle, 60, 118, 293
Tilt-trains, 276, 277
Train Masters, 159, 160, 188, 246, 247
  fires, 160
Train orders, 76, 77, 108, 109, 143, 257, 258, 268
Tres Pinos, 4, 5, 7, 39
Troop trains, *see* Military trains
Tunnel collapse, Cuesta, 60, 61
Twelve Wheel engines, 114, 117
Union Oil Co., 47, 119
Union Pacific Railroad (UP), 69, 83, 86, 105, 106, 108, 154, 262
Union Sugar Co., 19, 20, 46, 203
Van Nuys, 25, 151, 271, 275
Van Nuys Branch, 147
Van pools, 245
Ventura, 1, 2, 11, 17, 20, 23, 47, 51, 55, 58, 59, 61, 71, 157, 164, 170, 233, 271, 274-276, 300
Ventura and Ojai Valley Rail Road Co., 21
Visitacion, Visitacion Point, 33-35, 37, 70, 190, 279
Waldorf, 56, 264, 295
Watsonville, 7, 46, 48, 58, 83, 112, 142, 143, 151, 168, 169, 197, 262, 272, 287
Watsonville Junction, 10, 56, 84, 88, 107, 109-112, 117, 118, 143, 154, 157-159, 164, 170, 171, 180, 199, 200, 203, 250-252, 260, 262, 263, 267, 269, 287
West Colton, 260
Western Beet Sugar Co., 46
Western Pacific Railroad (WP), 48, 84, 165
White Hills, 19, 46
White Hills Branch, 47
Wrecks
  barkentine *Robert Sudden*, 63
  Hasson, at, 139, 140
  Honda, at, 56, 57
  Metz, at, 56
  Navy destroyers, 64, 65, 260
  steamer *Santa Rosa*, 63, 64
  steamer *Sibyl Marston*, 63
  Tunnel 7, at, 255
  Waldorf, at, 56
Wunpost, 164, 291
"Zipper," 150, 183, 193, 250, 262, 303

This book was set in Adobe Caslon,
a modern rendition by Carol Twombly of the
classic typeface cut in England in the 1720s
by William Caslon. Titling faces are
Cooper Black and Cheltenham Italic.
Book design and endpapers by John R. Signor.

Southern Paci
SAN FRANCISCO
To Ogden
Oakland
To Tracy
Niles
San Bruno
Burlingame
San Mateo
Belmont
Redwood City
Palo Alto
Sunnyvale
Los Altos
Santa Clara
San Jose
Lick
Coyote
Madrone
Morgan Hill
San Martin
Gilroy
Los Gatos
Santa Cruz Mtns.
Sargent
Hollister
Tres Pinos
Watsonville
Aromas
Davenport
Santa Cruz
Watsonville Junction.
Castroville
Gabilan Range
Salinas
Spence
Chualar
Gonzales
Camphora
Soledad
Metz
Monterey Bay
Spreckels
Del Monte
Pacific Grove
Monterey
Carmel Mission
Salinas River
Coburn
King City
Welby
Docas
San Lucas
San Ardo
Santa Lucia Range
Jolon
Bradley
Nacimiento
San Miguel
Paso Robles
Templeton
Atascadero
Pozo Range
Santa Margarita
San Luis Obispo
Edna
Pismo
Oceano
Callender
Guadalupe
Casmalia
Narlon
Tangair
Surf
Honda
Arguello
San Simeon
Cambria
Cape San Martin
PACIFIC
Pt. Sal
Pt. Purisima
Pt. Arguello
SIGNOR
SAN FRANCISCO M.P. 0.00
(Third St. Station) Elv. 13
Bayshore Elv. 18
South San Francisco Elv. 14
SAN BRUNO Elv. 23
Burlingame Elv. 27
San Mateo Elv. 23
Belmont Elv. 34
San Carlos Elv. 23
REDWOOD CITY Elv. 11
Redwood Jct. Elv. 18
PALO ALTO Elv. 61
California Ave. Elv. 28
Mountain View Elv. 78
Sunnyvale Elv. 96
SANTA CLARA Elv. 72
SAN JOSE Elv. 99
Luther Jct. Elv. 129
LICK Elv. 153
Edenvale Elv. 179
Oak Grove Elv. 190
Coyote Elv. 252
Perry Elv. 301
Morganhill Elv. 344
San Martin Elv. 285
Lonoke Elv. 207
GILROY Elv. 193
CARNADERO Elv. 169
Corporal El. 148
Sargent Elv. 138
Logan Elv. 115
Aromas Elv. 95
Eaton Elv. 60
WATSONVILLE JCT. Elv. 22
Elkhorn Elv. 6
Moss Landing Elv. 24
CASTROVILLE Elv. 21
Cooper Elv. 25
SALINAS Elv. 45
SPRECKELS JCT. Elv. 60
Spence Elv. 80
Chualar Elv. 103
Penvir Elv. 110
Gonzales Elv. 127
Molus Elv. 162
Camphora Elv. 165
Soledad Elv. 184
Harlem Elv. 204
Metz Elv. 235
Coburn Elv. 262
Elsa Elv. 286
KING CITY Elv. 334
Welby Elv. 319
San Lucas Elv. 399
San Ardo Elv. 455
Wunpost Elv. 494
Bradley Elv. 541
Nacimiento Elv. 568
McKay Elv. 586
San Miguel Elv. 617
Wellsona Elv. 670
PASO ROBLES Elv. 724
Templeton Elv. 775
Atascadero Elv. 833
Henry Elv. 852
Eaglet Elv. 881
SANTA MARGARITA Elv. 998
10 20 30 40 50 60 70 80 90 100 110 120 130 140 150 160 170 180 190 200 210 220 230
0.477 0.492 0.579 0.399 0.113 0.552 0.685